CROWNED HEADS

Kings, Sultans and Emperors:
A Royal Quest

CROWNED HEADS

Kings, Sultans and Emperors:
A Royal Quest

VERONICA MACLEAN

Hodder & Stoughton
LONDON SYDNEY AUCKLAND

British Library Cataloguing in Publication Data

Maclean, Veronica, Lady
Crowned Heads: Kings, Sultans and
Emperors – A Royal Quest
I. Title
929.70922

ISBN 0-340-56214-5

Published by Hodder and Stoughton,
a division of Hodder and Stoughton Ltd,
Mill Road, Dunton Green, Sevenoaks, Kent TN13 2YA.
Editorial Office: 47 Bedford Square, London WC1B 3DP.

Book designed by Behram Kapadia

Photoset by Rowland Phototypesetting Ltd,
Bury St Edmunds, Suffolk

Printed in Great Britain by Butler and Tanner Ltd,
Frome and London

Contents

CONCLUSION AND POSTSCRIPT

List of Illustrations

F

'What I have is yours; what I have
to do is yours; being part in all I have
devoted yours.'

V

Author's Acknowledgements

I have not drawn up a formal bibliography as my sources have been so varied and so wide-ranging that it would be impossible to do so usefully. But there are a number of writers, historians, and friends I am especially grateful to for their works and their assistance. They include:

David Ambrose, Ambassadeur Gérard André, Noël Barber, Ruth Benedict, Thomas Crump, Dr T. K. Derry, Lord Hailsham, Prince Hassan bin Talal, Sir Donald Hawley, Sir Charles Johnstone, Lord Menniker, Robert Lacey, Lady Longford, Sir Harry Luke, Major-General Sir James Lunt, Geoffrey Madden, Dr J. S. M. Matsebula, Margaret Meade, James Morris, Sir Harold Nicolson, Alan Palmer, Navendra Raj Pandey, Dr Nuri Rustomji, Rev. Dr John Stair, Lord St John of Fawsley, Giuseppe Tucci, Sir Robert Wade-Gery.

I would also like to thank my husband, Fitzroy, for his encouragement, his advice and, above all, his patience, which was often sorely tried.

I am enormously grateful, too, to Sheila MacPherson and Ruth Park who somehow made sense of my manuscript mazes; and to Ina Black, Jill Campbell and Ruth McFadyen who manned the duplicator and sent faxes from Argyll to strange addresses all over the world.

Strachur   V.M.
September 1992

Author's Foreword

There are twenty-five ruling monarchs in the world today: ten in Europe; three in Africa; four in Central Asia and the Middle East and eight in Asia and the Pacific. They reign over their countries in diverse ways, as absolute kings, as constitutional monarchs or as mere ornaments of state. That they should exist at all in this, the age of the common man, is something of an anomaly. That so few not especially talented people should command the attention, the respect or at least the insatiable curiosity of so many might also seem irrational, but that they *do*, is incontestable. Six hundred million people, worldwide, watched the Prince of Wales's wedding on television, by far the greatest 'audience participation' ever then known, and the most trivial activities of the world's royal families fill every newspaper and screen in every country's media every day. Republicans complain about it and intellectuals scoff. But how many people, when asked, have actually *refused* to dine with a king?

Sociologists and anthropologists have long puzzled over this mystery and have come up with different explanations – mostly to do with the fascination people have with their past, what is fashionably called 'roots'. For kings and queens are essential milestones in that past: its various periods are identified by their names and style, and our roots, whether acknowledged or unknown, are inevitably tangled with theirs.

It was our ancestors, who, at some moment in time, chose leaders, made them kings, and gave them sovereign power to rule over us.

Kings and queens stand apart; they are the role models, the shining symbols of man's final achievement, his greatest success. Every little girl wants to dress up 'like a queen' and every little boy sings, 'I'm the king of the castle'.

Kings and queens are part of nostalgia; that backward-looking quest for answers we have lost. They make people feel secure. In the growing insecurity of a changing, frightening world people long for simple certainties, for the loyalties and affections of ancient tradition, for a link with what, they imagine, was a happier, safer past.

Kings and queens are food for fantasy. They are the dreams of women who see themselves, but for a misdirected stork, as Princess Di dancing with President Clinton at a glittering White House Ball.

Kings and queens are Aunt Sallies whom in democratic countries it is fun to knock down although we, a parlour-partisan public and semi-republican press, always hope they will bob up again.

Kings and queens, for many peoples, are still the focus of their nations' identity. Patriotism, though thought of in Brussels as politically 'incorrect', is still alive and for them love 'of King and Country' remains inextricably, if illogically, mixed.

'The rise of monarchy appears to be the essential condition of the emergence of man from savagery,' wrote Sir James Frazer in *The Golden Bough*. Certainly, monarchy is the most ancient of all systems of government, and has existed on this planet for six thousand years.

The word comes from the Greek *monarkhia*, rule of one, and it means the undivided sovereignty of a single person.

Its dangers are obvious, but so were its advantages when nations needed strong leaders and warrior kings to survive and grow. With the evolution of nation states monarchy too has evolved and, though elected governments have now robbed it of some of its dynamism, they have also created safeguards against its abuse.

Walter Bagehot, the great constitutional historian of Victorian Britain, summed up his nineteenth-century belief in it in these words: 'the best reason why monarchy is a strong government is that it is an intelligible government. The mass of mankind understands it and they hardly anywhere in the world understand any other.'

The world has changed since Bagehot came to that rather olympian conclusion. The 'mass of mankind', angered by injustices or swayed by ideologies, has toppled many kings from their thrones – whether from comprehension or incomprehension is an open question. And those that are left have also changed: no longer do they lead us into battle, cut off our heads, or reshape the boundaries of nations.

Modern kings, shorn of power, are apt to be, with a few exceptions, a quiet, busy – even a humdrum – lot, more like welfare officers, environmentalists or businessmen, indeed, than tyrants or despots. Yet a question mark still hangs over their future. Can they survive?

I believe that they can, and will – as long as a nation's loyalty to its own history and traditions lives on in its people's minds, and its monarchy is seen to be an integral part of its heritage.

For royalty is an intangible conception, more thought than substance. It has changed and evolved as time has passed, but it is still the very stuff that nationhood, nostalgia, and nowadays, more dangerously perhaps, even soap-operas are made of. Yet selling newspapers and bringing people out on the streets to cheer is not its only function. Society today may be materialistic and irreligious but there is a kernel of simple folk within it, perhaps even a quiet and silent majority, who still hold old-fashioned views on values that have been handed down to them by older generations, and they are swelled by younger people who are instinctively searching for the same values. They stand a million miles from the chattering classes, the Channel 4 debaters. To them monarchy can be what they want to think it is – defender of the faith, bastion against what is bad and ugly and greedy in the modern world: a rock that stands above meretricious politicians, a too-often trivialising and corrupting media and sometimes even a fashion-following, dangerously drifting Church. And when, on State occasions, the Queen, Elizabeth II, rides out in her golden carriage wearing a golden crown or, on the other side of the world, the Emperor of Japan communes with ancient Gods in his solemn *Daijosai*, for them the pages of history turn back, and, for a moment, they glimpse the magic and mystery and sureness of an earlier kingship which their ancestors once shaped and shared.

For me that is enough, although I know that it is an emotional and perhaps an insubstantial view of monarchy.

The hard questions to be asked in the final decade of the twentieth century are more searching and practical: besides having an enormous 'fan-club', does monarchy still have an influence or use in today's hard-nosed society? Can it still unite a nation's divided factions when politics and politicians fail to do so? Can constitutional kings contribute ideas and values to their country that are beyond the remit of an elected government, and should they be given more scope to do so? Is there really such a thing as a truly democratic king? And, if there is, what does he (or his subjects or anyone else) really mean by 'democracy'?

In countries where they reign or rule, what makes a king outstanding? Heredity? Upbringing? Historical inevitability? Or simply character and charisma?

Will there be more of them in future, or fewer? And finally, do any of them retain that mysterious power that made them once win battles and cure scurvy, a power that set them apart, as true descendants of the gods?

To find the answers to these questions I decided to visit all twenty-five of the remaining kings in the world to see for myself how they were faring and whether their survival could be justified. My journey would be a quest, an adventure, and one that I would greatly enjoy. Technically, I was not very well equipped for the task, not being an historian or a journalist, but I am at least a good traveller and, after all, I reminded myself, 'a cat may look at a king'.

Author's Introduction

Interviewing kings and queens and summing up their chances of survival was, I soon found, rather more difficult than I had imagined.

Making contact through webs of protocol and bureaucracy, then finding windows in their busy lives that would correspond with my own, was the first problem. I overcame it by operating on two levels, correctly through the embassies involved, who almost invariably showed me great kindness and courtesy, or directly, if I had a friend who had a friend who knew a king or queen.

I made many mistakes and often a fool of myself, but after a while I learnt the ground rules of interviewing. Rule I: do your homework before you start. Even the most modern monarch has an historical background which matters. Rule II: don't talk, but listen. Rule III: while waiting around, take in as much of the surroundings as possible – without actually opening drawers. Rule IV: courtiers, who are usually charming people, can be over-protective and muffle their sovereigns – don't be too charmed. Rule V: don't pay too much attention to the parameters of permitted conversation. The monarch will soon forget them and so can you.

I confess I was taken aback by the grandness of some of the monarchs I visited and by the luxury or strangeness of their courts, which surpassed anything I had ever seen before, but I don't think this inhibited our conversations – once we started to talk. I was helped by having seen my parents being polite and at ease with the very grand. My father, Lord Lovat – a clan chief, occasional lord-in-waiting to King George V, Convenor of the Inverness-shire County Council and government minister in the House of Lords – and our home, Beaufort Castle, were obvious targets when it came to finding a roof and a hot meal for visiting dignitaries to the north of Scotland, so that royalty, both British and foreign, quite often visited my parents when I was a child. We were not unduly impressed or overawed by these occasions, though best feet were certainly put forward and a general sprucing up took place, for the honour of the house. 'It's a funny thing,' Princess Margaret once told me years later, 'but whenever I visit my friends in the country there's always a smell of fresh paint!'

We were a large and merry family and before the royal arrivals a good many jokes were told and tricks played. Indeed, her children's levity, rather than her household's 'nerves', were my mother's chief concern at these times. I remember Maurice Baring, the novelist and poet, an irrepressible jokester and our adopted 'uncle', declaring with the utmost gravity that King Edward VII and his offspring all spoke English with a strong Teutonic accent and would respond to any conversational gambit with a guttural 'Ach, so?' His sister, Lady Reid, had been a lady-in-waiting to Queen Victoria, so we children felt he ought to know, and practised pidgin-German – '*Was ist das?*' '*Gott im Himmel*,' and 'Pass me the butter, *bitte*,' for days beforehand. We were all the more disappointed when the story turned out to be a myth, though King George V *did* have a rather deep and rumbly voice.

His visit, the first I can clearly recall, passed without incident, except that my eldest brother, Shimi, deposited a small and rather elderly brown trout on Queen Mary's blue silk lap, telling her, 'You'd better eat it at once, because I caught it two days ago.' Whether this was an act of allegiance or *lèse-majesté* I have never been quite sure, for we had been brought up by a Gaelic-speaking Nanny in a spirit of ardent Jacobite romanticism and our attitude to the House of Hanover was decidedly ambivalent. 'Will ye no' come back again?' and 'Wae's me for Prince Charlie' were the songs we sang in the nursery, and we called the odious yellow weed that grew in front of the castle, and on the battleground of Culloden some twenty-five miles away, 'stinking Willie', after William, Duke of Cumberland.

The fact that Queen Mary did not wear a golden crown under her sky-blue toque (what else could it possibly be *for?*) was also a source of disappointment. But my greatest disillusion with British royalty came a few years later, in 1931, when the visiting Prince of Wales (later Edward VIII) failed to take me up in his private aeroplane and loop the loop, after he had promised solemnly to do so.

Our home was a large pink sandstone castle which stood high and proud on a hill above the River Beauly and was the quintessence of that unjustly derided style of architecture known as 'Scottish Baronial'. Our river was a salmon river, one of the best in Scotland, and distinguished by the family's ancient right to 'net' salmon in the artificial pools of a weir or 'cruive' which crossed the water just above the castle. This performance, much to the sorrow of fishing tenants, took place once a week and, on this occasion, had been laid on as an opening entertainment for the prince's visit.

My father was a punctual man and, when the prince's aeroplane failed to turn up at the appointed hour (HRH, who was playing golf at Nairn had, rather typically, chosen to go an extra round), he decided to start the netting without his royal guest. The local police had assured him there would be plenty of time to reach the landing ground when the prince's aeroplane was sighted, but such was the enthusiasm of everyone, including the police, as the heaps of flapping, fat beauties mounted on the cobblestones and the fishing ghillies' long poles searched the deepest crannies of the cruive pools, that no one noticed the small bi-plane of the King's Flight as it began its descent to a field on the other side of the castle, where one solitary policeman waited beside the orange drogues. No one, that is, except our cousin's Nanny, who had been placed in charge that day of us, the younger Fraser children. Known as 'Napoleon' Tansy, because of her remarkable powers of improvisation and command, she summed up the situation at a glance, for from the windows of the castle she could see both venues and knew that disaster threatened. Scooping up a trio of Fraser babies and my nine-year-old self and loading us into my uncle's 1920 Model T Ford, she rocketed down to the landing field and lined us up in formation just as the door of HRH's plane opened. The policeman saluted, we curtsied carefully, in line, and Nanny Tansy stepped forward and explained that his Lordship had been unfortunately delayed, but that the 'Major's' car was at HRH's disposal and could she drive him up to the castle?

The handsome young prince was delighted by such an unconventional welcoming party and promised me a ride in his aeroplane the very next day. We piled into the old Ford and headed for the castle, the two family cars (my father's travelling at what was then a Silverstone speed but was probably only 60 mph) and 'Napoleon's' nearly colliding on the drive.

In the post-mortem after the visit my mother was untypically censorious of the prince's behaviour; his facile charm had failed to move her. 'He actually asked me to re-arrange the "placement" at dinner so that he could sit next to Mary again [one of her lively Lindley nieces]! It's all very well liking pretty faces, but it was his *duty* to sit next to Lady Hermione [the wife of Lochiel, then Lord Lieutenant of Inverness-shire].'

Five years later I listened to the ill-fated prince as he made his famous abdication broadcast and once more, at least to our family's mind, abjured his obligations and his duty. My parents were in London, but at Beaufort we all gathered round the little crystal set in the schoolroom to listen. What I remember were not the often-quoted words, 'without the help and support of the woman I love' but the tears which rained down the cheeks of our old housekeeper, and the shocked white faces of our

Highland household. It was as if the roof had fallen in on their safe, comfortable and predictable world. 'And what will happen now?' they asked me, as if the end of the world were about to begin.

What had happened was that without knowing it we all had had a lucky escape, that the Duke and Duchess of York became King George VI and Queen Elizabeth, and that I grew up to be their fervent admirer, devoted servant and friend.

I believed then in monarchy as an institution and I still do, both by instinct and conviction, but it wasn't until I married and began travelling round the world with my husband, the best education that anyone could ever wish to have, that I became fascinated by history in general and by monarchies in particular. To ferret out the interlocking parts of their story through the pictures and peoples and countries I have visited and to fit them into the great sweep of world history has given me never-ending pleasure, and the more I delved into the past the more I have realised that until only recently – and sometimes even now – a country's destiny has been largely dependent on the character and behaviour of its monarchs, including even its constitutional ones.

Part One

EUROPE

1

GREAT BRITAIN

Queen Elizabeth, the Queen Mother

'Monarchy does not only symbolise and help to promote the unity of a nation . . . it serves to remind them of their ideals.'

EDMUND BURKE

I started my quest with our own royal family, and with Queen Elizabeth, the Queen Mother, the monarch I know and love the best. She first came and stayed with my parents in 1929 when I was still a schoolgirl and she was still Duchess of York. My first impression, carefully recorded in my small red diary, was: 'What fun she is!' and 'How easy to talk to!' – not at all like other royalty I had met whose formality usually created a kind of frozen space around them, paralysing all normal, and certainly youthful conversation.

It was a happy and informal weekend, for the 'Yorks' then bore the burden of royalty very lightly and, having dutifully done what was expected of them in Inverness, they drove out to Beaufort and relaxed, without seemingly a care in the world, or any idea of what the future held for them.

But eight years later, the 'pretty Bowes-Lyon girl', the 'sweet little duchess', who was such fun and whom everyone loved, had started playing an historic role on a world stage, as Queen and Consort of His Imperial Majesty, King George VI, Emperor of India, King of Great Britain, Ireland, and its Dominions over the seas.

Life seldom turns out as one expects it to.

Queen Elizabeth, the Queen Mother, is the fountain-head of the British royal family. She is still called 'Queen Elizabeth' by her household and her family, as distinct from 'The Queen', which is reserved for her elder daughter, Elizabeth II, but to her admirers all over the world, she is simply 'The Queen Mum'. This title, the one she likes best, has a larger significance: it was coined by the

British people, her subjects, and in three words it demonstrates the filial love of a nation and a commonwealth and its belief that, at heart, the Queen Mother is really 'one of us'. The phrase could not have been used for any of her predecessors and, in my opinion, the modern royal family is largely her creation.

Queen Elizabeth was not born a royal princess. She is of Scottish and Highland descent, the daughter of the 14th Earl of Strathmore, whose lineage is as ancient and as interesting to genealogists as that of the royal family, bringing more Norman, Irish and Stuart blood into the heredity of the present Queen.

There is no doubt that Queen Elizabeth's happy childhood had an enduring effect on her character and brought a breath of fresh air to the formal atmosphere of the court. When she first married, even King George V, that most punctilious of men who liked to run his palace like a battleship, succumbed to her pretty but as yet undisciplined ways and when she would arrive, breathless and apologetic, at his dinner table, would pat her hand and say, 'You aren't late, my dear. We simply started three minutes early.' It was the beginning of a deep and uninhibited affection between the two. After his death in 1936, she wrote to a friend, 'I miss him dreadfully. Unlike his own children, I was never afraid of him.'

For part of the year Lady Strathmore brought up her large family (six sons and three daughters) at The Bury, St Paul's Walden, in Hertford-shire, and in Bruton Street in Mayfair. But every summer they moved back to Glamis Castle in Angus, the ancient home of the Lyon family, a beautiful, romantic and sensationally haunted castle.

The Strathmores were a large, close-knit and happy family whose only shadow was the widespread local story of a mysterious curse that always affected the eldest son. But, as it had to do with an egg-shaped monster who, if he ever existed, had quite certainly died several generations earlier, it did not weigh very heavily on Lady Elizabeth or her sisters, or stop them enjoying the lovely freedoms of a Highland childhood.

They were brought up as other lairds' children of that generation: the boys at Eton, the girls at home by governesses, who taught them French and German, the English classics, a little history and geography, the rudiments of arithmetic (enough to add up household 'books' when they married), to play the piano and to sing, to dance reels, recite poetry and sew, or knit shooting stockings with fancy tops. Their mother taught them to pray, to arrange flowers, to be polite, kind and unselfish, to order a good dinner and look after visitors. The ghillies and keepers taught them to fish and shoot. There were always ponies to ride, picnics to carry, crofters and villagers to visit, cricket weekends to help organise, parlour games and charades and family feasts and children's parties at Christmastime. It was the ideal country childhood and, if it now seems privileged and paternalistic, that was what people on their estates wanted and expected from 'the Family' and 'the Castle'. For in the Highlands of Scotland responsibility and devotion to their 'own people', a legacy of the old clan system, was still felt very strongly by many lairds and chiefs. Certainly the Strathmores – who lived by a simple, classless code which made them at once fun-loving, unaffected, considerate and totally self-confident – did not lack local patriotism or a pride and affection for the people who lived round them, an affection just as certainly returned.

So, very early in her life, Lady Elizabeth Bowes-Lyon became used to visiting people who were poor, talking to people who were ill, attending village funerals and weddings and whist drives and bazaars. But, as well as learning, or, more probably, having been born with what she calls 'the knack' (of getting on with people), there was another side to the children's upbringing.

Her parents were devout Christians and each morning there were prayers before breakfast in the chapel at Glamis, where servants, family and guests (encouraged no doubt by the small white crocheted veils tactfully left in visitors' bedrooms) would meet and pray together. On Sundays, when the local minister from Glamis or Kirriemuir came over and preached, Lady Strathmore would play the organ. She passed on to her daughter not only her own conviction and deep spirituality, but also a very clear concept of what is right and wrong.

When war was declared in 1914, the Strathmores turned Glamis into a hospital and one of the most formative backgrounds of Lady Elizabeth's young life must have been the pain and the partings, the anxieties and the sorrows of those four years, seen close to in her own family – two of her brothers were killed on active service – and in those of the soldiers she helped to nurse.

By 1918 Lady Elizabeth was old enough to put her hair up, the war was over, and there were London balls and houseparties, followed the next autumn by the county ball at Kirriemuir which was the local equivalent of a hunt ball but with wild reels and piping and glamorous Highland dress.

I have been told by her contemporaries that many people fell in love with and proposed to Lady Elizabeth, and I can see why, for she still gets on wonderfully well with men and has a deliciously provocative, gently flirtatious way of teasing them that is irresistible. 'Bertie', as Prince Albert, Duke of York, was then called, King George V's sailor son, was only one of many suitors and at first he was turned down. 'I do hope he will find a nice wife who will make him happy,' Lady Strathmore wrote to a friend. 'I like him so much and he is a man who will be made or marred by his wife.'

Many people have wondered, but few will ever know, whether Lady Elizabeth had already fallen in love with a more dashing character before Prince Bertie proposed, or whether she mourned a first love who had been killed in the war. I believe myself that, beneath all her high spirits and love of fun, there existed a romantic and very serious girl who wanted, above all, to be absolutely sure and who would only commit herself to a man who regarded marriage in the same way as she did herself – as a union to last for life, of total fidelity and love.

Little by little, in Prince Bertie's very patience and steadfastness, she began to see qualities that others missed: goodness, staunchness and courage. She came to believe in him and to sense that she alone could bring out those virtues that others had barely glimpsed. She must also have known, poor girl, how much her life would be changed and how much she would have to sacrifice of the happy freedoms she valued. It is no wonder, really, that she kept him waiting.

Prince Bertie courted Lady Elizabeth for two long years until, on 10 January 1923, she finally accepted him in the garden at St Paul's Walden. Then, 'supremely happy', he sent the following laconic telegram to his parents at Sandringham: 'All right – Bertie'.

The Duke and Duchess of York settled down to a happy and not particularly demanding life in London at 145 Piccadilly and White Lodge, Richmond Park, and later at Royal Lodge in Windsor Park. This was the delightful Regency folly that George IV had built among the oak trees of the park for his own and the aged Lady Conyngham's amuse-ment, but which was later altered as much as possible by King William IV's wife, Queen Adelaide, in order to expunge what she thought of as the wicked excesses of the former Prince Regent. When the Yorks were given it, the house was almost a ruin but a fine Regency drawing-room on the ground floor was discovered and restored, and the young couple spent two happy years planning and rebuilding the house, clearing and planting the grounds to create a lovely woodland garden, of which the Queen Mother is justly proud today.

Apart from noticing that the young duchess smiled much more than any other lady in the royal family, the press and public at that time left her and her husband very much to themselves; for the Duke of York was, after all, a younger son and led a much quieter and less newsworthy life than his elder brother, the Prince of Wales. But when the duchess gave birth to their first child, a daughter, at her mother's house in Bruton

Street on 21 April 1926, attitudes changed. The baby, christened Eliza-beth Alexandra Mary, was very bonny, with speedwell blue eyes and the perfect pink and white complexion that is still the first feature one notices about Queen Elizabeth and her sister.

The duchess stayed in London during that early summer – there were many visits from the royal grandparents, King George V and Queen Mary, who were delighted with their first grandchild; the Prince of Wales, the new baby's Uncle David, also came and went as if was his own home, for the brothers were great friends.

Such happy domesticity was not to last for long. The king wanted his son and daughter-in-law to undertake a six-month tour of the Antipodes. For the duchess it meant parting with her baby daughter, while for the duke it meant what he dreaded most: making public speeches, and overcoming his natural shyness and the bad stammer that always afflicted him in public. Fortunately before their departure a new speech therapist, Lionel Logue, was found by the duchess, and all three worked hard and fruitfully together so that, partly through the duke's own efforts and partly through his young wife's charm and support, the tour turned out to be very successful – the first of many. It was also the first call for personal sacrifice that the monarchy had made on the young duchess.

The next trial was to be much more formidable. The royal brothers, particularly the Prince of Wales and Prince Bertie, had a close and affectionate relationship which the addition to the family of Prince Bertie's enchanting wife only made happier and more fun. Through a lonely and often demanding childhood, the princes had stood together, the happy-go-lucky, adventurous Prince of Wales often shielding his shyer and superficially less gifted brother, encouraging and teasing him and sharing his confidences. With manhood their ways parted and their lifestyles became very different, but the Duke of York and his siblings still loved and admired the debonair Prince of Wales, and he could do no wrong in their eyes.

Everyone in the royal family and 'society' knew that the Prince led a 'fast' life. Nearly everyone knew (and liked) the Prince's two mistresses: the beautiful Freda Dudley Ward, the wife of a Liberal MP, and latterly Lady Furness, the American wife of a shipping magnate. But in 1934 these two relatively circumspect ladies were suddenly and, in the case of Freda, cruelly cast aside by the prince who had fallen in love once again, this time with an American of a much more ambitious kind, Mrs Wallis Simpson. During the next two unhappy years a wedge was slowly driven between the brothers; the prince's character changed, and not for the better, becoming morose and even more undependable, while Mrs Simpson's adhesive grip on his life grew even stronger and more exclusive.

Wallis, whom I met long after the débâcle, had the brightest, deepest blue eyes that I have ever seen, like best-quality sapphires, and was very chic. She had an abrasive quality about her, a lacquered gloss that was the exact opposite of the Duchess of York's gentle, natural style; her values and manners shocked the good and dutiful Yorks and, although a polite front was kept up, the brothers saw less and less of each other. It must have been a deeply sad time for the Yorks, with loyalty and love being slowly eroded and with the gradual realisation of what we all now know: that the Prince of Wales had never understood the qualities which the British expect from their royal family; had never accepted that his freedom would be restricted; and did not share the high principles, nor even the down-to-earth common sense of his father or brother. In addition he had of late made some dangerous and quite unconstitutional contacts with Germany where, in 1933, Hitler had come to power.

At Balmoral in October 1935 the old and failing king told the Archbishop of Canterbury, 'After I am gone, the boy will ruin himself in twelve months.'

When George V died in January 1936 and the prince succeeded him as Edward VIII, the new king seemed hell-bent in the ten months of his reign on fulfilling that prophecy. All warnings were ignored, his family were shut out and by December the prince's obsession had become almost paranoid. When the story finally broke in the British press the reaction of a hostile people and parliament forced him into a final decision: to abdicate or give up the 'woman he loved'. He told the Prime Minister, Stanley Baldwin, of his decision on 5 December 1936, but what must surely have added to the hurt and anguish of his younger brother (and Queen Elizabeth herself has told me this) was that, for two whole days afterwards, the King avoided seeing him or telling him what was happening and it was only late on 7 December that Prince Bertie finally forced a meeting. His diary that night recorded: 'The awful and ghastly suspense of waiting is over. I found him pacing up and down the room and he told me his decision that he would go.'

The Duchess of York was ill with influenza then and one can imagine the loneliness of the future king as he came to terms with the cataclysmic change not only to his own life, but also to those of his beloved wife and children. The next day he went to see Queen Mary and when he told her what had happened, he broke down and sobbed like a child. The duchess's reaction was more positive. To the Archbishop of Canterbury she wrote: 'I can hardly now believe that we have been called to this tremendous task . . . the curious thing is that we aren't afraid. I feel that God has enabled us to face the situation calmly . . .'

If anyone had misgivings that George VI, as he chose to be called, was not equal to the task, they were soon to be proved wrong. Though a modest man and given to self-doubt, the new king grew in stature as the weeks passed. He was fully aware that the monarchy had passed through its greatest crisis in modern times and had written: 'If the worst happens and I have to take over, you can be assured that I will do my best to clear up the inevitable mess, if the whole fabric does not crumble under the shock and strain of it all!' And from the moment of his accession on 11 December 1936, King George VI dedicated himself totally to what he saw as his principal responsibility: 'to make amends for what has happened'.

The press reacted sensibly and patriotically. After Christmas Day they scarcely mentioned the king in exile. There was no censorship, but people wanted to forget and the nation held together like a good family does when there has been a bad scandal. As has been said, 'Abdication was Britain's vote for Monarchy', and a proposal by the Independent Labour Party Member of Parliament, James Maxton, 'to replace the crown with government of a republican kind', was defeated in the Commons by 403 votes to 5.

There was much to be done, and not only in restoring confidence in the monarchy. As the new owner of a dozen draughty and old-fashioned palaces and the new master of several thousand servants and dependants whose lives and conditions had scarcely changed in the last hundred years, George VI realised that the whole creaking machinery must be modernised and drastically pruned.

He had a talent for organisation, and when that spring he moved his family into Buckingham Palace he started on a major overhaul. Queen Elizabeth told my sister (whose husband, the Earl of Eldon, was a lord-in-waiting) that when she first slept in Buckingham Palace she was surprised to find a bottle of whisky on a side-table in her bedroom. She did not say anything, thinking it was a mistake, but the next night and the night after the bottle was still there, though she noticed that it was of a different brand. On making enquiries, she found that the custom of putting out a new bottle of whisky every night when she was in residence had existed ever since Queen Victoria, having a sore throat, had asked for a hot toddy some time back in the 1890s!

Queen Elizabeth's chief worry, other than the multifarious engagements and duties that were now becoming a daily routine, was the welfare of her two children. The Yorks had always hoped to bring up

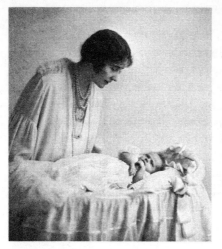

Left   HRH The Duchess of York with her first-born daughter, Princess Elizabeth, April 1926.

Right   A private visit to Beaufort Castle, 1946. HM Queen Elizabeth, with the author and her two eldest children.

HM King George VI and Queen Elizabeth after the bombing of Buckingham Palace, 1940.

the princesses as normally as possible, but Princess Elizabeth was now the heir presumptive to the throne and both her status and her parents' plans inevitably changed. Luckily, the eleven-year-old princess was a serious and conscientious child and a much-admired model whom Princess Margaret, four years younger and by nature more light-hearted and fun-loving, always tried to emulate. Their sensible and down-to-earth governess, Miss Crawford, was a competent teacher who took them on visits to museums and art galleries. There was a special Buckingham Palace company of thirty-four Girl Guides and Brownies, whose activities they joined in enthusiastically and who met once a week in the old summerhouse in the palace garden but, otherwise, the only young people with whom the princesses now came into contact were cousins and the children of courtiers and friends.

All manner of pets were kept and devotedly cared for, and perhaps the present Queen's love of animals goes back to the time when they filled the gap of ordinary companionship and rough and tumble with other children which the princesses were inevitably denied.

The coronation of George VI and Queen Elizabeth took place in May 1937 and the deeply religious king and queen felt uplifted and strengthened by the sacramental moments of the beautiful ceremony, * as well as much comforted by the enormous enthusiasm of the crowds. For everyone it was a healing day.

On 3 September 1939 Great Britain declared war on Germany. It is in days of national peril and disaster that monarchy is most truly significant. It is then that it is appreciated anew and fully understood; it becomes a comforting hand held out in the dark and a guiding light to follow. The British public were in the front line of the Second World War, and in the five and a half long years that followed, the king and queen led the nation and shared all the agonies and dangers of their subjects. Queen Elizabeth's saying after Buckingham Palace was bombed in September 1940: 'I'm glad we've been bombed. It makes me feel I can look the East End in the face,' will always be remembered by Londoners who endured the Blitz, and when the evacuation of the princesses to Canada was suggested: 'The children won't leave without me; I won't leave without

* The meaning of the Coronation Service is the same as it was in the year 973, when the first King of All-England, Edgar, was crowned at Bath Abbey – 'that an anointed king and his people are a partnership unto God'. In the coronation oath the king promises 'to do justice, stop the growth of iniquity, protect the Holy Church of God, help and defend widows and orphans, restore the things that are gone to decay, maintain the things that are restored, punish and reform what is amiss, and confirm what is in good order'.

the King; and the King will never leave,' was another remark (and decision) that endeared the royal family to the people and brought them much closer to their subjects. More clearly than ever before, the British monarchy symbolised the unity and courage of a nation who at one time stood alone against the powers of darkness.

I shall always remember VE-Day. My sailor husband had been reported missing, then killed on active service in November 1943. Among the cheering crowds and happy, reunited couples, bereft mothers and war widows tried their best to rejoice, but we made a poor fist of it and by evening it was thought best to ship me back to the country. Jack Eldon, my brother-in-law, dropped me off at what was left of Paddington Station on his way to the Palace. I sat on my suitcase on a deserted platform and waited for a train that did not come, and wept.

Indeed, once the cheering had stopped, the mood of the country was one of sadness and exhaustion. 'How did you feel when the war ended, Ma'am?' a mutual friend asked Queen Elizabeth. 'We felt,' and she put her head on one side and thought carefully, 'we felt absolutely *whacked*.' And once again she spoke for us all.

But that autumn, after the general election (the 'demob' election) had been declared and a new, Labour, government was in place, the king and queen escaped to Balmoral where they spent their first relaxed and completely happy family holiday since the outbreak of war six years before.

Queen Elizabeth, in waders and one of her timeless felt hats, fished the rivers and lochs to her heart's content between organising the household and the fun. The king taught his elder daughter to stalk, a sport which provides long hours of quiet and often silent companionship and collaboration. There were lunchtime picnics in the heather, parlour games and Highland dancing at night with 'the Bodyguard' (Queen Mary's name for her granddaughters' ball-partners and friends) and the young officers of the Scottish regiment on duty. It was a perfect and almost carefree holiday, but the following year, a year of austerity and rationing, of withdrawals and restrictions, new and deep anxieties overshadowed the lives of the royal family: the king was feeling unnaturally tired, he had seen his doctors, and what the royal physicians had told Queen Elizabeth in private was extremely worrying.

The king too was worried, though not about himself. The forthcoming independence of India and Burma appeared to him not only to herald the break-up of the British Empire, but the start of a decline which might well leave Britain without a voice in world affairs and her king-emperor without a role. Nearer still to George VI's heart was the prospect of another and equally inevitable loss. Princess Elizabeth had fallen head over heels in love with her dashing young cousin, Prince Philip of Greece, and wished to become officially engaged. Her parents agonised over their decision and at first withheld their consent, her father on the grounds that she was still too young and inexperienced to marry, her mother because she felt she had not yet met enough young men to be sure of her choice. There was also a constitutional difficulty about Prince Philip's nationality, and the problem of cancelling a planned family tour of South Africa. Besides all this, the king was not well and decidedly tetchy. He had set his heart on the entire family ('us four') visiting South Africa to show his gratitude to General Smuts and that country for their loyalty during the war, and he also wished to reaffirm the ties and affection which still linked Britain with her Dominions under the Crown in a bewildering world of change and uncertainty. Queen Elizabeth was also looking forward to escaping what turned out to be a harsh winter at home as she was worried about the king's health and thought the sunshine would do him good.

As it turned out, the king was unhappy, nervous and irritable during most of the tour. With the news of appalling weather and shortages of food and fuel in Britain, he felt he should never have left and might be criticised for doing so. Behind the scenes, as so often before, Queen Elizabeth soothed and smoothed. She could always make him laugh and sometimes, to defuse an explosion, she would take hold of his wrist and count the pulse beats like an anxious nurse, with invariably happy results. In public she radiated charm and interest, while the princesses thoroughly enjoyed the adventure of it all, so that what might have been a disaster was neatly turned into a great success.

From the first moment of her marriage Queen Elizabeth had made a deliberate decision never to upstage or outshine the king. Though they would often work as a team, hers, she decided, was to be the supporting role and she never deviated from this intention during his lifetime. In practice, however, things would sometimes turn out differently.

It was Queen Elizabeth who always bore the strain, filled the awkward gap and, ever vigilant when things looked like going wrong, carried off the day. It was partly her childhood training at Glamis, partly 'the knack', as she called it, partly her genuine interest in people, and partly her amazing vitality and energy that made it possible. Loyal courtiers return drained and exhausted from royal tours (after one gruelling royal visit to Canada my brother-in-law had to go to bed for a week), but Queen Elizabeth has always seemed to thrive on them.

Events moved fast after their return from South Africa. Although the official announcement of Princess Elizabeth's engagement had to wait another two months, on 10 July 1947 it was finally made, allowing barely four months' preparation for the doubly royal wedding which brought more crowned heads, reigning and exiled, to London than had been seen there since Queen Mary's dancing days. The old queen wrote in her diary after one of the many pre-wedding receptions: 'Saw many old friends. I stood from 9.30 till 12.15 am!!! Not bad for 80.'

For a ball at Buckingham Palace Nancy Astor lent me her dummy tiara, which was made of false diamonds and looked well enough except that, when we met on the ballroom floor, she gave its elastic an affectionate and proprietorial tweak. Later on I was brought up and presented to the king, who asked me to dance. Suitably flattered, I accepted and we hopped around for a bit, but when the music stopped I did not know whether I was meant to curtsy and move away or whether this would be lèse-majesté. The king went on talking, the music started up and round we whirled again, but when this had happened for a fourth time, and there was still no husband or courtier available to deliver His Majesty from me, I remember seeing Queen Elizabeth across the room and steered my royal partner towards her like to a port in a storm. I later learnt that part of His Majesty's shyness (and charm) was his great difficulty in saying goodbye.

King George VI may have stalled over his daughter's engagement but, once it was announced, he threw himself wholeheartedly into the wedding plans. He liked his new son-in-law, whose war-time service and career in the Royal Navy gave them so much in common and plenty to talk about. Nevertheless, as he wrote to his daughter some time later: 'I have watched you grow up all these years with pride under the skilful direction of Mummy, who, as you know, is the most marvellous person in the world in my eyes, and I can, I know, always count on you, and now Philip, to help us in our work. Your leaving us has left a great blank in our lives but do remember that your old home is still yours and do come back to it as much and as often as possible – I can see that you are sublimely happy with Philip, which is right, but don't forget us is the wish of Your ever loving and devoted Papa.'

'Adapt and evolve' is all very well as a principle for the British monarchy but life in the close-knit little family would never be quite the same again.

The next autumn, shortly after the birth of his first grandchild, who was christened Charles, the king's health deteriorated and his doctors confirmed that he was suffering from arterio-sclerosis, a form of thrombosis, and ordered a long period of complete rest. In the spring of 1949 he seemed better, but the improvement was short-lived. In March 1951 he was operated on for cancer of the lung and, although the operation was a success, there remained the risk of a further thrombosis which would probably be fatal. His wife and family kept this from the king and continued their endless round of public duties, Princess Elizabeth and Prince Philip undertaking a major tour of Canada and the United States. When they returned they were much relieved to find the king's health a little improved. There was a day of National Thanksgiving on 2 December 1951 and the royal family moved to Sandringham for Christmas.

The king came up to London in January to see his doctors and to say goodbye to Princess Elizabeth and Prince Philip, who were flying off on another long tour of East Africa and the Antipodes. It was a sad parting. A week later he had a good day's shooting at Sandringham with some of his tenants and the local farmers, about twenty guns in all, who, walking in line across fields of frozen stubble and winter wheat, accounted for a bag of 280 hares. He was tired and happy when he went to bed that night, but when his valet called him the next morning, the king was dead.

A photograph showing the three mourning queens tells better than any words the tragedy that suddenly, prematurely and irrevocably altered their lives. Dignity and duty sustained them – mother, wife and daughter – each in their private world of grief; sustained them throughout the accession formalities, the funeral ceremonies and beyond. There was no time for Queen Elizabeth or her daughter to indulge in sorrow, except in private. But the following autumn the Queen Mother went alone to the Castle of Mey, a house among the clouds and the bare hills of the Caithness coast which she had bought on impulse that mourning year, and perhaps it was there that she came to terms with her loss. The woman who had ceased to be reigning queen and empress, ceased to be the focus of a nation's adulation, is essentially a private person and it has only been by chance that a corner of the veil over those solitary days has been lifted, for Queen Elizabeth wrote to an old friend, Edith Sitwell, who had sent her an anthology of poems she had made:

'It is giving me much pleasure, and I took it out with me and I started to read it, sitting by the river, and it was a day when one felt engulfed by great black clouds of unhappiness and misery, and I found a sort of peace stealing round my heart as I read such lovely poems and heavenly words. I found a hope in George Herbert's poem, "Who would have thought my shrivel'd heart could have recover'd greennesse? It was quite

Three mourning queens,
Westminster Hall, February
1952.

HM Queen Elizabeth, the
Queen Mother, 1990.

gone underground," and I thought how small and selfish is sorrow. But it bangs one about until one is senseless, and I can never thank you enough for giving me such a delicious book wherein I found so much beauty and hope, quite suddenly one day by the river.'

Queen Elizabeth's story in essence has been a love story. She married because she believed in Prince Bertie when no one else did and, as Robert Lacey has written: 'Under the warming influence of her faith he unfolded and grew. In her marriage she gave him strength, and he repaid her with total love.'

The story was now over, the strength seemed exhausted and only courage was left. She returned to London and was once more engulfed in the daily round of family and public duty. 'Royalty is a job for life,' she had learnt from Queen Mary in the early days of her marriage and now Queen Mary too, the grand old trouper who had always been her loyal ally and friend, was failing. 'I am beginning to lose my memory,' she told Osbert Lancaster that winter, 'but I mean to get it back.' She had never once let the monarchy down in life, nor would she in death, and when it came on 24 March 1953, three months before her grand-daughter's coronation, her wishes were observed: the court did not go into mourning; the funeral procession to St George's Chapel at Windsor was a quiet and simple one; and no shadow was cast on the glorious events to come.

Queen Mary's death left a gap in the public image of the British royal family. Within living memory there had always been a matriarch behind the throne, a Queen Mother whose ultimate wisdom and experience both the family and the nation somehow, perhaps atavistically, relied on. What could be more natural than the promotion of Queen Elizabeth into that position? The formal announcement of her new title as 'Queen Elizabeth, the Queen Mother' was made on 14 February 1952. She fitted neatly into the gap that the hierarchy demanded, and her role from then on was assured.

Since the coronation of her daughter, Queen Elizabeth's most important work has been the official tours she has undertaken on behalf of the monarchy. She has carried out an average of one a year, thirty-six in all and, in 1991, in spite of everyone's advice, was contemplating her ninth visit to Canada. I can hear the echo of her voice: 'They really do seem to want one. I can't think why. And one can't, really can't, let them down.' This was said in that gentle, confidential, joke-sharing, deprecatory, vulnerable way of hers which makes strong men wobble and all men want to spring to her defence and undertake impossible feats of valour.

Sir Martin Gilliat, her Private Secretary of thirty years' standing, and Sir Alistair Aird, the Controller of her Household, though fiercely loyal, are sometimes more practical. It takes Queen Elizabeth's household – secretariat, dressmakers, modistes and others – nearly a year to complete the arrangements for a major tour, which are detailed down to the last bouquet and button, and although electronic miracles have recently speeded up communications, they are not always available in the far-flung outposts of what used to be empire to answer such questions as: 'Should Mrs Eleanor J. MacWhinney's gloves be buttoned or left undone when – and if – she is presented to Her Majesty?'

In between her tours, the ordinary routine of the Queen Mother's slice of royal duties continues unabated. As well as having to deal with a vast correspondence, she is president or patron of 312 organisations, colonel-in-chief of eighteen regiments, commander-in-chief of the women's army, navy and air force, Master of the Bench of the Middle Temple and, until recently, Chancellor of London University and Lord Warden of the Cinque Ports, two roles which had never before been held by a woman and which she has greatly enjoyed.

She is usually at her desk in the light and sunny sitting-room of her London home, Clarence House, by 10.30 a.m., having already made her personal telephone calls to her family and friends from her bedroom, where breakfast is brought to her on a tray by her personal maid and dresser. Sir Martin Gilliat soon joins her and the business of the day begins. It will seldom end until midnight. If there are no public or personal evening engagements, after a simple supper she returns to bed, sometimes with more papers and letters for there is always a mountain of reading to be got through. She writes all her personal and thank-you letters by hand, and they are very good letters indeed. Her personality jumps off the page and, like all good letter-writers, one hears her voice in every vivid, quirky phrase or *mot juste*, a voice that often inspires and always amuses. This sensitivity for language is part of her native wit and quick intelligence – an *intelligence du coeur* which can follow almost instinctively the thoughts of much more intellectual or academic men and women (but mostly men) like a good amateur can sight-read an accompaniment for professional musicians. Indeed she delights in their company almost as much as they do in hers. She is not always a sugar and cream lady, and can on occasion, and when she feels strongly about something, offer as sharp a judgment or opinion as any heard around smoking-rooms or high tables.

Her personality and personal taste are also reflected in her collection of pictures, particularly at Clarence House, where it is surprisingly wide-ranging in provenance and style. Family portraits, classical and modern paintings, a splendid mix of Old Master drawings, Paul Sandby water-colours of eighteenth-century London, Henry Moore's huddled figures of the Blitz, a good Duncan Grant, and a wonderful early Augustus John: each is the long-considered, much-valued choice of a discerning collector, or (and here she has an unfair advantage) the prime offering of a devoted artist-friend.

In music her taste is wide and uninhibited. Because she is truly musical and not a musical snob, she can find delight in almost any of its forms, provided they are good. She has always loved dancing, so a good dance tune or Highland reel will set her feet tapping. And singing, as naturally and unaffectedly as birds sing, has always been a happy feature of off-duty life at Royal Lodge, Windsor, or Birkhall. But it was not until I happened on an old book, Lord Frederick Hamilton's memoirs, that I realised Queen Elizabeth's remarkable musical pedigree. Here is his account of a visit to Glamis in the 1880s, in her grandfather's day, as it appears in *The Days before Yesterday* (1920):

'The seven sons and three daughters of the family were all born musicians. I have never heard such perfect and finished part-singing as that of the Lyon family, and they were always singing – on the way to a cricket match; on the road home from shooting; in the middle of dinner, even, this irrepressible family could not help bursting into har-mony, and such exquisite harmony, too! The dining-room at Glamis is a very lofty hall, oak-panelled, with a great Jacobean chimney-piece rising to the roof. After dinner it was the custom for the family pipers to make the circuit of the table three times, and then to walk slowly off, still playing, through the tortuous stone passages of the ancient building until the faint echoes of the music had died away. Then all the lights in the dining-room were extinguished except the candles on the table, and out came a tuning-fork, and one note was sounded – "Madrigal 'Spring is Come', third beat," said the conducting brother, and off they went, singing exquisitely: glees, madrigals, part-songs, anything and every-thing, the acoustic properties of the lofty room adding to the effect.'

There can be little doubt that the royal family have inherited their talent for music and acting – especially burlesque – from the former Lady Elizabeth Bowes-Lyon.

Once, when Queen Elizabeth visited Beaufort, my family home in Scotland, we persuaded her, somehow, on a *very* relaxed evening, to do a short cabaret turn at the piano, which turned out to be her very own interpretation of a Scottish ballad we had all learnt as children and long suffered from: 'Ca' the yowes to the knowes', beautifully sent up and sung with an extra poignancy not originally intended by Sir Walter Scott. It was very funny and extremely professional.

It may have been that evening when it first dawned on me, without any knowledge of her musical inheritance, that Queen Elizabeth is a born *performer*, and that it is easy and natural (and fun) for her to project herself before one, two, three or ten thousand people. This inborn talent has been immensely useful to her in public life, and I suspect that she knows all its advantages and, equally, its dangers.

Pretty, soignée, gentle and feminine, she can still turn herself on like a light and outshine everyone else in the room – a gift that has not always been appreciated by cleverer and by even more beautiful women.

How does she do it? In public, when she is on walkabout, it is partly spontaneous but it is also a deliberate and concentrated projection of herself to her audience which is as exhausting and demanding as any great actress's performance, but which cannot be denied, as the people love it and she really loves the people, both for themselves and for their loyalty to what she represents. And in private? One might as well chase a moonbeam as analyse charm. To most people it is just her own unique and inimitable way of being herself.

The question of her public image and style is another matter. Nowadays public figures, in America and elsewhere, have image-makers, but that would have been unknown to George VI in 1936 and, anyway, to Queen Elizabeth a laughable concept; yet almost by chance the new king created for his queen an 'image' which has lasted through the years and, aided by Cecil Beaton's timeless talent, immediately springs to a million people's minds whenever they think of her. Before a state visit to France King George asked Norman Hartnell, an up-and-coming young couturier, to design some ball-dresses for the queen that would look exactly like those that the other empress, Elizabeth (of Austria), had worn in the many portraits of her that hang on the walls of Windsor and Sandringham. It was an inspired choice, for they are possibly the most romantic and queenly portraits ever painted. And so the 'Winterhalter Look' – clouds of tulle and diamonds and a backward-sweeping crinoline – was born and Queen Elizabeth took it to Paris with her the following year, and it took Paris by storm. That it happened also to be the antithesis of the hard chic and vulgar jewels of the Duchess of Windsor was incidental.

The daytime 'look' was something else. When war came, Queen Elizabeth was nearly forty, with the beginnings of a motherly, if not matronly, outline. She was sensitive about her appearance and about the feelings of bombed-out, shelter-dwelling Londoners whom she visited almost daily, anxious not to look too smart and yet knowing she must be recognisably their queen. Why not capitalise on a simple, comfortable and approachable look and dress in soft, clear colours? The result, according to Winston Churchill's wife, Clementine, was 'very soignée and sweet, like a plump turtle dove'. And who does not love turtle doves?

Of Queen Elizabeth's many homes (Castle Mey in Caithness and Birkhall in Aberdeenshire, Sandringham in Norfolk, which the Queen lends her every July, Clarence House in London and Royal Lodge at Windsor), Royal Lodge is where her young and happy days were spent and where she can now enjoy the things she likes best, a country mixture of family, dogs, gardening, strolling round the park and friends. Clarence House is a base for work, Royal Lodge is a base for fun. There used to be weekend parties throughout the summer, but now Queen Elizabeth has rationed herself to only a few on either side of Royal Ascot for, as owner, enthusiastic spectator and perhaps the most popular figure in the horse-racing world, racing dates are fixtures which inevitably come first.

My husband, Fitzroy, and I are always bidden to the weekend which revolves around one of her oldest friends, the Very Reverend Bishop Horace Donegan, CBE, late Episcopal Bishop of New York, who has been an annual guest of the Queen Mother since 1955.* He is now nearly ninety but still preaches an excellent sermon on Sunday in the royal family's private chapel in the park, which is only two minutes' walk from Royal Lodge and where the Queen and the other members of Her Majesty's family often join Queen Elizabeth in her special side 'box' in the sanctuary of the high Victorian chapel. It was built as a memorial to Queen Victoria's own children by that queen herself, whose long life outlasted those of several of them.

Our Royal Lodge weekends are invariably happy ones. Queen Elizabeth is an inspired hostess, and as we are nearly always the same group of old friends, our company is very relaxed. There is walking and talking (occasionally shouting), swimming and sleeping, eating and feasting – and, yes, singing. It may not be of the same high quality as at Glamis, but we do our best.

Our royal hostess is tireless: there are practically no visible signs that Queen Elizabeth's years have in any way diminished her, or have dimmed her enormous capacity for having – and making – what she calls 'fun', but which is nearer to what philosophers might call enthusiasm, or pure happiness.

---

* Bishop Horace died in November 1991. We all miss him.

On her ninetieth birthday there was a tribute to Her Majesty the Queen Mother on Horseguards Parade which I attended and which Michael Parker, its co-ordinator, said was the easiest pageant he had ever organised. The only difficulty was *stopping* people from participating – people from every sphere of our national life – from every corner of the British Isles and its Commonwealth. 'I didn't have a single refusal,' he told Sir Martin Gilliat. Between the tears and the cheers of what was, in fact, the Queen Mother's triumph, it seemed to me that a bit of history was being made as well as re-enacted.

I did not care, nor was there need to look very much forward from that happy day, but looking back I remembered that on her *eightieth* birthday there had been a Service of Thanksgiving in St Paul's Cathedral and the banner that had hung across the nave proclaimed what I believe to be Her Majesty's personal credo. They were the words of Julian of Norwich, a fourteenth-century mystic: '*All shall be well and all manner of things shall be well.*' It was a good device to live by, and to die by too: cheerful, optimistic and founded on the certainties of Christian faith – and hope.

2

GREAT BRITAIN

Queen Elizabeth II

'Ours is a traditional rather than a revolutionary constitution. One may be more logical, but the other appears to keep out the weather more successfully.'

WILLIAM PITT (THE YOUNGER)

The British monarchy has served our country well. It has lived through many vicissitudes, survived many crises and adapted to many changes. I have little doubt that given our present Queen's proven courage and robust common sense it will survive the latest one, but what makes the events of 1992 particularly sad is that the British monarchy has been shaken, not by the actions of its sovereign, but by the failed marriages of too many of her children.

In the past royal marriages were often unhappy in private yet seen to be successul in public. With the spotlight of an intrusive media permanently focused on them, this is no longer possible. And times have changed. Today's partners have different priorities, different codes.

Queen Elizabeth II is an admirable and representative monarch. To most of her subjects she still represents old-fashioned principles and family virtue. But the question which the monarch and Parliament, who both represent her people, must now address boldly is: 'What went wrong and how can it be remedied?'

I have a theory that one's children turn out to be much more the sum of their four grandparents than of their two parents – that is, unless environment steps in and mixes things up. It happens in bloodstock lines, so why not with human beings?

Queen Elizabeth II is very much the amalgam of a Scottish aristocratic and an English, albeit Hanoverian, family. Lady Strathmore was a large, positive matriarch of great character with a gift for spreading happiness and fun around. She was also, in a quiet way, a deeply religious woman who was never solemn about the high standards she set for herself and for her children.

Lord Strathmore cultivated a certain deliberate vagueness and delegated the running of most things to his wife, but he too had the high sense of duty and obligation to the people on his estates that was traditional among old-fashioned Highland lairds and chiefs. His family had been strongly Jacobite and his ideas were regarded by some as behind the times, but this did not prevent them from flocking to Glamis in August for the shooting, or to St Paul's Walden in June for the friendly and often hilarious cricket matches which he delighted in organising. For the first ten years of her life, Princess Elizabeth spent long and happy holidays at St Paul's and at Glamis. She basked in their free and easy atmosphere and revelled in all the dressing-up, the music-making, the fun and games and expeditions that her grandmother and her uncles and aunts organised around the children.

It must have been quite a contrast to the visits she made to her other grandparents. At Windsor the soldiers and the servants, the magnificence of the apartments and the formality of the court must have spelt out to the little princess the grandness of her heritage, while the bracing East Coast air of Sandringham, where she would walk out to join the guns for lunch, or stand behind her father, collecting spent cartridges to stick on her small fingers, must have underlined its privileges. The great pheasant shoots at Sandringham started in the reign of King Edward VII, and were continued by his son. The best shots in the country would be invited and it was supposed to be an honour to take part in the slaughter. My father, Simon Lovat, often did; but the enormous bags at Sandringham sickened him, keen sportsman though he was.

Nursery protocol when the princesses were at Windsor or Sandringham was almost as formal as in other parts of the court. 'Alla', or Mrs Knight, the head nanny, and Margaret Macdonald, known as 'Bobo', her nursery maid, saw to that. Bobo is still with the Queen and must by now have served her faithfully for almost sixty years as nanny, chief dresser and friend. The children would be washed, brushed and dressed up after nursery tea and then would 'come downstairs' to visit their grandparents. Holding on to Alla's hand, they passed along many dark passages, under the watchful eyes of the Winterhalter portraits of their ancestors, until a door at the end of one would finally open, revealing the softly lit, flower-filled, comfortably armchaired world of the grown-ups. A cheerful fire would be burning and, sitting on a chair beside it, would be a short, rosy-cheeked old gentlemen with a grizzled beard. Princess Elizabeth would climb on to his knee and begin telling him about the events of her day. King George V was a good and simple man and, more rarely, a genuinely humble one, virtues that children recognise. Princess Elizabeth loved her 'Grandpapa England', as she would later call him, and always listened carefully to what he had to tell her.

And so, more surprisingly perhaps, did the nation. Towards the end of his reign King George V had become the very model of a national grandfather. He reflected every one of those virtues the British people believed they still, and had certainly once, possessed: a sense of duty, dignity, courage, honesty, prudence and common sense. In this, he created a new role for modern kings and queens just as their old one was vanishing: *representation*, a role which his granddaughter has succeeded in following and fostering.

With the exception perhaps of George IV, whose qualities offered a mixed bag of blessings, it has long been accepted that the House of Hanover was the least cultivated dynasty to rule over any major nation in modern history, and certainly George V did nothing to reverse this judgment.* For him, 'highbrow' was a pejorative word – he thought when he first heard it that it was spelt 'eyebrow', which puzzled him. He preferred whist to bridge; 'Rose Marie' to *Così fan Tutte*; and his own family to clever outsiders. Harold Nicolson, who wrote his official biography, found considerable difficulty with his subject. 'For seventeen years,' Nicolson complained in a letter to his wife, 'he did nothing at all but kill animals and stick in stamps.' Yet he not only survived a major war, crises and revolutions throughout Europe and the rest of the world (during his reign five emperors, eight kings and queens and eighteen minor dynasties came to an end), but he also grew in popularity, largely because he represented the innate beliefs and standards of every decent British man and woman. An attack on their king would be an attack on the nation.

As she grew older, he taught his favourite grandchild the simple virtues that he believed in and which had served him so well: duty, hard work, including the really boring kind, and, as Robert Lacey puts it, 'a strong instinct for the ordinary as opposed to the extra-ordinary in life'.

---

* The lines

> 'Prince of Sportsmen,
> Peerless shot,
> But happiest
> Aboard his yacht.'

penned, I believe, by a grateful visitor to Sandringham, could be described as a short biographical sketch of the king, and also serves as an excellent example of his favourite kind of verse.

Queen Mary was also a strong influence and, as the young princess grew up, her grandmother became one of her greatest friends and confidantes. Princess May of Teck had been engaged to Edward VII's eldest son, Prince Eddy, a weak and unprincipled young man who, it was believed, she would 'steady down', but, perhaps fortunately, he died of influenza shortly before their wedding. It was then announced, somewhat surprisingly, that she would marry his younger brother, George, for when Queen Victoria got hold of a good idea, she did not easily let go.

Princess May had been brought up in England, under the wing of the queen-empress, but the Tecks were always what she called 'in short street' and when her mother's debts became insurmountable they had been packed off to Florence by Queen Victoria to economise. Florence was exile and Princess May was only too pleased to return to England and the royal fold. She had been brought up to be royal, to marry royalty, to serve the royal cause and she believed till the end of her days that there was no finer calling.

Unfortunately the mixture of shyness and severity in her character, her lack of sophistication and of conversation, did not endear her to her jovial father-in-law, and the Yorks, as they were called at this time, never took part in the high jinks and worldly romps of Edward VII's court. Indeed, as soon as her husband succeeded his father as King George V, the romping stopped. A stern respectability and even a deliberate dullness descended on court life. Large-scale entertaining ceased and 'society' complained that King George and Queen Mary preferred the company of their own family to any other. Sadly this was not so, at least not exactly so. For, in spite of their excellent characters and innate kindness, King George and Queen Mary were shockingly bad parents. With the best intentions in the world, they arranged for their children to be brought up by a series of nurses, governesses and tutors within a rigid and unimaginative routine of work and duty more like a corrective institution than home life and, what is more, they hardly knew them. They met rarely, and only in the most formal way, and when they did, the parents were quite unable to communicate, let alone play with their children. When they were little the children were starved of affection. It left its mark on the more sensitive ones and almost inevitably caused friction and rebellion in the bolder sons. Queen Mary's stiffness was one of the troubles; her lifelong reserve and shyness always came between her and them. It distressed Lady Airlie, her closest friend and companion, who wrote: 'She loved them and was proud of them, but they were strangers to her emotionally.'

Once they grew up and married, however, Queen Mary's inhibitions disappeared and she got on wonderfully well with her daughters-in-law. As for the grandchildren, they were a constant source of interest and delight. She took a hand in all aspects of their welfare, including their education, informing Crawfie, their governess, that they should spend more time on their history lessons for 'she felt that genealogies, historical and dynastic, were very interesting to children, and for these children *most* important'.

She believed she was the only member of the royal family who had an eye for what she called 'good things'. It may have been Florence that educated it, or just living among the treasures of the royal palaces, but she was determined to share her appreciation and knowledge with her grandchildren, not least in regard to the historic collections that Princess Elizabeth would one day inherit. Queen Mary had become a keen collector herself and she enjoyed nothing better than antique hunting in Norfolk or Bath, which meant acquiring a great many sometimes dubiously authenticated knick-knacks and 'good pieces' – the dealers' only defence against her almost oriental belief that she should be presented with everything she admired!

When Edward VIII signed the Instrument of Abdication on 10 December 1936, Princess Elizabeth's life was radically changed. Overnight she became the heir presumptive to the British throne. She was ten-and-a-half years old and, though rather proud that her father and mother would soon be crowned king and queen, she did not relish her own new title. When it was explained to her that 'heir presumptive' was only a kind of holding position, and that if a son was born to her parents he would automatically be the heir *apparent*, she began to add to her evening prayers, poor child, a fervent but unanswered one for a baby brother.

That spring her family moved from the cosiness and familiarity of 145 Piccadilly to the chilly vastness and immense discomfort of Buckingham Palace, which has been her London home ever since. In those days it had a 'vermin man' employed solely to catch the rats and mice which scampered behind the wainscots, footmen in powdered wigs who lined the steps of the Grand Staircase whenever her parents gave state receptions, and messengers who carried notes from one end of the palace to the other as there was no internal communication system. But the palace did have a back garden which was almost the size of a nature reserve, and a lake, and a hill, and a hut which had once been Grandpapa England's summerhouse and which was now turned into the HQ of a newly formed palace troop of Brownies and Girl Guides. There were, after all, *some* compensations.

The new king and queen had always wanted their children to be brought up as normally as possible (I found on my travels that all royal families wish the same) and not suffer the isolation and loneliness of the king's own childhood. But inevitably, after the coronation, their small world shrank. It was only at Glamis or Royal Lodge that they would really run wild and behave like 'normal' children, and when, two years later, war was declared, even these limited freedoms were diminished. For the next five years the future Queen and her sister grew up in a kind of royal purdah which brought them into closer contact with their parents and with Alla, Bobo and Crawfie, but cocooned them in an artificial chrysalis which had nothing to do with the real world.

By all accounts, Princess Elizabeth was an exceptionally dutiful and responsible child, but she was also intelligent and precocious and eventually she began to chafe against the restrictions that had, of necessity, been imposed on the little group. The quiet determination which is part of her character, and which is perhaps a variation of her father's patience and steadfastness, was beginning to emerge.

On her sixteenth birthday – 21 April 1942 – she was required, like any other girl in Britain, to register at a labour exchange and then, unless circumstances forbade it, be called up for war work. She did this at Windsor, informing the family with evident delight that she was thinking of 'joining up' immediately. But the king would not hear of it. He insisted that she should continue her education, which by then had been supplemented by occasional lessons on constitutional history with Henry Marten, the Vice-Provost of Eton, and remain within the shelter of her family. She did not rebel, as many girls would have done; she bided her time. She had already made up her mind about much of the future: whom she was going to marry, and how. She knew that there would be other battles ahead, and more important ones. She was growing up to be a disciplined, quietly determined young woman.

I remember very clearly the long, hot summer of 1939. I suppose because of what was to follow, it will always seem an idyllic time, bathed by memory in a golden light. I was eighteen and in love with every young man who was in love with me, and even with some who were not. We had not yet known sorrow, or care, and we seemed to stand on the brink of something stupendous, not a cataclysm, we innocently thought, but an adventure.

Princess Elizabeth was only in her fourteenth year as, that same summer, the Royal Yacht steamed up the River Dart to anchor below the Royal Naval College, for her father was paying Dartmouth an official visit. On board *Britannia* were King George VI, Queen Alexandra of Greece (later Queen of Yugoslavia), Lord Louis Mountbatten, and four excited young teenagers, Lord 'Dickie's' daughters, Pamela and Patricia, and the two royal princesses. While the king and his cousin, both ex-Dartmouth cadets, were carrying out a cheerful inspection of their old college, the girls walked up to the Admiral's House and it was there that a newly joined eighteen-year-old cadet turned up – on the Admiral's orders – to help entertain them. He had fair hair, very blue eyes and all the assurance of a handsome young Viking, which, in fact, he more or less was.

Prince Philip of Greece's nationality and status in the pecking order of European royalty was far from simple. He was really a Dane, of the Royal Danish Schleswig-Holstein Sonderburg Glücksburg family; he had Russian and German but not a drop of Greek blood in him and he was related to nearly every royal family in Europe. Greece had invited his grandfather, Prince William of Denmark, to be her king in 1863 when she finally broke loose from the Ottoman Empire. But in 1913, after a long reign, King George I of Greece, as he had become, was assassinated and his family and descendants have had to play musical chairs with Greece's politicians and people ever since, on the throne at one moment, off it the next.

Prince Philip's father, Prince Andrew of Greece, a professional soldier, had been arrested in the latest revolution, nearly shot, and then exiled, first in Paris and then in Monte Carlo. His mother, Princess Alice of Battenberg, was Dickie Mountbatten's elder sister. She had brought up four daughters who had all married German princes but, when her youngest child and only son was still quite small, Princess Alice and her husband, having very different outlooks on life, had drifted apart and the boy had been taken under the wing of his two naturalised English uncles, his mother's brothers, while she herself retired to a life of prayer and good works in Greece. The elder uncle, Lord Milford Haven, sent young Philip to Cheam, a private school in Surrey, and later to Gordonstoun, Kurt Hahn's innovative public school which had been evacuated (because of Nazi persecution) from Salem in Germany to near Elgin in Morayshire. Dr Hahn used to come over and lunch occasionally with my mother at Beaufort and we thought him impressive, though not particularly likeable, and Prussian, rather than Jewish, in many of his theories.

The ambitious and dynamic Lord Louis Mountbatten ('Uncle Dickie') then took over Philip's career and obtained for him a temporary commission in the Royal Navy through the special entry scheme which allowed public schoolboys into Dartmouth at the age of eighteen. But on that happy summer's day Prince Philip's antecedents could not have mattered less to Princess Elizabeth. She had been bowled over by his easy, rather off-hand charm and she was only interested in his future. From that day onwards she began to day-dream about that future, and her own.

Day-dreams and hero-worship were all that sustained her during the long and dreary years of her adolescence when the war and national security imprisoned the two princesses in gloomy, dust-sheeted palaces, with precious few distractions. Cousinly letters were exchanged with Prince Philip and she occasionally saw him when he was on leave, for as soon as his training was over (he won the King's Dirk as the best all-round cadet of his term) the Prince had begun active service in destroyers and in the battleship HMS *Valiant*, where he made a name for himself as a bright and courageous young sub-lieutenant. He took part in the Battle of Matapan in 1941, in which his ship, though holed, managed to sink two Italian cruisers, and he was mentioned in dispatches.

In 1940 I had married a young naval officer who had already had two destroyers sunk under him during the first year of the war, and on the rare occasions when I was able to 'follow the flag' I would listen idly to wardroom gossip. An eventual royal engagement was rumoured and thought to be a good thing, but in HMS *Ivanhoe* and HMS *Faulknor* it was known that Philip was an extremely able and ambitious officer with a burning desire one day to command his own ship (every young Royal Naval officer wished the same) but it was also believed that, after the dangers and demands of active service in destroyers, Philip would never settle down to the restricted life of a prince consort.

The letters between Princess Elizabeth and Prince Philip continued, but when the Greek royal family made the first tentative suggestion that a courtship might ensue, it was brushed aside by an almost indignant King George VI. His daughter was far too young to know her own mind, he felt; she had not met enough young men, and so on. Lady Airlie, on the other hand, quotes Queen Mary as saying that Princess Elizabeth 'would always know her own mind. There's something very steadfast and determined about her'. The two old ladies also suspected that behind King George's delaying tactics lay an instinctive and scarcely realised possessiveness. Like many rather lonely men who had found complete happiness and fulfilment in marriage and a close family circle, he could not bear the thought of his daughter leaving it.

The queen simply wanted her daughter to be happy, but I know that she too agonised over whether Prince Philip was the right choice and whether, when and if it came about, he would ever accept the role of First Lieutenant to Elizabeth's captaincy of the ship of state.

Towards the end of the war, Princess Elizabeth realised at least one of her ambitions. She would be eighteen in April 1944, and her father at last accepted the inevitable. She joined the Auxiliary Training Service (ATS) as No. 230873, 2nd Subaltern Elizabeth Alexandra Mary Windsor, and started a course at Camberley in vehicle maintenance. As with everything she did, she took her training very seriously and emerged as an efficient driver and mechanic who could handle a ten-ton army lorry with the best of them.

With the victory of the Allies and the end of the war in Europe, life changed dramatically for everyone in the British Isles. The tensions and fears, the dangers and sorrows had eased, if not ceased, and an exhausted nation lay back to lick its wounds and count the cost.

For the princesses it was different. Life, so to speak, began on VE-Day when the drawbridge was at last let down and the king and queen deliberately encouraged them to meet as many people as possible, no doubt hoping that some attractive young man from a suitable British family would sweep their elder daughter off her feet. There was plenty of party-giving and party-going, but although she happily joined in the fun, Elizabeth's single-mindedness remained unchanged and her determination never faltered, even though new problems presented themselves. Quite apart from her father's objections, there was the question of Prince Philip's naturalisation, his new British name, the post-war plebiscite in Greece and, because of it, the effect of his actions on the Greek royalist cause. More worrying still was the direction of his naval career which was still of great importance to him, and the traditional distaste of the British public for foreigners – even for brave ones who had fought in the war alongside them. There could be no question of an immediate engagement.

Princess Margaret was firmly on her sister's side, but Queen Elizabeth knew from her own experience how long 'Prince Bertie' had waited for her and so thought the delays were no bad thing; but there must have been moments when her daughter felt once again that life was passing her by.

That year there was little contact between the two, but the following autumn her patience was rewarded. Prince Philip, on a few days' leave from the Navy, had joined the 'family firm' at Balmoral. He took Princess Elizabeth out for a drive and proposed to her. She accepted him immediately, and that was that. 'I have never seen anyone so much in love,' reported my sister to me – she was married to a lord-in-waiting to King George VI, Jack Eldon – but the young couple had nevertheless to agree that their engagement remain a secret until all the difficulties had been overcome. Once more it was a question of patience, discretion and self-discipline.

At last, when she was twenty-one years and three months old and Lieutenant Philip Mountbatten, as he was now known, was twenty-six, an official announcement from Buckingham Palace was finally made: 'It is with the greatest pleasure that the King and Queen announce the betrothal of their dearly beloved daughter, the Princess Elizabeth, to Lieutenant Philip Mountbatten, RN, son of the late Prince Andrew of Greece and Princess Andrew (Princess Alice of Battenberg), to which union the King has gladly given his consent.'

It was not until the morning of his daughter's wedding, on 20 November 1947, that King George gave his future son-in-law three new names: Lord Greenwich, Earl of Merioneth, and Duke of Edinburgh.

The period between her official engagement and her father's death three years later must have been among the happiest in Queen Elizabeth's life. Perhaps *the* happiest, if happiness can be measured on any time-scale. Shortly after Prince Charles's birth she joined her husband in Malta as an (only fairly) ordinary naval wife. The Duke of Edinburgh was then serving as First Lieutenant in the destroyer HMS *Chequers* and his uncle, Lord Louis Mountbatten, who commanded I Cruiser Squadron, Mediterranean, invited them to stay in his house overlooking the Grand Harbour at Valetta. Malta was always a happy station for the Navy. Even after the battering the island had taken during the war, the sun still shone, Valetta harbour still looked beautiful, everybody was delightfully 'foreign' and there was the usual round of parties, polo and picnics to enjoy.

'Uncle Dickie's' influence on his protégé and his protégé's bride was at that time unquestionable, and the fact that he was the Navy's foremost war hero and, as always, cut a tremendous dash, did nothing to diminish it. One of my favourite war-time stories about Mountbatten was told to me by an admiring sub-lieutenant who had served with him on HMS *Kelly*. Mountbatten liked having boiling hot water in his cabin for his morning shave, and when it was pointed out that because of a refit and a necessary readjustment of plumbing to accommodate new weaponry this would no longer be possible, the brains of the whole ship's company were put to solving the problem. The solution finally adopted was completely 'Heath Robinson'. The arrangements included: a new pipe, which

led directly to the captain's wash basin from the deck above; an Able
Seaman standing by it; a whistle; and a jug. When Lord Louis blew his
whistle the Able Seaman would rush to a nearby galley, fill his jug with
boiling water and pour it down the new pipe. The captain would turn
his hot water tap on and, bingo!, boiling water would flow from it, after
all.

Such determination always obtained results. Lord Louis's men adored
him and all his ships were happy ones.

The princess's visit to Malta was repeated after the birth, only a year
later, of Princess Anne. By this time the Duke of Edinburgh had been
gazetted Lieutenant-Commander and had realised his first great ambition
– the command of his own ship, the frigate HMS *Magpie*. It was, if
possible, an even happier time for the young couple. The Commander-
in-Chief, Mediterranean, had given Princess Elizabeth the use of his
dispatch vessel, HMS *Surprise*, and the Foreign Office and Admiralty
had agreed that the glamorous pair should jointly 'carry the flag' on
diplomatic visits to several Mediterranean ports – Athens included.

The two vessels enjoyed endless ragging and competition as they
steamed along and the signals passed between them are still preserved in
their ship's logs. Example: *Surprise* to *Magpie*: 'Princess full of beans'.
Magpie to *Surprise*: 'Is that the best you can give her for breakfast?'

The end of such fun came far too quickly. As his father-in-law's health
deteriorated, new responsibilities fell on Prince Philip's shoulders, and
he left the Navy 'on indefinite leave' to begin the series of overseas tours
with his wife which have been part of his duties ever since.

The first American tour, in 1951, was a tremendous success and, as
the king's condition seemed to be stabilised, they embarked on another,
much longer one to the Dominions. The young couple were only on the
first leg of it, in Kenya, when King George VI died suddenly of a heart
attack on 6 February 1952 and the shattered duke had to break the news
to his wife. 'I never felt so sorry for anyone in my life,' Michael Parker,
Prince Philip's Private Secretary, told Robert Lacey years later. 'He
looked as if you'd dropped half the world on him.' But what he and
Martin Charteris, then Private Secretary to Princess Elizabeth* remember most of all is the princess's amazing composure and her command of

* Martin Charteris (now Baron) was Private Secretary to Princess Elizabeth, 1950–2, Assistant
Private Secretary to her as Queen, 1952–72; Private Secretary to the Queen, and Keeper of Her
Majesty's Archives, 1972–7; a permanent lord-in-waiting to the Queen since 1978; and Provost of
Eton, 1978–91.

the situation. No doubt she had rehearsed it in her mind many times during the last year of her father's grave illness, but her decisiveness and the controlled calm of her public face were remarkable for someone so young.

As soon as a king dies, the burden of his kingship falls on his heir immediately. There is no pause or respite. *'Le Roi est mort. Vive le Roi!'*, and on it must go. Elizabeth had always known and still knows that this must be so and that until she herself lays down this burden or breathes her last, her duties as monarch will always be paramount – before those of daughter, wife, parent or friend. From the moment when she returned to the Sagana Hunting Lodge from a light-hearted fishing expedition to be told that she was Queen of Great Britain, its Dominions and Possessions beyond the Seas, she played her royal part with a calm dignity which did not falter until she stood beside the Lord Chamberlain at her father's graveside and watched him hold aloft his Staff of Office, break it in two and consign it to his royal master's grave.

From now on nothing would ever be the same. The emphasis of her relationship even with her family would change, and this was underlined by what Queen Mary had to say as she drove over from her own home to Clarence House, to which the Queen had returned: 'Your old granny and subject must be the first to kiss your hand.' From now on her mother and sister would curtsy to her on formal occasions and raise a delicate eyebrow if anyone dared to call her anything other than 'The Queen'. And even with her own husband, who certainly knew all about royalty and its exigencies, there would be moments when she would have to talk with him – or not talk – as Queen, rather than as his obedient and dutiful wife.

The coronation of Queen Elizabeth II was celebrated, we are told, not only by the whole British nation and Commonwealth, but by nearly one-quarter of all human beings then living in the world. It is a remarkable assumption, but then high-flown and remarkable assumptions were flying around the world like confetti in the general euphoria that led up to the great event. Even *Time* magazine, which had splashed the Queen's coronation portrait across its cover, believed that the young Queen was 'recapturing the mysterious power which ancient monarchs possessed, to represent, express and effect the aspirations of the collective subconscious'. This came rather ironically from a great republican nation that had once rebelled against one of those ancient monarchs, the Queen's own great-great-great-great-grandfather.

The crowds that day – 2 June 1953 – were enormous, the pageantry

The engagement photograph
of Princess Elizabeth and
Prince Philip, 10 July 1947.

The Coronation
procession passing
through Admiralty Arch,
2 June 1953.

superbly organised, and the processions to and from the Abbey 'as good as a play'. Inside the great mediaeval church the solemn and sacred coronation ritual unfolded like the stanzas of some epic poem. The Presentation, the Recognition, the Derobement, the Anointing, the Symbols of Power, the Enthronement and, finally, the Crowning. As St Edward's golden crown descended on Elizabeth II's head a great shout of 'God save the Queen!' roared out from every side, was echoed by the crowds outside, was wafted across the parks and down the streets till it seemed all London, all Britain, was cheering. Trumpets blared, bells pealed and cannons roared out their salute. The street parties, the fireworks and the dancing lasted long into the night.

When my sister sneaked into Buckingham Palace to join her courtier husband behind the scenes, the Queen's shining eyes told her of the extraordinary impact which the crowded streets and cheering people had had on her. She had never guessed it would be like that, she said, the feeling of elation and joy, of being carried forward on a great wave. She would never forget the tangible affection her people had shown her that day.

The new Queen found little difficulty in settling down to her new job. Every morning she would tackle the official boxes and correspondence with her Private Secretary, Michael Adeane. She was orderly and organised, indeed both her Private Secretaries have testified that at first they had been surprised by her almost professional ability to pick out the salient points of any memorandum or report they brought to her. She would muster her answers or solutions to problems in such a clear and decisive way that it often astounded them. Winston Churchill, then Prime Minister, who had declared himself nervous of discussing such serious matters of state with someone so young – 'a mere child' – soon became her greatest admirer and her willing slave, and he was only the first of a series of Prime Ministers who turned, it would sometimes seem, almost overnight into chivalrous champions of the monarchy, Socialists as much as high Tories. I have seen the same proprietorial, fond, even maudlin look on both Harold Wilson's and Jim Callaghan's faces when the Queen's name has come up in conversation – both, no doubt, rather touchingly thinking of her as 'their Queen'.

The young Queen was still basking in the afterglow of her coronation when she was faced with two almost simultaneous crises. Both Winston Churchill and Anthony Eden, his designated successor, fell seriously ill at the same moment and it looked as if she would have to use the Royal Prerogative and appoint either a new Prime Minister or a deputy one who would stand down if either of the invalids recovered. It was a

delicate situation, beset with political dangers, but it was compounded
by a second crisis, far closer to home.

Princess Margaret's ill-fated romance with Group Captain Peter
Townsend had been sniffed out by the world press, who were now threatening to blow it up into a major sensation.

There is little to add to a story that has already been told too often.
It is, after all, a simple story of a love affair that did not end happily,
but the other day I experienced – quite by chance – what might be called
a postscript, for I met Peter Townsend, now in his seventies, under
circumstances that might have been designed to encourage confidences.

We were fellow-passengers on a Yugoslav ferry boat, travelling from
Bari to Dubrovnik to support an internationally organised peace concert.
The night-crossing was long and tedious and there was nothing else to
do but talk to one's fellow-passengers. He was accompanied by his wife,
a good-looking Belgian lady who has something to do with UNICEF. I
suddenly recognised this frail, elderly, but still good-looking man, and I
asked him if he was indeed the Peter Townsend who had been an equerry
to King George VI. We talked, gingerly at first, about the old 'court',
mutual friends, death and then, without embarrassment, about his ill-
starred romance.

I asked him if he had any regrets, meaning perhaps did he feel, in
retrospect, any guilt and he answered simply and with conviction, 'Oh,
none. It had to go on, you see, to be played out until the end. We had
fallen in love, and there was no going back once we both knew that had
happened. The Queen Mother was very kind to me. We all loved her
. . . she was such fun. I wish I could send her a message . . . but . . .'
and his voice trailed off. 'The older courtiers,' he went on, 'simply didn't
understand. Tommy Lascelles* saw me and said, "You are either a fool
or a knave." I think if there had been some sympathy, even a little
understanding of my situation, it might have been resolved sooner, but
perhaps it was just as well.' There was nothing more to say and I changed
the subject, and thought, no-one could call him a bad man, but surely
rather a naive one, and how much easier it was for him, how *very* much
easier . . .

Princess Margaret's emergence from her war-time chrysalis had been
much more dramatic than that of her quieter and more serious sister.
The circle of friends she gathered around her was different too – they

---

* Tommy Lascelles had been Principal Private Secretary to King George VI and had stayed on
for the first year of Queen Elizabeth's reign.

were at first curious, then intrigued by the uniqueness of her position, then captivated by the brilliance and sparkle of her personality and by a beguiling charm which she would wickedly turn on (or off) at will. Her friends were not the wastrel children of an effete aristocracy, as they have often been painted, but on the whole a talented, clever and original crowd. She could have married almost any of them and lived happily ever after, but there burnt in her a spirit of romantic adventure, a dissatisfaction with the limitations of her life, a search for something different, yet at the same time a fierce awareness of who she was and what she and her family stood for. Until these contradictions were resolved they were bound to bring trouble to the warm-hearted, impulsive young princess.

Group Captain Peter Townsend, DSO, DFC, was fifteen years older than she was. He was also a newly divorced man with two young children, and the Anglican Church, of which the Queen was the titular head, at that time did not countenance the remarriage of divorced persons. After much thought and prayer, Princess Margaret renounced what was seen as an 'impossible' marriage by churchmen, the court and most conventional opinion of the day. She made the decision herself, without pressure from her family, and it was a turning-point in her life. After it she was left vulnerable, without direction and very much exposed to the public eye. That many of her friends told her conventional opinion was hypocritical, and that the Church would one day change its mind, was possibly true, but of very little help.

It was then the turn of the Queen to give her sister all the loving support that Princess Margaret had once given her when the fulfilment of her own dreams had seemed so uncertain. She did so in full measure, but it was the first time that Queen Elizabeth, a very private person, had to face up to a personal dilemma in the full glare of the public's gaze and it had been an unpleasant, painful experience for her and for the whole family. Their fear and dislike of the gossip-hungry media can, with good reason, be traced back to that time.

Prince Philip also found it difficult to settle down after the coronation. His career in the Navy had ended and he too had to find a role that satisfied his energies and employed his undoubted talents. It was not easy. If he or 'Uncle Dickie' had ever expected to change the two-steps-behind traditional role of British royal consorts, they were wrong. The royal family and the British public saw to that and in spite of his splendid war record, they watched him at first with mild suspicion. Had he ever put a foot wrong in that direction, and he never has, the British press would have pounced on it. They had already noted with some satisfaction that his aunts – 'Uncle Dickie's' sisters, who had all married German princelings, some of them thought to be Nazi sympathisers – were *not* asked to attend the coronation of his wife.

So strong a character as Prince Philip's was bound to chafe occasionally against the limitations that the Queen's pre-eminence and the British constitution imposed, but before long they worked out separate spheres of interest that neither overlapped nor conflicted. Wisely, he chose the realms of science, design and technology as ones that had been least encouraged by post-war British governments and could benefit most from royal patronage. He foresaw that efficiency and productivity in British industry were of equally vital importance and many of his speeches on the subject can now be read as prophetic. He was a good athlete, polo player and cricketer, so sport, athletics, adventure-training, exploration, conservation, wildlife have all benefited by his enthusiasm and ability.

Before long he had captured the nation's imagination and become a character – an able, bluff, witty, outspoken man's man, who could be guilty of the occasional peccadillo or gaffe, but who could put politicians on the spot, make a speech that produced a headline, coin a phrase that would be remembered, and generally say things which needed saying. Not long ago a poll was held by a national newspaper which asked people, as a lark, who would make the best British dictator. Prince Philip came out top, a somewhat ambiguous compliment, with the Queen nearly at the bottom of the list.

I do not suppose the duke has been an easy husband, nor an easy father, but his wife and children have remained devoted to him and they are a very united family. I even suspect that Her Majesty chuckles at the furore her husband sometimes creates, even when she distances herself from the controversy.

Walter Bagehot's definitive advice on a constitutional monarch's role *vis à vis* the Prime Minister's is this: 'to be consulted, to encourage and, occasionally, to warn'. This, and no more. It has been followed by Queen Elizabeth throughout her reign. She does not like playing politics, any more than her father or her grandfather did, and the few occasions when she has had to use the Royal Prerogative – the only part of the constitution which everyone has heard of, but few people quite understand – have not been happy ones.

In 1957, after Anthony Eden's resignation, she was criticised for choosing his successor solely on the advice of two elder statesmen whom she trusted, one of whom was the experienced, aristocratic and, one would have thought, well qualified Marquess of Salisbury. Yet it gave rise to an anti-Establishment movement and accusations of a 'magic circle' from which less well-born advisers were excluded. Later, in 1963, when Harold Macmillan was forced to resign, she was criticised for acting as referee between the rival claimants and for relying solely on the advice of her outgoing Prime Minister, again, through his marriage and lifestyle, an Establishment figure.

Although Her Majesty distances herself from involvement in politics, she has always been fascinated by the drama of parliament, by the rise and fall of political causes and by foreign and commonwealth affairs which she follows closely not least by the contents of the boxes which she receives and works on every day. Harold Macmillan was another Prime Minister who was surprised by her professionalism, by her grasp of detail and her calm appraisal of complicated situations. Churchill and R. A. Butler both thought her a clever woman and the former was amused by her interest in sophisticated smoking-room gossip. What I find interesting in their memoirs is their unconscious condescension. They all seem to start from the wrong end: to expect the Queen to be stupid and uneducated and then, to their surprise, find out that she is not. This is possibly the fault of the Queen herself, who, having a rather shy and thoughtful nature, worked out at an early stage in her life that she would never deliberately project her own image or 'put on an act'.

It may have been a reaction to her mother's consummate ease in being instinctively what her interlocutor wanted her to be, of being able to meet people halfway, of having 'the knack', or it may have been her generation's addiction to honesty at all costs; but for the first years of her reign the hard-working and dedicated Queen did not, in public, go out of her way to charm and it was only when things went accidentally wrong or she was genuinely moved, that her private face would show through and she would momentarily be recognised as the attractive, amusing and compassionate young woman that she really was.

Years of experience and, no doubt, the exigencies of a large family have mellowed the Queen's severity and now she smiles and quips in public more easily than she used to do. But she still dislikes public attention being focused on herself as a person rather than as a sovereign representing the monarchy of her country that she so passionately believes in, and woe betide the organisers of a public occasion who introduce a 'surprise element' into the programme, hoping to catch the Queen off-guard. The Queen is *never* off-guard, and both she and her sister, when displeased, can look right through the person they are talking to, or even an audience they are confronting, which is distinctly unnerving for those concerned.

Above The Annigoni portrait of HM The Queen in Garter robes.

HM Queen Elizabeth II on the fortieth anniversary of her accession, 1992.

On the other hand, the Queen's imperturbability has often saved the day on royal tours when things, by mistake, have not gone according to plan, for then she is adept at improvisation and in smoothing over awkward moments.

One such moment – which might better be described as dangerous – was when an 'intruder' broke into Buckingham Palace early one morning and the Queen woke up to find him literally sitting at the bottom of her bed. It needed imperturbability – and courage – of a very high order to keep him quietly talking until some fifteen minutes later when the foot-man on duty, who had been exercising the Queen's dogs, answered her bedroom bell, set up the alarm, and led the poor fellow gently away.

Elizabeth Longford has written about her: 'Elizabeth II is a close-up Queen. The nearer people get to her, the more impressed they are by what they see.' This is true in more ways than one. One's first impression on meeting the Queen is that she is surprisingly small, but that is com-pletely overcome by the next one – that she is surprisingly vivacious. The brilliant blue eyes, blue as a gentian in spring, the pink and white complexion, so porcelain-perfect that until one looks again one cannot believe it is natural – it is – can only be appreciated at close range, as can her sudden 'monkey grin' or her quick and quite sharp sense of humour. In private she makes jokes, quite good ones like 'I have to be seen to be believed', or, when asked what would happen if ever there is a revolution in Britain: 'We'll go quietly.'

What only friends and family know is that she has inherited a lot of her mother's sense of fun, loves parties and huge family gatherings, is quite uninhibited when not 'on duty' and dances like a dervish when the occasion allows her to.

Royal Ascot Week is the time when Her Majesty has the most fun – friends, family, and racing every day and sometimes dancing far into the night. The nearest thing to a royal court – or, if you look at it another way, the *last* vestige of one in the world today – is held during that week at Windsor Castle. The procession of open carriages down the 'private' race track (Ascot race-course lies within the Queen's Windsor estates),*

---

* In Queen Victoria's day my grandfather, Lord Ribblesdale, a Lord-in-Waiting and 'Master of the Queen's Buckhounds', led the royal procession down the course, riding a showy horse called 'Sparkler'.

In fact, the Buckhounds had ceased to exist, but that did not matter: together they put on such a good show and he looked so distinguished that the crowd waiting for the fun to start would cuff their inattentive offspring and yell: 'Look sharp, Tommie! 'Ere comes *the Ancestor!*'

Ribblesdale had no male descendants, both his sons were killed on active service, and the title has died out, but the appointment by the present Queen of another of his grandchildren, Lord Westmorland, as her 'Master of the Horse' would no doubt have greatly pleased 'the Ancestor'.

the protocol of being admitted to the Royal Enclosure or (even more rarely) to the Royal Box, the splendour of the very grand dinner-parties, the intimacy of the small ball, these are the moments when the Queen is seen to fulfil another function, as the head of our society, and when even the grandest and richest in the land aspire to be her guests.

The court's display then is theatrical, yet its pageantry, while it reaffirms the monarch's position, is not designed to keep others down, but to invite them to come on up. British society has always been an unequal, competing, and now only partially aristocratic mix, and today's Royal Ascot 'list' is very different from what it was a generation or two ago when it was scrutinised by the Earl Marshal's office to weed out the divorced and the 'unrespectable'.

What is perhaps most interesting about Queen Elizabeth's private life is not that she is a secret intellectual, far from it, but it is the high degree of *professionalism* she has acquired in all the things that interest her, whether it be pageantry, music, breeding and racing horses, riding, stalking, gun-dogs, party politics, or knowing about the history of her regiments or the contents of her royal palaces. She enjoys the challenge of being best among experts. She has always done her homework and after forty years of it, through fourteen different administrations and nine different Prime Ministers, * she has become a very professional constitutional Queen.

The Queen's relationship with the press and television gradually improved as her reign progressed, chiefly owing to her genuine and serious desire to modernise the monarchy. It was not easy, for neither she nor any member of the royal family possesses the knack, as Princess Diana undoubtedly does, of manipulating press opinion – while, understandably, the actual phobia of some of its members produced occasional outbursts which only resulted in more hurtful headlines.

Efforts to modernise were made in other directions too: greater access to the royal collections, informal lunches at Buckingham Palace, more and more 'walkabouts', two excellent television films, *Royal Heritage* and *Elizabeth R.*, which for once captured Her Majesty as she really is. But even these initiatives (which, with hindsight, seem too timid and

---

* The Queen has had longer experience of constitutional government than any senior minister, or head of state in Europe. Sir Ivor Jennings recalls that on one occasion Queen Victoria gave Mr Gladstone information which the Duke of Wellington had given her about Mr Pitt. Queen Elizabeth could probably give Mr Major information Winston Churchill had given her about Mr Gladstone.

too late) carried with them their own dangers. Letting the cameras in
let some of the mystique of royalty out and though Her Majesty now
appears in every living room in the land as a human being with whom
her subjects can possibly – though remotely – relate, she has also become
someone you can criticise like any other public figure – and nearly as
easily switch off.

As her large and normally wayward family grew up and became the
objects of inevitable gossip and petty scandals there was also the danger
of trivialising something precious and irreplaceable and, worse still, of
'linkage', which could do real damage to the monarchy.

The tornado that finally hit in 1992, and made it Queen Elizabeth's
'annus horribilis', blew up as many squalls do, from distant but worrying
clouds on the family's horizon. She had already realised that both her
sons' marriages had been unwise, and that in the case of Prince Charles
and Princess Diana, both parties were deeply unhappy; she had already
agreed to her strong-willed yet admirable daughter's separation and divorce although she had insisted on two years of waiting to see if it could
mend. That was bad enough, but I think that none of the royal family
realised the extent of the dangers that lay ahead. A new and much more
radical form of commercial and republican journalism had arrived in
Britain with a younger generation of non-deferential 'royal watchers'
who used electronic equipment to snoop, and imaginary informers to
infer.

The scene was thus set for the curtain to rise on an orchestrated royal
soap-opera, in which each member of the family was in turn blown up,
exploited, 'investigated', excoriated and 'put down'. They had perhaps
contributed to it themselves by the style and glamour of the royal weddings – but once started it could not stop – the film-star beauty and
suffering saintliness of Princess Di, the daring and dash of red-haired
Duchess 'Fergie' were novelettes fed daily to an avidly curious public,
who always wanted more.

Who cared if they diminished the dignity of the Queen and the monarchy? They filled the coffers of a thousand tabloids all over the world.
And then, with the publication of Andrew Morton's book *Diana, Her
True Story* and its serialisation in the *Sunday Times*, came the horrid
revelation that it had been written with her daughter-in-law's friends'
help, and substance was added to fantasy. This was quickly followed –
or was it preceded? – by the scandal of 'Fergie's' blatant infidelity, caught
on camera by voyeur paparazzi and blazoned around the world.

In Britain 1992 was a year of recession, unemployment, insecurity and
fear. Belts were tightened and public expenditure cut back. Not for the

first time in her reign Queen Elizabeth heard rumblings of public discontent with the size of the civil list and her own contributions to the public
purse. This time she heeded them. In early summer she told her Prime
Minister that she wished to pay Income Tax on her personal fortune
and curtail the Civil List. Inexplicably, her decision was not immediately
made public.

On the night of 2 December a fire broke out in the private chapel of
Windsor Castle, which blazed for twenty-four hours and destroyed nearly
a third of the Queen's much loved home, including the great Banqueting
Chamber of St George's Hall, which was reduced to ashes. The Queen,
a small figure in raincoat and 'wellies' stood sadly by and watched it
burn.

The following night at a Mansion House Dinner to celebrate the
fortieth year of her reign, she announced with typical directness that it
was time for the monarchy to adjust to the financial conditions that now
prevailed, then spelt out what she had already put in train. She also
asked for the nation's patience and understanding in what had been a
terrible year. But her gesture was not welcomed as generously as it might
have been: owing to a political miscalculation a row immediately broke
out over who should pay to rebuild her castle, though everyone agreed
it belonged to the nation and not to her.

And Queen Elizabeth's 'annus horribilis' had still not come to an end.

On the afternoon of 9 December the Prime Minister read out to a
hushed and sombre House of Commons an announcement he had
received from the Palace. It began: 'With regret the Prince and Princess
of Wales have decided to separate. Their Royal Highnesses have no
plans to divorce and their constitutional positions are unaffected . . .'

The Palace announcement was timed as a brave effort in damage
limitation, and it is a fact that there are no constitutional or ecclesiastical
complications that will prevent Prince Charles from one day succeeding
his mother as King. But, inevitably, there are other sad consequences:
the effect on the children of the marriage, a faint question mark over
the succession; the disappointment of the public (though one in three
marriages now ends in divorce they had been led to believe the 'royals'
were 'different'); the republican press's delight and their now open hostility to the monarchy.

The hurricane has now passed over, but it has left some bruises and
some sober thoughts behind. The Queen has every right to expect more
protection for the monarchy in future. The nation has every right to
grieve over a lost ideal, but neither has any reason to believe that the
end of the House of Windsor is in view. Queen Elizabeth has established

herself as a figure of rock-like integrity, but most thinking people know that the institution of monarchy is more important than the individuals who compose it. Such has always been Queen Elizabeth's belief, and such is the Prince of Wales's too. In a shifting world, where few nations can agree on their own future, Britain needs its monarchy more than it has ever needed it before. Now is the time to stand up for it, and be counted. The alternative is unthinkable.

3

GREAT BRITAIN

The Prince of Wales

'The British monarchy has always adapted to changing circumstances.
That has always been its strength.'

HRH THE PRINCE OF WALES

Sir John Riddell had rung up to say that the Prince of Wales was
having a busy day in Kent the following week with his Prince's
Trust activities and would I like to come along and see how it all
worked? And would I please be very punctual, as everything was timed
to the last minute? And so I caught the 8.50 p.m. from Victoria to
Faversham, near Canterbury, a small town surrounded by fruit orchards,
and spent the night there, just to make sure I was very punctual. The
next morning, at 9.00 a.m. prompt, I left the Railway Inn and drove
out to Brogdale, the experimental fruit farm where I was to meet the
prince's party. It was threatened with closure, or with 'rationalisation',
which in government terms is usually the same thing, and the prince's
visit and declared interest in its work was a recognition of its unique
position as keeper of ancient records and the national collection of fruit
trees, which might, as my taxi-driver hoped, stay the minister's axe.

At exactly 9.20 a clattering red helicopter crossed the horizon and
disappeared off to the right. The ladies in the welcoming party pulled
on their gloves and preened; the men straightened ties and shoulders;
the small talk faltered . . . At exactly 9.30 the three royal cars drew up
in front of us and Prince Charles, in a smartly cut green tweed suit, got
out and shook hands with the director, the top scientists, horticulturalists
and plantsmen, and then, together with the Under-Secretary from the
Ministry, the charming Baroness Trumpington whom we all suspected
of being Public Executioner Number One, and Lady Mountbatten, Lord
'Dickie's' eldest daughter who is Lord Lieutenant of Kent, proceeded to
inspect row upon row of beautifully cordoned apple trees and to ask
knowledgeable questions about their breeding and qualities.

It was the beginning of an extraordinary day, when I followed in the
Prince of Wales's footsteps like a good gun-dog follows his master, for a

gruelling ten hours of non-stop public engagements, speeches, visits, committees, inspections, receptions, etc, and which ended by our flying back together to Kensington Palace in the same red helicopter as he had arrived in, munching sandwiches and conducting a hilarious, but also quite serious, interview above the noise of the whirling propellers.

I had been trying for a long time for a joint interview with Prince Charles and his grandmother, the Queen Mum. They get on so well together that I hoped they would chatter away and almost forget my being there. 'She teases him and brings him down to earth, and he teases her and makes her laugh like no one else can – *and* tell stories,' Princess Margaret had told me, but although they had both agreed in principle, their separate programmes had never allowed it, so when Prince Charles suggested a campaign-follower's day in Kent, I accepted with alacrity.

My family knew Prince Charles much better than I did. My husband had accompanied him on an official visit to Yugoslavia, had taken him to see Tito at Igalo in Montenegro and had followed him on a walkabout in the old city of Dubrovnik. There he witnessed an unsuspected hazard in the life of royalty. A British mother with small boy in tow had patriotically waylaid the prince, who presented a friendly finger to the little fellow, who, horrid child, immediately bit it. The paparazzi, somehow managed to miss this splendid photo opportunity, and begged His Royal Highness to 'do it again' – but Prince Charles, wincing from the encounter, muttered 'not bloody likely!' and strode on.

I had met him only occasionally, at other people's houses, but I had danced at his wedding, or rather at the great ball the Queen had given at Buckingham Palace on the *eve* of his wedding, when, towards the end of it, the first silver heart-shaped balloons that London had ever seen floated gently down upon the dancers and when, in an unforgettably comic scene, be-tiaraed duchesses and be-ribboned ambassadors had pounced on them, some seizing the same bit of string, and hissing at each other, 'I only wanted this one for my little sick/blind/lame grandson – surely you wouldn't . . . ?' I had also sat in St Paul's Cathedral to watch him get married, squeezed between a tail-coated Spike Milligan and a kilted Lochiel, the Chief of Clan Cameron, whose granddaughter was performing as the smallest bridesmaid (and whose mother had been the Lady Hermione the prince's great-uncle would not sit next to at Beaufort). I had wept sentimental and patriotic tears when Kiri Te Kanawa's flawless voice floated up into the great dome to join the hovering angels there, but I had never got closer than that. I was, therefore, a little apprehensive about how the day would go.

The answer was, and I should have guessed it, 'like clockwork'. No sooner were the Brogdale speeches and presentations over than I was whisked discreetly into the third car with Sir John Riddell and Guy Salter, the private secretary who specifically looks after the Prince's Youth Business Trust (PYBT) work, and in careful convoy we drove off through cheering crowds to the next appointment. This was to inspect some new workshops which Tesco had built for the PYBT behind one of their supermarkets. None of their young tenants could have afforded to lease work-space on their own but, with the help of the PYBT, they were beavering away happily and productively at an amazing variety of small enterprises, from traditional painted pub-signs to dried-flower floristry. The third stop was before a huge factory complex where HRH was to meet regional activists of the PYBT and hold a committee meeting, unveil a plaque and attend a buffet lunch.

Before lunch I followed Lady Mountbatten to our private 'comfort stations' where we found the prince had preceded us. He greeted me very matily and asked if I was enjoying myself and, if so, 'good, because there is lots more to come'. I sat in on the committee meeting, quiet as a mouse, in a dark corner, and was impressed by the way he conducted it. He has a courteous and polite, but also a confidential super-salesman's manner, which is difficult to resist; his enthusiasm and dynamism are infectious but, most important of all, he sounds knowledgeable and well-informed, as if he has done his homework – knew the details and difficulties, sympathised with them, but was certain they could be overcome.

We lost him after lunch as he was whisked off to do a television interview and to visit certain local government dignitaries. The cavalcade moved off without him and stopped at an old people's home in Whitstable, where I had a happy time talking to some sprightly old ladies and a local councillor in a sunny back garden, till the prince arrived, when all was bustle and excitement, balanced cups of tea and home-made cakes, and life stories for which there was never quite enough time to reach the end.

Outside the home a large crowd of schoolchildren had gathered, some waving paper Union Jacks. The prince grinned and waved, then walked up to them, hands clasped behind his back, Navy style, and, looking serious, stopped in front of three ten-year-olds. He asked them a stern question, about school, I think, and received a sheepish answer. He then added something I could not hear but which obviously pressed the button as they doubled up with laughter and shot a whole fusillade of questions back at him. But he, smiling, moved on to surprise, establish contact with and win over groups of mothers and teachers further down the line.

His technique is superb and, it seems, effortless, as if he is really enjoying it, varying sympathy, jokes, and serious attention with jolly badinage when the girls are pretty or the kids are cheeky. He obviously likes meeting individuals and feels enormous empathy with them, the people who will one day be his subjects, his people. When he is seriously interested he looks anxious and worried, the effort of concentration, of sorting out one face from another and one problem from a hundred showing on the very open and unguarded countenance of this extraordinarily receptive and sympathetic man. His face shows it too when matters are not quite as they should be – an electric tension is communicated to aides and officials by the twitch of an eyebrow. The prince, like a nervous racehorse, must then be handled with care, or he might possibly bolt.

There was an example of this at the next place we visited in Canterbury, for too much time had been allocated to a community project portraying the city's history and not enough to walking among and talking to the cordoned-off crowds. Crowds, the Chief Constable assured me over yet another cup of tea, were a nightmare on these occasions. The royals disliked safety barriers, but the people who are in charge of their security . . . it only needs one over-excited or rough element . . . Prince Charles's crowds had doubled since he made his famous 'carbuncle' speech . . . but the crowds that turn out for Princess Di . . . now they are really frightening.

For myself, unused to travelling in a royal car and to the acclamation of crowds, I found the cheering enormously stimulating and the enthusiasm infectious. I practically had to sit on my hands to resist waving back.

The last visit of the day was to Canterbury Cathedral, to see how the multi-million-pound programme of conservation and repair there was progressing. It meant visiting a stained-glass workshop in one of the crypts and talking to young stonemasons from the North of England who were re-carving missing bits of the capitals as skilfully as the native masons of the twelfth and fourteenth centuries. I found this the biggest thrill of the day: to walk round that great echoing house of God and history *alone*, without services, or music, or tourists to distract one, with only a few of the top experts to tell me all about it and to answer all my questions. I thought to myself that this for me unique experience is an everyday occurrence for royalty and realised that perhaps there *were* some compensations, after all.

Then it was time to go. I snatched up my bag, with its notebook and tape-recorder, that a kind detective had been carrying round for me all day, and followed the prince up the ladder and into the insect-like object that was to transport us back to London.

'No coffee today, Sir, the machine has packed up. Sorry about that, Sir,' said the second pilot, who also acts as steward, 'but I've got some sandwiches and the drinks are here.' We settled into the two back seats of the red helicopter and delicious, savoury sandwiches, brown bread of course, were handed round.

'You're never going to record me on *that!*' said the prince and he ended my feeble fumblings by taking over my little box and starting off the tape. 'Well, it may be worth a try, but these machines make one hell of a noise.' He was shouting by this time and the earth was slipping sideways beneath us. 'I'll hold on to it and speak close up to it, if you'll bellow your questions in my ear – so fire away.' I was too full of sandwich and nervousness to bellow anything, but I did begin to laugh, and the best bit of the tape, I found later, is our combined and helpless laughter.

I asked Prince Charles whether the various schemes and activities of what is now called the Prince's Trust simply evolved or whether its whole conception happened at once and was primarily a way of giving him more freedom of action in matters he cared about.

He told me that, for some time, he had been president of the Royal Jubilee Trusts, which helped voluntary youth organisations, and of his own Prince's Trust, which he himself had set up in 1976 to help disadvantaged and disabled young people. But it was not until a few years later when, immediately after the Toxteth riots, he had driven up to Liverpool and looked at what had happened there, that he realised, 'I had to do something, something different, and to do it quickly, to help the truly disadvantaged of this country, those who had been "left out" for too long, the young without hope, the alienated. Other countries had somehow managed it, but nothing seemed to be happening in Britain and I knew the situation couldn't wait, so I collected the very best people I could think of and we put our heads together and they came up with this idea of community help, of big firms and companies, rich individuals, financial institutions, all banding together to give a kick-start for young people who wanted to work, had good ideas, but hadn't the money or the know-how to get organised on their own. We felt that if they could be given a boost at the beginning, a loan, a place to work in, the best advice, quite a few would succeed – at the very least they would be given hope.'

'A door marked "this way" that could lead them out of their waste land?' I suggested.

'Exactly. It took a bit of time setting up local committees, de-centralising, merging and re-shaping, but in the end we came up with the Prince's Youth Business Trust. And it *worked*, better than any of our wildest expectations – it just seemed to take off.'

I asked him how he cut through red tape and avoided bureaucracy when what he wanted were quick solutions, quick results, and he answered that at first the Social Services people, the Home Office and other institutional bodies 'weren't too keen, but we persuaded them, and soon they saw it could be made to work, after which they gave us terrific back-up, as did many organisations and institutions. Margaret Thatcher had been enthusiastic and since her day, the ministries have learnt to trust us. In fact the government is now copying a lot of our ideas for their own training schemes. Their White Paper on the training of unemployed youth is very much on the lines we pioneered.'

I asked him how he persuaded employers to co-operate and to contribute their time as well as their money when the government had so often failed to do so. He gave me a lop-sided smile. 'It wasn't too difficult. I saw a great many people and worked very hard at it. Most of them wanted to do something but hadn't followed that wish through; didn't know where to start . . . once we had told them, the response was infinitely better than I had hoped for. ICI, Marks & Spencer, Pilkington, Sainsbury's, IBM, Shell, many banks, hundreds of other companies as well as individuals. They seemed to *like* helping, especially locally, in their local branches and their home communities. But, of course, we needed a great deal of money, more than could ever be raised by direct contributions. Then someone had the idea of organising a rock concert at Wembley and the first one was such a fantastic success that we have repeated it every year. The artists, the stadium, everything is given for free and the money rolls in.'*

I bellowed into his ear something about idealistic goals and did he want to change our materialistic society?, and immediately felt him bristle. 'I don't know about young people being materialistic,' he protested. 'In the community work I've been doing, I'm amazed how many good people one meets, people who haven't much, but who want to help others who have less.'

'So, with the eighty per cent success rate of the PYBT, you're not frightened of creating more and more yuppies?'

'Certainly not. They've got to work damned hard to begin with, day in, day out, and they sacrifice a lot when they start out on their own –

---

* Shortly after I talked to the prince, a £40 million appeal was launched which the government promised to match pound for pound. It has been very successful, but will probably go on for ever, for as soon as one target is reached another is aimed at.

pension rights, sickness benefits and all that – and remember, the Trust is based on *community* effort. We have twenty regional boards which cover the whole country and nearly four thousand voluntary business advisers who help. We've found many of the young people who succeed plough back money or know-how into the Trust to help others in their community on their way up. Success breeds success and that's the kind of economic activity the country needs.'

I asked him whether he thought the pendulum had swung too far from the permissive sixties and seventies to the opposite extreme – too many laws, too much bureaucracy?

'One always has to resist bureaucracy, but British people on the whole have a great sense of proportion, of balance. If they think things are going too far in one direction they are quite capable of redressing the balance. There were many factors in the sixties and seventies that don't exist today.'

I asked him if he minded being 'different' – apart, extraordinary and unable to equate with the man on the Clapham omnibus – and he answered politely that he was perfectly satisfied with his identity, 'and if I hadn't got used to it by the time I was forty I'd be a pretty good chump, wouldn't I?'

I also asked him if he felt our monarchy was threatened by the great changes that joining Europe would entail. He answered seriously that the British monarchy had always adapted to changing circumstances – 'that has always been its strength' – and that he saw it as the sheet anchor of our democracy, our rights and freedoms, that monarchy guaranteed stability and fair government better than a republic, and that he saw no reason for this to change.

He told me that he had hated being a schoolboy and that he thought it both unnecessary and brutal to separate small children from their parents and send them off to boarding school. He and Princess Diana hoped to send their own to day-schools. 'And after that?' They had not made up their minds. He told me that he had enjoyed being at Cambridge, but that the famous tutorials Lord Butler had given him had left very little impression. 'Though, I suppose he may have taught me to think independently.' He told me Balmoral was his favourite home and that his heart was 'definitely in the Highlands of Scotland'. For him they were 'the most beautiful place on earth'.

I began asking about his battles with the architects and his ideas about community architecture, with which I strongly sympathised, and we were just swapping horror stories when the flying machine bumped gently to a standstill and it was all over. We had landed in what seemed a field

Prince Charles on the hill, photographed by the author's daughter-in-law
Susan Crawford; *below* at his work for the Prince's Trust.

behind the kitchen gardens of Kensington Palace and Prince Harry, holding his nanny's hand till the propellers stopped whirling, came forward to welcome us. At least, that was the idea, but actually he did not, he was a great deal more interested in whether his friend, the pilot, had brought him the right kind of sweets, which he had not, than in his father's arrival. But Prince Charles picked him up and hugged him into submission, after which he trotted along beside us, chattering away about his friends in play-school like any cheerful toddler.

We passed through a gate in a wall, then through one of the many doorways of the sprawling old building and the little prince disappeared with his nanny, still talking. Prince Charles nobly asked me if I wanted to come upstairs for a cup of tea and looked immensely relieved when I begged to be excused, saying that I would have one in the equerries' room where Guy Salter could give me more information about the Trust.

This is where the younger members of the prince's household work, gossip and wait. It is a large room off the front hall with desks and files and comfortable sofas, early-nineteenth-century paintings of racehorses and a brass and leather club fender in front of the fireplace. While we were talking the pretty young lady-in-waiting, who was to accompany Princess Diana that evening, drifted in and checked with the equerry, who is in charge of logistics, about the timing of what sounded like a complicated schedule. Pinned to her shoulder was the personal badge of Princess Diana's household, a pink bow of watered silk with a 'D' in diamonds on it that the princess has given to all her ladies-in-waiting.

The prince's household then consisted of Sir John Riddell, who had overall responsibility, and three private secretaries, one of whom acts as a liaison officer between Whitehall and HRH and another who is entirely occupied with the Trust and its business ventures. The prince's office, whose workload is rapidly becoming as heavy as that of a government department, has moved to St James's Palace as it had run out of space in Buckingham Palace, its original home.

Guy Salter, * who was seconded from one of the big merchant banks in the City to help the prince with the PYBT and other ventures, explained to me exactly how they work in a language and with concepts that were entirely new to me. After I had taken aboard such phrases as 'good practice which can be replicated' and the idea of 'enablers', he told me about the prince's other initiatives which all come under the umbrella of the Prince's Trust. There is Community Venture, now

---

* Guy Salter has now returned to merchant banking and has been replaced by Hugh Merrill, an equally whizzing kid from British Telecom.

called the 'Prince's Volunteers', whose aim is to make young people better citizens and which throws plus and minus young folk together within groups of ten for a gruelling ten months of training and community work, usually among the old and ill. Its results have been spectacular, especially with the young unemployed and the hard-case 'thought-to-be-unemployable'.

There is Business in the Community (BIC), which promotes liaison between pupils, schools and employees but also assists economic regeneration of large areas, like Calderdale in Yorkshire, where the Halifax carpet industry had collapsed and where BIC was so successful that other towns were soon clamouring to be advised and helped. For example, and most spectacularly, the Lea View Housing Estate in Hackney was transformed in a very short time from an unpopular and grim concrete jungle to 'Hackney-in-Heaven' to which everyone on the council's housing list wanted to be moved.

The principle of Community Architecture – that people should be directly involved in the planning and construction of the buildings they live and work in – had been given full rein in Lea View and Prince Charles from then on became its champion.

There are Prince's Trust Enterprise Centres, which lease workshops and mini-factory space and give grants to small businesses who might not otherwise get off the ground in many towns and cities.

There are residential camps for young unemployed people, the Advisory Group on Disability, and proposals for the regeneration of Inner City Aid, whose balance sheets and reports, facts and figures all testify to their achievements, but the Prince's Youth Business Trust is without doubt the most spectacularly successful of all these initiatives. In five years it has grown to be 'the largest voluntary seedcorn finance organisation in Britain', or, for that matter, the world. In 1987 it had set up 3,500 new businesses and created 5,000 new jobs; four years later the figures were 12,000 and 15,000 and still growing, while the spin-offs are immeasurably greater.

At exactly 6.30 p.m. Prince Charles and Princess Diana came down the stone staircase together – she looking elegant and soignée in a black faille evening suit, a poised, self-confident beauty now, and she and her lady-in-waiting were whisked off to another engagement in a chauffeur-driven royal car.

It was time for the prince's reception and he and Sir John led me down a dozen passages and through as many inner and outer doors – what a rabbit-warren the palace is! – until we came to some narrow stairs and, climbing them, arrived on the *piano nobile* at the ante-room of its great Christopher Wren saloon. Here some two hundred people, trustees, regional co-ordinators, business advisers and committee members were waiting to talk to the prince and to have their hard work and generosity rewarded by his fleeting smile and, with luck, a few minutes of conversation. The speeches were short and to the point. In that year's budget the Trust will have raised another £2 million and, thanks to the generosity and co-operation of banks, institutions and commercial organisations, and the seconding of staff from them, its overheads are less than 4½ per cent of its income.

The clapping had hardly died when Prince Charles slipped away for yet another appointment that evening. We said a quick goodbye at the bottom of the stairs and he dashed off, not in the best of moods, to change into a dinner-jacket and turn up smiling as the principal guest at a musical charity function. My feet were killing me – thank goodness I was not royal. It had been a long day.

I am sure Prince Charles would rather be judged by what people know he has done than by what people think he is. But what he *is* is something so very unusual – such a 'one-off' or 'turn-up' in what we have come to accept as our conventional and predictable ruling family – that it is an irresistible challenge to try to discover a little, just the smallest cog in the machinery that makes the royal leprechaun tick.

Lord Deedes, once a government minister and a former editor of the *Daily Telegraph*, has suggested that the royal family would be better off on an island inhabited by republican cannibals and surrounded by piranhas than be, as they are, wide open to the attacks of the British press. Prince Charles had been called many unkind things: spoilt, foolhardy, adolescent, loopy, opinionated, out of touch, etc. I suppose one could make out a case that all our royal family is spoilt, if you are convinced that the advantages of the job outweigh the disadvantages (which include assassination, for 'these are among the little uncertainties of our profession', as Prince Umberto of Italy was heard to exclaim before he was shot through the head at Monza). But to suggest that Prince Charles was indulged by his parents or allowed to have his own way more than other children is a fantasy. His childhood, and certainly his schooldays, were a great deal harsher, lonelier and more disciplined than those of the average schoolboy, and by the time he graduated to the freedom of university life he must already have accepted that his own was forever circumscribed. Growing up cannot have been easy for him, for he was often misunderstood and undervalued by his parents. Though two more dissimilar characters could scarcely be found than those of Prince Philip

and his eldest son, they now get on well and admire each other's achievements. But, I suspect, the young prince's early desire to prove himself by
physical acts of bravery and to excel in dangerous sports ('Action-man'
was what young friends called him) stemmed from a very sensitive boy's
wish to please and emulate a demanding parent of proven courage, in
whose eyes he longed to shine. It has taken a different kind of courage
to stand on his own two feet and put space between himself and his
family and if it has taken a little longer for him to do so, it can be
explained by a highly developed sense of loyalty and filial duty and by
the natural diffidence which is a part of his charm.

Prince Charles's idealism, which at times is almost visionary, stems
partly from the decade he grew up in and the friends he then made, and
partly from an inborn kindness and generosity of nature which has always
made him believe in other people and want to help them. It is a creative
idealism. He is an ideas man, a born leader and teacher, even a utopian,
but one who possesses the necessary guile and determination to make
his ideas work. He also has the rare gift of listening well and he has
chosen some of his advisers and experts with intelligence and sensitivity
while others, it cannot be denied, have laid themselves open to criticism.
But then, when have experts who have their royal master's ear not been
pilloried by rivals who have not?

There is no doubt that Prince Charles's years in the Royal Navy, and
his own command of a frigate, taught him how to get on with people
at close quarters and often in adverse conditions. It may account for his
remarkable and almost uncanny talent of knowing what the man in the
street thinks about controversial subjects, and frequently being on his
side. As he feels passionately about any number of these, his spontaneous
outbursts have considerable impact. This is obviously both a temptation
and a danger; but the Prince of Wales has probably influenced opinion
and achieved more in the last fifteen years of his life than most of his
royal ancestors in a lifetime. The list is endless: from archaeological
innovation (the raising of the *Mary Rose*) to new concepts of urban
architecture which put the occupier first and scare city planners; from
the reborn appreciation of classical style to the creation of the 'perfect
model village' on his Cornish estates; from community self-help to the
solution of Inner City problems; from prevailing attitudes towards the
disabled and disadvantaged to the regeneration of the economy; from
education, business and jobs being interlinked, to a campaign for the
teaching of the proper 'Queen's English' and Shakespeare, and the cru-
cially important environmental questions of our day. He has written two
books, is an all-round sportsman and an amateur artist and musician.

He can fly his own aeroplane, sail his own boat, captain his own polo team (and break his own arm). It is very unlikely that he could have achieved so much if he had been king, and I would guess that this is one reason why Her Majesty the Queen is never likely to abdicate in his favour. Another, of course, may be that she agrees with her grandmother, Queen Mary, who commented on Queen Wilhemina of Holland's retirement at sixty-eight, 'That is no age to give up your job!'

As Prince of Wales, Prince Charles has the double advantage of being able sometimes to side-step the rigid limitations of a constitutional monarchy and also make demands which, because of his position, are seldom refused. He strives to remain above party politics but also to address important social issues, and he has been surprisingly successful in doing so.

I originally intended to leave Prince Charles's troubled marriage out of these pages, regarding it as his own and no one else's business, but it has now become the subject of national debate, and the announcement of a formal separation between him and Princess Diana has ended hope of the marriage being mended. It is indeed a sad ending to such a pretty, hopeful start, but also, in a way, it is a relief, a release, and even perhaps a beginning of something better for both. With a certain amount of hindsight, and unblinded by the romantic hype that surrounded their 'fairytale' romance and wedding, one can now see that it was indeed a fairy tale, a marriage that was almost certainly doomed to fail.

When two young people come together with totally different backgrounds and with totally different visions of what they want from the union, it is bound to be difficult.

Prince Charles was not only years older than his bride, he belonged to a different generation. A kind and sensitive man, he had nevertheless been brought up in an old-fashioned aristocratic mould where wives play second-fiddle to their husbands' duties and career and are presumed to find fulfilment in loyalty to it, child-bearing and entertaining their husbands' friends. He was used to the court life of his parents' world – with its unique mix of luxury and privilege, hard work and discipline, duty and obligation. He had never packed a shirt, ordered a taxi, posted a letter or stood in a queue in his life, but he could face endless public dinners, boring protocol and punishing schedules without a murmur. What he wanted from marriage was a companion with whom he could relax, share his idealism and occasionally his jokes, who could discuss serious issues, sympathise with his frustrations and supervise an old-fashioned country home which (like his grandmother's) would be full of dogs and children, gardening tools, fishing-rods and friends. He did not wish to change those or his adventurous, action-crammed life, which was that of a happy bachelor, who needs must produce an heir.

Princess Diana, on the other hand, had just found happiness of a totally different style. After a peripatetic, insecure and unhappy childhood and a dull school life, she had discovered the freedoms of a (not too hard) working girl and all the dizzy excitements of London life, flat-mates, girl-gossip, dancing, dreaming, flirting and fun. When she fell in love and married her handsome prince, she thought she was exchanging those carefree days for something even better. The disillusionment, bewilderment and loneliness that followed must have been very hard to bear for someone so young.

For learning to be royal is a tough assignment, as the Queen Mother had found in the early days of her marriage. There is no easily charted way through the intracacies of Court life and royal habit for those who have been born outside its stiff and limited horizons.

Princess Diana went outside them for help, which was a mistake, but communication, the most vital ingredient of any marriage and something that no member of the royal family seems good at, had irretrievably broken down; the rest is history.

I do not believe unhappiness in life is wasted time. Princess Diana has emerged a stronger, tougher, more mature woman who now knows what she wants and what she is capable of achieving. Her star quality, which has made her the darling of the public and the press, has complicated her life, and at one time turned her head. It is a dangerous gift, but, as long as she uses it wisely, and not in competition or indeed rivalry, it can only help her perform the work she is so good at. Her husband will return to his bachelor ways and to his never-ending work for the British people which he has always found absorbing.

The altruism which is a major part of both Prince Charles's and Princess Diana's nature, their genuine compassion for the weak and suffering and their devotion to their children, are all links which may grow stronger now that distance has cleared their view. It is not likely, but it is not impossible, that separation may lead one day from armed truce to peaceful reunion. The nation would like that, and the papers be left with nothing to say.

4

SPAIN

King Juan Carlos

'Democracy is a demotion . . . Government should see to the needs of
the people, but be watched and supervised by the monarch. His view
is always the balanced one, for he has nothing to gain.'

LYTTON STRACHEY

*Of all the European embassies that I approached the Spanish one in
Belgrave Square proved the most practical and helpful. Whether it was
because of the cat's cradle of strings I simultaneously pulled or the
direct intervention of the Spanish ambassador I shall never know, but
within a remarkably short time the most glamorous king in Europe
had agreed to see me. I was off to a good start.*

*Don Juan Carlos of Spain is the only monarch who has ever been
chosen by a republican dictator to succeed him as king.*

*General Franco, or the Caudillo ('The Chief') as he was called
by his supporters, had been the victor in a long and vicious civil war,
and after it he ruled Spain without compromise, as a right-wing, fascist
dictatorship. He had no son, and he was too wise anyway to believe
that dictators' sons can succeed their fathers. Before he died, he decided
to restore the monarchy in Spain, but for a long time he kept his own
counsel and his options open as to how this should best be achieved.
There were several contenders, for, in the past, succession has seldom
been an easy process for the kings of Spain.*

I t was a large, long, sunny room with one wall all window and the
other three panelled and lined with light wood bookcases, on top of
which a splendid collection of nefs was displayed, a silver armada in
full sail. From a desk at the other end King Juan Carlos rose and came
forward to greet me.

My first impression was of height and of that natural confidence and
authority of bearing that can only be described as regal. My second was

of rugged good looks, very well-cut clothes and the dynamism of someone who is used to command and to being obeyed. For a moment I was reminded of Machiavelli's Prince and his definition of that princely quality, *virtú*: 'inflexible will, quick powers of decision and a capacity to act with ruthlessness and speed'. But then King Juan Carlos smiled and the illusion of an absolute monarch, a formidable prince, vanished. He is urbane and charming, relaxed and very informal. He definitely belongs to the twentieth and twenty-first centuries, not to the Renaissance.

He sat me down at a table and began talking, and my carefully prepared questions vanished like the morning dew. It was King Juan Carlos who was conducting the audience and he was telling *me*.

Two days previously the Spanish ambassador's secretary had rung me up in Scotland at teatime. I was walking my two young spaniels on the hill, a long walk to take the bounce out of them, and came back late to find the message on the hall table: 'The King of Spain can see you at eleven, the day after tomorrow.' There was a train strike, a bus strike, a flight controllers' go-slow, but somehow I managed to arrive in Madrid at eight o'clock the next evening and, sighing with relief, settled into a comfortable hotel near the Prado.

The King has two palaces in the capital: the vast and imposing Palacio Real, built in the eighteenth century on the site of the Arabs' Magerit and the mediaeval Alcazar (both of which mean 'fortress'); and a modern palace outside the city at Zarzuela, which is more of a country house and family home. King Juan Carlos was at Zarzuela and the next morning at 10 a.m. sharp his smart saloon car with grey-uniformed chauffeur rolled up to my hotel to drive me there. A few kilometres out of the city we turned down a side road and stopped at a small gate-house. There was a short confabulation, the royal guards grinned and saluted, an Alsatian wagged its tail and the barrier was lifted. A long drive through scrubby grassland planted with pine and ilex leads to the palace, which is built on a small hill overlooking the Castilian plain and is a low, square, no-nonsense modern building with large plate-glass windows. It looks not only modern, but new.

The car swished to a standstill and a liveried servant opened the door. Before I had time to button my gloves a major-domo came out of the palace and ushered me into a black and white entrance hall – black marble floor, white walls with a very splendid royal coat-of-arms in bas-relief on one of them. A footman led me up a staircase to the *piano nobile* and a small ante-room, furnished halfway between stiff palace and modern comfortable; yellow striped silk on the side chairs and an eighteenth-century chandelier, but the pale, cool Spanish carpets that are woven with the royal cipher and look like needlepoint rugs, a feminine touch no doubt added by the queen, are pretty and informal. A good, rather dashing portrait of the king's father, Don Juan, in bright, brave colours, hangs above the directoire settee, a token of filial loyalty. Soon Don Fernando Gutierez, the charming and delightfully informal press officer, came bustling in and explained in a fatherly way that things were running late 'as His Majesty is being filmed and we all know what cameramen are like'. I asked him whether I could tape-record my interview and he advised me not to – both the King and Queen Sofia hate being taped, but they permit photographs.

The media men emerged with a clatter of equipment and he hurried off to deal with them. A smart young aide-de-camp in Air Force uniform appeared and bade me follow him. We crossed a lobby with a desk at which another officer was sitting, towards large double doors which mine opened, politely ushering me into the king's presence. After which he saluted, turned on his heel and left me on my own.

King Juan Carlos told me that he was leaving that afternoon for Saragossa as his son Don Felipe, Prince of the Asturias, though already at Madrid University, was returning to his military academy for the passing out parade which would make him a full-blown lieutenant in the Spanish army, and his anticipatory smile told me how much he was looking forward to it. Juan Carlos is obviously immensely proud of his son, whose contemporaries say is not only very nice, but also bright and, it would now seem, extremely independent. 'Of course, he will reign in a different way to me when he succeeds,' he told me. 'Each king must do so, and a king who reigns successfully in one country would not be able to do so in another. You will find that out from your researches. I could not be King of Siam, but I know my own country and my own people and I show myself all the time so that they know me. That is what I tell my son. You must know the people *better than anyone else* in the whole country. My grandfather, Alfonso XIII, told me when I was a very small boy: "Always be a nomad in Spain, go everywhere, meet everyone."' The king went on to say how General Franco had said much the same to him when he was being tutored for kingship by the dictator. At this point he turned to me and said, almost fiercely, 'I did not approve of all the things Franco did, but if anyone speaks ill of him in my presence I shut them up immediately.' Any thoughts of disparaging the Caudillo vanished immediately from my mind and I hope I looked suitably impressed.

Franco began grooming Prince Juan Carlos as a possible successor in 1948 when he was ten years old. He sent him in turn to a military and then to a naval academy as well as to university and personally taught him many lessons in statesmanship and government. Later, as heir presumptive, honorary ADC, and sometime representative of the Spanish dictator abroad, Juan Carlos slowly gained experience. 'You will do it differently when you are king,' Franco told him. 'This is my way, but you must find your own.' It was not always an easy way.

After a first official visit to America when the young prince unwisely sounded off to a correspondent of the *Washington Post* about his ideas for the Spain of the future, he was carpeted by the old man on his return. 'There are things you can say inside your country to your own countrymen and things you can say outside. They are not the same.' And another time he told him, 'There is an old Spanish saying – if you don't open your mouth no fly will buzz in.' There were many lessons in discretion, in moderation, and in statecraft. On one occasion Franco was due to drive from his palace to address a meeting of Falangists, the Fascist party of Spain. He came down the staircase in his Caudillo's uniform (little black shiny hat like an inverted saucepan) and was greeted with the Fascist salute by the waiting assembly of army officers. He spotted Prince Juan Carlos, who expected to accompany him, among the young men below and, signalling him out, told him sternly to return to base. Later that evening the anxious prince demanded an audience and asked what he had done wrong to be so summarily dismissed. 'I did not want you to be seen with me dressed up like that,' was the remarkable answer.

It was not until 1969 that Franco declared Juan Carlos to be 'Principe de España', or official heir apparent. By that time he was married and his third child, a boy, had been born. The old dictator was not taking any chances.

'And when Franco died and you finally became king,' I ventured to ask, 'were there still divisions, bitterness or disillusionment in your country, in the aftermath of your terrible civil war?'

'Not really,' he answered. 'Franco's greatest gift to Spain was the creation of something that had never existed before – a middle-class – an entrepreneurial class which concentrated on rebuilding the country and giving it something it had never known in all its history: prosperity and peace. People were simply too busy making money to let old quarrels or politics interfere. Foreign money poured into Spain after World War II and foreign investors were bribing everyone, right and left, to get their concessions and their deals in first. Do you know, they even attempted to bribe *me?*' He looked at me quizzically and grinned. 'Lucky I was rich enough to resist the temptation!'

King Juan Carlos's first aim when he became king was to lead Spain towards a new form of government based on British lines: a multi-party parliamentary democracy, with one man, one vote – and to give his country a new constitution, a more liberal constitution than it had ever known, but one in which the monarchy still retained independent, though limited, power, whatever the political complexion of the government. Today, Juan Carlos has the right to dismiss a government and call a general election, to approve or veto the choice of Prime Minister, to be consulted on the formation of its cabinets, and when I asked him how he would deal with a controversial political decision that he disapproved of, he told me he would send for his Prime Minister, Felipe Gonzalez, a right-wing socialist who is said to have excellent relations with the king and, 'We would discuss it.'

I could not help feeling that the Prime Minister might get the worse of such a discussion but, though a liberal and overtly democratic, that is the kind of monarch Juan Carlos is: a king who still rules as well as reigns and is very conscious of that fact. He is also the supremo of all three armed forces.

'I had three problems to deal with when the monarchy was restored,' he told me. 'The old court of my grandfather, the families who expected the clock to be put back and their functions and privileges to return; then the different, but equally expectant people who had gathered around Franco and constituted *his* "court", the army, which expected to hold on to their power; and lastly the Communist Party, which had been declared illegal by Franco but of course had only been driven underground.

'The first problem I dealt with by simply not having a court at all, in the old-fashioned meaning of the word. The queen has no ladies-in-waiting. When she attends functions she chooses one of her friends, the wife or daughter of an official or a professional woman she likes, to accompany her. I have my ADCs, my private secretaries, my chamberlain, and that is all. I work three days a week in the Palacio Real in Madrid, where I hold councils, give audiences. We also do our official entertaining there; and I spend three days in the country here, where I also hold audiences and work at my papers. I travel round the country as much and as informally as possible. To be seen and to see. There is little grandiose pomp and ceremony about our monarchy today. At the opening of parliament or at military reviews perhaps, but no golden coaches.' As he said this he looked so regal that one felt golden coaches

would be superfluous. 'A Spanish king is not crowned like your Queen
Elizabeth in England. He attends a High Mass in the Church of San
Jeronimo el Real in Madrid and a solemn Te Deum is sung.' One of his
titles is still 'His Most Catholic Majesty', though he only uses it on
special occasions, such as the Pope's visit to Spain.

'I get on very well with my government and I have no trouble with
the Church – far from it. As for the Communist Party, I will tell you
how I managed that. While Franco was still alive he sent me on a state
visit to Romania, where Ceausescu was already head of state, and we got
on rather well together. As soon as I succeeded, I sent him a message
proposing a deal and the man I chose to take this message to him was
Carillo, the Communist leader, head of the proscribed Communist Party
in Spain. I told him I would like to make a "gentleman's agreement": "I
will recognise the Communist Party in Spain if you promise not to bring
your people out on the streets and start shouting". Carillo went off to
Bucharest like a lamb and came back and agreed to my terms. He was
one of the guests at the banquet I gave after the first elections. He kept
his promise, but the party (here he gave a very Gallic shrug) is not very
significant any longer.'

El Rey – I have written 'El Rey' but this is a title that neither I
nor the general public would normally use. His intimates do, although
sometimes they call him by his nickname as a boy, 'Juanito'. The rest
use the resounding 'Don Juan Carlos'. But when he signs his name at
the bottom of a document or letter it is Yo, el Rey: I, the King.

Don Juan Carlos likes talking and, when he is talking, one is conscious
that he is a child of the Mediterranean, articulate, involved, acting out
every story with gestures and swift changes of expression. He is amused
by others and by himself and he himself is both amusing and stimulating.

'And the 23 February coup?' I prompted him. Apparently it was more
serious than the outside world realised, and more sudden. King Juan
Carlos had just come in from playing squash and was about to take a
shower when the telephone rang in the room where we were sitting and
the army delivered its bombshell and ultimatum – more power, a less
liberal constitution, or else . . . adding that their tanks surrounded the
capital. The king's immediate answer was that he was a soldier too, that
tanks needed fuel to make them move and this was in his power to
withhold.

I cannot help thinking it may have been fortunate that politicians of
all parties were incarcerated in the chamber of the Cortes by the civic
guard (which was commanded by Colonel Antonio Tejero) and could
not for once interfere, so that the handling of the crisis devolved entirely

HM King Juan Carlos of Spain; with Queen Sofia and their family: Don Felipe, Prince of the Asturias; Princess Elena; Princess Cristina.

on the young king. He certainly rose to the occasion and showed wisdom and judgment beyond his years. 'First of all I changed my clothes,' he told me with a smile, 'and then we made a video in which I broadcast to the nation and told them what to do.' The navy and the air force were loyal. The officer in charge of the squadron defending Madrid, when ordered to join the rebellion, had answered: 'I only take commands from my king.' As did the troops guarding the capital's television tower. 'We only had a minimum of equipment out here and I remember a frantic search through every drawer in the palace to produce a second tape, for safety's sake, in case the first was captured. When it was all over there was no purge. Only the top brass and the officers responsible were punished. The rank and file only needed good leadership to return to their senses.'

While we were talking the telephone rang twice. The first caller was Don Juan, the king's father, and there followed a lively and intimate family conversation in Spanish. The second was Prince Charles, speaking in English from his car phone in London. He was trying to arrange a weekend's sailing with Juan Carlos in Majorca, which is the king's and the prince's favourite place for summer holidays in the sun. Juan Carlos is very fond of the Prince of Wales and considers himself a kind of benevolent Dutch uncle to him. In spite of being so very Spanish he is quite proud of his British blood, through his grandmother, Queen Ena, who was Queen Victoria's granddaughter.

It was time for me to go. We had been talking for nearly two hours and, as I curtsied and took my leave, I marvelled at the fate that at last had given Spain, after so many dud rulers, a very remarkable king.

That afternoon, as I walked around the Prado which is like paying a call on all of Don Juan Carlos's ancestors, with my head still buzzing from all that the king had told me, I reminded myself that it could not have been as simple as all that. It hardly ever is.

Juan Carlos's education under Franco's stern eye must have been something to be endured, not enjoyed. He was only ten when his father, Don Juan, and the dictator came to an agreement: Franco would bring up the boy in his own way, in his own 'court', as a likely heir to an eventually restored monarchy, if Don Juan would renounce his own claim to the crown and remain in exile. It was not so much an 'if' as an 'either/or'. At first it was not made clear whether the Duke of Cadiz, the son of Don Juan's elder but deaf-mute brother, who was married to Franco's daughter, was also in the running; and it was only when, in 1969, Franco gave Juan Carlos the one-off title *Principe de España* that it was more or less certain he would eventually succeed.

It speaks well for both father and son, that in spite of their enforced separation, family ties and family loyalty and affection were never broken, and the young prince survived what must often have been a desperately anxious, lonely and tough adolescence in a formal and alien environment. Every summer the dictator's 'court' and the whole of 'official' Spain would move from Madrid to San Sebastian on the cooler and bracing Atlantic Coast, and, it is said, this is the reason why Juan Carlos now prefers his Majorca estates for his own happy and relaxed vacations. Solitary holidays without one's own family could not have been much fun. Neither could the period of the transition of power have been an easy one.

Franco was ill, then better, then ill again, and when he finally died, in November 1975, he left Spain with a constitution of sorts but an illiberal and undemocratic one, and an illiberal and undemocratic Prime Minister to match. The new king's far from simple task was to get rid of both.

In 1976, Juan Carlos dismissed the three men who constituted Franco's Council of the Realm – a sort of inner cabinet – and chose his remarkable old tutor, Torcuado Fernandez-Miranda, to be chairman of a new council which he would appoint. The next stage, for change could not be pushed too far or too fast, was to ask Carlos Areas, Franco's Prime Minister, to produce a democratic constitution. A commission sat for six months under Areas and produced a wholly *un*democratic document, with no universal suffrage and many reserved powers.

The king refused to sign it and the Cortes, which was divided between 'Left' and 'Right', refused to ratify it. By July 1976, there was an impasse and a constitutional crisis. Then the young king for the first time showed his mettle. He dismissed Areas and replaced him with a clever but surprising choice, Adolfo Suarez, who had been one of Franco's supporters, indeed the minister for the Falangist party, but whom he knew well and trusted.

Under Suarez a democratic constitution – one man, one vote – was produced, the Council of the Realm was wound up. There was a referendum in December 1976 and a period of necessary blood-letting: dismissals, resignations and gory carpets, but the middle and entrepreneurial classes stood firmly behind the new government and a crisis that might well have become a revolution was brilliantly averted. Again, it was on 23 February 1977 that King Juan Carlos personally defused the rebellion of the army under General Millans del Bosch, a crisis on a knife-edge which might also have turned into a revolution. He spent all night on the telephone, reminding his friends in the services of their loyalty to the crown, to himself, their king; cajoling, arguing, persuading, listening and, by sun-up, winning back their allegiance by his particular blend of sympathy and toughness. It was a remarkable feat and added enormously to Juan Carlos's prestige and popularity.

Don Juan Carlos's marriage and family life is a different story. Queen Sofia and the two young infantas had already left for their summer holiday on their private estate in Majorca, so I missed them. Queen Sofia is almost as popular in Spain as is the king – and goes about her multifarious duties in a simple, unaffected style, and with obvious intelligence and common sense.

The daughter of King Paul of the Hellenes and Queen Frederika, and the sister of the exiled King Constantine, Sofia met Juan Carlos before he became king at the wedding in England of Prince Richard of Gloucester. They were both twenty-four at the time, exceptionally good-looking and refreshingly uninhibited and independent-minded. Her brother was a king, albeit a shaky one, and Juan Carlos was likely to be one, one day. There were high spirits and high jinks in the royal carriages that had been tacked on to an ordinary passenger train that was bringing them both to London – Prince Charles, who had been sent to escort the foreign royals, and Don Juan Carlos borrowed the attendants' jackets and went up and down the train announcing a dinner that did not exist. Princess Sofia told the Spanish prince that she was learning judo. 'That can't be much use to you, surely?' was his reaction.

'You don't think so? Then give me your hand!' answered the princess, and before he knew what had happened he was lying prone at his future bride's feet.

They were married in Athens in 1962, and their two daughters, the Infantas Elena and Cristina, were born in 1963 and 1965 – followed by Don Felipe, Prince of the Asturias, in 1968. Queen Sofia is a pretty, beautifully turned-out and soignée woman, but she has also strength of character and a happy, sunny nature which seem to communicate themselves to everyone who comes her way. She was educated in Greece and at Salem College in Germany, and is very musical. Concert-going is her chief relaxation. When she was a girl she trained professionally as a children's nurse, and child welfare is still a great interest.

Her eldest daughter, the Infanta Elena, has a teaching degree and came to England to attend Exeter University in 1990 to learn more about teaching handicapped children. The Infanta Cristina also has a degree, but in political science, which she took at Madrid University. It is a happy family, a hard-working family, that aims at 'knowing our people better than anyone else'. They all have a good rapport with the Spanish press.

'You are young, popular and photogenic royalty, what do you do about the occupational hazard of all modern monarchs, being tormented by the media?' had been my last question to the king.

'Inside this palace,' he waved a hand round the room in which we were sitting, 'I am a private man: no one is allowed here without my permission. But when I step outside the door I belong to the Spanish public – as does my family. *I am a public man*, I have accepted that, it's part of the job. And once you have accepted it, it is not so difficult.' El Rey really does have an answer to everything.

Spain's economic and political maturity is very recent. For close on a hundred and fifty years she was regarded by the rest of the world as largely ungovernable; a disunited country with an almost mediaeval outlook; an unworkable constitution; an autocratic monarchy which failed to rule and squabbled endlessly about the succession; an undisciplined, ill-equipped army; a hungry peasantry and overbearing clerics; and a land whose foreign visitors were preyed upon by bed-bugs and brigands. In the 1914–18 war Spain remained neutral, but suffered economic hardship and political unrest in its aftermath, culminating in a terrible civil war (1936–9) in which both sides were cruelly manipulated by the protagonists of the greater European war that was to follow. Both Russia and the Axis powers had been eager to try out their fighting machines in a cynical dress rehearsal for the real thing and were totally indifferent to the suffering or to the ultimate fate of Spain.

Her geographic position – cut off from the rest of the continent on three sides by sea and on one side by high mountains – and her nearness to Africa may have had something to do with the turbulence of Spanish history and in particular with the story of her monarchy. The Iberian peninsula suffered in turn invasion and conquest by Carthaginians, Romans and Visigoths until, in the eighth century AD, it was overrun by a wave of Muslim Arabs from North Africa, who swept northwards in an unstoppable jihad (holy war) until they were confronted and defeated by the Frankish Christian king, Charles Martel, grandfather of Charlemagne, founder of the Holy Roman Empire, at the battle of Poitiers in 732. But in Spain the Saracens and then the Moors had come to stay, establishing a Muslim Caliphate in Córdoba, from which they ruled almost the whole of Spain for the next three hundred years, after which the 'Reconquest' slowly began. It was not achieved until the second half of the fifteenth century.

In northern and central Spain, however, several small states and cities remained independent, ruled by their own princes and counts; the stories of the struggles of their Christian heroes against the infidel are as famous in Spain as those of King Arthur and his knights are in England.

Castile, in central Spain, and Aragón in the north-east slowly emerged as the most powerful of these states and, when they were united by the marriage of Queen Isabella of Castile and Ferdinand of Aragón (the Catholic sovereigns), a new period began in Spanish history. The voyages of discovery of her navy, and the conquest of Mexico and Peru soon after, brought untold riches to Spain and before long her armies and fighting men (in particular the invincible *Tercios* of her infantry) were the most disciplined and formidable in all Europe, her civil administration the most competent.

After the 'Reconquest' the power of the Catholic Church greatly increased and during the reigns of Isabel and Ferdinand and of their great-grandson Philip II, it was used to a large extent as an instrument of government. Indeed, the Spanish Inquisition itself was a department of royal government, employed not only to ensure religious unity and obedience but also to enforce national unity and the authority of the crown.

All professing Jews and Muslims, the two most industrious classes in the country, were expelled from Spain. Many converted Jews (*Conversos*) and Muslims (*Moriscos*) and all suspected 'infidels' were subjected to persecution and often torture and death, so that the period of the Inquisition, though it eventually produced religious orthodoxy and a flowering of great Spanish mystics, artists, poets and saints, also considerably weakened the strength and economic progress of the country.

And so it was that, despite her possessions in the New World, her near-monopoly with its trade, and her conquest of Portugal; and despite the brilliant victories of her armies and navies in Italy and the Netherlands, culminating respectively in the battles of Pavia and Breda, Spain never managed to build a sound base to her economy at home, nor achieved even a degree of political will and unity among her people.

In 1520, Charles of Hapsburg, grandson of Ferdinand and Isabella of Castile, had barely succeeded to the Spanish throne through his mother (Isabella's daughter) when he was also 'elected' to be Holy Roman Emperor, and so Charles I of Spain became the great Emperor Charles V, or 'Charles-Quint', and Spain was drawn ever more closely into the politics and wars of Europe.

Philip II, who was Charles's son, married Henry VIII's daughter, the Catholic queen, Mary Tudor of England, to bolster his quarrels with France and with the Pope; but he only visited England once, and then for a matter of months. When Queen Mary died childless and was succeeded by her Protestant half-sister Elizabeth, the conquered Netherlands looked to England as a Protestant ally for support in their revolt against Spain, and Philip, just like Hitler, some five hundred years later, decided on an invasion. In 1588 his redoubtable army, under the Duke of Parma, waited in the North Sea ports for the great fleet which was to carry them to England, but the Spanish Armada was defeated in a sea battle by Sir Francis Drake and dispersed off Plymouth Sound and all over the Western Approaches in a great storm which changed the course of Spanish and British history. It was the end of Spain's monopoly of sea power, and of Philip's territorial ambitions.

In later life he retired into the Escorial, an austere monastery/palace outside Madrid, where he worked himself to death in the administration of his country and its enormous possessions, though some say he was eaten alive by the vermin that infested the hair shirt he always wore, as an act of piety, to achieve sainthood by mortifying the flesh.

Then began a less fortunate period for Spain; a period of moral and material decadence. Europe was bedevilled by religious wars and their aftermath, famine and plague and, in 1618, Spain was drawn into the terrible Thirty Years War by the Austrian Hapsburgs, the cousins of her own kings.

The Spanish Hapsburgs reigned for nearly two hundred years, but in 1700 the imbecile Charles II, dying without an undisputed heir, left a vacancy which Louis XIV, King of France, hastened to fill by declaring his grandson Philippe, Duc d'Anjou, King Philip V of Spain (Louis XIV's wife, Maria Teresa, was a Spanish princess). Austria, with a similar candidate for the empty throne, protested and there followed the War of the Spanish Succession, which lasted throughout the Sun King's declining years, cost a great many thousand lives, severely impoverished both countries, but in the end left a branch of the Bourbon family firmly established on the throne of Spain.

At first the Spanish Bourbons did not produce a much better run of kings than had the Spanish Hapsburgs, nor were they, at least according to Goya's portraits, handsome to look at. But they did have one advantage – they brought with them able French and Italian administrators who, besides partly relieving the monarchy of the intolerable burden of direct rule (Philip II was said to have spent all his life either at his desk or on his knees), were also responsible for legal and many other reforms.

Both Philip V and his grandson, Charles IV, had Italian wives, whose scheming on behalf of their families, and their lax morals, rivalled those of the French court, as did the Spanish court's grandness, rigidity and excessive formality. Surprisingly Charles III, Philips' third son by the formidable Elizabeth Farnese, proved to be the best king Spain had had since the Emperor Charles-Quint; under his enlightened despotism many reforms were carried out and the country made both material and political progress. The Jesuits were expelled, secular courts of law were established, shipping and industry flourished, public works and communications were improved.

Charles III was a true countryman, as is revealed in Goya's wonderful portrait that hangs in the Prado, keener on hunting and fishing than praying and gallivanting like so many of his forebears; but even so, and in spite of an exemplary marriage, his eldest son had to be bypassed owing to the hereditary curse of imbecility, which so darkened the lives of the Spanish monarchy of that period.

His second son, Charles IV, was as stupid as his wife, Queen Marie Louise of Parma, was ugly, although this did not seem to worry her lover, the handsome Don Manuel Godoy, who was also the favourite of the King. The inseparable trio was known throughout Spain as the *Santa Trinidad*.

Charles IV – good-natured, vacillating, easily bullied and yet wholly despotic – was a disastrous king, totally incapable of steering his country through the dangers of a tumultuous period in European history. The story of his forced abdication, of his wife Marie Louise's and his son Ferdinand's intrigues with Napoleon, of the latter's coup which replaced the Bourbon kings by the Emperor's own brother, Joseph Buonaparte, of the defeat of the Spanish navy by Nelson at Cape St Vincent and Trafalgar, and the eclipse of her merchant fleet, of the French invasion and long Peninsular War, of the junta of 1814 which split the nation in two, is one long chapter of ineptitude, failure and defeat, the saddest, perhaps, in all Spanish history. Nor did matters improve when the despicable Ferdinand succeeded, for he immediately embarked on a series of repressive policies which aimed at snuffing out the faintest spark of nascent liberalism. His subjects rebelled, there were risings and suppressions, followed by a period of near-chaos, a situation which threatened the peace and dearly won balance of power in Europe. So anxious were the great powers that they collectively re-affirmed Ferdinand on his Spanish throne by sending in the Duke of Angoulême with a detachment of French troops to put down incipient revolution.

Towards the end of an unhappy reign which saw, among other disasters, the gradual loss of the American colonies, Ferdinand, short of an heir, altered the Salic law to make it possible for his three-year-old daughter to succeed him instead of his younger brother, Don Carlos, whom everyone had expected to be his heir, once more confusing an already confused succession.

When the child, Isabella, was declared Queen of Spain in 1843, the country was again divided by a successional squabble, half of it supporting the Carlist faction and fighting three separate wars to reinforce their claim, and half remaining loyal to Isabella, the legitimate queen. 'Spain is a hopeless mess,' wrote Princess Lieven to Metternich and for nearly forty years this seemed to be the case, until the jovial, promiscuous and grossly self-indulgent queen finally abdicated and her son Alfonso, later known as *El Pacificator*, became King Alfonso XII.

Isabella's, or 'the Spanish' marriage, had been the cause of much anxiety and intrigue in the courts and councils of Europe, for on it again depended a possible shift in that balance of power so carefully preserved by the great statesmen of the day. The choice of her cousin, Francisco de Asis, was accepted as a coup for Louis-Philippe of France, whose son had married Isabella's younger sister and had every intention of producing an heir, whereas the queen's bridegroom was generally thought to be congenitally incapable of fatherhood. 'What can I say about a man who wore even more lace than I did?' she is supposed to have answered to discreet enquiries about her wedding night.

But in spite of, or more likely because of, an unhappy marriage and a reign which was one long battle between her autocratic nature and the growing wish of the people for parliamentary government, Isabella produced no fewer than nine children before she was deposed in the revolution of 1868. For the next six years, Spain was in a state of total anarchy. The political incapacity of her people seemed endemic. They did not want a republic, but could not decide on a king. In the end Isabella's son, the young Alfonso XII, was chosen by a military junta, and the Spanish Bourbon dynasty was returned to the throne of Spain.

He was an admirable choice and under his tragically short but firm rule (1874-5) the end of the Carlist wars and the beginning of parliamentary government brought Spain at last into the modern world. Six months after his death his widow, Marie Christine of Hapsburg, gave birth to a posthumous son. The child grew up to be King Alfonso XIII, the grandfather of the present King Juan Carlos. He married Queen Victoria's grand-daughter, Princess Victoria Eugenie (Ena) of Battenberg, but was forced to abdicate when Spain became a republic in 1931.

*   *   *

King Juan Carlos was the European monarch who impressed me most by his majesty and he was not in the least self-conscious in doing so. Nearly all the others have been conditioned by the fashion of the day to play down the essential apartness and dignity of monarchy, to 'democratise' it, which is a contradiction in terms, quite apart from being futile; they talked to me about their children going to ordinary schools, being just like ordinary children, having ordinary toys and ordinary careers. Not so El Rey. He is proud of being Spain's king and he enjoys being different. He knows that his people, after a long run of feeble and venal kings and one dictator, want to see a *great* king and he does his best to gratify their wishes. He has enormous influence in his country and plays a discreet but important part in its politics; his key role in aborting the right-wing coup of 23 February 1977 made him a hero and established confidence in the monarchy. In a country once famous for its political volatility and immaturity, he has provided strong leadership and stability. It will be interesting to see, with Spain now a full member of the European Community, how far his leadership will be allowed to count. It certainly contributed to the enormously successful Olympic Games staged in Barcelona in 1992 when Spain's new confidence and ability impressed the whole world.

5

SCANDINAVIA

The Scandinavian monarchs are so inextricably mixed by consanguinity and history that one must consider them all together and then go back to Viking days to discover their common roots.

Of the three kingly houses that reign in Denmark, Sweden and Norway today, only the Danish Oldenburg line of Queen Margrethe is an unbroken and ancient one. The Swedish House of Bernadotte is French, with a mixture of German, and only started in 1814; while the Norwegian line is really Danish and only began in 1905 when Norway at last became independent from Sweden and chose a Danish king.

Christian IX of Denmark (1863–1906) had so many beautiful daughters that he was called 'the father-in-law of Europe' and Queen Margrethe is probably related to more royalty than any other queen in the world, except our own.

There is a strong 'cousinage' between Danish, Spanish, Greek, Norwegian, Belgian and Luxemburg relatives and sometimes the younger members of the royal families of Europe get together when they are on holiday, if only to retreat to some private estate or mountain as far away from the paparazzi as possible, but, as with every extended family, it depends very much which part of it visits which.

The British are probably the most stand-offish; none of Queen Elizabeth's children have married foreign princes or princesses, but Prince Charles and Princess Diana see a lot of their royal relations when they stay with King Juan Carlos and Queen Sofia in Majorca on their private estate. But even this retreat has recently been invaded. It really does seem ridiculous that royalty are hunted like big-game, without any national or international law or convention to protect them. Even animals have the World Wide Fund for Nature. I suggest that there should be a closed season every August when no one can hunt royalty (and maybe an open season in December when royalty can shoot photographers?). It would at least redress the balance!

The Scandinavian monarchs are businesslike and efficient, but in fact they have comparatively little to do and very little influence on the governance of their countries. King Karl XVI Gustaf of Sweden probably has less power than any other king in Europe, though this may one day change, for the Swedes have suddenly woken up to the fact that socialism, even their quite mild brand of it, doesn't work, and they have voted in a Conservative government for the first time in forty years.

King Harald V of Norway may well follow in his grandfather, King Haakon VII's footsteps by becoming so popular with his subjects that his opinions really matter, but officially he is equally hamstrung by Norway's constitution, while Denmark, which has a clever and able queen, has a constitution which does at least allow her Prime Minister and ministers to consult her frequently, though she will not admit they follow her advice!

It is the *shape* of Scandinavia, I believe, that has accounted for most in its history, and the position of that shape: all those rocky islands, and long sea lochs which cut off families and villages from each other and made them self-sufficient and independent; all that snow and ice which made them extra-hardy; all that land-locked water and those narrow straits, which pressure-cooked their desire to burst out into the open sea, and then all those trees which gave them the wood to build the boats in which to do so.

Certainly Scandinavia's most glorious moment in history has been that of her common ancestors, the Vikings. 'Men of the creeks', pirates, sea-robbers, murderous vandals, fearless explorers, warrior-kings, call them what you like, the Vikings' impact on the Western world from the eighth to the eleventh centuries was formidable, and whether it was cupidity, economic necessity or sheer love of adventure and fighting that inspired them, there is no doubt that they delivered the last great pagan . assault on Christendom in the West and nearly succeeded in snuffing it out.

Brave, cruel and lusty, the Vikings were also good colonisers, sharp tradesmen, imaginative entrepreneurs, but above all that they were *experts*. They carried the skills of seafaring, of boat-building and of fighting to the ultimate limit that was possible in their day and age, and later, when the descendants of these hirsute warriors wrote about it all – having learnt the art of poetry from Irish court bards – they translated the deeds of their forebears into *sagas*, which many people believe surpass the entire literary achievement of pre-Dante Europe.

Having listened, a long time ago, to the last of the Barra Senachies reciting the history of ancient clan battles – exactly as his ancestors had recited them generation after generation after generation before him – I like to think that it was an infusion of Celtic genes that heightened the Icelanders' sense of drama, improved their imagination and made their poetry sing, for the two civilisations have much in common, and owe much to each other, the earlier culture of the Gaels having had a profound and pacifying influence on the wild Northerners.

'From the fury of the Northerner, good Lord deliver us,' was the prayer most frequently heard in churches and abbeys up and down the British Isles during the Viking Age. The Norseman's religious beliefs encouraged brutality towards the followers of the 'White Christ', and their military tactics led them to cow resistance by acts of deliberate cruelty, operating as they did in small numbers in the midst of hostile populations. The rich coastal abbeys, which had no defence except a sacrosanctity which the pagans did not recognise, were sitting targets, and the terror of their lightning hit-and-run attacks soon spread like wildfire across the land. Nevertheless the Viking expeditions during the ninth to eleventh centuries were much more than a series of murderous raids which ransacked Christendom for plunder; wherever possible they organised settlement, and where piracy did not pay, the Vikings were eager to trade.

Perhaps the most astounding thing about them was their cosmopolitanism, which ironically may in the end have contributed to their downfall. It is indeed amazing to think that any race, let alone one from the borders of the Arctic Circle, should, in the brief period between the fall of the Roman Empire and the first Crusade, have established contact with all the great trading routes of the then-known world, and even ranged outside it to discover new worlds of their own.

The Vikings traded with Arab merchants in Bolgar, Byzantium and Cordoba; with the principalities of Novgorod and Kiev; with the Normans of France, and the Mediterranean islands. They reached the shores of the Black Sea and made portages across the Caspian coast to Iran. They sacked Hamburg, sailed up the Seine to Paris, and founded the city of Dublin. They left settlements in the Faeroes and districts of Normandy and the Loire; overran and conquered the Orkneys, Shetlands, Hebrides and large parts of England, including York and the Isle of Man. They colonised Iceland and Greenland, and took the first-ever* look by Western explorers at the coast of America.

The list is endless, and it was all achieved in small, beautiful clinker-

---

* Hebridean scholars may dispute this – claiming that Celtic sailors got there first.

built boats like the Gokstad ship which lies today in an Oslo museum, or the Oseberg ship in Sweden. Masterpieces of maritime design, with high, sweeping prows and retractable keels which, given a fair wind (and this has recently been proved), could cross the Atlantic in an easy fortnight.

No one has explained why this surge of almost superhuman enterprise should have arisen simultaneously in three essentially different countries which, though at first they may have shared a common language and culture, soon developed separate identities and monarchies of their own. And too many monarchies. The early Viking rulers had the self-weakening habit of dividing up their conquests between their heirs – and as polygamy was the practice in pagan Norseland there was always a superabundance of them. Harald Haarfager (or Fairhair), for example, the mighty warrior who united most of Norway under one crown, destroyed his achievement by giving about twenty of his sons the title of king, which inevitably led to jealousies and a fratricidal struggle for power.

It was not till the end of the tenth century and a second wave of Viking expeditions that Christianity began to make an impact on Scandinavia. The Danes supplied 'the first Viking leader to be admitted into the civilised fraternity of Christian Kings'. He was Cnut, the Great King of England, Denmark and, briefly, of Norway and Sweden and parts of the Baltic coast. 'The great' is really an understatement, and it is a pity that British children have been led to believe that he was an old man who sat on a throne on a beach and told the waves to retreat – an unlikely story, as any six-year-old will tell you.

Norway was converted by two Olavs – the first, Olav Triggvesson, used force. He sailed along the coast demanding submission and conversion from both chieftains and 'lag things' (early courts of law), and as the penalties for refusal included mutilation and death, his mission was a singularly successful one, though he did not live to see it prosper, being himself killed in a battle five years later.

The second Olav, the saint, set sail from England with only two shiploads of Christian warriors. He had fought an average of two battles a year since the age of twelve and he eventually won a decisive one at the mouth of Oslofjord which made him king. Olav reigned for ten years as the first king of *all* Norway, and he passed laws which greatly assisted the work of the missionaries who had followed him from England and Denmark. Olav's battle-cry was 'Christ's men!' but he was nevertheless defeated and killed at the battle of Stoklistad in 1030.

In Sweden, the spread of Christianity was slower and later. By the beginning of the twelfth century there were six missionary dioceses in southern Sweden and, in 1157, King Eric and an English bishop, Henry of Uppsala, felt strong enough to launch a crusade for the conversion of Finland.

The Vikings' foothold in England ended at Stamford Bridge in the year 1066 when Harald Hardraada's expeditionary force was defeated by the Saxon King Harold (less than three weeks before the invasion of the Normans). They held on to the Isle of Man for a little longer and kept a firm grip on the Orkneys, Shetlands, the Hebrides and much of the coast of Argyll until the middle of the thirteenth century.

In 1263, the aged Norwegian King Haakon IV was manoeuvred into fighting a land battle near Largs by the wily Scottish King Alexander III. The Vikings lost and Haakon escaped to Kirkwall in Orkney where he died a few months later. Magnus VI, his son and successor, then sold back the Hebrides and the Isle of Man to the Scottish Crown for a lump sum and an annual rent, a transaction which was ratified at the Treaty of Perth, a somewhat pedestrian end to the great Viking adventure.

6

DENMARK

Queen Margrethe II

'The Queen is head of our society: the Crown is head of our morality.'
WALTER BAGEHOT

I waited for Queen Margrethe of Denmark in the pretty, sunny draw-ing-room of a house in Belgravia and tried to imagine from its comfortable and country-house atmosphere what its resident would be like. There had been no fuss in arranging my interview and when she came in, hatless and rather out of breath from a Christmas shopping expedition that had made her five minutes late, there was no fuss about Queen Margrethe herself. Her lady-in-waiting took over the parcels and her coat and she settled into one of the armchairs, looking very elegant in a burnt-orange cashmere jersey with a high polo-neck and a light tweed skirt. She is tall and slim, with an unquestionably Nordic face, pretty fair hair scraped back into a Grecian knot, a high natural colour, grey-blue eyes and good, regular features. Her small, neat head is carried on a graceful neck and the ramrod-straight back reinforces a natural air of dignity, even regality, of which she seems quite unconscious but which is there, however informal the *mise-en-scène*. I was immediately aware of a strong, sharp, confident personality, and this first impression was reinforced by our conversation. There are no ambiguities and no diplo-matic evasions. She comes straight to the point, and makes some very good ones at that.

I told her I had read up Denmark's history and quoted a particular source. 'He is good,' she agreed, 'well balanced. But,' she added, smiling a little, 'one must be careful . . . usually when one likes an author it means he agrees with one!' It struck me then that fairness, not an easy quality for reigning queens to practise, but a very Danish one, would come high in Her Majesty's priorities. Yet higher still, I soon realised, from a change of tone or sudden animation, was her feeling for her country and its people.

When Princess Margrethe was thirteen, laws were passed changing the Danish constitution in order to allow female succession to the throne.

'People,' she told me, 'wanted my father's (King Frederik IX) family to go on reigning – so, as he had no sons, there had to be a plebiscite and close to eighty-eight per cent of the votes cast were for me to succeed. Naturally, I did not realise all the implications, but I guess I was pleased. Most princesses know they will marry and almost certainly live abroad, which I would have hated, but I knew then that I would stay in Denmark and this made me very happy.'

It was her French husband, Henri Laborde de Monpezat (now Prince Hejnrik of Denmark) who had to be uprooted, but it was a love match and the marriage is a good one. By the time Queen Margrethe succeeded her father, King Frederik, whose reign ended in 1972, there were two small sons, Crown Prince Frederik ('All Danish kings are Frederiks or Christians, it's very muddling,' she told me), and Prince Joachim.

HM Queen Margrethe II of Denmark.

The boys are now twenty-four and twenty-three. The Crown Prince, having finished his military service, is attending Aarhus University. Prince Joachim, having so enjoyed a soldier's life that he volunteered to stay on in the army for an extra six months, has started a new career as a student in an agricultural college. 'Both boys,' said their mother, 'are much more mature since they have done their military service. They entered the army as privates, were treated exactly like all the other recruits, and had to mix and get on with everyone. They did well, became sergeants and eventually officers. They are very close to us and we see them all the time, but they have their own apartments in the Amalienborg.' The Amalienborg is the magnificent eighteenth-century palace, or rather, four elegant rococo palaces, built for four noble families in the reign of Frederik V in 1746 in the heart of Copenhagen. It is one of the architectural gems of the city.

Although she conducts the affairs of state from the Amalienborg, Queen Margrethe and Prince Hejnrik live for part of the year at Fredenborg, a palace in the country forty miles away. It is a very hospitable palace, famous in the days of Christian IX for its enormous three-generation family gatherings, which his sophisticated son-in-law, Edward, Prince of Wales, used to find 'a dreadful bore'.

Queen Margrethe is very conscious that her own and her family's privileges carry with them definite duties and obligations, and says that her sons too have already learnt that lesson. She is a constitutional monarch and though there are practically no ceremonial duties attached to the job in Denmark, her working days are full. As well as all the social and charitable projects she is involved in, she holds public audiences for her people every fortnight in Christianborg Palace, for 'since time immemorial' Danes have had the right to meet and talk informally to their king or queen.

Queen Margrethe is also responsible for all decorations, awards and honours given to Danish citizens. She sees her Prime Minister and Foreign Secretary every Wednesday and presides over the Council of State regularly. Although there are few state occasions, no ceremonial coronation (a proclamation is simply read from a balcony), Queen Margrethe attends the opening of parliament and would have to choose a Prime Minister in the event of a hung vote between level-pegging parties. She is obviously interested in both national and international politics and reads and signs every order and Act her government passes.

There is no formal court but she has a Lord Chamberlain, a private secretary, and ladies-in-waiting when she needs them. Her day starts at her desk in the Amalienborg: state documents with her private secretary, consultations and planning with any number of people, discussions with her Chamberlain. She has a light lunch, sometimes just a sandwich in her upstairs apartments and then there are always engagements in the afternoon. The evenings are usually spent at home, which means with her family.

'Are you able to have a reasonable private life, as well as a public one, Ma'am?' I asked.

'Oh yes, especially when the children were growing up. It needs organising, but it *can* be managed.'

Nowadays she often visits London where she has many friends and relations including her younger sister, Queen Anne Marie, and her husband, the exiled King Constantine II of the Hellenes. Indeed, the two sisters are related to practically every crowned head in Europe and do a lot of visiting. It was their great-great grandfather, Christian IX (he of the houseparties) who was called 'the father-in-law of Europe'. His first daughter, Alexandra, became Queen of England; his second, Dagmar, Tsarina of Russia; while his son William was chosen to be the first king of Greece as George I of Greece 'and Prince of Denmark'; and when Norway and Sweden parted company in 1905 his grandson Karl was elected King of Norway. In addition, the Queen Mother of Denmark who, now retired from public life, lives for most of the summer in a small 'dependance' at Fredenborg, was Princess Ingrid of Sweden, the daughter of the late King Gustav VI Adolf, so the family circle is immense.

Queen Margrethe is also one of the best educated monarchs in Europe. She went first to a boarding school in England, North Foreland Lodge. 'I was one of those unoriginal children who really loved their schooldays,' she told me, and she was equally modest about her university career. This included reading philosophy, constitutional and international law, archaeology and sociology at two Danish universities, as well as at the Sorbonne, Cambridge and the London School of Economics. 'But I never took a degree at any of them. I only wish there had been more time and that I had matriculated – especially in archaeology, which I'm still passionately interested in.'

She does admit, however, to speaking five languages, as well as a little Faeroese. I asked her what she thought about the 'eternal' students and hippies who squat in the disused barracks in the centre of Copenhagen, to the outrage of some of its senior citizens. Her attitude towards them was engagingly relaxed and lenient. She was equally tolerant of the feminist movement, which is strong in Denmark, but less so of its all too frequent result, one-parent families. She believes passionately in families being balanced two-parent units, but even then I felt she was able to see the other person's point of view. She said, 'It isn't good for children to be brought up in a family where two people are always at war with each other. I'm glad that women can now fulfil their potential. It's easy for the privileged to talk about their place "in the home". We both,' she said, fixing me with a direct and mist-piercing Viking eye, 'had nannies to help look after our children – and thank God for them – so we had the best of both worlds' . . . *'and can't talk.'* I knew she meant, though she didn't say it, and I felt suitably and deservedly reproved.

We talked about Denmark's links with Scotland. Scotland's James III married Margaret of Denmark in 1460 and the Danish King Christian I mortgaged the Orkneys and Shetlands in order to provide his daughter with a handsome dowry when she married a Scottish heir apparent.

I asked Her Majesty next about Denmark's links with Greenland, Iceland and the Faeroes and she explained that, in the eighth century, a Viking sailed westwards from Norway till he came on land which impeded further progress. He had discovered Iceland, and from Iceland, the Vikings could see the mountains of 'Greenland' and realised a great country lay beyond. Today Iceland is independent and both Greenland and the Faeroe Islands have self-government, but they recognise Queen Margrethe as Queen. In the fourteenth century, when the Danes were at the height of their power, Margrethe I of Denmark, the 'Semiramis of the North', ruled over all the Nordic countries, Norway, Sweden and Denmark, as well as Schleswig-Holstein, but Sweden broke away in 1523, and Norway was lost in 1814. The Oldenburg line was elected to the throne of Denmark in 1449 and the same family has ruled over it ever since.

'Do you remember the war?' I asked Her Majesty.

'Only a few things,' she answered. 'Mostly my grandfather being very ill and the victory parades.' She was only five in 1945. In April 1940 the German army invaded Denmark, breaking their mutual treaty of neutrality on a trumped-up charge that the British were about to establish bases on its coast. How this small country, occupied by the enemy, managed, for the next three years, to retain the essential aspects of her national sovereignty was the result of an amazingly skilful combination of diplomacy and determination. Jurisdiction over her people remained Danish, and all German negotiations and proclamations were channelled, as to a foreign country, through the Danish Foreign Office. Germany sent Denmark iron and coal and Denmark had to send back her entire export of farm produce. Though news was censored (almost every citizen listened to war-time BBC news on secret radios), schools and universities remained under Danish control, as did cultural institutions and youth organisations. Some pro-Nazi Danes were content to sit out the war as a German protectorate, but the vast majority were not.

In October 1942 King Christian X suffered a severe accident by being thrown from his horse and thereafter was too ill to play a leading part,

though he remained highly revered as a symbol of the continued existence of the national spirit. For a time he hovered between life and
death, but later he was able to transmit his wishes through Crown Prince
Frederik (Queen Margrethe's father). When, in September 1942, Hitler
sent him a congratulatory telegram on the occasion of his seventy-second
birthday, he replied, with minimum courtesy, 'Thank you', a put-down
which is said to have enraged the Führer. Certainly, the Germans began
stepping up reprisals against the proliferating underground resistance
movements in Denmark. 'It was only natural,' commented Queen Margrethe, fair as usual. But the nation's patience had begun to wear thin
with the deliberate caution of its politicians and leaders, who were anxious to avoid a complete and premature break with Germany, and in the
spring and summer of 1943, the people's open defiance was shown by a
series of strikes in the shipyards and factories, by increasing sabotage and
by the total non-cooperation of the townsfolk to civic authority. Of
course, in return, more punitive action was taken by the Wehrmacht,
who moved in fresh units and a new general to command them.

Finally, at 4 a.m. on 29 August 1943 a State of Emergency was
declared which allowed the Germans to impose martial law: curfews,
drum-head courts martial, executions and transportations. Then all party
chairmen and trade union leaders met and agreed to protest as one united
nation and refuse to comply with the new order. The Danish fleet, at
the same time, in a brilliant and gallant gesture, managed to scuttle
itself rather than fall into enemy hands and, though retribution followed
swiftly, the Germans were never able to control the country again or to
form a new government.

A clandestine Freedom Council was set up which was also in close
touch with the Free Danes in England. This gradually turned into a
military command committee which played a significant part in the
liberation of their country. But not before the Germans had murdered
thousands of prominent Danes and sent others to Buchenwald. When
the Nazis tried to round up the Danish Jews, only five or six hundred
out of many thousands were captured, the rest being smuggled out of the
country or hidden by people from all walks of life. With the king at their
head, all civilian leaders protested against the persecution of the Jews
'because,' as a Bishop's pastoral letter stated, 'Christ was a Jew, because
the persecution violates Christian ideals and love of mankind, and
because it violates the Danish sense of justice'.

One is very conscious as one talks to Denmark's present queen of her
belief in that justice and in democracy and, although this may seem
contradictory, I believe that she sees herself – the constitutional monarch

of a country where justice and democracy really work – as their fiercest guardian, for she is above party and politics and has no personal ambition other than to further her country's interests. After all, she was chosen by the Danish people and although she would be the last to claim it, her popularity with them has increased ever since.

I have often wondered what Queen Margrethe thinks of the Maastricht Conference and Treaty, which hadn't happened when I saw her last. She favours referendums, for it was one that made her Queen, and although she is above party and politics, I imagine she would approve of her people's hard-headed realism and caution. It has taken enormous courage for a small nation to stand up to the might of eleven others. But the Danes stood fast against Nazi Germany, and haven't forgotten it.

Their intransigence has made the rest of Europe pause, consider and have second thoughts.

7

SWEDEN

King Karl XVI Gustaf

'You cannot have progress without continuity; you cannot have continuity without progress. Continuity is a condition of progress. Revolution points the contrast.'

QUINTIN HOGG

Stockholm is a capital in which the history of its kings is written large, and the story conveniently lies within the forty-two hectares of Gamla Sten, the old walled city, which once clustered round the defences of a mediaeval fort. John III (1568–92) turned the fortress into a Renaissance castle, the Tre Kronor, named because of the three golden crowns on its summit, and then, after a disastrous fire, it was metamorphosed once more into Charles XII's (1697–1718) immense and imposing neo-classical palace which stands today as both a reflection of Sweden's eighteenth-century glory and a suitable habitation for the Swedish king's new status in the world.

It was to this great building, divided now into royal museums, secretariats and the private apartments of the royal family, that my husband and I drove one sunny afternoon in the spring of 1991, in the resplendent comfort of the embassy Rolls-Royce, courtesy of our British ambassador to Sweden, H.E. Sir John Ure.

A quiet inner-courtyard in classical style led to an unassuming entrance where a footman was waiting for us. He ushered us in and hurried off to fetch Baroness Elizabeth Palmstierna, Their Majesties' Chief of Protocol, whom we had already met at a dinner party with the Ures.

We found ourselves in a long, light gallery of Italian Renaissance style, with tall windows reaching from vaulted ceiling to the chequered stone floor on one side of it and colonnaded embrasures, inhabited by white marble gods and goddesses, on the other. Whether this was the Museum of Antiquities of Gustaf III (1771–92) or a mere overflow from it I do not know, but it was evidently the side door that the palace staff use and this was reinforced by the arrival of the charming Elizabeth Palmstierna, who is multi-lingual and might easily be mistaken for one of our own sovereign's ladies. She hustled us along passages, in the dim corners of which rather touching royal family detritus lingers: a pram, what looked like an antique sledge, two brightly painted rocking horses . . .

The suite of rooms we finally came to were modest compared with the seventeenth-century audience chamber in the now public part of the palace, whose walls are hung with bosky Dutch tapestries, ordered by Queen Kristina for her coronation in 1650, and where a magnificent throne and golden canopy (probably brought from Florence by John III's wife, a member of the Sforza family) dominates the room.

It is just as well. King Karl XVI Gustaf is a modest man, and the comfortable but businesslike office we were shown into is furnished in his own plain and masculine style, with just a few museum pieces and objets d'art scattered around to remind one of the extraordinary richness and diversity of Sweden's culture and of the Swedish royal family's possessions and history.

That history must surely begin with that remarkable woman, the first Queen Margaret of Denmark. In 1397 the Union of the Three Crowns of Denmark, Sweden and Norway under Queen Margaret brought peace and prosperity and, above all, order to Scandinavia for a short time. It came about because this remarkable Danish queen, the widow of a Norwegian king, had a son who was elected king of Sweden. During her long double regency of both Norway and Sweden, Queen Margaret of Denmark ruled all three countries at the same time. The union of her own country and Norway lasted for four centuries – that with Sweden was more restless, and briefer.

After Queen Margaret's death there followed a period of trouble and uncertainty, which in Denmark ended in 1449 when the Danish nobles elected Christian of Oldenburg to be their king. Sweden was not so fortunate. The unruly Swedish nobles were divided in their allegiance and in October 1471 a fierce battle was fought on the Brunkeberg hill outside Stockholm, which historians have compared to Agincourt. The pro-Danish nobles and the Danes were defeated and Sten Sture, the rebel leader, became guardian of a briefly independent Swedish state.

A generation later, Christian I's grandson, Christian II, a more formidable and cruel character than his patronym, reconquered Sweden by force of arms and, in 1520, was crowned its hereditary king. Three days after the coronation festivities were concluded, he started to purge the country of all opposition. Eighty-two of his enemies, mostly nobles from the great families of Sweden, were rounded up, accused of heresy and, after a brief trial, executed one after the other in Stockholm's Market Square, whose gutters, an eye-witness tells us, 'ran with blood'. The corpses were then burnt and, as a further disinducement to rebellion, Sten Sture and his little son's exhumed bodies were placed on top of the pyre. The bloodbath of Stortorget has never been forgotten by the people of Stockholm. Today every citizen can tell you the place where the royal executioner stood.

These were rough times and, as King Christian had once told Erasmus (who had deprecated Martin Luther's violence): 'Gentle medicines produce no results; the best and most effective remedies are those that shake up the entire body.' Be that as it may, in 1523 Christian II was deposed in both Sweden and Denmark and the Union of the Three Crowns came to an inglorious end.

The man who led the rebellion in Sweden was Gustav Ericsson Vasa, a relation of the Stures, who was to rule Sweden for the next thirty-seven years. Gustav Vasa was the first of two remarkable Vasa kings and one high-handed and mysterious Vasa queen, who brought their country from relative obscurity to the forefront of the European stage.

In all Western civilisation, this was an era of change and of new ideas, of re-organisation and reform. In Sweden the impact of the Reformation, which affected every man's life, was far greater than that of the Renaissance, whose illumination touched only the few. Gradually the Swedish Church was separated from the monasteries and from Rome and was organised into a State Lutheran Church which, in all essentials, survives to this day – the riches and lands of the monastic communities and the Catholic sees passing into the possession of the Vasa family and their supporters, greatly increasing their power.

In Sweden a basic national code of law had already been established by the end of the fourteenth century, which aimed primarily at safeguarding an individual's peace and security. Acts of violence in church, or the Thing (the early parliament of Sweden, which preceded the Riksdag), personal attacks on another man's house or against a defenceless woman, made a man an outlaw without rights or property, and the 'law of the land' also included a short written constitution delineating the separate powers of the king, his councillors and his subjects. One of its phrases is as simple but, to my mind, as perfect a definition of Christian monarchy as can be found: 'The King shall all justice and truth strengthen, love and preserve, all wrongs and falsehoods destroy, both by law and by his Royal power.' You only have to add 'under God' and there you have it.

On the whole Gustav Vasa lived up to this high ideal, but he was also a down-to-earth, practical man. Under his able rule, government administration was reorganised and reached unprecedented efficiency; local interests were set aside for the common good, and foreign policies were aimed firmly at Sweden's aggrandisement and eventual control of all the Baltic. To this end, Gustav I waged war against Poland, Denmark, Lübeck and Russia, and soon Estonia was added to Sweden's growing empire.

All three of Gustav Vasa's sons succeeded him as King – John III married a Polish Catholic princess and fathered a son, Sigismund, who first became King of Poland and then King of Sweden – but Sigismund's religion and long absences from the country, as well as his efforts to create a new 'northern' union, made him much disliked in Sweden and, in 1599, he was deposed by his uncle, Karl, after a Swedish reign of only seven years. Far from bringing the two countries together, the net result of the brief dual monarchy was to make Sweden and Poland implacable enemies for the next two hundred years.

Karl's son and Gustav Vasa's grandson, Gustavus Adolphus, was a king of kings. He was called *il Re d'oro* by Italians, because of his fair Nordic good looks; the 'Dragon King' by Charles I of England, because of his martial genius; and the 'Lion of the North' by his embattled Protestant co-religionists in Germany. He brought Sweden into the Thirty Years War on their behalf, but also raised her to the status of a great power, eclipsing the ablest of Danish rulers and making the dominion of the Baltic a natural goal for his successors.

He spoke eight languages fluently and was equally eloquent in all of them. He combined royal dignity with comradely kindness, and was loved by all classes of his rapidly expanding kingdom, but more especially by his soldiers, with whom he was prepared to share every danger and hardship. Although a devout Lutheran, he believed, even in those days of polarised belief, in the merits of religious toleration. It was a tragedy for Sweden when he fell in battle at Lützen in 1632.

Gustavus Adolphus was succeeded by his six-year-old daughter, Kristina, and a long regency followed his death. Queen Kristina may not have been as beautiful as Greta Garbo's unforgettable, dreamy, celluloid queen, dressed in sexually confusing clothes and suffering pangs of mysterious love, but in real life she was a good-looking woman of strong character and fine intellect, with a delight in power and a weakness for romantic intrigues. No one has ever completely understood her enigmatic character, but one thing is certain: she awoke the upper classes in Sweden from their cultural barbarism and brought new ideas and foreign talents of the highest order to the Castle of the Three Crowns, where she established a brilliant and extravagant court.

The long campaigns of her father had brought the Swedish Crown and State to the verge of bankruptcy, and they had only been sustained by the sale or transfer of Crown lands to the nobility. As a result during Kristina's long minority, the noble families ruled the country. They were in possession of over seventy per cent of Sweden and Finland's land, the Crown and independent farmers only owning twenty-eight per cent, or the rump. It was a situation which endangered the free husbandmen of the country (who greatly feared they would be turned into serfs) as well as inhibiting any kind of central authority.

At the meeting of the Riksdag which preceded Kristina's coronation in 1650, the three Lower Estates demanded the restitution (*Reduktion*) of alienated lands and rights, so that the state could meet its necessary expenses. Though the young queen listened and agreed to the demand in principle, she never in practice seemed able to grasp the nettle of economic reform. She loved embellishing her palace, entertaining on a lavish scale, being patroness of academia and the arts. Her court rivalled that of a Medici palace (without their hard-headed bankers' grip), while her plans for improved education and enlightenment in her country were equally grandiose. Yet land alienation continued and, in the ten years of her reign, the Swedish nobility, far from being reduced, multiplied; the number of counts and barons rising from eighteen to eighty.

When, at the age of twenty-eight, Kristina decided not to marry her cousin Charles, Count Palatine of Zweibrücken (an eminently appropriate suitor, whom she had already designated as her heir), and at the same time was converted to Roman Catholicism, which was proscribed in Sweden, she found herself boxed in by too many problems, which her free and somewhat imperious nature could not sustain. In a 'complex quandary of conscience' she took the only way out she could think of, and abdicated. Her half-German cousin was crowned Charles X Gustavus of Sweden the following day.

The House of Pfalz – or Palatinate – produced two famous warrior-kings, Charles X and the even better known Charles XII, and it introduced autocracy to Sweden. Charles X, having taken on both Poland and Denmark in a series of brilliant campaigns, died suddenly when he was only thirty-seven, and had no time during his six-year and soldierly reign for economic reforms at home.

It was left to his son, Charles XI, an autocratic but sagacious king, to bring about the *Reduktion* of the nobles which Queen Kristina had notably failed to achieve. Under his absolute rule, Sweden at last enjoyed two full decades of peace, and her trade and economy not only recovered but began to flourish. His son, Charles XII of Sweden, was the very model of a warrior king: an autocratic and decisive ruler at home, a great leader and thoroughly professional soldier abroad. From his first teenage campaign until the day he died, cut down by a sniper's bullet in the trenches before Fredriksten, he lived a life of spartan discipline and constant danger. He had killed his first bear, his father proudly noted, at the age of eleven years and seven months, and he defeated Russian forces five times as great as his own at the Battle of Narva when he was eighteen.

A coalition of Russia with Poland–Saxony and Denmark had been mounted against Sweden by Peter the Great in the year 1700, and before he had even come of age the young Charles planned and conducted a series of brilliant defensive campaigns whose initial success was unparalleled in the history of warfare – they not only routed his opponents, but led his small army into the heart of their territory. Then, however, in pursuit of the 'Grand Design' he always talked about, he made the classic mistake that Napoleon and Hitler both made, centuries later. In 1704, he invaded Russia.

Instead of his campaign leading to the fall of Moscow and the end of the Russian Empire, it led to his defeat at Poltava (1709), the capitulation of his army and his own precipitous flight into Turkey. Poltava was a turning point in the history of Europe as well as 'the great Northern wars'; from then on, Russian power in the Baltic was assured.

Charles remained in Turkey for more than five years, first as a guest, then as an exalted prisoner of the Porte. In almost a modern Lebanese situation, it was the under-cover influence of the Emperor Charles V that obtained his release, but he had to travel back to Sweden incognito, covering a distance of 1,500 miles in fourteen days, two-thirds of it on horseback.* It was only to find a desperate situation awaiting him. Frederik IV of Denmark, a redoubtable king with a cool head and powerful will, had now been joined by Hanover/England and Prussia in an anti-Swedish coalition. Charles attacked Norway, hoping it would act as a springboard for a leap into Denmark, but he was killed as he besieged the Norwegian fortress of Fredriksten, only four years after his return to his own country.

The disastrous end of the great Northern wars led to a violent reaction of the Swedish people to royal absolutism. During the next fifty years

---

* How he did this while bringing back with him a small army of Turkish cooks and their 'batterie de cuisine' defies the imagination!

the country underwent a kind of bloodless revolution which drastically trimmed the king's power, reducing it to only two votes in the Council (*Cabinet*) and giving the nation an embryo constitution which at least laid the foundations of democracy. It was known as the 'Era of Liberty'.

But liberty was brought to an abrupt end by the accession in 1772 of Gustavus III, followed a few months later by a royal *coup d'état* which brought the governance of the country firmly and decisively back into the hands of an autocratic king.

Gustavus' father, Frederick, was a weak-minded, vacillating Danish princeling, but his mother, Louise Ulrica, was sister of Frederick the Great of Prussia and a consort of very different calibre. She was a child of the Enlightenment, and in Prussia had been used to being surrounded by clever people and beautiful things. She had good taste and grandiose ideas, and the courage and energy to act on them. She considered the royal palace in Stockholm 'provincial' and immediately embarked on the reconstruction and embellishment of a second palace, outside Stockholm, that had once been the home of a rich merchant. It was called Drottningholm.

As well as adding wings and a new façade to the building, she laid out its formal gardens on a grand scale, with vast parterres, fountains, oaken avenues and clipped hedges surrounded by an 'English park'. But what made Drottningholm one of the most delightful palaces of the Western world were such appendages as the monarch's private theatre and ballet school, a Chinese pavilion in the park which grew like a mushroom in the night, and was presented to her by her husband as a birthday surprise – a striped iron tent in the Turkish style for her guards to shelter in when it rained . . . and other delectable follies.

No wonder a little prince, growing up in this hothouse of culture and privilege (and foreign influence) which effectively cut him off from the aspirations of his proletarian subjects, would decide, when he later ruled over them, that his wishes always came first. After a second *coup d'état*, in conjunction this time with some of his nobles, Gustavus introduced what became known as 'Gustavian absolutism', which remained in place for the rest of his reign. It was an enlightened despotism, and many of Gustavus' reforms were positive achievements which have lasted to this day. He abolished torture, purged and reorganised Sweden's bureaucracy and insisted on religious tolerance – like his uncle Frederik, he was a freemason – but there was a dark side, too, to his administration: he introduced censorship and recruited a secret police which was modelled on the one that already existed in France.

French influence on the Swedish aristocracy reached its zenith at Gustavus III's court, which became a kind of northern Versailles, and the king's passion for the theatre (he wrote and directed many amateur productions himself) resulted in a Royal Opera House being opened in Stockholm in 1782, while a Swedish Academy was founded only a few years later 'for the encouragement of poetry, scholarship and rhetoric'. At its opening the king emphasised that it should also act 'as a bulwark of traditional values' but these did not include liberty or equality, and the Revolution in France was only three years away.

Gustavus brought Sweden into the Russo–Turkish war in 1788. He fancied himself in a martial role. But by so doing he offended a proportion of his army and his nobles, who had violently opposed intervention, and whether his victory over Catherine the Great's fleet in the Gulf of Finland outweighed the cost in lives and money of the two-year war was openly doubted by an increasingly rebellious population.

In 1792 he was shot by a former captain of the Royal Guards during a masked ball at the Opera House, a *coup de théâtre* that he would have appreciated himself had he not been the victim. He died a painful and lingering death some two weeks later from his wounds.* The opinion of his subjects on his reign was evenly divided. To some he had seemed an immoral, ruthless tyrant; to others 'the enchanter on the throne'. But, when a statue commissioned in his honour was finally unveiled in January 1808, its sculptor made the following little speech, which was recorded for posterity: 'Gentlemen – hold me up, blast you – our Sun was drowned in blood, but he has risen again to shine in another world. Devil take me if Gustav III was not a ray of the Light Eternal. The statue I have made is trash, but we have his image in our hearts and there he will live as long as we have a drop of blood in our veins. A health to the memory of Gustav III, our father and benefactor!'

It was a handsome tribute, and goes to show that royal patronage of the arts usually pays.

Gustavus III was succeeded by his son, but Gustavus IV's absolutism and foreign policy was a great deal less successful than his father's. After a disastrous declaration of war on France and the irrevocable loss of Finland to Russia, the Swedish population rose against him in another bloodless revolution and he was removed from the throne in 1809. A new constitution was then adopted which was based on Montesquieu's

* Not so painful, however, as the death of the regicide, Count Ankerström, who was scourged with whips of iron thongs, had his right hand cut off, then his head, after which his body was impaled.

theory of the 'separation of power' – the king in future was to be the sole sovereign of the realm but would have at his side a Council of Ministers who must approve or countersign all his decisions. It was ratified by the Riksdag in 1809 and became the code by which, in essence, Sweden was governed until only a generation ago, when the king's powers were still further diminished.

The deposed king's uncle, Duke Karl, was then asked by the Riksdag to accept the crown as Karl XIII. He was elderly and childless and it was important that an heir should soon be found to succeed him. A Danish prince was the government's first choice, but he died shortly after his arrival in Sweden. Then a most surprising decision was made by King Karl and his Council. A Gascony sergeant, named Jean Baptiste Bernadotte, had risen from the ranks in Napoleon's army to become a Maréchal de France, and had been appointed the temporary governor of Swedish Pomerania, where he earned the goodwill and respect of the people by his fairness and genial disposition.

On this slender evidence, Bernadotte was now formally invited to be Prince Héritier to the Swedish throne. After consultation with Napoleon he accepted the challenge and, having changed his name to Charles John, he arrived in Oslo in 1810 as Prince Karl-Johan of Sweden. The desire for an alliance with Napoleon, and the slender hope of obtaining the latter's support in regaining the lost provinces of Finland and the Baltic coast had been behind the Swedish choice, but Bernadotte, who almost immediately assumed the duties of Crown Prince and the direction of the country's foreign policy, now showed his independence of mind and also his nerve. He persuaded his new country to join a coalition *against* Napoleon, a shrewd and well-timed move for, in the Treaty of Kiel that followed the Emperor's defeat, he prised Norway away from Denmark and, after a short campaign, the issue of which was never in doubt, he forced Norway into a union with Sweden which was not to be dissolved until the beginning of the next century.

In the eyes of the rest of Europe, in the short period of peace that was to follow the Napoleonic wars, the principal change which had been brought about in Scandinavia was the change in sovereignty – the transfer of the Norwegian crown in 1814 by a defeated Frederik, King of Denmark to Karl XIII of Sweden and his able Prince Regent, and the acquisition of Finland as a grand duchy by the idealistic, if mistaken, Tsar of Russia, Alexander I. The result was a twofold alteration of the balance of power in the north – from then onwards, Russia would always overshadow Norway–Sweden, and within Scandinavia itself a reduced

Denmark would never again be strong enough to challenge a Norway–
Sweden union. A less obvious result, which can more easily be seen in
retrospect, was the introduction into both Norway and Sweden of political institutions which have lasted to the present day, and in Finland too
a special form of self-government that was put into place at the beginning
of the nineteenth century.

Bernadotte, an active, decisive Frenchman who never learnt a word
of Swedish during his twenty-six years on Sweden's throne, had found it
difficult even as Prince Regent to accept the restrictions of the 1809
constitution, and he had been frequently at loggerheads with the more
independent members of his Council. After Karl XIII's death in 1818,
as King Karl XIV John, he increasingly chose his ministers from among
royal bureaucrats whom he could trust to carry out his orders, for the
former revolutionary had evolved into a traditional monarch with distinctly autocratic tendencies.

Sweden, under the Bernadotte dynasty which followed, fought no
more wars and steered a careful course of non-involvement in the power-
bids, squabbles and revolutions which the rest of Europe indulged in
during the next hundred years. Their own struggle to retain their personal
power against that of the State, which increasingly encroached on it,
was the question which largely dominated Swedish politics during the
same period.

Under Oskar I, Bernadotte's son, ministers had largely been the servants of the king, but under governmental reforms of the 1840s they
became heads of their own ministries, with considerable clout, and
further reforms in 1866 abolished the old Riksdag of the Estates and
introduced a bi-cameral assembly which could always be depended on to
support the Council vis-à-vis the King. Things came to a head when
King Gustaf V, in February 1914, delivered his famous Courtyard Speech
to 30,000 of his subjects, who had gathered on a cold winter's day for a
so-called 'Farmers' Rally' in one of the courtyards of the royal palace; but
his well-argued speech fell on deaf ears.

The struggle for royal power was lost and, from that day onwards,
Sweden's future belonged to democracy, to parliamentarianism and, as
later decisions were to show, to neutrality. It was a near-run thing then,
and again after the general election of 1917, that Sweden was not in
fact declared a republic.

The personal popularity of both Gustaf V and Gustaf VI who, between
them, occupied the throne of Sweden for the next sixty-six years, was
the reason that the monarchy survived. It was a new kind of monarchy,
without power, or pomp, or ceremonial – but it seems to have suited the

people of Sweden and not even the most rabid republican politicians that the country can produce look like dislodging it today.

King Karl XVI Gustaf* is tall, good-looking and, behind his steel-rimmed designer spectacles, he has large, very blue eyes, crinkly at the corners, like all good sailors' eyes should be ('It comes from drinking gin,' I was once told). He and I sat down on a rather stiff sofa and began a rather stiff conversation which was saved, minutes later, by the arrival of Queen Sylvia, who breezed in looking extremely pretty in a green and white silk dress, and with her recently broken arm in a sling which matched it. 'The traffic was awful, I'm so sorry I'm late,' she announced, and from then on everyone relaxed, my husband perked up visibly, and the conversation became lively and fun.

Karl XVI had been barely a year old when his father was killed in a plane crash; he was brought up by his German mother, Princess Sibylla of Saxe-Coburg and Gotha, and was taught to be a king by his elderly grandfather, King Gustaf VI Adolf, who died in 1973 at the age of ninety and whom he succeeded when he was twenty-seven years old. Sweden had got used to two very old gentlemen on the throne, King Karl's great-grandfather had lived until he was ninety-one, and Sweden's neutrality in both world wars had isolated her from the mainstream of European royalty. I asked if he saw much of his British royal relations, and he confessed that he was much closer to his French and German cousins, with whom he had been brought up.

At first the nation was suspicious of a young and untried bachelor king and once more there was talk among republicans of bringing the monarchy to an end. The young king's first few months on the throne must have been uncomfortable ones, especially as, in the spring of 1975, a new constitution, which had been many years in preparation, at last became law. It supplanted that of 1809 and, from the point of view of the monarchy, it was a pretty deadly document for it reduced the sovereign to little more than a figurehead. Even in a hung parliament situation he would no longer be able to choose a Prime Minister, nor was he able any longer to take part in government meetings, sign bills or appoint or dismiss ministers, and the Riksdag would have the right to decide, if he failed to fulfil, or was prevented from fulfilling, the few duties that were left to him, whether or not 'he shall be considered to have abdicated'.

Of all the monarchs in Europe, the King of Sweden now has the least

---

* At first I was puzzled by Swedish nomenclature, then discovered that often the reigning monarch's name is followed by that of the deceased king.

HM King Carl XVI Gustaf of
Sweden and Queen Sylvia.

power, even constitutional power. He does act, however, he told me, as a roving ambassador in his country's interest, he has many duties and he is able to hand out decorations and orders, of which the Swedes have a great many. Queen Sylvia interrupted here to tell us that, on the eve of their marriage, he suddenly remembered the Order of the Seraphim, which can only be given by a Swedish king to foreigners; a frantic hunt through the palace produced one and he decorated her with it on their wedding day. Queen Sylvia was born Sylvia Sommerlath. She is the daughter of a West German businessman and his Brazilian wife. Much of her childhood was spent in Brazil, but she graduated in languages at Munich, and was chosen as Chief Hostess for the Olympic Games there in 1972 – it was then that she met the Swedish Crown Prince and that they fell in love.

It has been a particularly happy marriage and Queen Sylvia's sunny, extrovert nature and effortless charm have made her very popular and helped the king to overcome a natural shyness and, at the beginning of his reign, a certain lack of confidence (no wonder!). He was a dyslexic child whose education had to be tailored to overcome this disability, and his grandfather's 'act' has been a difficult one to follow, especially when a socialist government cuts your wings just as you are learning to fly.

King Gustaf VI Adolf had succeeded in fighting off republicanism by getting on with the man in the street, and by being a learned and impressive character in his own right whom no one could lightly dismiss. * He kept in step with Swedish society of the day, which was (and still is) a mixture of folksy traditionalists, proud of their Viking ancestry and their brief moment of glory under warrior kings, and at the same time, and quite illogically, a 'green' population of ardent environmentalists, keen socialists and dedicated pacifists. Sweden's few remaining nobles, or aristocracy (about six hundred families out of a population of six million), though impoverished and without any political power, take themselves very seriously. They meet once a year for a formal dinner in a mediaeval hall, where their fading banners and coats-of-arms still hang in mute testimony to their feuding, fighting and glorious past. For the rest of the year they live in enchanting manor houses and small castles whose beauty can only partly compensate for their lack of servants or modern amenities.

King Karl told me that, with the enormous number of refugees that flooded into Sweden when it was pursuing an open-door policy, the

---

* He was a serious archaeologist, much respected among international scholars, and was never happier than when doing field work in his own and other countries.

republicans among the population have been very much diluted, and that he felt the monarchy was now more secure than in his grandfather's or great-grandfather's time. Nowadays, many big businesses, big conglomerates straddle several countries, Sweden/Norway/Finland, or Sweden/Denmark/Norway, and this in a way is a curious revival, though in less idealistic form, of the 'Scandinavianism' that was Oskar I's dream.

We talked about their children and how the eldest girl, Crown Princess Victoria, who was born in 1977, will one day inherit the throne instead of his son, Prince Philip, who was born two years later. 'Surely that will create problems?' I suggested. But neither of them seemed to think it would – their youngest child, Princess Madeline, is only ten and unconcerned about questions of succession.

King Karl trained as a naval officer after he left school, and he is still a keen yachtsman. He took courses at Uppsala University and later an economics course at Stockholm University. His grandfather sent him all over Sweden to learn for himself the workings of Swedish industry at every level, and he worked for a time at the Ministry of Foreign Affairs, and then in London at his own embassy, and at Hambro's Bank in the City.

It seemed to me, as we said goodbye, that if an independent company was drawing up a balance sheet of the Swedish nation's potential, Karl XVI Gustaf, its under-used king, would go down in the column marked 'Wasted Assets' – and that someone should do something about it.

In September 1991 Sweden's Social Democratic government fell, and in the ensuing general election the Conservative Party was returned by a large majority. For the first time in years Sweden will be being governed by a right-wing administration. It may well be the one to recognise the considerable advantages of a constitutional monarchy.

8

NORWAY

King Harald V

'Nations touch at their summits.'

WALTER BAGEHOT

On 15 May 1990, I received the following message from Mrs Barbara Iliffe, private secretary to HM King Olaf V of Norway, sent on to me by his embassy in London: 'HM has suggested that you lunch with him at his country house. You will be the only guest, and you can decide whether you wear a hat or not. HM loves pretty ladies and pretty hats . . . You will drive with HM from the Royal Palace to his country house, Kongsgaard, at Bigdsy (which means "settlement on the peninsula"). The drive will take about fifteen minutes, and lunch will be served immediately.'

How more welcoming can a king be? I firmly reminded myself that in his youth Crown Prince Olaf had often sailed and skied and danced the Charleston with my cousins, the Lindley girls, when an aunt of mine had been British ambassadress in Oslo, and that he had probably kept a soft spot in his heart for our family – King Olaf was known far and wide, in royal circles and outwith them, for having a very large heart with a great many soft spots in it. Nevertheless, I immediately went out and bought myself the prettiest hat I could find.

Alas, the meeting I had so looked forward to was not to be. King Olaf suffered a stroke only weeks before my visit, from which he never fully recovered, and he died on 17 January 1991.

Six months later, the Norwegian ambassador in London very kindly arranged an audience for me with his son and successor, King Harald V.

Our British NATO general had lent me his car for the occasion and his RASC driver, a nice young corporal who greatly enjoyed scattering a crowd of startled tourists and sweeping up to the *porte-cochère* of the royal palace, which is built plumb in the middle of Oslo, so that where the main shopping street ends, the palace avenue begins. And there formality ended. No powdered flunkies, no sword-clanking equerries, not

even a concierge in sight. There was no one to open the front door or
tell me where to go. This is Norway! So I walked through two towering
glass doors, up a short stone staircase to a small lobby, where I waited.
Eventually I was joined by a youthful palace attendant in a striped waist-
coat that looked like some sort of livery, who asked me shyly if I would
sign a visitors' book, which I did. Ten minutes later an intercom buzzed
and someone must have given instructions down it, for with a polite and
more confident 'Follow me', the young man led the way up a grandiose
stone staircase to a wide landing above, which had fine reception rooms
leading off it, to left and right.

An ADC in air force uniform came quickly forward and shook hands,
and we proceeded to a small ante-room where, again, we waited. It was
lined with rather grim nineteenth-century paintings of rocks and pine
trees, but the ADC, who spoke impeccable English, showed me another
picture, one in a book which was lying open on one of the tables in the
room. It was a war-time photograph of King Haakon VII and Crown
Prince Olaf in a birch wood, taken during their flight from Oslo to the
north; it was only a snapshot, but it gave a remarkable sense of the
urgency and drama of the time.

Suddenly the inner door opened and a stout and bustling matron
emerged, wreathed in smiles, whom I wrongly assumed to be a protocol
lady and shook warmly by the hand. She answered by more smiles and
a flood of friendly Norwegian, which the ADC tried to stem by making
signs to me behind her back. Having finally succeeded, he led her politely
but firmly out of the room. When he returned, he looked at me as if to
say, 'Ready?', shot his cuffs, felt for his tie and escorted me smartly
through the half-open door and into King Harald's presence.

King Harald V is much better looking than one would think from his
photographs, where he tends to appear wooden and dull. In fact he is
lively and has considerable charm. Tall and trim, with a deep tan, he
looks every inch an outdoors man, super-fit and a lot younger than his
age. He is easy to talk to, but keeps the conversation very much under
his control. He was wearing a dark suit that looked as if it had been
made by one of the last good tailors in Savile Row, and a dark tie, as
the royal family's official mourning had not yet ended. As we sat down,
the thought flashed through my mind: Why are young European monarchs so much better dressed than our own Royal family?

It happened to be the day after the abortive coup in Russia against
Mikhail Gorbachev, and our conversation rather naturally started by
comparing notes on the latest news. Norway has 196 kilometres of frontier with Russia in the very far north, where the North Cape dips down

HM King Harald V of Norway.

into Finland, well inside the Arctic Circle. It is mostly inhabited by reindeer, and once, I suppose, by NATO spies.

We talked about NATO, the dangers of a Soviet military coup, or, possibly even worse, of chaos and anarchy spreading throughout the Russian Empire. I said I had been surprised that there was so little security in these dangerous times around his own palace; it was nice and refreshing, but all the same, Sir, I might have been carrying a couple of hand grenades in my handbag! He answered, with a distinct twinkle, that an American ambassador had asked his father the same thing: 'Can you tell me why, Sir, in Norway the king has no bodyguard?' and that the old king's answer had been a proud one: 'You are mistaken, Mr Ambassador, I have four *million* bodyguards!' King Harald apparently has equal confidence in his subjects' devotion.

He told me that there had been no formal crowning rituals when he succeeded his father, but that he and Queen Sonja were blessed in a simple ceremony in Oslo Cathedral, 'like my father had been – it seemed a good way of beginning'.

We talked about his schooldays in Oslo, when science was the subject that interested him most, of his years in the Norwegian Military Academy, and how he had ended his military service as a fully fledged cavalry

officer. After his army training he came to England, where he finished
his education at Balliol College, Oxford, reading political science, history and economics. His grandfather, King Haakon VII, died in 1957
and Harald, having been made Crown Prince by his father, King Olaf,
had immediately started sharing with him the duties of monarchy,
attending state councils, presiding over committees and even acting as
regent when King Olaf fell ill.

Holiday visits to England were frequent but, from his schooldays
onwards, the young prince, like nearly every other Norwegian boy, was
able to sail and regatta-race in Oslo sound and in the fjords and lakes of
his own country. This soon became a ruling passion, and eventually an
Olympic-class skill. As an experienced yachtsman he has represented
Norway several times at the Games, and five years ago he won a World
Championship in his one-ton yacht *Fram X*, which the Norwegian business community had given him as a present for his fiftieth birthday.

He asked me what I had seen of his country and I told him I had
previously visited Bergen and the country further north, but had been
converted to loving Oslo by staying with the ADC of the NATO general
and seeing it through his younger eyes. 'You seem, Sir, to have tamed
your climate and organised your country into one vast outdoor play-
ground!' Indeed, Norway is a paradise for the young and healthy (and
everyone in Norway seems bursting with health): sailing, swimming,
wind-surfing, aquaplaning all summer; langlaufing, ski-jumping, lugeing,
tobogganing all winter – and everything so easily reached and so easily
affordable. 'What is it that makes Norwegians so *practical*?' I asked him
rather plaintively, thinking of our very different distractions in Scotland.

'We have had to be practical,' he answered. 'There was no alternative,
for we are still a poor nation with a difficult climate, and we have to
make our own fun.'

'But surely,' I protested, 'since North Sea oil and fish farming were
discovered, people in your country are *rich* by comparison with other
small countries. Just look at the standard of living! The houses! The
boats!'

'Well, that is possibly one of our worst problems,' he answered with
a smile, 'the very high living standards and consequently high wages that
Norwegians now expect as of right; it has led to unemployment . . . and
the cost of social welfare is always . . .' We were off on an animated
discussion of the country's economy.

We talked about forestry and Norway's enormous potential for energy
production and conservation; oil, gas, hydro-electricity – how long they
will last and which type is best. These are subjects which obviously

interest him and I soon realised I was talking to an expert and listened with growing interest. When we switched back to family affairs I said I was very sorry not to have met his queen, of whom I had heard so much. His face softened as he told me that nowadays she was almost busier than he was himself, reorganising and modernising the living quarters of the palace, which they intend to use more than his father had done, and planning the cultural side of the Winter Olympic Games which are to be held in Norway in 1994.

Meanwhile the king and queen live outside the city on a dairy farm which supplies Oslo with a lot of its milk. His son, Crown Prince Haakon, is still at school in Oslo, but his daughter, Princess Martha Louise, was then in England. 'She's a keen horsewoman and has begun to ride in various horse trials and competitions. At the moment she is learning with one of the best teachers in the world.'

'Practising for the Olympic team?'

'Well, who knows? But you have to be pretty good for that – and have good horses.' Her father, who is a gold medallist himself, would, I felt sure, provide all the encouragement she needed – but whether he could supply the horses was another matter for, according to a newspaper 'Monarchs and Mammon league table', the Norwegian family is one of the poorest in Europe.

The impression he left me with was of a strong, active man who is very much in touch with his people and the technocracy of a modern state, who is aware of the limitations of his power but also of the competence of his knowledge and influence – a family man who enjoys life, but whose pleasures are simple and unsophisticated. When I asked him a specific question about some future policy, he answered: 'Give me time! I've only been in the business for six months!' And time alone will show if he will be as popular a monarch as were his father and grandfather. For in Norway, that is important – the legitimacy of its present monarchy is not rooted in an existing nobility (one of the big differences between Norway and Sweden is that in Norway there is no aristocracy), nor a kingly line that goes back to Viking gods, but in the hard-headed choice of the people's representatives, in an honestly elected parliament.

When Norway finally split away from Sweden, in 1905, the principle which she had already fought for and won, under the first Bernadotte, was even more clearly defined: the Constitution stood above the king, and it was this principle that was first adopted. The choice of a king came later. The years that followed have shown that the people's choice was a good one, and that Norway's system of government and its monarchy are two separate sides of the same coin that have needed each other equally in times of trouble. One could almost say that the democratisation of the monarchy was succeeded in the Second World War by the monarchisation of the democracy – and this was due not only to the personalities of two remarkable kings, but also to the institution itself, which held firm when everything else was falling apart.

The story of Norway in the Viking age is the story of Scandinavia as a whole. But the Viking kings – who conquered large parts of Britain and most of Scotland, and were defeated at the battle of Largs in 1263 – were *Norwegian* Vikings. They have left many place names, burial cairns and folk memories in the west of Scotland, and a Viking chief lies buried only a few miles from my home on Loch Fyne. Some indeed stayed behind and settled in the Hebrides and the green coastlands of Argyll and the north-west. They became the progenitors of Highland clans among whom were the Macdonalds, 'Lords of the Isles'. (Scottish clan chieftains who claim descent from Viking chiefs bear a galley on their coats-of-arms, while those who descend from the Celtic princes of Ireland bear a salmon.) There has always been, and still is, a great affinity between our two countries.

After the glories of the Viking period had faded into history, Norway became the poorest and the least important of the Scandinavian kingdoms. Until the thirteenth century she had largely depended on the punitive raids of her fierce and daring warriors, who had brought back not only booty but also prisoner/slaves who significantly increased her tiny population, and on whom, to a certain extent, the agriculture of the country had depended. With the coming of Christianity, and the 'White Christ' of the Benedictine abbeys, slavery, though it lingered on for a time, was finally abolished, and with it cheap farm labour. According to the records of its provincial laws, slavery in mediaeval Scandinavia presents a grim picture, even after the introduction of Christianity. Icelandic law required owners to refrain from killing slaves on legally prescribed Holy Days and throughout Lent. A Western Norway Code of Law allowed the children of a dead slave to be exposed in a grave in the churchyard, 'provided that the last survivor is kept alive . . .'

With the rise of the Russian principalities, Norway's valuable fur trade collapsed, and the newly formed Hanseatic League of German and Dutch traders encroached upon and eventually took over the best of the fishing harbours of her western coast; Bergen, which was the main entrepot for the dried cod brought down from Lofoten, being gradually dominated by the League, whose traders, by the middle of the thirteenth century, had taken up permanent residence in the port.

The 'Atra Mors' or 'Terrible Death', which was the first name for the Black Death (or bubonic plague) that swept through Norway in the fourteenth century, nearly halved her already meagre population and was another source of her decline.

Magnus Ericsson was the last of the unchallenged independent kings of Norway. His election to the crown of Sweden, and the marriage of his son, Haakon, to the ten-year-old Danish heiress, Princess Margaret, paved the way to the Union of the Three Crowns, which took place under the regency of the grown-up Queen Margaret, and also to a Dano–Norwegian union that lasted for four hundred years.

The Union was always dominated by Denmark and by the time the Oldenburg dynasty took over, its first king, Christian I, hardly even bothered to consult the Norwegians when he mortgaged the Orkneys and Shetlands to give his daughter Margaret a handsome dowry at the time of her wedding to Malcolm VI, the future King of Scotland. In the ensuing centuries, Norway seems to have done little else than supply soldiers and pay taxes to support the wars of the Danish kings or defend herself against their enemies, while they squabbled incessantly with Swedes, Germans, Russians and Poles for supremacy in the Baltic. Soon she was being treated as a mere province, and the flame of her identity and national pride burnt low.

In the seventeenth century, however, under Danish absolutism, Norway's position slightly improved. The new legal code and reorganised bureaucracy that Frederik III and Christian V introduced put Dane and Norwegian, in theory at least, on the same humble footing, as equal subjects of an all-powerful king, and by 1680 the number of peasant freeholders in Norway began to increase again. With the mining of iron, copper and silver, and the industries that follow it, Norway's economy began to expand and, after the Great Fire of London, there was considerable demand for Norwegian timber, which put that industry on a very healthy footing.

Yet it was not until the beginning of the nineteenth century, after the Danish government had foolishly committed Norway and Denmark to Napoleon's lost cause, after the British and Swedish navies had bombarded Copenhagen and had almost starved Norway to death, that a treaty was signed at Kiel on 14 January 1814, between the Swedes and Danes, in which Frederik VI of Denmark, without consulting the country which had been part of his kingdom for four hundred years, handed over Norway and its entire population of 900,000 souls to his Swedish victor, Karl XIII, and his Prince Regent and heir, the Maréchal Bernadotte.

It was then that the Norwegians once again found their independence, and their soul. They refused to acknowledge the treaty, declaring that while the Danish king might renounce his right to the Norwegian crown, it was contrary to international law to dispose of an entire kingdom without the consent of its people. A meeting of delegates was convened at Eidsvold where, on 17 May 1814, a constitution framed on the constitutions of America, France and Spain was adopted. Among its most important provisos, which still obtain today, were that the Storthing, or National Assembly, should be a single-chamber institution, and that the king should not be given an absolute veto, nor the right to dissolve the Storthing.

At first the Danish governor of Norway, Prince Christian Frederik, was elected king, but when Bernadotte, with a small Swedish army, invaded Norway, he slipped quietly over the frontier and into oblivion. After only a fortnight's almost token hostilities, Bernadotte opened negotiations with the Storthing.

A new convention was held, and it was proposed that Norway should accept the Swedish king as their sovereign provided that their constitution of 17 May remained intact. This was agreed and Norway was then declared to be 'a free, independent and indivisible Kingdom, united with Sweden under one King'. A year later the Treaty of Kiel was formally abandoned and an Act of Union was accepted instead by the national assemblies of both countries. The Union was, in effect, a voluntary offensive and defensive alliance under a common king, each country retaining its own government, parliament, army, navy and customs.

You would have thought that from then on everything would run smoothly. Norway had retained both monarchy and independence, both of which her people wanted, but the decades that followed were scarred by a lengthy and complex struggle between the king in the Union, who was supported by Sweden, and the Norwegian national assembly, the Storthing. On the surface the conflict raged round the minutiae of practical politics, but it was really about the right to define the centre of gravity in the system – in other words, the power – and it ran parallel to an emerging but very real antagonism between the two peoples. Things finally came to a head in 1905 over a silly dispute about consuls and the heavy-handedness first of Bostrom, the Swedish Prime Minister, and then the king, Oskar II. After negotiations had finally fallen through, the Storthing took the matter into its own hands and passed a bill for the establishment of independent Norwegian consuls in May 1905 – which Oskar II refused to sanction. The Norwegian ministers in his government then resigned and the king refused to accept their resignations.

On 7 June the Storthing met in Oslo and Christian Michelsen, the canny and able Norwegian Prime Minister, informed its delegates that *all* the members of his government had resigned in consequence of these events and that, as the king had refused to exercise his constitutional right and ask someone to form a new administration, the union with Sweden, based upon a monarch in common, was consequently dissolved. This was a bit of chicanery on Michelsen's part. The king had actually said he could not *now* form a new government,* and Michelsen deliberately left out that word.

King Oskar protested, the political parties in Sweden were outraged, but after meetings of the Swedish government and the Riksdag it was agreed that Sweden would, after all, enter into negotiations towards the severance of the two countries' union, after Norway had justified its intentions by a national referendum. A general plebiscite was held in Norway in August, when 368,211 Norwegians voted in favour of dissolution and only 184 against it. After further negotiations had taken place between the two governments, King Oskar issued a proclamation to the Norwegian Storthing in which Sweden finally and for ever relinquished the crown of Norway.

To mollify Swedish and world opinion, Michelsen had originally offered the Norwegian crown to a cadet member of the House of Bernadotte, but the wounded feelings of the king prevented its acceptance. The Storthing was then able to authorise Michelsen to negotiate for the candidate they really wanted – Prince Charles of Denmark, the grandson of King Christian IX, who was married to Princess Maud, a member of the British royal family. There followed a good deal of behind-the-scenes royal-families shuffling, King Edward VII rather naturally supporting his son-in-law's election. Prince Charles, however, showed the remarkable prudence that was to serve him so well in later life. He did not accept the offer until the candidature of Oskar's second son had been formally refused (it was reported that the king rejected the offer without consulting his son, remarking angrily that if he was not good enough for the Norwegians, neither was his son) and a plebiscite had been held in Norway, which happily resulted in a 4–1 vote in his favour. He thereupon took office as King Haakon VII of Norway, and Queen Victoria's granddaughter became Queen Maud.

On 25 November they arrived in Norway to assume their duties as the King and Queen of Norway. In an almost symbolic snowstorm they

---

* The king, being the sovereign of both countries, was constitutionally bound to consult with both governments.

boarded a Norwegian ship about thirty miles south of the capital and sailed up the Oslofjord. King Haakon landed in the city with his two-year-old son, Olaf, dressed in white, in his arms. It was a historic and happy moment; the country had at last re-won the freedom and independence it had so long desired.

But it was not all plain sailing for the monarchy in the years ahead. A 'democratic monarchy' is something of a contradiction in terms; there was (and still remains) a fairly strong republican party in Norway, and there was the legacy of the country's long struggle against Denmark and Sweden and their autocratic kings. Haakon and Olaf had no formal power but they could still exert influence, and this they proceeded to do most skilfully. Their pronouncements, which were few and always tactful, carried weight. And on one of the few occasions when the constitution calls for the intervention of the sovereign, such as when parliamentary succession is unclear, as it was in 1928, King Haakon had no hesitation in acting: he appointed, against the advice of the outgoing government, the first Labour Party government, for it had a good programme and sensible leaders – a decision which no doubt also contributed to an alteration in the Party's basically anti-monarchical line.

In the national crisis of 1940, the king and the Crown Prince played an even more central role. Hitler had launched his Blitzkrieg and Europe was in turmoil. On 8 April the Crown Prince, listening to a radio newscast, heard that a ship transporting German troops had been torpedoed off the coast of Norway. What had actually happened was that the German battleship *Blücher*, heavily laden with troops, high command officers, tanks and civil servants, was passing through a narrow strait on its way to a pre-arranged invasion area, further up the coast, when the young Norwegian gunnery officer who was on duty that night suddenly perceived its enormous hulk looming out of the dusk in front of him; it was within easy reach of his battery's guns and he realised at once its identity – so, no doubt muttering a prayer that he would not be cashiered, he swung his sights into the right position and fired his only two torpedoes at her, broadside. The *Blücher* sank within minutes, and he then rang up the Norwegian admiralty to tell them rather nervously what he had done.

Throughout the night there were more radio broadcast warnings of impending invasion. By daybreak Olaf arrived in Oslo with his family and joined the king. The Germans had suborned Quisling, a disloyal member of the Norwegian government, and they now demanded that their puppet should be made Prime Minister and that Norway should negotiate for peace. The King's personal answer was a resounding 'No'

– and his statement to his government, when they met at Nyberssund, was equally simple: 'The decision is yours, but if you choose to accept the German demands I must abdicate, for I cannot appoint Quisling as Prime Minister.'

The next day King Haakon, Crown Prince Olaf and his family, the cabinet and most of the members of the Storthing left Oslo by special train. The royal family parted company at Hamar – Crown Princess Martha and her three children crossing the border to Sweden where they stayed for four months before sailing to America. (They settled in Washington, where they were President Roosevelt's guests for the rest of the war.) Crown Prince Olaf continued north together with the king and the cabinet.

The advancing German army chased them from one place of refuge to another until in June 1940 they were rescued by a British submarine and brought over to England. Olaf wanted to stay on with the Norwegian Resistance, but his wishes were opposed by Haakon and the cabinet and, instead, he played a leading role in the Norwegian government in exile, which set up its headquarters in London. In 1944 Olaf was appointed Commander-in-Chief of the Norwegian forces, a position he held until his country's final liberation in May 1945, and the royal family's triumphal return.

The Norwegian monarchy had been the nation's symbol of unity and continuance during five long years of war, and it was more popular than ever in the peace that followed.

Crown Princess Martha died in 1954 when she was only fifty-three, a tragic loss for her family, and three years later King Haakon died at the splendid old age of ninety. King Olaf then reigned for thirty-three years. He was a simple and genial king, a happy man who had the gift of making others happy. He identified very much with his people; they could meet him langlaufing on a Saturday afternoon on the myriad ski runs in the woods around Oslo, or exercising his dogs in the public park that surrounds his palace. But he could also, with his great height, good looks and imposing figure, be extremely regal when the occasion demanded. He stood out among his many royal relatives at family gatherings in Copenhagen, Windsor or Athens, and was much loved by all of them. He once said in an interview: 'I have tried to maintain a balance between being an elevated symbol and at the same time being a sort of receiving station for human contact. Perhaps it has become a way of life, learning to distinguish between the official and the casual.'

When he lay dying in the royal palace in Oslo, many people from all over Norway kept vigil outside it. Someone stuck a candle in the snow banked up on either side of the steep avenue which leads from the town to the palace gates. Soon there were a thousand candles, then two thousand, flickering on through the night; their symbol of love and hope and perhaps gratitude was only extinguished when the old king's life flickered out and the blinds in the palace were drawn down.

9

LIECHTENSTEIN

Hereditary Prince Hans Adam

'I've learnt the way a monkey learns – by watching its mother.'
THE PRINCE OF WALES

My next three interviews were not with kings but with the princely rulers of three small European countries whose independence has been jealously guarded by their royal families over the centuries. I had entrée to two of their courts – Monaco and Luxemburg – and had already visited the tiny principality and the grand-dukedom, but Liechtenstein was another matter. I had no idea what to expect from a country whose income I was told is chiefly derived from false teeth and postage stamps.

When I wrote to Her Serene Highness, Princess Gina of Liechtenstein, I had not realised that she was dying of cancer. It was a closely guarded secret, known only to the family and a few friends. I thought, when she very courteously answered that her husband, Prince Franz Joseph, would be in Austria on the dates I had proposed and suggested I should talk instead to her son, Hereditary Prince Hans Adam, that she was merely protecting the old prince, who was eighty-three and had been in poor health for some time. I wish I *had* met them, for they were a very remarkable and much-loved couple and one cannot fully understand the story of Liechtenstein without understanding theirs.

Born in 1906, Prince Franz Joseph Maria Aloys Alfred Karl Johannes Heinrich Michael George Ignatius Benediktus Gerhardus Majella of Liechtenstein, Duke of Troppau and of Jagendorf and Count of Rietberg, succeeded his great-uncle, Prince Franz I, in July 1938 as twelfth Hereditary Prince von and zu Liechtenstein, a country so poor that it was said his father had to sell family jewellery to bail out an administration which could no longer pay its civil servants' wages. When he died, fifty-one years later, it had been transformed, largely through his devotion and enterprise, into a country with one of the highest per capita incomes in the world.

He was the first of his line to live permanently in Vaduz, the principality's capital, but he was born in Austria where his family have, to this day, retained property twice the size of Liechtenstein (their Bohemian property was twelve times its size, but disappeared behind the Iron Curtain)*, as well as palaces in Vienna and outside it. His mother was the Archduchess Elizabeth Amalia of Austria, niece of the Emperor, Franz Joseph, and half-sister of Archduke Franz Ferdinand (Sarajevo) and Prince Rudolf (Maierling).

Part of Franz-Joseph's childhood was spent in Vienna but most of it in the family castle on his father's estates in Moravia, now Czechoslovakia, which was then still part of the Austro–Hungarian Empire. Prince Franz Joseph received an excellent education at one of the best Viennese *Gymnasiums*, then graduated in forestry at an agricultural college and was trained to be a forestry engineer. He occasionally visited Liechtenstein with his great-uncle, Prince Franz I, who was the first of the family to spend regular periods there, and he formed an attachment to the unspoilt and beautiful country and its stout-hearted, friendly people.

In 1938 his uncle, Prince Franz II, abdicated. Prince Franz Joseph succeeded him (his father having renounced his claim to the throne) and Adolf Hitler marched into Austria.

One year after the German Anschluss with Austria in 1938 Franz-Joseph was crowned Hereditary Prince von and zu Liechtenstein, and immediately moved into the semi-ruined castle above Vaduz to begin rebuilding it as well as the country he was to rule over for the next half-century. It was a dangerous time for the principality and the situation needed delicate handling, as the German army and Hitler's Reich had become, overnight, its closest neighbour. To preserve their independence and neutrality, the two political parties of Liechtenstein (traditionally one Catholic and one Protestant) formed a coalition government, under the leadership of Prince Franz Joseph II, and for the rest of the war he became the pivot of national unity.

In March 1939 the prince paid an uncomfortable but necessary official visit to Berlin (the Führer, he reported, was 'ill at ease' during their ninety-minute interview, and made 'no impression at all') but he wrote

---

* Since Czechoslovakia regained its independence Prince Hans Adam has been in a quandary: whether to reclaim his estates and pay out a fortune to support them, or to let things be.

later, 'it helped make the Nazis leave us alone, because it flattered Hitler's ego'.

Throughout the war years the prince managed to safeguard Liechtenstein's neutrality, and to put down any attempt by the few local Nazis to join the German Reich. He also managed to form close ties with Switzerland, and perhaps most amazing of all, to seize his moment, in the chaos of 1944, to save his family's great art collections from destruction and bring them out of Austria in a caravan of illegally commandeered lorries and privately driven trains. They included some 1,400 Old Master paintings, tapestries, carpets, armour, porcelain and ivory, a treasure house of beautiful things collected by the family over many generations.

In 1943 he had married Countess Georgina von Wilczek, fourteen years his junior and as beautiful as she was good. In the First World War her mother, Nora, Countess Kinsky, had been conspicuously brave in rescuing White Russians from the Bolsheviks under cover of the Austrian Red Cross, and, in the Second, her daughter, Princess Gina, founded the Liechtenstein Red Cross which became famous not only for helping Allied POWs escape into Switzerland from their camps in Germany and Austria, but, in 1944 and 1945, giving shelter and food to the thousands of refugees who had been caught up in the advancing armies' momentum and brought up short against the closely guarded borders of Liechtenstein.

After the war ended, Prince Franz Joseph bravely refused, despite strong pressure from Russia, to extradite and hand over to the Soviets some five hundred soldiers of the 'First Russian Army of the German Wehrmacht' (including among others Grand Duke Vladimir Kyrilovich). In May 1945, they had evaded the French and Russian armies and had arrived at the Liechtenstein frontier in the middle of the night, where they had sought and been given sanctuary. The tiny principality's determination, despite strong Soviet pressure, not to hand them back demonstrated a moral courage and unshakeable principles – which could put a hundred times more powerful countries – including my own – to shame. 'A proud chapter,' the prince recalled, of his country's history.

Liechtenstein emerged from the war comparatively unscathed and its prince, parliament and people, seizing this advantage, immediately started on an ambitious programme of reforms designed to convert their poor and undeveloped, largely rural land into a highly industrialised and economically sophisticated nation. The war-time link with Switzerland was strengthened, new methods of forestry and agriculture were introduced, huge electric works were built. In addition, the royal family's private banking interests were expanded and diversified, foreign banks were invited to open branches in Vaduz, and relations with Swiss and international institutions developed.

Free trade, plus liberal company laws and favourable taxes, induced many foreign companies to register in Liechtenstein, or to trade as 'mail-box' companies from Vaduz. New factories were built which specialised in small and easily transportable products: sausage skins for Germany, false teeth for all Europe. The result was an upsurge in agriculture, tourism, services and industry. Liechtenstein boomed.

Meanwhile the prince's art treasures, which included da Vinci's famous portrait of Beatrice Cenci, and master works by Raphael, Rubens, Franz Hals, Breughel, Van Dyck and many other Dutch and Flemish painters, absorbed more and more of his interest and time. His knowledge and taste were proverbial, and he enjoyed arranging public exhibitions in Vaduz and abroad. He had written theses on thirteenth- and fourteenth-century art and was recognised as a serious art historian. His other inter-ests were ecological and sporting. He was a member of the Olympic Games Committee, enjoyed four-in-hand carriage driving and downhill ski-ing, which he went on doing well into his seventies. He had more Hapsburg blood in his veins than any other reigning monarch and he was also one of the richest princes in Europe (his art collections alone being worth more than £300 million). He was extremely popular, both with his own people and with that grandest of clubs, the royal families of Europe, to most of whom he was closely related.

A difficult act to follow? I wondered, as my train pulled eastwards into the mountains of the Vorarlberg, and I wondered also if his good-looking son would be forever inhibited by his talented father's image.

The train journey from Zürich to Sargans is one of the prettiest I know. The railway meanders between lake-shore and mountain-foot, offering tempting side glimpses of alpine valleys, till it chugs into a small village dominated by an ancient castle on a neolithic hill surrounded by apple orchards. Here one de-trains and either looks for a taxi – there were none the evening I arrived – or climbs into the local bus for the forty-minute journey through the upper valley of the Rhine to Vaduz. The road follows the river and Switzerland lies on the other side of it, but there are no formal frontiers or frontier guards between Switzerland and Liechtenstein.

The valley is scattered with small factories, competing for space with tidy crops and the neat villas of its well-to-do inhabitants. Its sides are clothed in a rich tapestry of broad-leaved trees, till the alpine meadows take over and lead the eye up to craggy mountain peaks.

The bus stopped between the church and the Museum of the Postage

Stamp – Liechtenstein has made the issue of connoisseur stamps one of its many attractions, and sources of revenue, and it has become the Mecca of stamp collectors from all over the world.

I had no qualms in leaving my luggage by a municipal flowerbed and walking a hundred metres towards the Hotel Engel, whose café terrace I could see at the end of the street. I was shown into a small but comfortable room whose window, rather disappointingly, looked on to a cliff face (the castle's?). A porter was dispatched to fetch my suitcase and I settled in to bone up a bit more on Liechtenstein's history.

It is a long one, for the territory has been inhabited since 5,000 BC, first by Celts, then by Rhaetians who came from the south-east. Passes through the Alps were important to the Romans, who needed to control them to keep out the barbarians and, in 15 BC, Tiberius's legions pushed over the Julian pass and established the Roman province of Rhaetia, which it held on to for nearly eight hundred years until, in AD 750, the Alemanni invaded and drove them out. Christianity probably came via the Romans, as did the Romanisation of the language – Rhaeto-Romance, which eventually was superseded by German. Then came the Ostrogoths and the Franks and, after the break-up of the Roman Empire, Central Rhaetia, the Alpine valley of the Rhine, was absorbed into Charlemagne's Holy Roman Empire. It was then ruled by a succession of feudal lords and barons, under the suzerainty of the Hapsburg emperors of Austria, Charlemagne's successors, but these small territories were too weak to prosper and frequently changed hands. The Thirty Years War, the plague that followed it and the terrible witch hunts of the seventeenth century (somebody had to be blamed) in which three hundred people were tortured and executed out of a population of three thousand, brought the country to its lowest ebb. The people appealed to the emperor, an Imperial Commission was appointed and the last Count of Hohenems was deposed. But the country was so deep in debt that the only solution was to sell the County of Vaduz and the Lordship of Schellenberg – which were immediately snapped up by Prince John Adam of Liechtenstein, Hans Adam the Rich, who had been looking for just such a bargain.

This was a prince of quite a different calibre. The princes of Liechtenstein were originally knights who protected the frontiers of the Holy Roman Empire on the Danube, and were made Lords of Donauwörth and later Lords of Liechtenstein, after their castle in Lower Austria. They were created princes in 1608 but, though a rich and distinguished family, they lacked the lands to be made Princes of the Empire, which entailed a seat and vote in the Assembly of Imperial Princes, a much desired status in the highly stratified hierarchy of the Hapsburg Imperial Court.

The acquisition of first Schellenberg and then Vaduz changed all that. The two territories were united and, in the year 1719, Prince Anthony Florian of Liechtenstein became a Prince of the Imperial Principality of Liechtenstein – and, his ultimate ambition, a Prince of the Empire.

For a country whose destiny had been so largely dependent on the fortunes of its hereditary rulers, it is remarkable that no single member of the Liechtenstein family set foot in their new territory until 1842, 143 years after their acquisition! But the family were committed to quite another world – that of high office and personal service to the Emperor, in Vienna. Prince Joseph Wenceslas was the Field Marshal who defeated the French and Spanish armies at Piacenza in 1796, and he was Ambassador to the Prussian court at Berlin and the French one at Versailles. He was a friend of the Imperial family, and was given the unusual task of driving Princess Isabella, the betrothed of the Emperor Joseph II, from Parma to Vienna in a golden carriage for her wedding. In the nineteenth century, Prince John of Liechtenstein was the general who represented Austria at the peace talks after Austerlitz – and much impressed Napoleon.

And so throughout the eighteenth and most of the nineteenth centuries, the Liechtenstein princes continued to live in Vienna, in the two magnificent palaces built by Prince Charles I's grandson, and had little interest in their tiny principality on the upper Rhine, a poor and backward country known to them only through the reports of their bailiffs.

In 1799, however, the 'poor and backward country' experienced further trials when General Massena's army retreated through the upper Rhine valley, and the French soldiers commandeered its meagre food supplies and looted and burnt its villages.

Then in 1806, as a member of the Rhenish Confederation, Liechtenstein enjoyed a busy period of sovereignty under Napoleon's protection. Prince John I, though a fighting general in the Austrian army, was the first of his line to concern himself with the welfare of the principality. In 1808, he abolished both serfdom and the office of the *Landammann* (high bailiff), and in the following years carried out many reforms.

After Napoleon's defeat, Liechtenstein became a member of the German Confederation, but only in 1866 did she achieve complete independence when Austria, defeated by Prussia, seceded and the Rhenish Confederation was dissolved.

Under the reign of Prince John II (the Good) great progress and economic improvements were made. He was the first prince to grant his subjects a constitution, which established government through an elected Diet (or Assembly). Many reforming laws were passed during his long reign (1858–1929), a savings bank was founded as a state institution, communications were modernised; a postal treaty, giving Liechtenstein the right to produce its own stamps, was signed with Austria. The good prince, great art lover and benefactor, is said to have given over 75 million francs to the principality during his lifetime.

Liechtenstein remained neutral during the First World War. After it her customs treaty with Austria was annulled and in 1923 a similar treaty with Switzerland was ratified, the Swiss franc became Liechtenstein's official currency, and the two countries drew closer.

Prince Francis I (1929–38), Franz-Joseph's uncle, was an Austrian diplomat, scholar and historian, and also the first prince to spend regular periods of time in the country. But the thirties was a sad period for Liechtenstein; like most of central Europe, it suffered greatly from the unemployment and the economic stagnation of the times.

The next morning, a pretty young woman drove up in a taxi to take me to see Francis I's great-nephew and Franz-Joseph's son in the family's ancient stronghold, the Castle of Vaduz. It is perched on the mountain bluff, immediately above the town, and the drive up to it is so steep that it takes fifteen minutes to negotiate all its hairpin bends. It is a proper mediaeval castle, with towers and bastions and a moat and a drawbridge. The moat today has been filled with flowering shrubs and flowerbeds, and little emerald green lawns which form a pretty contrast to the stark grey stonework and massive bulk of its huge, round towers. In the inner courtyard there are many doors, but the narrow windows, framed by wooden shutters painted with the bold red and white heraldic stripes of the family's coat-of-arms, only begin high up on the castle's façade. There is no main entrance: a little wooden staircase with an iron balustrade leads to a simple doorway which opens into a small vestibule, off which a wooden staircase leads invitingly upwards.

The old castle, I soon realised, has been skilfully converted into an elegant modern palace – woodwork and panelling, staircase and floors are of honey-coloured wood, beautifully crafted. On the landing of the first floor a magnificent *millefiori* fourteenth-century tapestry is hung above a fine refectory table with Old Master paintings on either side of it. The drawing-room is a long, low room with windows on both sides, whose diamond-paned windows and armorial glass look out on to parkland. There were several groups of comfortable sofas and chairs upholstered in pale yellow silk, into one of which I lowered myself and nervously awaited developments.

A door at the far end of the room opened and His Serene Highness, Prince Hans Adam of Liechtenstein, came in. He is tall, very good-looking, smartly turned out, smooth – but in no way effete. He looks every inch a businessman or successful merchant banker (which he is not) who has done his stint in the army (which he did, at Sandhurst). He has that indefinable quality, presence. We sat down on one of the yellow sofas and I told him about the book I was writing and he told me about himself and his family.

He had been acting as executive (but not titular) Hereditary Prince since 1983, when his father's health failed. He believes strongly in the system of monarchy, and that the unusually wide powers that the Liechtenstein constitution grants its hereditary princes are entirely beneficial. Prince Hans Adam shares power with the Diet which he can convene or dissolve at will. He can choose his Prime Minister, has the final say over legislation and can issue emergency decrees, powers unparalleled in any other European country. He is his country's representative abroad and the source of all honours at home. His hand on the helm contributes to the country's 'continuity, neutrality and stability'. He believes firmly and without any apologies that unbridled democracy is not necessarily good for a country and that it is better for power to be stratified and the responsibility of governance shared.

'In mediaeval times,' he told me, 'absolute power was shared between the emperor, princely heads of state, the nobles and the people.' It wasn't such a bad system and it survived for many centuries.

I asked him if he thought that monarchy might return to some Central European countries. 'possibly,' he answered. 'Certainly, it has given Spain far greater stability.' There have always been fashions for different systems of government; different countries, different desires and aspirations. After the First World War all countries in Europe freed from Turkish rule wanted to become, and succeeded in becoming, monarchies. And then the fashion changed again.

Princess Marie now joined us. She is an attractive woman, not strictly beautiful perhaps, but elegant with pretty hair, nice eyes, neat legs and a charming smile. She wore a yellow slub silk suit and a wide gold necklace, which became her. She caught her husband's eye and smiled. There is an obvious sympathy between the two. When we talked about their eldest son, Prince Aloys, who was briefly a young officer in the Coldstream Guards, she glowed with maternal pride: he had been chosen (with young Prince Jean of Luxemburg) to ride beside Queen Elizabeth

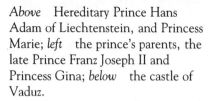
Above Hereditary Prince Hans Adam of Liechtenstein, and Princess Marie; *left* the prince's parents, the late Prince Franz Joseph II and Princess Gina; *below* the castle of Vaduz.

at a Trooping the Colour ceremony in London. He is now at the University of Salzburg.

We talked about bringing up their family and they both insisted that their four children (three boys and a girl) attended the local school in Vaduz – had friends, played games, ate out, skied and danced with their grandfather's subjects 'just like anyone else's children'.

The prince told me that while his father looked after the family's business concerns, he was responsible with his Prime Minister and cabinet for a major reorganisation of the country's economy and for a campaign to join the United Nations Organisation.

'We are now one of the most highly industrialised nations in Europe, with the highest per capita income, but Liechtenstein has such a small indigenous population that our industries have had to import workers from other countries. Sixty per cent of our workforce are now of foreign nationality.'

Apparently this caused few problems. 'Like native Liechtensteiners they are predominantly German-speaking, and their standard of living here is much higher than in their own countries. Average wages in Liechtenstein are only matched by those in Geneva or Zürich. In fact we are the *only* country in Europe who can afford to employ Swiss *Gastarbeiter* – and we do!'

'You have flourishing schools, a good transport system, a welfare state; in such a tiny country, how on earth do you manage to balance the national budget?'

'Because we have always had low taxation in Liechtenstein, and the lowest company tax in Europe, we have attracted some eighty thousand "brass-plate" companies to register here – and that provides a considerable part of the country's income. So, of course, do our postage stamp issues. We are a neutral country and don't have to pay for a standing army, and because we are such a small country we have a very small bureaucracy. Do you know that the whole population of Liechtenstein is smaller than the entire number of Swiss bureaucrats? Many officials here work part-time for the state and some even work for nothing. Of the five ministers in my government, three only work part-time.'

'I understand you have only two political parties. Are there no "Greens" in Liechtenstein?'

'Only a few. Greens in most countries are strongly radical and there are no socialists here, no left wing. The parties traditionally have been either pro-Austria (or Catholic), or pro-Switzerland, and both have always been middle-of-the-road politically. People in the past were "born" into their family's party, but of course this division became weaker after 1918. During the crisis of 1938 my father insisted on a coalition and to some extent we still have one.'

'Does that mean you have government by consensus?'

'Far from it! Normally there is a general election every four years, but latterly I had to dissolve parliament earlier than usual as the heads of the two parties were quarrelling. I thought then a "Green" faction might emerge, but it didn't.'

I asked about the family's famous art collections and he told me that, quite apart from the pictures in Vaduz, the bulk of which are in the castle vaults, with rotating exhibitions at the Municipal Art Gallery, there are considerable collections in the family's two palaces in Vienna, though some pictures from those were on permanent loan to a museum.

His father had done little in the way of conservation and this was now being remedied. 'I am not an art expert myself,' he added. 'I haven't the time for it. But we have stopped selling and are even adding occasionally to the collection.'

We talked about Women's Lib (women's suffrage was introduced in the 1920s and there is now one woman in Liechtenstein's parliament, 'and our Chef de Protocol is a lady,' added Princess Marie); about abortion, which is forbidden by the state unless a mother's or a child's life is at risk, for Liechtenstein is a Catholic country and the royal family, though ecumenical in outlook, are practising Catholics; and lastly, about the power of the press, with which the princely family seems to deal with firmness and equanimity.

There is no doubt that the new Hereditary Prince is articulate and intelligent, with firmly held opinions and considerable charm. He struck me as an efficient, unpretentious modern businessman, rather than the princely descendant of a long line of Austrian art-lovers and military heroes; probably, with all that is to happen to Europe in 1994, this is the metamorphosis that Liechtenstein needs. His skills have already been put to the test because Liechtenstein's economy (and Luxemburg's) have suffered badly in the world recession.

I explored Vaduz that afternoon, screened the shops and visited the art gallery and small museum. In the evening I dined out at a rather good Italian restaurant, one of the happier tourist traps that lurk round every corner of the little town. Admirable though its people's initiative and ingenuity are in making a silk purse out of a sow's ear, or millions of Swiss francs out of a brass plate and a postage stamp, the impression of Vaduz that I took to bed with me was one of oversell, of too many bank managers, too many souvenir shops, too many Wiener schnitzels and chips. The next day was Sunday and, after Mass in the fine modern cathedral of the town, I boarded a tourist bus and explored a little more of the country's sixty-two square miles.

It was a sparkling day; the mountains and the mountain villages were unbelievably picturesque; everyone looked prosperous and clean and happy; before long my faith in human nature and the principality was reborn. I remembered Prince Franz Joseph's words: 'I am ruling over a happy country; it is a happy country because it is small.' And, more soberly, those of a philosophical Swiss politician who lived at the beginning of this century. 'A small country nowadays has to be a moral force if it desires the right of continuity.'

Four months later I read that Princess Gina had died, in a small nursing home on the other side of the Rhine Valley in Switzerland. From her room she had seen the same range of mountains she had looked out on for so many years from the castle above Vaduz. She and the prince had moved there to be alone and to wait for the end together. It came on 24 October. When the old prince visited her that morning she could no longer speak to him, but gave him her hand, which he kissed. On returning to his own rooms he suffered a stroke, from which he never recovered consciousness. She died, without his knowing it, the evening of that same day. It was, in a way, a happy ending to their love story.

10

LUXEMBURG

Prince Jean, Grand Duke

'The first of earthly blessings, independence.'

EDWARD GIBBON

I am not very good at sticking photographs into albums – mine tend to be stacked away in bursting cardboard boxes waiting till I break a leg or am bed-bound by my 'terminal'. I regret this because, quite apart from the happy narcissism they engender, they rekindle one's faltering memory and fix dates.

I had already written to HRH Prince Jean, Grand Duke of Luxemburg when, in an old folder marked 'Keep', I came across a faded box-Brownie snap of some people grouped rather stiffly around a sundial and simpering self-consciously. A deerhound and part of a honeysuckled porch identified it as Eilean Aigas, my mother's dower-house in Scotland. It is wartime, for the three men are all in uniform. My brother, Hugh Fraser, is wearing the chequered bonnet of the Lovat Scouts; the dog-collared captain, with the maple-leaf insignia of the Canadian Forestry Corps, is their chaplain, Father Austen McGuire, a Redemptorist priest of great saintliness and charm; and the third is a tall young man with a small, neat head, Irish Guard buttons to his tunic and a shy but engaging smile. Of the three women in the picture, one is tall and wistful, my mother, Laura Lovat, and the other tall and sedate, the Grand Duchess Charlotte of Luxemburg. The last figure, squeezed in between the boys and shamelessly grinning, is me.

Memory came flooding back. During the late summer of 1943 the exiled grand duchess had rented Eskadale House, a few miles up the river from my family's wartime home, so that her eldest son, Prince Jean, could join her and some of their family on his last leave before training began in earnest for the D-Day landings. She badly needed a rest for, ever since Hitler's invasion of Luxemburg and her dramatic escape to France, she had worked tirelessly for her country's and her subjects' welfare, travelling all over Canada, the USA and Britain to visit them and, at the same time, keeping in touch with her government-in-exile in London. She loved Scotland and Eskadale was a perfect refuge. There was fishing on the Beauly at the bottom of the garden, a little rough – very rough – shooting and lovely walks up the glens, over the hills and far away from the worries of war-time. She became a frequent visitor to my mother's house and enjoyed talking to our resident invalid, the same Maurice Baring who had encouraged us when very young to misbehave during King George V's visit.

It was one of those chance war-time meetings when people come together, establish sympathy and break up to go their different ways, usually never to meet again, rather like the characters in a Maurice Baring novel, but here I was, nearly fifty years later, shaking hands with Colonel Germain Franz, KCVO, the Grand Duke's Chamberlain, and following an ADC up the very grand marble staircase of the Palais Grand Ducal in Luxemburg to a *piano nobile* of magnificent proportions, where nineteenth-century *fauteuils* covered in pale silk brocade stood stiffly around in formal groups and life-size portraits of Prince Jean's Orange-Nassau and Nassau ancestors looked sternly down at me as I nervously pulled on my gloves and prepared to live up to my surroundings. Leaving the grander reception rooms behind us we proceeded down a wide corridor to a door on which the officer knocked twice. '*Entrez*,' was called from within and there was Prince Jean, Grand Duke of Luxemburg, the boy by the sundial in Scotland. He had altered so little in forty-eight years that I shook my head in disbelief, forgot about formality and almost forgot to curtsy.

He is taller than I remembered and ruddier, but otherwise just the same. He was dressed smartly in a dark suit with a blue and red striped tie, not a brigade one, though the impression he immediately gives is soldierly, indeed, Brigade-of-Guards-type—soldierly; easy and sure of himself and 'comfortable in his own skin', as the Italians say. He has a very warm personality. He called me by my first name, asked after my brother's health and told me he had read all my husband's books – gambits guaranteed to give pleasure, but there is a sincerity and kindness behind them that goes a long way beyond good manners. He manages to establish immediately an intimate and informal atmosphere and remains at the same time fully in charge. 'The confidential manner,' my husband calls it, sometimes adding, 'don't be fooled by it'; but it is a great and rare gift for sovereigns to possess, especially when they mean what they say.

We sat down on either side of the fireplace and chatted amicably about Yorkshire and Ampleforth, the Benedictine school where he and my brothers were educated, where the monks were friends as well as teachers

HSH Prince Jean, Grand Duke of Luxemburg.

and where the boys lived an amazingly free and old-fashioned country life that was perhaps unique in British public schools. His schooldays were very happy and he made many friends. The most exciting moments in the war, he told me, were escaping from Luxemburg to Unoccupied France just in front of the German armies in 1940; fighting in Normandy and Belgium; and then marching back at the head of the Allied contingent who liberated his country, marching back through wildly cheering crowds to his own city, his own palace, his own home.

That had been the greatest, the most unforgettable moment in his life. Another proud moment came years later when he was made Colonel of the Irish Guards; indeed he often comes over to England to their parades and functions, to see some of his old sergeants as well as the officers, and several times he has asked them back, with their wives, for a holiday in his own country.

Luxemburg is a Catholic country and the Grand Duke and his family are a very Catholic family. He told me proudly he was the godson of Pope Benedict XV and without his saying much more about it one gained the impression that his religion is very central to the life of this simple, genial sovereign.

There was a pause while coffee and delicate little sandwiches were brought in, then he went on to tell me about his ancestors and his children. He pointed to a full-length portrait of his great-grandfather, Prince Adolphe of Nassau, which hangs on the wall behind his desk. 'He was a great old boy who, when about to succeed to the Grand-Dukedom, was asked to shake hands with his neighbour, the Kaiser. He was outraged, and at first refused; then he relented on the understanding that it was not the *Duke of Nassau* who was touching the hand that had stolen his heritage (Bismarck had demoted him after absorbing Nassau into the new Germany) but the un-insulted prospective Grand Duke of a new and better Duchy, *Luxemburg.*'

I had already met Prince Jean's two oldest sons. Prince Henri, or to give him his full title, Hereditary Grand Duke Henri, is a good-looking young man who has already made a name for himself in the international business world. He is also Sandhurst trained (Irish Guards, of course) but he is not as soldierly a figure as his father. Relaxed and easy to talk to, friendly and unassuming but obviously extremely intelligent – he has a Master's degree in Political Science from the University of Geneva – he struck me as being the very ideal of that new breed, which rather frightens me, the young European.

There are two more princes and two princesses, one married to an Austrian archduke, the other to the brother of Prince Hans Adam of Liechtenstein. Prince Jean and Princess Josephine-Charlotte have already quite a brood of grandchildren.

When we first got in touch they had asked me to lunch with them at their home, the Castle of Colmar-Berg which looks, at least from the outside, as if it had been designed by Bismarck and built by Walt Disney, but the sudden death and funeral of Prince Franz Josef II (of Liechten-stein) had prevented this and so I never met the Grand Duchess, who is a sister of King Baudouin of the Belgians. I asked Prince Jean why he thought that monarch had turned down my request to visit him.

'They never give interviews, it's their policy,' he answered.

'But neither do you,' I pointed out.

We both hastily agreed that this was NOT an interview but just a friendly visit, and I tucked into another delicious sandwich to prove it.

We talked about Luxemburg and the extraordinary position his small country has achieved in Europe today. It is the seat of the European Coal and Steel Authority, of the Secretariat of the European Parliament, of the European Court of Justice, the European Investment Fund and the European Monetary Fund. There are so many grand initials on the grand brass plates of the offices all around the Grand Ducal Palace that I wonder if it does not sometimes feel swamped, and the royal family feel squeezed by so much Olympian bureaucracy, which is perhaps why they use the Palais Grand Ducale only for official entertaining and as their secretariat.

'How has it happened,' I asked Prince Jean, 'apart from the iron ore that Luxemburg so conveniently sits on?'

'It is partly our geophysical position,' he suggested, 'and also the hardiness and hard-headedness of our people, who have had long practice in the art of survival, and then they positively *like* hard work!'

Luxemburg lies at a crossroads where ancient trade routes intersected and nomadic peoples settled. First Celtic, then Gallo–Roman, Germanic, Frankish and Holy Roman Empires succeeded each other in this part of Central Europe, but it was only in the tenth century that a well-connected count of the Ardennes (he was related to the Emperor of Germany and the King of France) built a great château-fort on a rocky promontory above the river that was to grow into the town of Luxemburg and the country and dynasty of that name. Though their possessions were small, the family was of consequence and by the end of the Middle Ages the Luxemburg dynasty had given four emperors (including Charles V) to Austria, four kings to Bohemia (including John the Blind) and one king to Hungary. The Emperor Charles V had, by double inheritance, united the Hapsburg dynasties of Austria and Spain and he set up in Brussels a central government for all the provinces of the Low Countries, of which Luxemburg was one. But Luxemburg, with its great fort and central communication system, was a rich prize and it was fought over continuously for the next four centuries by Burgundians, Spaniards, French, Austrians and Prussians. The fortress itself was besieged and devastated more than twenty times. The French were in possession of Luxemburg at the end of the eighteenth century and Napoleon's rule over the Duchy was benevolent. He introduced *Le Code Napoléon* to the country and attempted to impose conscription to reinforce his armies, which was stoutly resisted.

The Congress of Vienna raised the status of the Duchy of Luxemburg to *Grand* Duchy, and then proceeded to give it, as a present, to the new King of the Netherlands, William I, Prince of Orange-Nassau, 'to be owned in a personal capacity by him and his legitimate successors for ever'. The victorious Great Powers certainly had some strange ideas and, like nearly all peace conferences, their deliberations only sowed the seeds of future conflicts and future wars.

King William I was a disappointment to the people of Luxemburg. He did not grant them a constitution, nor indeed did he visit them more often than he needed to. William II and William III, however, served the country better and during their reigns there were significant changes and progress.

William II, in his youth, had courted Princess Charlotte, the Regent's daughter ('A Frog he would a-wooing go. – Hey ho, says Rolley'). He was called 'Young Frog' in London and he was turned down, but his fortunes recovered, unlike those of the poor princess, and he married Tsar Alexander I's sister, the Grand Duchess Paulowna. He made French the official language of Luxemburg, as well as German, which was popular, and has left as legacy every Luxembourgeois' ability to speak two, if not three languages. He gave the country independence and a Constitution of Estates and he made it a member of the *Zollverein*, the German Customs Union.

The fortress that had caused so much trouble in the past was sensibly dismantled, the Prussian garrison sent home, and Luxemburg at last achieved full independence and perpetual neutrality.

Under William III the constitution was revised, giving the people greater liberties, but the monarchy a still firmer grip. The 'William' Railway was built and foundations were laid for a strong economy, based on the country's nascent iron industry, to which it still owes its great wealth, although recently production has been halved by the recession.

William III of the Netherlands died in 1890 without leaving a male heir, and the dynasty of Orange-Nassau that was the younger branch of the Nassau family died with him.

In accordance with an eighteenth-century family pact, the Grand Duchy then passed to the male head of the *elder* branch of the family, Adolphe of Nassau, who had been divested of his Duchy by Bismarck in 1866 as punishment for being too friendly with Austria. Adolphe was succeeded by his son William, who had six daughters though no son, but by a further family agreement the Salic law was broken and the eldest of the daughters, Marie Adelaide, succeeded her father and became Grand Duchess just as the First World War was starting. The Germans invaded Luxemburg, as they did Belgium and Holland. Being a neutral country there was no army in Luxemburg to resist them. The twenty-eight-year-old Marie Adelaide bravely drove to the frontier to order the German army out of her country – an order which, having other plans, they politely rejected and Luxemburg was occupied for the duration. At the end of the war there were political intrigues and power struggles and Marie Adelaide was accused of being pro-German. The French would not parley with her government and in 1919 she abdicated after a referendum which declared the country 80 per cent in favour of her sister, Charlotte.

Grand Duchess Charlotte married Prince Felix of Bourbon Parma in

1919 and their five children were only teenagers when the Second World War against Germany broke out. As Hitler's armies invaded Luxemburg on 10 May 1940, the family escaped first to France, and next to Portugal. Grand Duchess Charlotte then fled to London, where she was welcomed by King George and Queen Elizabeth and established the Luxemburg government-in-exile while the older children, accompanied by their father, sailed for America in the warship that President Roosevelt had sent to Lisbon to rescue them. Prince Jean eventually reached Canada, where he was to finish his education by reading Law and Political Science at the University of Quebec. He volunteered for the Irish Guards in 1942 and after his training at the RMC, Sandhurst, he was commissioned lieutenant in 1943 and promoted to captain in 1944.

Prince Jean landed in Normandy with his regiment, part of the Guards Armoured Brigade, five days after D-Day and he took part in the Battle of Caen and the Liberation of Brussels; then, on 10 September 1944, he joined his father, Prince Felix, who had been attached to an American unit and together they marched into Luxemburg at the head of the first Allied troops to liberate their country. Four days later he rejoined his regiment and they moved up towards Arnhem and took part in the terrible battle to capture the town and the fighting that followed it.

After the war he began learning the statecraft that he would one day need, serving as a member of the *Conseil d'Etat* for ten years before his mother, the Grand Duchess, appointed him *Lieutenant Représentatif* in 1961. When, three years later, she abdicated in his favour he became Hereditary Grand Duke of Luxemburg.

There is no coronation ceremony in Luxemburg. The new Grand Duke takes a solemn vow and is sworn in by the elected deputies in parliament and is then presented to the people from a balcony. A few speeches are made, and that is that.

In Luxemburg sovereign power lies in the nation. The Grand Duke exercises it in conformity with the constitution and the laws of the country. Though a constitutional monarchy, the powers provided by the Luxemburg constitution are very flexible and there is a great deal of interaction between the legislature (the Chamber of Deputies) and the executive – the grand duke. The judiciary alone is completely independent.

This means that Prince Jean, who alone among European monarchs exercises his executive power (within the law), has a great many serious responsibilities and a lot of work, though he is assisted in it by government departments. He did not dwell on this but talked to me lightly about being Chief Scout and a member of the International Olympic

Committee. His duties, in fact, are much more important than these peripheral ones. He is responsible that the laws of his country are carried out and that order is maintained; in other words, he makes the regulations and decrees required for this to happen; he is head of the army; he administers all public property; no Bill can be exacted without the common consent of the Grand Duke and the Chamber and he can, under certain conditions, adjourn the Chamber, or dissolve it and call an election. He concludes treaties and appoints diplomats and other officials. He can preside over the Council of State (the cabinet) when he judges it right to do so and has as his royal prerogative the right of mercy, the right to issue coinage and the right to confer titles and medals. It is all a considerable workload, but it seems to lie easily on the shoulders of Prince Jean, who, like his subjects, positively enjoys hard work.

As we said goodbye, an ADC was already waiting to escort him to a meeting of the Old Comrades Association, of which he is President.

Prince Jean is one of the few monarchs in Europe who rules as well as reigns, but the character and personality of such a kindly and obviously good man must disarm even the keenest republican minds in Luxemburg, and make them think it would be difficult to do better under any other arrangement.

11

MONACO

Hereditary Prince Rainier III

'Royal families suffer the same personal trials, dramas, tragedies as other families. What makes them different is their visibility: a visibility which is not complete, because it is never more than a partial lifting of the veil.'

WALTER BAGEHOT

The royal dynasties of Liechtenstein and Luxemburg are rooted in the Holy Roman Empire. Their survival and growth into nationhood were due to the grim determination of their peoples to remain independent in spite of the Great Powers that surrounded them, and to the financial perspicacity of their rulers.

Monaco is altogether different – more bouillabaisse, so to speak, than sole meunière. Tough, no doubt, as their ancestor, the original Grimaldi brigand from Genoa must have been, but this princely family, their tiny country and its mini-population are extrovertly and irrepressibly Mediterranean, with all the fun-loving charm and scant attention to marital parameters that this sometimes implies. Few royal families have had so much scandal and drama in their past, beginning with the highly questionable activities of Prince Louis I (a godson of Louis XIV) and Madame de Monaco (a sister of the Comte de Guise), Monsieur's' lover at the court of Versailles, and continuing the scandal, the sensational glamour and also the tragedy right into the present day. *

At the time of the French Revolution Monaco was annexed to France – Prince Honoré III was deposed in absentia and arrested in his palatial Hôtel de Matignon in Paris. His daughter-in-law, dressed and made up as if for a ball, was paraded in a tumbril and taken off to the guillotine – but her husband and her son, Honoré V, survived the Terror and later, as a soldier of the Grande Armée, became an

* Since my visit, Princess Caroline's husband has been killed in a horrific speed-boat accident.

*equerry to Napoleon, and then to Josephine. When Honoré set out
to reclaim Monaco in 1814 it is said that he met with the emperor, who
had just landed from Elba. 'Where are you going?' asked Buonaparte.
'Home, sire, to take possession of my estates.' 'I, too,' answered
Napoleon, 'of mine.'*

Honoré found his estates and the great fortress on the rock in a
lamentable condition – and there was little money to improve things.
It was only when his successor, Prince Florestan, had the happy idea
of introducing gambling into Monaco (it was banned in France) that
things began to look up.

But it was Florestan's son, Charles III, who proved the entrepreneur of real genius. After a plebiscite in which he consulted his subjects
he sold the provinces of Roquebrune and Mentone to Napoleon III
for four million gold francs. He then allowed the Genoa–Nice railway
to run through his country and, in return, France built him a magnificent coastal road which was a tremendous feat of engineering in those
days, and is still known as 'the Corniche'. He then had the capital
and the communications necessary to go ahead with his plans, and,
with the help of a clever businessman, Monsieur Blanc, a large-scale
real estate venture was launched. Two casinos were built, hotels
sprang up, visitors flocked and the resort flourished. The State, Prince
Charles and Monsieur Blanc grew rich and happy and the gamble
which was the smartest gamble in the town paid off. All three parties
remained majority shareholders in the venture, primly named Société
des Bains de Mer et du Cercle des Etrangers (SBM) which was given
the task of running it – which, with the help of Monsieur Blanc, it did
supremely well. For a time gossip about the Grimaldis died down, but
then Prince Rainier, Charles III's great-great-great grandson fell in love
with an American film star, Grace Kelly, and it all began again. Indeed
the whole family can be said to have been 'on camera' ever since.

Yet without the Famille Princière Monaco would be a dull place,
less important than Cannes, not so pretty as St Tropez. An eighteenth-
century traveller described it as 'a barren rock and some lemons'. Its
prosperity and its unique cachet are almost entirely due to the fertile
mind of Charles III and his successors and to the love of excellence
of the present prince.

Monaco's, I found, was the third royal family in Europe whose
destiny was very much part of their country's prosperity. I think of
them as the 'Entrepreneurial and Business Princes', and feel sure they
will survive, as all really good businesses usually do.

I first met Prince Rainier of Monaco and his sister, Princess Antoinette, in that long summer before the outbreak of war when we were,
all three, in our dizzy teens and as unsure of our adolescent selves as
we were of our grown-up future. The occasion was one of those huge
pre-war house-parties that Lord and Lady Londonderry collected annually
at Mount Stewart, their Northern Ireland home on the shores of Lough
Neagh.

Charlie Londonderry was Secretary of State for Air at the time;
'Cousin' Edie, his wife, was a famous political hostess who enjoyed
patronage and parties; and in August 1938 their great Georgian house
was crammed to the rafters with what seemed to me alarmingly clever
and distinguished guests, none of whom I knew.

We, his daughter's young friends, had been flown over to Ulster in
our host's private aeroplane – an adventure for most of us, in itself. My
special 'young man' (we did not call them boyfriends in those days) had
felt airsick over Belfast and I remember – how could I forget? – giving
him my best, prettiest – and only – hat to throw up in as we came in to
land.

The first day was spent discovering the delights of that enormous house
and wonderfully exotic garden (flamingos and macaws flew around its
sub-tropical and Himalayan plantations and there was a lake, and a
tamarisk-fringed swimming-pool where the garden met the sea). I think
we sat down at least twenty to dinner that night, the men in white tie
and tails, the girls in their best evening dresses and borrowed family
jewels – but there were still more visitors to come.

Prince Pierre of Monaco, who started life as Comte Pierre de Polignac
and changed his name to Grimaldi when he married the only daughter
of Prince Louis II, arrived the next morning with his two children. The
young Grimaldis seemed relaxed and self-possessed; 'cool' one might call
it today, but I think we were all pretending to be a lot more grown-up
and sophisticated than we actually felt.

Prince Rainier, still at school in Switzerland, quiet and a little shy,
had considerable charm and was certainly grown-up enough to enjoy
teasing and being teased by the girls of our party, while Princess Antoinette, just seventeen, was pretty, extrovert and *sportive* enough to take on
all comers. She adored Scotland, for she had often visited her Hamilton
relations at Brodick on the Isle of Arran; she liked dogs, games and a
good time and she was obviously going to cut a dash through life, and
blow the consequences. I suppose, because I was bilingual and Scottish,
we gravitated towards each other.

Before their arrival there had been a good deal of grown-up chat about their absent mother, Princess Charlotte, the love-child of Louis II who had been created Duchess of Valentinois by him in 1919 and was now Hereditary Princess of Monaco and heir to the throne. She had married Prince Pierre, produced our two young friends and then divorced him and was thought to be going to hand over the succession to her son, Rainier, on his twenty-first birthday. The general opinion of the lunch-table was that the Polignacs were a grander and more talented family than the Grimaldis – had Proust not been a friend of theirs and brought them into his novels? Or was it the Grimaldis? No one seemed quite sure.* The Polignacs had certainly been friends and patrons of Diaghilev when he brought the Russian Ballet to Paris in 1900 (and outraged half the *beau monde* of the dying *Belle Epoque*) – but then the Prince de Polignac was a composer, quite a good one too, and the family had more or less *adopted* the Russian ballet and made it their own . . . The subject was tossed around for a while, then dropped for a lively discussion about India as an ex-Viceroy was also one of the guests.

Prince Pierre, whom, because of Proust and Diaghilev, I had expected to be tall, languid and literary, turned out to be small and spry, very Gallic and very amusing. He wore a blazer and a silk cravat, his white flannel trousers were beautifully creased. When I sat next to him at lunch he talked about the Ballet de Monte Carlo and French politics, neither of which subjects I knew anything about, but in such a way that he made me feel I did.

Most of the talk that long weekend was above my woefully ignorant head. There were jokes about King Billy and Orangemen, who, I thought, might have something to do with Nell Gwyn, about Winston Churchill and his warnings from the wilderness – and where would that be, for goodness' sake? But at least I had heard of Munich and Monsieur Laval's politics, both of which, in my family's opinion and the prince's, were disasters, while the Maginot Line defences, I happily agreed, were definitely *une blague*. It was my French governess's brother's view, who lived in Dijon and was given to prognostication, not mine, but it got me by and formed a bond between us.

I was not to meet the Grimaldi family again until some fifty years later.

---

* Proust, in fact, was befriended by Albert I and his second wife, Princess Alice, an American heiress who features at the beginning of his famous novel as the raffish 'Duchesse de Luxembourg' – but his friendship with the family and the Polignacs turned to spite when Prince Pierre decided *not* to subscribe to a de luxe edition of the first novel. In the latter part of *A la recherche du temps perdu*, Prince Pierre becomes the pompous 'Comte de Nassau' who insists on every man rising when his wife enters the room. 'Her grandmother,' then comments a wit, 'made every man lie down. What a change.'

This time I flew into Monte Carlo by helicopter from Nice at Prince Rainier's invitation, also something of an adventure. It is an instructive form of travel, for the physical elements of the tiny principality are laid out below one like a map: the ancient fortress/palace and little post-Napoleonic town of Monaco 'on the Rock', its dark-green pine woods descending to the edge of Cape Monaco, a rocky nose pushed out into the sea, with Menton in France on one side of it and, on the other, Monte Carlo's Grand Harbour, a small bay that used to be surrounded by groves of lemon trees, then Monaco's only harvest and source of income. Now it is thronged with the yachts and motor-cruisers of multi-national millionaires and surrounded by buildings and boulevards. The other buildings are a mongrel mixture: jazzy hotels and immodest villas, tall sky-scrapers and concrete boxes, *Belle Epoque*, art nouveau and deco, tier upon tier of them, climbing up the mountainside behind the harbour right up into the bare rocks and precipices of the Alpes Maritimes. These constitute the new town, built by Rainier's great-great-great-grandfather, Prince Charles III, and called after him – Monte Carlo.

'Where does Monaco end and France begin?' I asked the pilot.

'Where the houses stop, Madame,' he answered, and indeed there is not a ninety-carat *inch* of Monegasque soil that has not had something built on it or been 'developed' in one way or another, either by Prince Charles III's *Société de Bains de Mer et du Cercle des Etrangers* (SBM), a euphemism for the real estate venture between sovereign and mammon which built two casinos, a sporting club, restaurants and hotels and started a company in which they have been shareholders ever since – though some say it is now owned by newer and somewhat less sedate international financiers, or by later developers. No citizen of Monaco is allowed to gamble, however, or even visit its own casinos (a law passed by Charles III to protect his Monegasque subjects *and* to prevent money leaving the principality), but then no citizen of Monaco pays direct taxes, a happy state of affairs that was decreed by law in 1869 and only achieved by the financial astuteness of its princes and, of course, the unrestrained, much-encouraged gambling of its foolish visitors.

The epicentre of Monte Carlo is the Grande Place (which, in spite of its name, is half the size of a London square) with its once glittering Casino now sadly debased by ugly Las Vegas style fruit machines and flashy neon strip lighting, the sugar-cake Hôtel de Paris, and the still stylish Sporting Club and Café de Paris. Another pearl of *Belle Epoque* architecture is the Hôtel de L'Hermitage, which is slightly higher up, on a quieter mini-square that overlooks the Bassin and the Rock. Both hotels, though pale ghosts of what they must have been under the direction of Monsieur Blanc and Charles Ritz, nevertheless retain an aura of Edwardian splendour and luxury. Cocteau wrote: '*On a bien tort de mépriser le style architectural de Monte Carlo; c'est le fin de courbe du style baroque . . . et un témoignage d'une époque heureuse.*' I found myself in total agreement as I settled in to the little-altered luxury and happiness of the Hermitage, though I could not help wondering when, later on, I dined on its starlit terrace and listened to a dreadful 'ensemble' of singing American students, whether we, the clients, were not also a *fin de courbe* and had not deteriorated sharply in the intervening years.

The next morning, having swum in the 'ozonised' (whatever that means) sea water of the Piscine des Terraces pool, together with one handsome young masseur and two fat Arab children, I was driven up to 'the Rock' by a young lady taxi-driver who stopped with a flourish and a splatter of gravel in front of our destination, Le Palais Princier.

It was much older, larger and more imposing than I had imagined. Set four-square on top of the Rock with a huge empty parade ground between it and the edge of the old town, it is a real *château-fort* that has been transformed through the centuries into an Italianate palace. The four great mediaeval towers and bastions are all that is left of the Genoese Republic's Gothic fort, but they still dominate its massive profile. The beautifully arcaded and frescoed inner courtyard, or '*Cour d'Honneur*', is late Renaissance Italian. It was built by the Grimaldis, whose exiled ancestor, François Grimaldi, first captured the fort from the republic by artful subterfuge in 1297.* They have managed, after many struggles and sieges, on their own and under the protection first of Spain and then of France, to cling on to it ever since.

A palace guard in smart uniform and white pith helmet inspected my credentials, saluted, and led me to Virginia Gallico's office behind the main gateway, where she soon joined me. Virginia first came to Monaco with her husband, Paul Gallico, the author, and from being just a friend of the Rainiers has grown in widowhood into one of those wonderful and indispensable British women whose lives revolve round a cause – her cause now being the *Famille Princière* of Monaco. She walked with me across the *Cour d'Honneur*, which was being prepared for one of the open-air concerts that are often given there. Concentric rows of little gilt chairs were beginning to cover the beautiful tessellated and cobbled pavement of the court and one could see that its Grand Staircase,

---

* According to legend, Lanfranco 'the Spiteful' captured the fortress by disguising himself as a poor monk seeking shelter. Once inside, he drew his sword, murdered his host and opened the great doors to let in his own soldiers.

HSH Hereditary Prince Rainier III
of Monaco; and the late Princess
Grace of Monaco.

aesthetically perhaps an unfortunate seventeenth-century addition, has now become the perfect theatrical prop for large orchestras and choirs. Leaving the public part of the palace behind us, we passed under a tunnel, gently sloped and cobbled for the passage of royal cavalry and princes' carriages, then, slipping through a small wicket gate at the end of it, we entered another world.

The private garden of Prince Rainier is more than theatrical: the towering wall of the oldest Gothic tower, the grey stone ramparts of the mediaeval fort, enclose an intimate and perfect stage set that is pure Noël Coward. Emerald lawns, an azure pool, tall, tapering king-palms and feathery acacias dapple it with light and shade; cypresses stand sentinel over riots of roses and geraniums, great clumps of agapanthus and hortensias slope gently down to a wild garden, then a darkness of dense pine woods ends in high cliffs above a cobalt sea. Off right is a rustic cocktail bar, around which hovers a palace servant in immaculate white mess kit. A circle of comfortable garden chairs clusters beneath a magnolia tree down stage while, off left and on a lower terrace, is an inviting luncheon table: sparkling glasses, bright silver and flowers on a cornflower-blue tablecloth. Centre stage and coming forward to greet us, Prince Rainier and his sister Princess Antoinette.

Antoinette looks smaller, daintier and frailer than I remembered her, but with the same indefinable air of spirit, and adventurous, indomitable pluck. Rainier is still handsome, but looks careworn and cuddly simultaneously – rather like a battered teddy-bear. I wonder briefly how I must look to *them* and whether they too are politely disguising an inevitable readjustment of perception and memory? Fifty years is a long time . . .

There were curtsies and kisses and then we sat down beside the pool and reminisced about Ireland and Arran and the war that came so soon afterwards and was pivotal in all our young lives. Monaco, though a neutral state, was invaded by three different armies, German, British and American. Prince Rainier left Les Rosiers to join the French army, Princess Antoinette the Red Cross. They pointed out to me a secret path and tunnel at the end of the garden which leads down to the town and was used as a shelter from the bombing. 'The British,' they told me, 'bombed targets in the port and avoided the town, but American B17s, the "Flying Fortresses", flew much higher and were more indiscriminate and many of our people were killed or wounded.'

I started my questions by asking Prince Rainier how much he is at present involved in the day-to-day running of Monaco, a state which could be said to have only survived and prospered owing to the perspicacity and shrewd business sense of his family. He told me that the 'business' of Monaco is nowadays managed by the government, the *Conseil National*, and not by his family. The operation of gambling in Monte Carlo is also something which neither he nor his predecessors have ever had anything to do with: it is run by the SBM. But he is heavily involved in the tourism, banking, cultural affairs and public relations of the principality and one of his prime interests today is the new development schemes for land reclaimed from the sea.

Prince Albert I, his grandfather, was the first Grimaldi to give the Monegasques a constitution in 1911, and, although this may have eroded some of the princely powers, Rainier is still a *Prince Souverain*. He can dismiss the government, choose the Prime Minister and has a *droit de veto* on all laws passed by the Council. As no Monegasque citizen pays rates or direct taxes, revenue for social services is raised by value-added tax, by foreign investors and by the same indirect taxation that exists in France. The upkeep of the palace, the ceremonial side of the business, is paid for by the government. 'But there is not much pomp or ceremony here. Maybe for the opening of parliament, at the opera or for a military parade, but no *real* pageantry as in England.'

I asked him how democratic was the *Famille Princière?* 'Oh, completely. My daughters went to the local day-school without any fuss and so do Caroline's children. I can walk anywhere I want to in Monaco and people can speak to me. I know many of my subjects by name and they know me. On special occasions they even dine with me.'*

I asked him about freedom of religion in a Catholic state.

'Catholicism is the *Religion d'Etat* in Monaco,' he answered. 'Unlike France it is not separated from the state, but here there is complete freedom for every religion to flourish and indeed there are other churches for other believers. We have a bishop and a cathedral in the Principality, but our cardinal is in France.'

Prince Rainier himself I knew to be a *croyant* Catholic, and a religious man, but he was obviously shy about talking about his faith and I bravely passed on to another delicate question and was relieved to find that he *liked* talking about Princess Grace. 'Where did you first meet?'

He pointed a thumb downwards. 'Here, in this very garden. She was brought over by some movie people for a drink from the Film Festival at Cannes. Sinatra, Old Blue Eyes, I remember, was one of them.' His glance fell on my glass, which had been filled with Jack Daniels and ice by his footman. 'He drank bourbon, like you, only much more of it. She

---

* During Prince Rainier's twenty-first birthday celebrations it is true that every single Monegasque was bidden to a huge tea-party-cum-banquet at the palace.

stayed for lunch that first day,' he stopped talking for a minute and looked at his own glass, then continued, 'and I suppose that was it. Of course, I went over to California a couple of times to continue courting her, but I fell in love with her here, the first time we met. Later she made the garden as it is today. She loved the palm trees, so that is why the pool is shaped like it is. She wouldn't allow our architect to cut any of them down.'

I put as many of my questions to the prince as I could before lunch as I suspected that, as with all good Mediterranean men, siesta-time would come after the coffee, and he answered readily, with assurance and authority. I had not realised he was so closely involved with the citizens of his principality and with everything that affected their lives.

We were joined before lunch by Princess Caroline, who also lives on 'the Rock'. She wore a deceptively simple long white cotton dress, with a minimum of Richelieu embroidery at the neck and bootlace shoulder straps. With her long, shining hair, that has as many colours in it as a tortoiseshell cat's, and her strong classical features, she is stunningly beautiful. The other guests were the new Director of the Monte Carlo Opera, Monsieur René Croesi, and Monsieur Choiseul, their very nice press officer. Luncheon, at which I sat on Prince Rainier's left with Princess Caroline on his right, and Monsieur Croesi on my other side, was as simple and delicious as only a good French private chef can make it, far better than the food at the Hermitage – a judgment which His Serene Highness was delighted with and promised to pass on.

We started with a cold roulade of salmon and spinach, served with a pale green remoulade sauce. It was followed by a perfect beef *daube* and a pretty platter of very fresh young vegetables. The dessert was fresh mango ice-cream with a dark red fruit coulis of mixed fruits which tasted as good as it looked.

We talked, once again, about the Ballet de Monte Carlo, of which Princess Caroline is an active president, about some new young Russian dancers and the inability of old ones to retire – 'And that goes for singers, too,' growled our host, no doubt thinking again about Old Blue Eyes. Monsieur René Croesi, who had just flown in from Vienna, had hoped to recruit new singers at an international singing competition there, but had returned disappointed and empty-handed. 'They just weren't good enough.' We talked about the swiftly approaching Europe of 1994, of the crumbling of the Russian Empire and the surprising nostalgia of many nations for the old Austrio–Hungarian one. I asked him if he thought that Bourbons or Orléaniste 'Pretenders' would ever rule again and he answered with certainty that France preferred presidents to kings – and anyway, which one? – but that Iran or Afghanistan might one day restore their monarchies. He told me about the amazing new technology of 'infill' schemes on the Monegasque seaboard which has already pushed back the sea and added 180 hectares to Monaco's land area, an increase of 15 per cent, and he described the plans he has for these new developments. He told me about his 'ranch' on the mountainside above the town, which is a very private retreat that he loves to escape to and 'camp out' in (I could not help wondering to what degree). He also has an estate in the north of France where he goes to shoot partridge and wild boar.

Prince Rainier told me about the Rose Garden of Remembrance he had built below the palace in memory of Princess Grace, 'because she loved roses,' and how rose-growers from France and all over Europe, as well as Monegasque townsfolk, had sent him plants for it; I promised to visit it the next day with Virginia.

I then asked him why Lady Mary Hamilton, his Scottish great-grandmother, had left Prince Albert after only six months of what seemed a suitable and suitably grand marriage for both of them.

'Prince Albert was a difficult man to live with,' answered his descendant. 'He was a charmer, and a great oceanographer, but he was more interested in his fish and his charts than his family. It is always said that what caused the final rupture was a cup of tea,' he smiled, 'an *extra* cup of tea.'

'What do you mean?' I asked.

'Well, it seems that Albert disapproved of the traditional Highland teas that his bride had introduced to the palace, scones and cakes and that sort of thing, and then one day a young cousin from Scotland turned up at teatime, but when she sent for another cup and was no doubt looking forward to a good gossip, the prince forbade the footman to bring it. Upon which a row developed which ended with the prince throwing cups and cousin out of the palace, and the princess packing her bags and following, vowing to return to her native land. Actually,' he confided, 'she only went as far as Baden-Baden, where her parents lived and where my grandfather, Prince Louis,* was born a few months later.'

After lunch we talked a little more over our coffee by the pool. I asked why a room in the palace was called the 'York room'. 'Because a young brother of your King George III, Edward Augustus York, was sailing from Genoa to Marseilles when he became very ill and was landed in

---

* The future Louis II.

Monaco and carried up to the palace. But our doctors could not save him and he died, poor fellow, in that room in 1767, I believe, aged only twenty-eight.'

I could see that the prince's eyelids were beginning to droop and that siesta-time had come, and I was preparing to say goodbye when an eruption of pretty blond children, Princess Caroline's, who had come to hug their grandfather and to swim, gave me pause. The eldest boy, Andrea, who is about five or six, having enthusiastically done so, said 'Bonjour' to me and kissed my hand. The middle one, Carlotta, climbed on to her grandfather's knee, asked for and was given a sugary 'canard' from the bottom of his coffee cup. After admiring their swimming styles (Pierre, the youngest, is a fearless floater) and watching some first brave bellyflops, they were lined up, dripping, to say a formal and very mannerly goodbye to the guests. Much impressed by this, I thanked everyone ten times over, curtsied to the Prince, kissed Princess Antoinette and took leave of the Famille Princière and their magic garden with real regret.

I walked down to the harbour on the old cobbled road which zigzags through the enfilades, redoubts and gun emplacements of the old fort and thought about my second encounter with the Grimaldi family. I had been most impressed by the grown-up Serene Highness, Rainier III. He struck me as an intelligent and dedicated man of the world, civilised and 'fin', with perhaps a spark of something else, could it be goodness? He obviously still mourns his beautiful wife, still has tussles with his lively children, but he is deeply involved in the fortunes and future of his tiny state, as well as those of his family. He is, I thought as I descended the last few steps of the long incline, without doubt a kind man, a dedicated and caring prince who, in a unique and old-fashioned way, is still the patriarch of his people.

There were fireworks and a formal dinner on the terrace that night. Spanish fireworks, let off from a fleet of small boats beyond the harbour and the possible winners of the Firework Stakes which different countries compete for throughout the summer season. I do not really like fireworks, but they were certainly a great improvement on the Harvard 'crocodillos' of the previous night and in that romantic setting they were very spectacular, a kind of elemental theatre that not only the privileged diners of the Hermitage, but all the town could watch. I wondered if the Prince Souverain, whose grandfather had been Diaghilev's friend, had not been involved in their conception, as 'the Family' is actively involved in so much of Monaco's glamour and fun.

Alas, the company did not match the display. There were no Russian Grand Dukes, no handsome wastrels, no desperate gamblers – and would-be suicides were conspicuous by their absence.

The next morning, after breakfasting in the happy baroque of the hotel dining-room and swimming in the 'ozonised pool', I joined Virginia Gallico for a tour of the town. She told me that Princess Stephanie, whom she loves, still suffered from the appalling shock of her mother's death-crash and could not forgive herself for being its survivor. Virginia herself will never forget the shock and horror of the accident. When she saw Prince Rainier the next day, she told me, 'he had aged by twenty years'. We were standing in Princess Grace's memorial rose garden, from which you can just see a corner of the prince's apartments at the Palace on the Rock. I wondered if he had copied the idea from Shah Jehan in Agra, and whether all princes with beautiful dead wives are as sadly and creatively romantic.

That Prince Rainier has a genius for planning became very evident when we visited the 'new' Monte Carlo that has arisen like Venus from the sea. The year-round permanent Circus, which looks like some Far-Eastern Khan's campaign pavilion and doubles as an exhibition centre (full that morning of ancient Rolls, Maseratis and Sotheby's salesmen); the beautifully planned children's kindergartens and crèches next to public housing which did not look very different from the ultra-expensive flats nearby; the open-air Olympic swimming centre, built on top of a huge complex of conference and exhibition halls which incorporates a hotel for the participants and which, in its classical simplicity, would pass even Prince Charles's critical eyes. The materials from which everything has been built, the roofs, windows and arcades, are in the traditional idiom of the Midi so that, despite their size, they fit quite snugly into the landscape.

'Nearly all the initiatives are his,' Virginia told me. 'He plans everything down to the last tiny detail. If he sees rubbish on a street, he will make a note of it and it will be cleared up within hours. And, thank goodness, he has the power to veto the horrors that are continually proposed.' Looking up at the sprawling town from the elegant Yacht Club dining-room, where we were lunching, I wondered nevertheless why so many horrors had slipped through the royal net, but I suppose that, even in Monaco, every care- and tax-free citizen wishes to build his own version of the Castle on the Rock, and in such a happy, nonsense town, after all, why shouldn't he?

Part Two

AFRICA

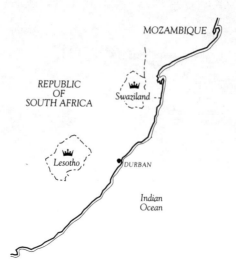

HM King Moshoeshoe II of Lesotho.

12

LESOTHO

King Moshoeshoe II

'I am surprised that my ancestors should ever have allowed such an institution to come into existence.'

JAMES VI OF SCOTLAND AND I OF ENGLAND

ON THE HOUSES OF PARLIAMENT

My next assignment would be a complete contrast, more of an adventure and for me a totally new experience.

I had never set foot on the African continent and most of my black friends came from the Caribbean, New York or London. I thought I had prepared myself by reading lots of books and talking to many friends and relations who had lived there and loved the place.

But the reality of Africa comes as a shock. It is more than an experience, it is a revelation, and it is so big and so overwhelming a revelation that at first it bewilders. I learnt a lot in a very short time, but most of it consisted in realising how little I knew.

I knew that both the African kingdoms I would visit, Lesotho and Swaziland, were small and shaky, threatened by the economic clout and politics of a powerful neighbour, but I had no idea of how big 'small' is in Africa, nor had I understood the enormous differences between black races, and how important their own race and their own race's history is to each of them and to the pace of evolution in Africa today.

The drive from Johannesburg to Lesotho takes six hours I was told by a pretty but scatty Avis Rent-a-Car girl ('I've never done it myself, but just follow your nose and I'm *sure* you'll be all right!'). It took me ten hours, and my nose must be circular, for it kept on bringing me back to where I had started from. But I finally managed to leave the huge sprawl of Johannesburg behind me and headed out for the open veldt and the great north–south highway that runs straight down the centre of what used to be the Orange Free State, towards Bloemfontein.

I was surprised by the huge distances between towns and even villages, the immense scale and awesome emptiness of the country; I was taken aback by the fierceness of the African sun, which is different from Asian or American suns and, until one knows how to cope with it, quite frightening. Then (I should surely have expected this!) I was stunned by the total absence of a white face. After I left Jo'burg, I didn't see one during the whole of my journey. And, lastly, I learnt, the hard way, that in Africa one must be self-sufficient to survive, and that one's luggage must always include a cold drink and a spare can of petrol, which mine didn't. Of course I broke down, waterless, in the high heat of the day. I was more than lucky to be saved by a particularly kind Transvaal policeman, who happened to pass by, and who drove me to his village, plied me with iced fizz, picked up a can of petrol from his own house and siphoned it through his teeth into my stalled Austin Allegro.

Much relieved, I continued on my way over the endless, rolling, empty plains until, four hours later, I crossed the River Caledon on a suspension bridge which also accommodates a one-track railway and, after filling in a great many forms at the frontier station, entered Maseru, Lesotho's capital and only town.

It is not too difficult to find one's way in Maseru. There is only one main street, which leads from the river to the Catholic cathedral at the end of the town. New buildings have mushroomed up on new roads on either side of it and a few high-rise concrete blocks tower above its one-storey shops. One could see distant and flat-topped mountains standing out from an ochre-coloured plain at most street corners; they looked like shipwrecked liners in the gathering dusk. No one was about and the police station was closed, but I found a willing boy there who directed me to the British High Commissioner's residence and came with me for the ride.

Her Majesty's representative, John Edwards, was in the bath and his wife was making last-minute preparations for a large cocktail party they were about to give for a visiting Foreign Office minister. Five British bishops were hovering and, owing to an administrative snafu, they hadn't expected me till the following week. Yet, with practised aplomb and extreme kindness they plied me with cold drinks and canapés, booked me into the Sun Hotel and promised to cope with my problems on the Monday. I gathered, however, in a brief conversation in between gulps that there had been no positive reply from the palace to my request for an audience with the king, and with a strong feeling of failure and doom my heart sank lower into my dusty boots.

The Sun Hotel proved to be an enormous hotel-cum-casino-cum-sports club, which is known as a 'leisure centre' in the tourist trade. It was solidly and grandly built in local basalt by the Hilton Company to ensnare South African weekenders (gambling is not allowed in the Union), but something went wrong with the venture and it is now jointly owned by the Lesotho government and the British-based Sun consortium. The food, overseen by a German manager and cooked by two excellent German chefs, is good and surprisingly varied, and the South African wine – and its price – a welcome surprise. The next morning I swam in the large outdoor swimming pool and breakfasted beside it on exotic fruits and good coffee, after which I drove down the hill, heard midday Mass in the Roman Catholic cathedral and then made my way round to the rectory. After queuing with several extended Lesotho families my turn came at last, but the exhausted rector, an elderly French priest who had already said four Masses, had no time for investigative journalism, if that is what you call my bumbling questions, and he directed me to the Dominican Mission which, he assured me, were 'much better at that sort of thing'.

On the outskirts of the town and off a dusty side lane I found the bungalow monastery, which consisted of a beaten earth campus dotted with rondavels, a chapel, mission hall and recreation room, where a bearded and laid-back prior gave me an admirably succinct and irreverent résumé of Lesotho's recent history, together with the parallel one of its Catholic mission, which was amusing, as well as honest and perceptive.

We were interrupted when the bell rang for Vespers and a group of bearded and rather scruffy young monks appeared from nowhere, chattering like starlings in what seemed a dozen different languages. They paused briefly to take me in, smiled friendlily, and hurried on towards the chapel. The prior rose, said 'Goodbye and good luck', and followed them, his head, as he passed from sight, already bent in prayer. The interview was over.

That evening I talked to Dr Mosebi Damane, a retired professor of history and a friend of Lesotho's royal family, who told me the story of the great Moshoeshoe, the founder of the nation and its royal dynasty. Any account of Lesotho's kings must start with him.

Bushmen and a few primitive tribes were the original inhabitants of South Africa. To the north and north-east lived the more highly organised Zulus, a strong and aggressive race who burst out of their own tribal area at the beginning of the nineteenth century led by Shaka, their formidable young warrior-king, and rampaged through their neighbours' lands. The explosion was short-lived but deadly, for Shaka was murdered by his half-brother Dugana when he was only about forty, in 1828, but from 1810 until 1820 his highly trained Impi regiments, using new techniques of war – short hand-to-hand fighting spears instead of throwing ones, larger shields, night attacks, calculated terror psychology before battle, rampaged through southern Africa, and the bushmen and settled tribes of the plains fled before them in confusion and chaos. Those times were called the 'Lifaquane' – or 'Wars of Calamity' – when tribe fought tribe for their herds of cattle, or merely in defence of their families and kraals, and famine, then ferocious bands of tribesmen turned cannibal, stalked the land.

King Moshoeshoe II's ancestor, the Great Moshoeshoe, was born in 1786; his father was chief of the Ba Mokoteli clan, a junior branch of the Bokoena (Bakwena), the largest Basutho tribe. The young Moshoeshoe emerged as a natural leader when he defeated the senior and more powerful Bokoena and founded his own power centre at Botha Betha, on the plains, but this was soon threatened by other warring tribes and his brother was sent to reconnoitre for a safer base. He reported back that he had found the ideal retreat (but not before their grandfather, 'Pete', had been waylaid and eaten by cannibals), and Moshoeshoe then brought his people out of the dangerous plains to the safety of Thaba Bosui, a rugged, flat-topped hill which still dominates the surrounding country and is set in a dramatic amphitheatre below the high Maboti mountains. It was a natural fort, easily defended and virtually impregnable, and it became the home and headquarters of the Bokoena for several generations. Soon many other clans and cannibal bands joined Moshoeshoe at Thaba Bosui where he was able, by a mixture of diplomacy and strength, to avert any further Zulu or Matabele attacks. By 1831 he was the acknowledged leader of all the Basutho clans.

A new danger to the independence of the emerging Basutho nation now threatened – and this time it came not from their own countrymen but from two foreign powers, the Dutch Boers who had landed in the Cape in 1830 and the British, who were already established there. The Voortrekkers were greedy for more land in which to settle and had marched up from the south in the Great Trek of 1834. They soon began nibbling at the frontiers of the Basutho homeland. For the next thirty years there were endless territorial disputes, raids and counter-raids, with the defending tribes eventually fighting with the guns and horses which their adversaries had introduced into their country and which they had captured from them. Moshoeshoe was assisted in his resistance to the Boers by a French Protestant missionary, Eugene Casalis, who identified himself and his followers with the Basutho and acted as the chief's adviser in his relations with the outside world. Apart from their support, Moshoeshoe was flattered at having erudite men as part of his court and indeed he appointed one of the evangelical missionaries to be his secretary. Advised by Casalis, Moshoeshoe asked the British Crown (then reposing on the head of the young Victoria) for protection from the Boers. An agreement was signed in 1843 with the Governor of the British Cape Colony, by which he became 'the friend and ally of Great Britain', the British in turn respecting the boundaries of his domain.

But in 1848 new settlers drove up into Basutholand from the south, and new boundaries, arbitrarily imposed by both British and Boers, caused more trouble. In 1852 the Basuthos inflicted a crushing defeat on the British Resident's men at the Battle of Tehela, and swift retribution followed. A British force of two thousand troops was sent up from the Cape and Moshoeshoe was ordered to pay a fine of ten thousand cattle and one thousand horses. The Basutho chief declared this impossible and so hostilities began again. As the 12th Royal Lancers were driving Basutho cattle down from the plateau Malopo, the king's son, attacked them from the rear and the British suffered heavy losses. Moreover, when encamped that evening, they found themselves surrounded by Basutho tribesmen whose whistling, shouting and singing caused many of the captured animals to stampede. Dawn brought wiser counsel and (perhaps because they had got most of their cattle back), they withdrew. A humble and diplomatic letter was then sent by Moshoeshoe to General Cathcart. 'I entreat peace from you . . . you have shown your power . . . you have chastised . . . let it be enough, I pray you: and let me no longer be considered an enemy to the Queen . . . I will try all I can to keep my people in order in the future.' It worked. It was now the turn of Cathcart and his forces to withdraw.

Nevertheless, skirmishes and sometimes outright war between the Boers (who in 1858 had proclaimed an 'Orange Free State Republic') and the Basutho continued for another decade until a crisis was reached when 'Free State' forces overran much of the country and captured every lowland fortress except Thaba Bosui. The new British Governor of the Cape, Sir Philip Wodehouse, was an intelligent man, and perhaps quicker to realise the dangers of the situation than his predecessors. After much prodding he secured the British cabinet's permission to annex Basutholand, and on 12 March 1868, Moshoeshoe's prayer was at last answered and the country that is now called Lesotho became British territory.

The British protection sought by Moshoeshoe proved, however, a mixed blessing, for Britain soon decided to administer Basutholand from Cape Colony which, in 1872, had been granted internal self-government. This did not suit the Basutho at all and angry reaction led to open rebellion, first from Mooros, an ancient chief who defied a Cape Colony army for many months from one of his country's formidable mountain fortresses and then, after a humiliating law called the Peace Preservation Act had been passed, and all Basutho firearms confiscated, by a real war in 1880–1 which came to be known as the Gun War and cost the Cape government dearly in men and money. But after a change of governors in the Cape, British direct rule was resumed and the Basutho won the right to have their country, now known as Basutholand, administered separately from other parts of Southern Africa, and in 1884 formal dis-annexation from the Cape marked another stage in the sequence of events which would finally lead to Basutho's full Independence.

From 1884 onwards a dual system of government evolved under which the Paramount Chiefs acted as Chief Counsellors, the British Commissioners as Presidents, and ninety-nine Basutho chiefs, or Headmen, as members of a National Assembly the 'Pitso', the tribal gathering or open-air assembly, remaining the main method by which the principal and Paramount Chiefs consulted with their people.

In 1910 Basutholand was left out of the Union of South Africa by the direct intervention of her people, who sent a deputation to London earnestly requesting the exclusion. But afterwards Basutholand found herself physically surrounded by three of South Africa's constituent provinces and from that time onwards she has, to an extent, become an enclave in a larger and more powerful state. Developments in the Union inevitably affected her people and the Union's Land Act of 1932–3, which restricted the grazing rights of her neighbours, affected them disastrously. Its consequences were that many Basutho were forced to return with their cattle to Basutholand, which resulted in the overpopulation and overstocking of their own country and serious land erosion. A drought, that same summer, made matters worse and led to wholesale starvation as precious cattle died in their thousands.

By the time Independence would be granted, or should one say restored to Basutholand, the prosperous country which the great Moshoeshoe had once entrusted to British rule was fast becoming an overpopulated and impoverished labour reserve, for the majority of its men, from sheer economic necessity, had become 'slave-workers' in the coal and gold mines of South Africa, dangerous work for which the annual wages then amounted to R200 (equivalent to about £40 by today's value, perhaps even less). Worse still, normal family life could not be sustained with husbands absent for such cruelly long periods – sometimes half a lifetime – and this too caused great unhappiness, and a lowering of moral standards throughout the country.

However, in the late 1950s, Harold Macmillan's 'wind of change' had begun blowing across all Africa, and Basutholand's longed-for independence moved steadily nearer. In 1960 a legislature was formed and a year later Moshoeshoe II (the great Moshoeshoe's great-great-great-grandson) was formally installed as Paramount Chief. A constitutional conference then agreed on a pre-Independence constitution; in 1965 elections followed, and in October 1966 Basutholand at last became an independent kingdom under the new name of Lesotho, with Moshoeshoe II firmly installed as its Paramount Chief and King.

Lesotho's pre-Independence history seemed complicated enough, but what I learnt in the next few days, as I patiently waited for King Moshoeshoe to receive me, was even more complex. John Edwards, my kind host, returned one morning from the Chancery looking decidedly worried. He told me that there were rumours of a political crisis brewing and he was beginning to doubt my chances of meeting the king. Nevertheless he and I kept on trying. One day we even caught the Chief of Protocol actually working in his office, but our hopes were dashed when he talked of a clerical error having been made and my name not having got on to a necessary list; but mostly he did not talk at all and, as the days went by and no one answered either telephone or note, even my optimism failed. The Foreign Office Under-Secretary had not been received by the king either, which was unusual and apparently out of character, for 'everyone', by which I mean the whole Lesotho establishment, assured me that His Majesty was the most courteous and kindly of men. Those who knew him personally also felt sure he would enjoy talking to me, informally, about Ampleforth, the Benedictine school in Yorkshire where he and my brothers and son had all been taught, and where many lifelong friendships had been forged with the monks and with village people who lived nearby.

At a lunch party at the Residency I met several Maseru old-timers including David Ambrose, the author of the only comprehensive and reliable guide book that has been written about Lesotho. In fact the experts unloaded such a wealth of information about the country, its politics and its monarchy that my mind reeled, especially as politicians, church and army all seemed to have changed sides as often as dancers in a Scottish reel. 'Do begin at the beginning,' I begged, and so they did.

The roots of Lesotho's two political parties go back to the days of colonial government and the Associations (embryo trade unions) which were formed by grass-root public opinion and supported by the churches in order to persuade the British government *not* to include Basutholand in the projected 'Union of South Africa'. One group eventually formed the Congress Party, which had, and still has the Evangelical Church's blessing and support. It started life as a Labour and Workers' Party, but it moved steadily towards the Right, eventually representing the traditionalist element in any crisis, and always backing the monarch. In the early days, however, the mass of uneducated Lesotho tribespeople felt that they had been left out of some of the most important deliberations and that their voice had not been heard, so they formed the National Party, in opposition to the Congress Party, and were at first supported by the Catholic missionaries.

The pre-Independence 1965 elections were narrowly won by the National Party of Chief Leabua Jonathan, but the Congress Party came a very close second. When Independence was declared, the Nationals quickly formed the first government (by a trick, it is sometimes said) and it soon became evident that Chief Jonathan, their Prime Minister, was a much more powerful and ruthless figure than the gentle, scholarly King Moshoeshoe II, and that his government would not be a democratic one.

Tensions rose between the two parties to such an extent that at one time opposition leaders were charged with public violence, were frequently detained and in some cases murdered, while the king, who had continued to speak out for the multi-party system and the democratic framework of the 1966 constitution, was required by Jonathan to submit to an agreement not to participate in politics.

Lesotho's economic position had deteriorated still further after Independence. A large part of its annual budget had now to be supplemented by Britain and considerable aid was sought and given by South Africa, who then seconded many technicians and officials from Cape Town or Durban to occupy senior positions in Lesotho. In January 1970, at the time of the first post-Independence elections, a South African Electoral Officer and a South African Chief Justice held these all-important posts.

These elections resulted in a defeat for the National (BNP) Party by Congress's winning 36 seats to their 23. Results were announced in the individual constituencies but not nationally. Instead, Chief Jonathan, backed by South Africa and the Police force, staged a military coup, and declared a State of Emergency. The constitution was suspended and Opposition leaders were gaoled. This seizure of power, cancelling all democracy or basic freedoms in the country, was opposed by the king, who then went into temporary exile (on the advice of the British government). His absence was treated as a kind of sabbatical, a holiday from kingship, and he visited several European countries and even settled for a time in Holland. But after pressure had been brought to bear on Chief Jonathan King Moshoeshoe returned to Maseru in December of the same year.

The fifteen years between the first and second military coups in Lesotho were marked by violence and repression and extraordinary *volte-face* by almost everyone concerned – the parties and even the churches (who, I am sorry to say, never ceased to meddle in the politics of the country). King Moshoeshoe, the only consistent player in the drama, attempted a balancing act, on the one hand working ceaselessly to persuade his own government to return to some form of democracy and stability and, on the other, encouraging national and international support for the (still illegal) ANC movement in South Africa.

It was of course South African politics that bedevilled the situation and ordained the fate of the South African 'refugees'. For a mass of schoolboy refugees had fled from Soweto after the uprisings there in 1976, and in the Basutho tradition they had been granted asylum and had been integrated into schools and colleges in Maseru. They were soon followed by fleeing ANC guerrillas, who also sought and were granted asylum. This, of course, was highly unpopular with the South African government, who accused them of mounting raids from Lesotho into Union territory.

Meanwhile, in 1973, a nominated *Interim* National Assembly had been created by Chief Jonathan, in which some former Opposition members accepted office while others remained aloof. There were uprisings by clan chiefs, and police reprisals, and a flight into exile of some of the Opposition leaders, who feared for their lives. Once outside the country a group of these announced the formation of a Lesotho Liberation Army, which declared war on their homeland and launched a series of guerrilla raids into it from bases in South Africa, where they had fled. The period soon became one of endless border raids, and rising tension between the two neighbours and the two squabbling political parties within Lesotho.

In the 1960s, Chief Jonathan's National Party had been right-wing and had been supported by the South African government, but after 1970 it moved gradually leftwards and began supporting the ANC movement, educating its young refugees in schools and colleges and, to the dismay of the Catholic Church, establishing links with the Eastern Bloc Communist Parties (the North Korean and Soviet embassies are the finest buildings in Maseru). An offer was now made by the South African government to curb the activities of the Lesotho Liberation Army (LLA) in return for the expulsion of key ANC refugees, but the offer was turned down. The government then lost patience and, on 9 December 1982, the South African Defence Force, supported by helicopters, attacked Maseru with the clear intention of killing the ANC refugees. Many were shot in their beds, several being High School pupils, and some innocent Basutho families and a university librarian were also among the forty-two victims.

The king appealed to the UN Security Council about the 'Maseru massacre' and although there was universal condemnation of the attack, no solution was found, and for the next three years the antagonism of the two neighbouring countries grew even greater, South Africa beginning a deliberate policy of destabilisation and harassment. Strikes, border raids and finally a South African boycott of Lesotho's produce and a frontier blockade precipitated a crisis. In January 1986 a second and right-wing coup against Chief Jonathan's left-wing government was mounted by the Lesotho Paramilitary Force (later sedately renamed the Royal Lesotho Defence Force), which took control and established a Military Council under the chairmanship of its leader, Major-General Justin Metsing Lekhanya. At first, from the king's point of view, the new government seemed a great improvement on the old one, and he hoped for a speedy return to democracy and free elections. Lesotho Order No. 1 of 1986, promulgated by the Military Council, vested all legislative and executive authority in King Moshoeshoe II, who remained Head of State. At the time I arrived in Lesotho, the king was in theory only *advised* by the Military Council who, together with the Council of Ministers, assisted him in the administration of the country. But, on looking through the list of this council's members, I noticed that its chairman (who doubled as Minister for Defence *and* Internal Security) was also Major-General Lekhanya and it seemed obvious that the general, through this office and through being chairman of the five-man Military Council, which shadowed every ministry, had a very firm grip on the reins of power, which he could tighten at any moment he chose. To many people it already seemed unlikely that the king – an idealistic and educated man with progressive ideas about economic development and strongly held views on democracy and corruption, military or otherwise, who was openly critical of the government's increasing accommodation with Pretoria* – would be the one to survive any confrontation with the general, but perhaps that is hindsight.

On the fourth day of my visit, I moved into the Residency and in between the telephone calls of desperation, when one counts pips up to one hundred, knowing full well that there is no one at the other end, I did a little sight-seeing, driving to the king and queen's village at Matsieng, thirty kilometres south of Maseru, where Moshoeshoe and his family lived in quite simple conditions as part of a village community in accordance with Lesotho culture and tradition. The palace in Maseru, approached by 'The King's Way' and guarded by soldiers, is strictly for entertaining and work.

Constantine Bereng Seciso, the King of Lesotho, is the son of the late Paramount Chief of Basutholand, Simeon Seciso, and was born in 1938, a direct descendant of the Great Moshoeshoe. He was educated first at a village school in the Mokhotlong district and then at Roma, a Catholic school near Maseru known for its uncompromising discipline and good teaching. His father died when he was only two and he was brought up by his uncles. To begin with, he was treated just like any other boy at school and there were no privileges, but when he was fifteen he attended Queen Elizabeth's coronation in London and the next year he went to Ampleforth. During his three years at Oxford (he read PPE at Corpus Christi) he returned to Lesotho only once, to be installed as Paramount Chief or *Motlotlehi* by an assembly of all the Basutho chiefs and the British High Commissioner at a great Pitso held in the meeting ground on the plain below Maseru.

King Moshoeshoe, who assumed the English title of 'King' when Lesotho became an independent state in 1966, married Princess Tabitha Mojela when he was twenty-four and they have two sons and a daughter. Queen Mamahato, as she is now called, is the daughter of a Lesotho chief who fought in the First World War with the Allies in France. She, too, finished her education in England. She was converted to Catholicism after her marriage and works for charities which concern women's and children's welfare. The family is very religious and goes to Mass every Sunday at the cathedral in Maseru; but they worship at a different time from that of the Mass attended by General Lekhanya, so the prior told me, with no comment but a wicked smile. In the early 1970s King

---

* One of the first acts of the Military Council was to expel the remaining ANC refugees.

Moshoeshoe returned to Oxford to finish his degree in PPE, as well as
to take another one in law. He is an excellent athlete, loves riding and
horse-racing, and has begun breeding race horses on his own farm outside
Maseru. But he is also a serious academic, and his greatest interest lies
in developing educational opportunities for his country's children and
in promoting and encouraging rural development of every kind in the
backward parts of his kingdom.

Having learnt all this about the king without even setting eyes on
him, I decided on my last day in Maseru on desperate measures. I would
storm the palace and demand to see the Chief of Protocol, and possibly
the king. I set out at 10 a.m. from the Residency (after His Excellency
had gone to work!) and drove as near as I could to the palace gates,
where there was a sentry in a sentry box and an office building just inside
them. I said I had an appointment and the sentry saluted and let me
through. I entered the rather ramshackle building where an uninterested
employee was sitting at a desk with a cup of coffee and an ashtray full
of fag-ends in front of her, making more rings on the desk's stained and
pitted surface. I said I wished to speak with the Head of Protocol, and
the girl nodded in the direction of swing doors ahead.

On the other side of them was a long passage with small rooms running
off it, some with half-open doors through which I could see mountains
of paper on groaning desks and laid-back secretaries gazing at them
gloomily. Everything was painted office green. I was shown into a waiti-
ng-room and I waited. After a very long pause and several cups of pallid
coffee, which three different young secretaries brought me, an elegant
and urbane young man appeared who seemed genuinely embarrassed and
distressed at my predicament. I told him that, after a long and thoroughly
punctilious correspondence, I had travelled all the way from London to
Lesotho to see the king and had to leave the next morning for Swaziland.
He said it was all the fault of the Protocol Department and its Head
who was now in another part of the country. The King was locked in
urgent discussions with the Military Council, but he would *try* and
get word through to him and have me somehow slotted in between
meetings.

At two o'clock he returned to say the king was now in the building
and hoped to see me on his way to another meeting in the palace. At
four o'clock he came back looking sad and troubled and said he did not
think it was likely after all, as the meeting still had not broken up. At
five o'clock the office packed up and I was swept out with the crumbs.

John Edwards did not say, 'I told you so', but gave me a strong drink
instead, and the next morning I was driven in his official car to the

airport to catch the early morning flight to Mbabane. Catching kings is not always so easy.

I was not sure, until later, that what I had witnessed that day in Maseru was, in fact, a third military coup. But three weeks after returning to Scotland, I heard that there had been an internal struggle for power within the Lesotho Military Council and that following it one group of its members (including, naturally, the general) had come out on top and that King Moshoeshoe II had gone into temporary exile. Hearing that this had brought him to London, I decided to try once more to realise my long-sought objective: an informal meeting, if not an audience, with the king.

It took a long time to arrange and by the time we met there had been a final confrontation between General Lekhanya, 'a modern Oliver Cromwell', as the papers now called him, and the king. 'Last month,' I read to my dismay, on returning from the Far East, 'King Moshoeshoe refused the job of constitutional monarch.' General Lekhanya therefore got rid of him by means of a decree called 'The Office of the King Order, 1990' presented to Lesotho's Constituent Assembly by the Military Council and accepted after due consultation with Lesotho's twenty-two principal chiefs. He announced the order 'with a heavy heart', regretting that his government had been forced to go to such lengths 'to preserve the nation from a man who did not have its democratic interests at heart'.

It did not, any of it, sound right to me.

The first answer I got from the switchboard of the Lesotho High Commission in London was also decidedly chilling. 'Chief Seciso, you mean? I don't know where *he* is!' and then a coarse snigger before the line was cut. A little later I ran the King to ground in a house in Hampstead which he was sharing with friends (although he spends a lot of his time among academics in Oxford, he has an official base and office in Belgravia). He very courteously accepted an invitation to lunch and turned up one morning at our flat.

He is much taller and more dapper than I had expected, dapper verging on elegant, with beautiful manners, and he was far more positive than I had been led to believe. I imagine a lot of the gentle kindness that he was known for has turned to determination, and probably anger at the shabby way he has been treated.

He told us over lunch that, before General Lekhanya's intentions had become clear, he and the majority of the Basutho people had welcomed the 1986 military intervention because they thought the general would

immediately form an interim government of national unity, which would
be widely representative and would bring back 'democracy and the basic
human rights and freedoms of the people, which they had lost in 1970'.

But the first thing the Military Council did was to expel the wretched
refugees and move closer to the South African government, whom the
king and most of his subjects still regard as the arch-opponent of Black
Liberation in Africa (I wonder what he thinks now?), and though King
Moshoeshoe had nominally been given executive powers, he soon found
that he was unable to exercise them without the agreement of the Military Council. All his protests were ignored (including some about the
widespread and increasing level of corruption in high places), as were
his impassioned letters to the Council, seeking a period of peace and
reconciliation which the nation desperately needed.

'For my part,' he wrote in one of his letters, 'I am ready, as before, to
play whichever role the people of this nation may require of me. I am,
as before, committed to a form of democracy which actively and genuinely serves the interests and welfare of our Nation and relies on the
effective participation of *all* of our people.'

'And how exactly do you see that role?' I asked him.

'I believe that this is as well defined in the 1966 constitution document
as is possible. In my view that document could well be used, as it stands,
as the first basis of returning power to the people. If there is a need for
amendment, it should be left to an *elected* government and parliament
to amend it.' Contrary to what has been said, he told me, 'I don't seek
any role that is not relevant to a constitution, decided upon and confirmed by a democratically elected body.'

'That doesn't sound to me like absolutism.'

'I'm afraid absolutism was all on the other side,' he answered sadly.
His first negotiations with the Military Council in October had foundered
because he could not accept a clause in the agreement by which the
general could *at any time* announce his abdication, without any form of
democratic consultation. In November 1990, just as all seemed to be
negotiable for his immediate return to Lesotho, he suddenly received a
message saying he *had* abdicated! And then, 'just as I feared, an order
was drawn up, *without consultation* either with the Constituent Assembly
or with the people of my country, which enabled the Military Council
to depose me and to remove from office any chief who did not co-operate
with it, again without notice and without a hearing.'

'Have you no legal redress?' I asked him.

'Oh, the Office of the King Order, 1990, is riddled with legal errors,
but that doesn't alter the fact that a military junta is in power in Lesotho,

that my family and many other chiefs have been silenced, and that no one dares challenge it. It suits our powerful neighbours, and even the British government seems content to accept the status quo . . .'

'For want of any solution without a great deal of shooting?'

'That could be so.'

He brightened a little as he said goodbye, and shook hands with a charming smile. 'And we haven't talked about Ampleforth. That must wait for another time.' Then, turning to my husband, 'If you happen to talk with anyone of influence in the Foreign Office, tell them what I have told you. All that I ask is that HM's government would withdraw British military or police presence, as a sign of disapproval . . .' He turned and left us, a sad, idealistic and somehow very admirable king, in a Burberry mackintosh, without a family and without a throne.

A week after Moshoeshoe was deposed, his son, King Lessie III, was presented to the Basutho nation by his mother, the Regent, Queen Mamahato, with the exhortation that he should rule 'in such a manner as to preserve the character of the monarchy, as a symbol of the unity of the Basutho nation, and cordially refrain from involving the monarchy in any way in politics'. As *The Economist* pointed out: 'Surrounded by South Africa, the Basutho need a king to remind them of their Sovereignty,' but that, for the moment anyway, was all, and I was frankly puzzled by the word 'cordially'.

However, in Africa, politics are more volatile than in most places, and less predictable. In April 1991 Major-General Lekhanya was overthrown by Major-General Elias Ramaema, the present head of the Military Council, who promised free elections in 1992. The Commonwealth Secretary-General then negotiated terms for the King's return with the Military Council, and in July 1992, after two years of exile, many rumours and several hitches, King Moshoeshoe finally returned home to an emotional welcome by the people of his country – ululating women wept, smothered him in hugs and kisses and strewed blankets on the ground to pave his way. The king wept too as he embraced his son Lessie who was at the airport to greet him.

The story for the moment ends there – and one can only hope that peace and reconciliation will now ensue. Moshoeshoe is a good and idealistic man and I am sure he will do his best to see that they do.

13

SWAZILAND

King Maswati III

'A monarch is a mirror. He reflects his people's religion, their history,
their culture. They can understand their collective identity better
through him than through any one or thing else.'

SULTAN QABOOS OF OMAN

There had been no difficulty in obtaining permission for my audience with the youngest king of them all, the dishy-looking Maswati III of Swaziland. Courteous letters had been exchanged, the
British High Commissioner had been very helpful and a meeting had
been arranged well in advance of my arrival. The exact timing of the
occasion was another matter, a cavalier attitude towards time, as I was
soon to learn, being one of the more endearing characteristics of the
Swazi people, and one which made me immediately feel at home.

For a country whose history has been roughly parallel to and often
part of the one I had just left, Lesotho, I had expected similarities. But
I was wrong.

The Swazis have a strong and very distinct culture of their own which
is not only upheld by its monarchy, but also in which the monarch is
absolutely central. Their land, too, is very different physically. Lesotho
is part of the high South African Plateau that stretches from the
Drakensberg mountains in the east of the Cape to the Atlantic Coast,
while Swaziland, on the other side of the range, tilts gently towards the
Indian Ocean, with lusher and more varied vegetation and tropical
jungles near the sea.

The drive to Mbabane from the airport is very beautiful, through
rolling grassland and densely wooded foothills above a broad green valley.
Sadly, John Flynn, the British High Commissioner, was on leave, but
his deputy, Roi Milburne, and his pretty and dynamic wife were the best
of hosts. They showed me a lot of the country and introduced me to
many old Swazi 'experts' as well as to the lifestyle of the expatriate Brit
in South Africa, which in Swaziland is a very comfortable one.

That first evening they took me to a meeting of the Swaziland Rotary

Club, where I met most of the foreign community: farmers, miners, professionals, businessmen and civil servants, who had all driven in to Mbabane in their Range Rovers and Toyota trucks to organise a charity golfing tournament (which my clever hostess eventually won) the follow-ing week. They were a polyglot but closely knit community who had lived in the country through most of the late king's reign, and the upheavals that followed his death, and they all had something to tell me.

I was curious to know how far a fairly homogeneous people like the Swazis could look back into their past, and at dinner I was lucky enough to sit next to a kindly and historically minded Scotsman who answered all my questions, 'The Ngunis moved south into Swaziland about 1700,' he told me. 'It was already inhabited by Sotho tribes (the same Basutho people as you saw in Lesotho) whom they call "those found ahead". They were led by their king, Ngwane III, who was of the Dlamini clan and a direct ancestor of young Maswati, the present king. 'Do you want any more?'

'Yes, please, lots more.'

'There were two Swazi kings,' he continued, 'who were outstanding warriors and conquerors. The first, Sobhuza I, was a contemporary of the Zulu king, Shaka. He gave two of his daughters to Shaka in marriage, and he was not unnaturally outraged when the Zulu king murdered them when they became pregnant. He never met Shaka, or there would no doubt have been a bust up, but later he took his revenge on Dugana, Shaka's half-brother and murderer – the *Zulus* were a rough lot! – and he defeated *him* in battle instead.

'The second of their hero-Kings was Maswati I, who was only sixteen when he became king in 1840. He reorganised the Swazi army Zulu-style, raided and conquered lands to the north of his country, let in the mission-aries and united all the clans into a formidable nation. But it was the discovery of gold in Swaziland, or rather the European discovery of its existence, that made the country suddenly one of the most coveted in all South Africa. In the regular gold rush that followed there was great rivalry between the Boers and the British to obtain land concessions from the Swazi kings, which they, in their innocence, handed out left, right, and centre. In fact, without realising what they were doing, they gave away nearly all their country – and, poor devils, they have been trying to get it back ever since.

'At first,' he continued, 'the Swazis got on well with the Boers, but goodwill gradually disappeared after they realised how much they were being exploited. Paul Kruger wanted the Transvaal Boers to have an outlet to the sea through Swaziland, and so Rhodes and Kruger, the two giants of the time, did a deal, Kruger allowing Rhodes, with his British sympathies, to expand into what became Rhodesia, while Britain stood by and let the Boers "administer" Zululand and Swaziland. The Swazis were upset by this and sent a deputation to Britain asking for protection and then, in 1899, came the Anglo–Boer war and the creation of a powerful country as their immediate neighbour, whom they could not, and still cannot afford to offend.

'When it comes to today's economy,' Mr MacDonald concluded, 'it is South Africa, I'm afraid, that calls the tune. They employ huge numbers of Swazis and they are this country's biggest market.'

The next morning Roi Milburne introduced me to George.

Major George Lys, Tutor Co-ordinator to His Majesty King Maswati III, is one of those remarkable yet frequently unremarked British soldiers who start their careers as exemplary regimental officers and then dis-appear for a time to reappear quietly as old colonels in some sleepy village in the Cotswolds, but who, in between, have often helped change the course of events, perhaps even the history, of some remote corner of the world.

George is the son of a Gurkha colonel, and was a Gurkha officer himself until he grew bored with the army. He was about to retire and sail round the world when the Foreign Office offered him a job which, as they say in the advertisements, you cannot possibly refuse.

He had been told about my book and was eager to see that I did his royal master and charge full justice. 'Meanwhile,' he said as he leapt out of a smart personnel carrier, 'I've come to take you out to lunch and to brief you on how to behave when you meet *him*'.

George is a great communicator and very good company. By the time we had finished lunch I had begun to understand why half the maidens of Mbabane, and probably their mothers and their grandmothers, were thought to be in love with him, and why he had been chosen for the job. On the way home we stopped at a toy shop and I chose a particularly nice black teddy-bear to present to the king for his youngest child's birthday. George said it was just the thing; HM would love it.

King Maswati is only twenty-one but the Swazis are a polygamous race and he already has four queens – one of them, to the disapproval of many a Mbabane matron, being Queen Poppy, the white daughter of a local missionary – and four children, including the Birthday Baby.

Over lunch George had told me how, when a Swazi king dies, his heir is chosen. It sounded a most complicated affair and one that must cause as many problems as it solved, the lengthy process being cast in a maze of tribal traditions involving scrupulously performed ancient rites and strictly observed taboos which are, seemingly, immutable, for if they are not carried out, some kind of National Disaster, it is thought, is bound to follow.

While the future king is still a minor (the heir is always young and unmarried) the mother of the *late* king, who had up till then been the Queen Mother, becomes the *Queen Regent* and rules the country with the help of the late king's senior brother till the Crown Prince comes of age and is crowned, at which point his own mother, the *Ndlovukezi*, begins joint rule with her son, and the Queen Regent retires.

The Swazi monarchy is a dual monarchy. The monarch is regarded as the father, the Queen Mother as the mother of the nation, and between them there is an undefined but delicate balance of power, the mother by tradition exercising a gentle but moderating influence over the son.

King Sobhuza II, Maswati's father, his biographer tells us, was one of the 'wisest, most patient and most circumspect kings that Africa has ever known'. He was certainly an educated and well-read man, who was converted to Christianity early in his life but, wisely perhaps, never let it be known which denomination he favoured. Rivalry among the early missionaries was intense, but they were never molested because King Sobhuza I, Shaka's contemporary, had had a dream about white-skinned people 'with hair like tails of cattle' who would arrive in his country bringing with them *Umculu* and *Indilinga*, which meant scrolls (or books) and 'round metal' (or money), and that no harm must come to them or the nation would be destroyed.

Sobhuza's minority was a long one and overshadowed by the vexed question of land ownership, mineral rights and the so-called concessions that wily Europeans and particularly, I am sorry to say, the Scots, had tricked his innocent forebears into giving away. He was installed as king in 1921 at the Royal Kraal in Lebamba after three years of training in the traditions of Swazi Dlamini kingship.

Colonial rule was not easily acceptable to the young king, but it was a prosperous period for his country and the economy moved from the purely pastoral to the starting up of small-time industries and the slow development of a middle-class. The king established a Swazi National Council which gradually moved from purely tribal administration to holding more sophisticated political discussions and making decisions on a national level. The British Colonial Office, whose policy in Swaziland was 'minimal involvement', nonetheless encouraged these and throughout the 1960s prepared the country's way towards eventual self-government. With Sobhuza's active participation, a legislative council was formed which led to political parties, a trade union movement and, in 1964, legislative elections. The old Swazi National Council, which had evolved into a conservative and monarchist political party called the 'National Movement', won this first election by a huge majority. It was very different from other emergent African nations. There were no Reds under Swaziland's beds during the 1960s and 1970s.

The new government's first action was to negotiate its country's independence from Great Britain and this was done with amity and speed, Swaziland finally becoming a sovereign state in September 1968. Constitutional problems, however, still remained. The Foreign Office had produced a 'Westminster-style' constitution for the new nation. It was not imaginative and was not a success. For as Dr Damane pointed out to me in Lesotho, African society 'cannot simply become a carbon copy of Western democracy overnight'.

Compromises had to be made with traditional infrastructures and decision-making processes. Something new had to be created which took careful account of the roots of the people – a system had to be found which would safeguard what was of value in the traditions and culture of the nation, but was also aware of the new conditions that existed in Africa in the 1970s.

King Sobhuza was fortunately the ideal king to make this difficult adjustment. His greatest gift was his ability to keep a foot in both worlds. He never lost touch with his ancestors' beliefs but was shrewd enough to understand and manipulate the politics of emergent Africa. In 1972 he repealed the 'Westminster Constitution', but kept a British-style judiciary, which he insisted must remain independent (and is still paid for by Britain). At the same time he allowed the old tribal courts, where the elders dispensed justice at sub-magistrate level, to co-exist with the High Court of properly trained and appointed judges. He called on the tribal elders to work out what they approved of and wanted to keep and what important tribal traditions they wanted to add to a new constitution. He even sent them abroad to study other countries' constitutions. He established a new and more reliable system of voting, called *Timkhundla*, for the elections of 1978. But in 1982, just before decisions could be made on the final draft of the new constitution or who the appointees to a new National Council of Elders (*Ligogo*) should actually be, King Sobhuza sadly died, and there followed a dangerous period of drift and confusion.

Prince Makhosetive, as Maswati was then called, was still a carefree

schoolboy when his life was abruptly and irrevocably changed. Within
a few hours of her husband's death his mother, Queen Ntombie, was
chosen by the Royal Council to be the new Queen Mother, making him
his father's heir. As he was a minor, Queen Dzeline, the late Queen
Mother, took over the duties of Queen Regent and his own mother
retired with the other widowed queens into the Mourning House. The
Queen Regent was a powerful character and she has been blamed by
some for the troubles and disorders of the next few years. In fact these
were due to a variety of causes: to the venality of the National Council;
to the frustrated ambitions of certain members of the royal family; to the
manoeuvrings of a tricky new breed – the emerging politicians – and
also, and perhaps most of all, to the relative inexperience of everyone
concerned. It was the latter, just as much as the autocratic behaviour of
the old queen, that caused the trouble. She does seem, however, to have
lacked tact.

She began by offending all the traditionalists in the country through
not carrying out her son's funeral rites in the correct manner, an omission
which many Swazis believed was the cause of a disastrous typhoon which
devastated Swaziland in 1983. She also appointed a favoured prince as
the 'Authorised Person' who would guide and speak for her during her
regency, instead of her senior brother-in-law whose duty and position it
should have been. The same year she offended not only the elders but
the whole nation by sending their future king to school (Sherborne) in
a foreign country without consulting them. Then she quarrelled with
parliament and dismissed her Prime Minister; and lastly she fell out with
the National Council, who had criticised such behaviour, and tried to
dismiss them too, whereupon the elders, whose patience was exhausted,
rounded on her and stripped her of her office, appointing the Crown
Prince's own mother, Queen Ntombie, as Regent in her stead. Then,
fearing a counter-coup from other factions, they abruptly cut short the
future king's British education and brought him back to Swaziland for
for the first of several times.

These dislocations and interruptions certainly damaged Maswati's education, and the anxieties the poor boy no doubt felt when separated from
his family must have been as great as the almost permanent crises he
found each time he was reunited with them. However, a Swazi king's
education into the rites and traditions of Dlamini kingship is just as
important in the eyes of his countrymen as European learning and takes
just as long to assimilate as preparation for 'A' levels.

The young prince returned four times to Africa from his school in
England and each time it was his very presence that bolstered his sup-

porters and averted crises; it was also during these visits that he began his gradual initiation into Swazi kingship.

First came the Showing Ceremony, when he was presented to the people in a great Pitso outside Mbabane; then his participation in the annual Reed Dance, his anointing, his initiation into the Royal Regiments and finally the traditional Royal Hunt when he disappears with his hunter chiefs into the bush, to be taught how to hunt and kill a lion. These and other ceremonies were all carried out with due publicity and according to tradition, as part of the making of a Swazi king.

At the end of the 1985 autumn term the Prince left Sherborne for good and, after a meeting of the Chiefs and Elders, as well as senior members of the royal family, it was announced that Makosetive, the Crown Prince, would be enthroned on 25 April 1986 as King Maswati III, four days after his eighteenth birthday.

Judging by the photographs in the Milburnes' family album, the coronation of the young king must have been a unifying as well as a happy occasion. Royal guests flew into Mbabane airport from every side and were ferried to the capital in fifty Mercedes-Benz limousines which the government of West Germany had lent as a kindly gesture. The first day and the actual crowning provided rather low-key entertainment for the privileged guests who attended this part of it. They sat in a specially built pavilion inside the 'cattle byre' of the National Homestead (or Kraal) at Ludzidzini, a large stockaded enclosure around the outside of which were grouped five smaller enclosures, three for the Royal Regiments and two for the royal family. The small sacred enclosure at one end of the 'byre' in which the actual crowning took place was screened from public view, and the distinguished visitors and the press sat gravely through several hours of hidden ritual, being entertained sporadically by the warrior dancers of three Royal Regiments. But at last the bugles sounded and Prince Mboni, the new and suitably chosen 'Authorised Person', emerged from his seclusion with all the male members of the royal family and announced: 'People of the Swazi Nation, I am instructed by the Elders to inform you that as you have been patiently waiting for the "sun" to rise, now it has risen.' Then the Crown Prince, dressed in loincloth and leopard skins and with the red feathers of the lourie-bird adorning his royal head, stepped forward and raised his stick in acknowledgment as Mboni solemnly declared, 'Here is your new King!' The regiments whistled and leapt and shouted 'Bayethe' – which is the Swazi equivalent of 'Long Live the King' – there was a traditional dance, in which the king joined with his warriors, and then quite suddenly it was all over.

The next day a much greater gathering took place in the Somhldo

HM King Maswati III of
Swaziland during his
coronation, 1986;
celebrating his twenty-
first-birthday, 1989.

National Stadium and King Maswati III, again in national dress, drove round the arena in a white Land-Rover. The huge crowds went berserk, the army fired off a twenty-one-gun salute, there were guards of honour, dancing, singing and pageantry. The young king made his first public speech and a good time was had by all. That evening there was a state banquet, and the next day the Royal Garden Party at the Lozitha Palace, at which the king appeared in British morning dress, rounded off the proceedings most elegantly.

The guests departed and the young king settled down to his duties, with the Queen Mother, in the role of joint ruler, acting as both parent and support. His newly acquired kingship, however, was incomplete until he had chosen and married a maiden from the Matsebula clan and had performed his first Newala Festival with his bride.

No doubt many candidates were presented and many more would have liked to have been, but by September *la Matsebula* had been selected and King Maswati was ritually and ceremoniously married to his chosen queen. After the ceremonial wedding dance (the 'Reaching of Manhood') the king left his bachelor quarters to live in his new *sigodlo*, or harem, the old dwelling-house, according to tradition, being dismantled and its material removed.

Newala is the main ceremonial that Swazi kings perform and preside over every year. It is a First Fruits ceremony and at the same time a religious festival of great ancientness. The Zulu once practised it, but it disappeared from their tribal customs with the disappearance of their kings. Only a king can open and close the ceremonial, and it launches all Swaziland on a week of national ritual and prayer, thanksgiving for the fruits of the year that is ending and a petition for the fruitfulness of the year that is to come. The Swazis from time immemorial have believed in an Almighty Being who exists outside time. His name in their language means 'He who appeared First'. He is the most good and expects His creatures to be good too and to lead good lives. He communicates with them and they with Him through their leaders and so the Swazi nation gathers together at every year's end to offer *through their king* their thanks to their God. They could no more renounce Newala than a Muslim could give up Ramadan.

Between his marriage and the first Newala the young king made two positive and far-reaching decisions. He summoned the nation's elders to the Ludzidzini national byre, thanked them for building his *sigodlo* and for his wedding presents, and told them he was appointing two governors to help him rule and that he was retiring the old Prime Minister and appointing a new one, an honest man who had been an Assistant Commissioner of Police. And six months later he dissolved the controversial and quarrelsome *Ligogo* (the National Council of Elders) which had caused so much trouble during his minority.

A lot had happened in the young monarch's life in a very short time and it could only have been when events quietened down that he realised what he had missed by not having been able to finish his studies in the UK. As a schoolboy, his greatest ambition had been to go to Sandhurst, the British Royal Military Academy that so many young princes have found invaluable as a training ground for organisational as well as military skills, and this was no longer possible. It was then that the avuncular status of the British Foreign and Commonwealth Office towards Swaziland produced the ideal solution. If King Maswati III could not go to Sandhurst, then Sandhurst must come to the king in the shape of a royal tutor and coordinator, a regular officer of experience and distinction, Major George Lys.

It was a success from the very beginning. There is a strong rapport between the two, a loyalty born of affection and, on the part of the royal tutor, respect as well as patience and understanding. He is good, George Lys told me, a thoroughly good and nice young man. Given time he will be a very good king.

And so the lessons continue and a certain amount of order is brought into the daily routine of the palace by the tutor-coordinator, though coordination is perhaps one of George's most difficult and delicate tasks in a job that is balanced on eggshells. And the question often is, which palace?

The traditional system of new houses for new kings was all very well when Dlamini royal palaces were reed huts, but now things have changed dramatically. Japanese or Filipino architects are sent for, smart interior decorators proliferate and the opportunities for million-dollar rip-offs are endless.

The king did not like the new palace and harem that the nation had built for him and he has recently commissioned a new one to be built at the very top of the highest hill above Mbabane. It has magnificent views on every side and must be pleasantly cool in summer, but although it was not finished when I saw it, I doubt whether its avant-garde Filipino architect would have won the Palace of the Year award from either Prince Charles or myself.

The Queen Mother lives in the valley in a palace of great charm, while the large one near the airport is now the seat of government administration. George, however, was much looking forward to moving into the new building, where he would have his own flat and offices.

*   *   *

The exact time of my audience had not yet been divulged and so, on the day it was to happen, I persuaded George to take me on a sweep through Reilly's Park, which is a conservation area full of wild game only a few miles outside the capital. It was bequeathed to the nation by a certain Mr Reilly, whose concession it had been, and covers a huge acreage of wooded hills and rolling grassland. Here, while we bumped over forest tracks and stopped to watch zebra, gazelle, monkeys, giraffe and other wonders, I learnt about Swazi notions of land tenure. In Swaziland, George told me, the land has always belonged to the nation. It is held in trust for both present and future generations by the king, who is in control of the *use* of it. Anyone who wants to settle and farm or build a house (provided it is for his own use) will be given land by the king, so long as it does not encroach on tribal grazing lands. It may run out one day, but meanwhile there is plenty of it and the king has his own Royal Fields which are administered by the Minister of Agriculture. In general, Swazi agriculture is not much more than subsistence farming and the land is badly overgrazed, for cattle are the riches of the people and wives are still paid for in cattle. Even now such concepts as individual ownership, heritable property or grants in perpetuity are hard for the average Swazi to understand, while in the nineteenth century, as Mr MacDonald had told me, they were quite unknown, which is how the indiscriminate land and mineral right concessions came about.

After many chiefs and tribesmen had been turned off what they still considered to be their lands by Boers and 'diggers', who believed they had bought it, the situation grew fraught and King Mbandzeni began to realise what he and his forebears in their generosity had innocently signed away. The help of a white advocate, Theophilus (Offy) Shepstone was sought and his services were retained as 'Resident Agent and Adviser in all matters in which white people are concerned in and about our country', but it was not for many generations, and legal battles and petitions, missions and commissions that some, but not all, of the damage was undone. Much of the concession land had ultimately to be bought back by the Swazis from the British Crown and much of it still remains in the hands of the descendants of the original concessionaires, but by now the Swazis have learnt to live with the problem and there is little hostility between the white settlers and their dispossessed hosts.

As we drove down again to the valley, George told me that it was in the wild country around Mbabane that a penniless young author called Rider Haggard had conceived the idea of *King Solomon's Mines* from listening to local legends and exploring the great limestone caves that riddle its hills, which are among the oldest in all Africa. Looking up at their fierce escarpments I could easily imagine the dreadful Gaghoul lurking in their depths.

We drove up to the queen's palace, and while George disappeared to telephone for news, I sat back in the Land-Rover and watched a timeless and happy country scene, a scene in which I was beginning to feel so much at home that I was almost a part of it.

The palace is a working farm as well as an administrative office. It was five o'clock, and the women and children who had been working in the fields, schoolchildren, civil servants, clerks and clerkesses were all going home. There was laughter and greetings, good-natured ribbing and gossip. Parcels and pails were lifted on to strong shoulders and curly black heads, bundles of fodder piled on to handcarts, bicycles mounted, phut-phuts kick-started and a stately procession that soon became silhouetted against the setting sun moved off down the grassy track that led to their kraals, somewhere beyond my view in those distant hills above the plain.

George came out and said we must drive on to Lozitha as he had not found anyone who could tell him anything, which I imagined, but tactfully refrained from saying so, must be more or less par for the course. The king's working palace is enormous. Dazzling white Monte-Carlo-1930s style with a significant touch of the oriental. Apart from the sentries at the gate, who presented arms but did not stop us, it was quite devoid of human life and had the feeling of an abandoned airport. We walked across a terrace the size of a football pitch covered by dozens of little cast-iron tables and rococo cast-iron chairs and entered a cinema-type foyer. It was totally deserted but we nosed around, George shouting for a key to the washrooms and loos, which were locked. Eventually a tired-looking housekeeper appeared and produced one. We were then joined by a crusty old courtier with grizzled, close-cropped hair and a tropical town suit and the three of us sat on the terrace, making polite conversation for the next hour or two. Just as the sun finally set a peacock picked his careful way across the empty lawns below us, the golden eyes of his display catching, as it were in sympathy, a last golden beam before darkness fell. After what seemed a long time some military cars rolled up the drive and a royal guard tumbled out of them. Lights went on in the pavilion by the side of the terrace and we perked up. Minutes later, with a splendid swoosh of sleek black cars, the royal party arrived, inspected the guard, who presented arms, and disappeared into the pavilion.

We drooped again.

Half an hour later a chamberlain walked over and, after shaking hands, announced formally that His Majesty was ready to receive us and would we please follow him. His message delivered, he then began joking and laughing with George as the courtier and I fell in behind. More sentries and salutes, a red carpet, then double doors opening on to a huge, high-ceilinged audience chamber, a group of over-stuffed high-backed 'herrlichen' chairs and a table arranged in a rather lonely circle at one end of it. Standing in front of the middle throne, his bare sandalled feet reposing on a beautiful Persian carpet, was His Majesty, King Maswati III, magnificent in full tribal rig and feathers, with a respectful half-circle of elders, equally, but slightly less glamorously, turned out, to one side of him. As we advanced across acres of carpet he gestured to the secondary thrones and explained with the most charming smile: 'I'm sorry I'm a little late, but the woman who usually does my feathers could not be found and the girl who replaced her wasn't any good at it.'

He speaks slow and rather careful schoolboy English and is still hesitant about tackling difficult or abstract subjects; when those arose he appealed to George for help, and immediately got it. He is very beautiful, paintable, rather than just 'a fine figure of a man', with the bloom of youth and vigour attenuated by a gentleness, a kind of innocent goodness, that is very touching. While we talked, it was delightful to watch natural high spirits struggling with a seriousness of purpose, and a determination to be dignified flit across his very unguarded face. Searching for political questions no longer seemed appropriate and we talked about Swazi traditions and those of Dlamini kingship, about conservation and cattle, his visits (with George) to Britain and America, his interest in the army and in military history, his contacts with his people at village level, the demands of tribal loyalties and finally how much time he gave to playing with his children – upon which he doubled up with laughter and I presented him with the black teddy-bear.

The Swazi national character, or so everyone told me, is non-aggressive, hospitable and happy. The men are inclined to be idle and vain, the women are the industrious ones. The whole nation is steeped in tradition, which is upheld by its monarchy and in which the monarch is of central importance. They are completely unselfconscious, indeed proud of their national dress because it is a clear statement of their nationhood – 'just like your kilts,' an English settler had told me. Looking at the old men opposite in their skins and feathers, with just one of them (our companion on the terrace) in a European suit, I realised it was true, for he certainly looked slightly embarrassed and was definitely the odd man out.

'What did you wear in America?' I asked George after we had taken our leave. 'Oh, the feather bit and all,' he answered blithely. 'I haven't the right kind of hair and it was fearfully difficult keeping them on, but we made it to the United Nations in New York and HM made an excellent speech. By the way,' he added, as if suddenly remembering something, 'have you got any old bits of leopard skin you could collect and send us? HM wants to join WWFN (the World Wide Fund for Nature) and it's a bit difficult if they go on shooting leopards to trim their own ceremonial gear.' I promised him leopard skins and that we could all meet again in Scotland, kilts, feathers and skins – the lot.

That night I tried to round up my impressions of Swazi kingship while they were still fresh in my mind. It was enormously complicated and yet more simple than anything I had come across before. Complicated by the apparatus of its ritual form, simple as total faith is simple. Everyone in this country believes in their king, and King Maswati quite obviously believes in himself without any more doubts than a daisy has in being a daisy. The monarchy here embodies the nation and the king's health and fertility relate directly to the health and fertility of the soil. His utterances have a deep and mystic significance to many of his people and the ceremonial he takes part in or leads is central to their survival and prosperity. He is a *necessary* king.

The next morning John Flynn, the High Commissioner, returned. He is an impressive Scotsman and had just been offered a new and challenging post in another part of the world. He was sad to leave Swaziland. He saw most of their problems, economic and political, in relation to what was happening in South Africa. He regretted not being able to see a final version of the new constitution drafted and adopted, but thought this was still some time away.

After lunch he drove me into Jo'burg so that we could talk a little more. It was the day that Nelson Mandela was released from prison, and the huge crowds at the airport thought he would fly up to Johannesburg that evening. As I waited for my aeroplane, excited ANC supporters were dancing and singing and waving banners on the parking lots below the terminus, every now and then being moved on by tough-looking Boer policemen. I don't know which of them alarmed me more. But that is another story, and one which is still to be continued.

Part Three

CENTRAL ASIA

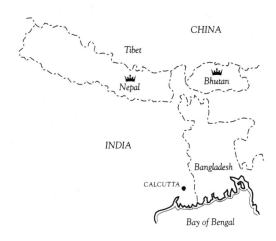

14

NEPAL

King Birendra Bir Bikram Shah Dev

'Subjects have no greater liberty in a popular than in a monarchical state. That which deceives them is the equal participation of command.'

THOMAS HOBBES

The two African monarchies I had visited had been very different. Their personalities, pace of development, their geography, their economic potential, were dissimilar, but they both faced the same disadvantage – a frontier with a powerful, overbearing neighbour, the Union of South Africa, and the economic necessity of their impoverished tribespeople to cross it to find work.

Their own independence and the future of their monarchies depend very much on South Africa's future, and that is still frighteningly uncertain. I witnessed, and can almost be said to have participated in the military coup which led to one of their kings' dramatic banishment – and that this was due to outside influence, as much as to inside feuding, there is no possible doubt. What I had not expected was that on my next visit to another king, another country and another continent, I should find a very similar situation.

My husband came with me to Nepal. Many years previously, in the summer of 1957, as a government minister, he had visited Nepal and together we had entertained King Birendra's father, King Mahendra, at Strachur, our home in Scotland. We had introduced him to the Highland sport of shinty and arranged for him to shoot a stag. He had been piped round our dining-room table and had met the neighbours. He was accompanied, I remember, by a dashingly smart Gurkha colonel, an elderly court official and some personal servants, including a faithful bodyguard who slept across the threshold of his bedroom door. He was found there, at daybreak, by my Argyllshire housemaid, who was deeply shocked: 'Not even a pillow and a' his clothes on,' she reported to me in stern disapproval. I do not know what King Mahendra thought of us, but we liked him.

We also liked his son, a chubby lad and fearless games-player who was at the same house at Eton as our son, Charlie. When young Birendra eventually succeeded his father and was crowned, Charlie, with half a dozen other old schoolmates, was invited to Kathmandu and spent an entertaining evening at the royal palace with the young king. 'It was extraordinary,' he told me later. 'We all reverted into being sixteen-year-olds again, including the king, the old jokes and buffoonery, the old alliances, prejudices, school gossip – and from sober city gents, soldiers, diplomats, journalists and an about-to-reign monarch! Birendra was totally relaxed and a marvellous host. He really is a very decent fellow.'

We were not entirely surprised, therefore, when the Nepalese ambassador in London told us the king would grant us an audience, and that we were to join him up-country at the Royal Camp in Pokhara, the official base he uses when visiting his subjects in the western region of the country. What was very exciting, though, was to hear that we were to accompany him and Queen Aishwarya on their visit to Damauli and would see the *Panchayat* system of government actually working.

The Panchayat system, a form of government adopted by Birendra's father, King Mahendra, in 1961, is based on the country's age-old traditions – the decision-making of village elders. Under Mahendra's rule, the elders ('Panchayat' means a council of five) were elected by adult franchise and secret ballot from village assemblies every five years. It was a three-tier system, the kingdom being divided, for administrative purposes, into village, town and district Panchayats. (The office-bearers of the village and town Panchayats were automatically members of the District Assembly, and from the District Assemblies the representatives of the National Assembly, or Panchayat, were chosen. Towards the top of the pyramid were the king's ministers, twenty per cent of whom were chosen by him and eighty per cent by the National Panchayat and the 'Class Organisations' (the other elected bodies which represent women, youth, farmers, elders, labourers and ex-servicemen). At its apex, the monarch himself was 'the ultimate authority for all legislative decisions' and in effect could dismiss or recall a Prime Minister or a member of the Council of Ministers whenever he liked.

Every year, for a period of two to three months, the king and queen, with a secretariat of government officials, fly by helicopter to the remoter parts of Nepal to hold audiences, discuss development problems and receive requests (and complaints) from the district and village Panchayats of the area – some of whom have trekked for days from their Himalayan homes to the meeting place. It all sounded quite reasonable to us and, like monarchy itself, remarkably easy to understand.

And so we flew from Kathmandu to Pokhara, where King Birendra and Queen Aishwarya use the Royal Camp and small lakeside palace as their official base when they are visiting their subjects in the western region of the country. Mr Pandi, the king's secretary and our trusted and amiable companion/guide, installed us in Pishti Lodge, a unique hotel on the wilder shores of the lake which one reaches by crossing on a raft, pulled back and forth by an 'endless' rope.

Its three circular bungalows, or rondavels, were designed by a Swiss architect who settled in Nepal, and are set in a ravishing lakeside garden where claret-coloured magnolias, creamy daturas and tree-sized poinsettias mingle with yellow jasmine, banana palms and scarlet hibiscus. It was presided over by a cheerful and efficient Goanese called Toni. Every bedroom led on to a little private lawn with its own comfortable garden chairs and hammocks, and ours had the inestimable bonus of a morning and evening spectacular – an uninterrupted view of the great Mahabharat range of the Himalaya, rose-coloured at dawn, ice-white and sparkling at noon, then lost in cloud to re-emerge in all its majesty as dusk falls, peerless, inviolate, against slowly darkening skies. Its central peak, the Pishti, or 'Fish-tail' mountain, rises high above the others; as pointed and idiosyncratic as the Matterhorn. We learned to love that mountain, greeting its every appearance as that of a shy, yet beautiful and friendly neighbour.

The third round-house encloses the restaurant and bar, where on cool February evenings customers sit in a cosy circle, sipping their pre-prandial drinks, round a huge blazing and aromatic log fire whose central chimney is suspended above it and rises to the roof.

That first evening, a breathless Mr Pandi pushed his head round our door announcing that we had been summoned by His Majesty to the Royal Camp across the lake. 'Just as we are?' I asked, feeling inadequate in track suit and sneakers. 'Just as you are,' insisted Mr Pandi, and we rafted over and hurled ourselves into the waiting jeep within minutes.

The drive to the camp was equally brief. It is run, as are all the logistics of Their Majesties' tours, by the military, with exemplary efficiency. The Royal Nepalese Army is entirely Nepalese, but apart from that there is little to distinguish it from British or Indian Ghurka regiments, also recruited from the foothills of the Himalaya. In each case most of the officers are Sandhurst-trained and speak excellent English.

A smart and obviously senior ADC, with the scarlet cap band of a major-general, stepped forward and saluted. 'His Majesty,' he told us, 'has just finished being briefed for tomorrow's programme – come this way,' and he led us down a lantern-edged path to a large Nissen hut, simply furnished with a desk and some chairs, office lighting and maps and charts pinned round all the walls.

We had not seen King Birendra for nearly thirty years, since his Eton days. Physically he had not greatly changed. I remembered a quiet, rather solid-looking boy with a shy smile, who had a reputation for courage on the games field. Here was a king with the same features, but with a confidence now that amounted to authority; no longer shy, but articulate and sophisticated, and, it soon became apparent, with a natural friendliness and shrewd intelligence.

He asked after Charlie, welcomed us to Nepal, and then explained to us the next day's proceedings, suggesting we drive by jeep to Damauli, the district capital, where the Panchayat was to take place, so that we could see some of the country on the way and witness his arrival by helicopter. 'May we take photographs?' we asked. 'Of course, as many as you like.' He asked us if we were fit for heights and, on being assured that we had not turned a hair when we drove over the Kunjerab Pass on the Karakoram highway (this from my husband – in actual fact I had felt both sick *and* dizzy) he announced that, if the weather held, he would fly us up to Mustang the following day, the Rajah and people of this tiny Himalayan dependency having expressed a desire to see him.

My husband was excited and delighted by the possibility of visiting Mustang – he told me that not only was it a restricted area, being adjacent to the Tibetan (now Chinese) border, but also that only two or three Europeans had ever visited it. Originally a small sovereign kingdom called Lo, or Lo Mantang, its rulers are now subordinate to the Nepalese monarchy, but they still consider themselves to be kings (and not rajahs) of the highest kingdom in the world. Since 1961 they have accepted the sovereignty of Nepal and were at that moment part of the Panchayat system, Mustang being one of the seventy-five districts of Nepal.

The drive from Pokhara to Damauli takes a Nepalese motorist two hours. We took more than three because it was so beautiful. A great effort has been put into improving the communication system of Nepal. There are roads now wherever there *can* be roads and the excellent macadam one we drove along links the major towns of the valleys and the Terai, the heavily populated southern plain that borders on India. Only ten per cent of the land in Nepal is arable, but the Pokhara valley is fertile and every inch of it is cultivated. As we drove from its lush vegetation into the foothills, we noticed that the earth became visibly thinner and is terraced into tiny fields which wrinkle up the sides of the mountains, eventually giving way to forest and then bare rock. Here poor farmers can only scratch a living in summer, a living which has to be supplemented in the long winter months by some of the family finding work in the tropical Terai region of South Nepal, or even the sub-continent itself. Mr Pandi, in answer to our many questions, gave us a lucid account of ancient and modern Nepal and a little of its recent history.

Folk memories of the Nepalese go back into the legendary times of the *Mahabharata*, he told us, but the squabbles over succession and mini-wars over territory between ruling rajahs and kings in more recent times were no different to those of other Himalayan kingdoms. Nepal has always been a free and independent sovereign state which has never been colonised by any foreign power. It is a Hindu state which embraces many other religions, including Buddhism, Tibetan Lamaism, and Christianity. Religious and racial tolerance have always been remarkable features of its culture (in fact, the only members of any religion that have ever been harassed have been proselytising Christians), as has its deep-rooted reverence for its monarchy. That is, until the middle of the nineteenth century. But in 1846, a massacre and political coup reduced the country's royal family to feeble figureheads and the Rana dynasty, who were Indian by origin, came to power in Nepal as hereditary Prime Ministers, and remained in power for the next 104 years. It was a corrupt and autocratic interregnum which held the country back for a century and caused its people much suffering; but finally, in 1951, a national revolution, spearheaded by Birendra's grandfather, King Tribhuvan, a strong character of considerable courage and a remarkable legislator, overthrew the Ranas and restored his own and the people's rights.

King Tribhuvan ('Father of the Nation') died when he was only forty-eight, and the task of translating his ideas into reality was shouldered by his heir, King Mahendra. A multi-party, parliamentary form of democracy was instituted and, by the rules of a new constitution given to the people by the king, a general election was held in February 1959 and the Congress Party (which was a radical and republican off-shoot of Nehru's and Mrs Gandhi's Indian Congress Party) swept to power in a landslide victory. It was representative of the new stirrings of political thought in the cities of the plains and the heavily populated Terai, but it was totally unacceptable to the Nepalese mountain peoples. What is more, it was as corrupt as the Rana family had been before it.

So, in December 1960, King Mahendra, after extensive tours to every
part of the country and consultations with all shades of opinion, dismissed the government and instituted the non-party system of Panchayat,
or Village Council Democracy, as the most practical and understandable
form of government for the poorly educated, multi-racial and multi-
religious peoples of Nepal. It was, of course, the very reverse of socialism
and centralised government and, although enthusiastically supported by
the more traditional mountain peoples in the north and north-west, it
was less than popular with the better educated and politically ambitious
inhabitants of the valleys and the Terai. King Birendra inherited the
Panchayat system when he succeeded his father in 1972. He immediately
started a series of five-year plans and reforms. However, the political
unrest in the south and the valley towns soon spilled over into open
revolt (encouraged by a left-wing government in India). In 1981, Birendra held a referendum asking his subjects whether they wanted to be
ruled by the non-party Panchayat system or revert to a party-political
one, with a new constitution, which would inevitably mean that the
country would take a radical and possibly republican lurch to the left.
By the barest of margins the traditionalists won and for a time there was
political peace, but now a customs and trade blockade by India was
heightening tensions and storm clouds were gathering once again on the
political horizon. Such was the situation as we drove towards Damauli,
the capital of the Western Development Region.

As we neared the little hill town, people were streaming into it from
every side and in every conceivable conveyance, but mostly on their
own two sturdy legs – men from the mountains in thick wool slung
jackets, pouched in front to accommodate, maybe, a couple of new-born
lambs, or townsmen in thin cotton tunics with the Nepalese striped
and brocaded *topi* set at jaunty angles over aquiline or moon-faced and
snub-nosed features. Women wore gay saris and heavy, silver-mounted
jewellery, some had gold nose rings or a bright jewel in one nostril,
which told which village they came from. Nearly all had scarlet *tikkas*
painted on their foreheads to proclaim their Hindu faith. Some were
young and pretty, but their exotic glamour was sorely diminished by very
Western woolly cardigans – just as the elegant, timeless lines of the
men's *kurta*, or tunic shirt and jodhpurs, have now been ruined in India
and Nepal by the addition of Western suit jackets.

'What did Nepalese wear in winter *before* you took to blazers?' I asked
Mr Pandi.

'I suppose we all shivered,' he answered as we drove under the welcome
arches and through milling crowd-lined streets. Our jeep, passing through

various checkpoints manned by smartly saluting soldiers, came finally to a halt on high ground on the other side of the town in what looked like another royal camp. There were neatly mown lawns, rows of barrack-like buildings and offices, several much larger buildings and a magnificent dais draped in scarlet, which faced a crowd of several thousands in a fenced-off area at the bottom of the hill; flags and bunting and tinsel and flowers wherever one looked; and away to the right where the ground sloped steeply down to the river valley, a grey square with a white circle painted on its centre – the royal helicopter pad.

And, as always in Nepal, on the far horizon and high up in the sky, range upon range of the greatest and most beautiful mountains in the world, standing quietly sentinel; watching, waiting; part of the scene from time immemorial yet sublimely removed from it, and making the antics of us poor mortals look flimsy, ephemeral, and of very small consequence.

We were just in time; the noisy crowd fell silent as a small red object appeared and circled twice above us, then with all the delicacy of a hovering dragonfly dropped gently down on to the exact middle of the circle and let its whirring blades come to rest. King Birendra emerged, in cream-coloured kurta and embroidered topi, Queen Aishwarya followed in a green and silver sari – dignitaries rushed to meet them, bowing low with joined palms in courteous *namastes*, and with schoolchildren scattering rice and flowers before them, they were escorted to the royal dais and installed on two thrones. The crowd below us went wild, we advanced discreetly with a posse of cameramen as far as we dared when, to our amazement, we were seized hold of by a couple of colonels and propelled towards two minor thrones, or armchairs, outside the dais, which had been prepared for us. It was like that all day: wherever the king and queen went we were squeezed in and made welcome as their guests, and occasionally, but only very occasionally, they would catch our eye and smile.

The performance started with the National Anthem, then a seemingly endless line of elders passed below the dais, performing their *namastes* with the utmost fervour and devotion, then placing their offerings on a table below the dais. These were immediately pounced upon and neatly piled into heaps by several uniformed Girl Guides (rather like Wimbledon ball-boys retrieving dead balls). A few carried small bunches of crimson *Rhododendron arboreum*, which gladdened my gardener's heart, for not only is it the national flower of Nepal, but it also grows in my own woodland garden in Argyll.

When the village and town Panchayats stopped processing, women's organisations followed, some in the grey-blue cotton saris of Red Cross and health workers, then representatives of the various class organisations. It seemed to go on for ever and no one was left out. Meanwhile, we and the crowd were simultaneously entertained by cheerful displays of folk-dancing and by the spirited singing of children's choirs.

When we finally broke for lunch, we talked to a representative of the Nepal Ex-Servicemen's Organisation – a tiny ex-British Army Gurkha in a smart uniform with a chestful of medals and a smattering of English, who had marched for three days from his mountain home and was as delighted to see us as we were to meet him. We ate our boxed lunches in a building like a cricket pavilion while the king received delegations from the class organisations in one of the camp's audience halls. After lunch we separated and I followed the queen's progress through a series of visits to new Red Cross and medical headquarters where she cut ribbons and addressed committee meetings of officials, then on, through happy, cheering crowds, to a district medical headquarters where two young doctors, one qualified, the other a paramedic, showed her how various development schemes and public health targets were progressing in the Damauli district.

There are paramedics and medical stations within reach of most communities in Nepal today, but outside the valleys there is only one qualified doctor for every 100,000 people. A system, therefore, has been set up of medical camps which, like travelling hospitals, tour the country once a year with a dozen doctors and surgeons who diagnose, treat and operate on the spot, or send back to central hospitals cases who need major surgery. Minor cases and terminally ill people are turned away and left to the care of local wise women. 'We are a Third World country,' the queen told me sadly, 'and we have to stretch our limited resources in the best way possible; there is still a lot of suffering that we cannot help.'

There was nothing hesitant or shy about Queen Aishwarya's approach to charitable work. Within minutes she had entered into lively discussion, questioned speakers closely, listened to replies and delivered what sounded to me like shrewd comment, as well as encouragement. For all her gentle femininity she is obviously a woman of practical intelligence, with a positive mind and a talent for summing up a situation and making decisions. Our last visit, before the queen too held audience in the Royal Camp, was to an orphaned children's school. The welcoming ceremony ended in one of the classrooms, where the Queen sat in dignified and inscrutable majesty (dark glasses firmly in place) on a raised platform, while one by one the teachers and members of youth and women's organisations filed past, performing their obeisances with the usual deep reverence. There were speeches, medal giving, a bag of money collected for a good cause, which Queen Aishwarya augmented by fifty per cent, and finally a song and dance performance by the children. Four nimble little boys and pretty little girls gyrated and clapped their way through innumerable rhythmic verses, while between them a deeply concentrated (and adorable) three-year-old kept perfect time with a tiny stamp in counterpoint.

When the dance was finished, all the children filed past the queen, performing their namastes with varying degrees of fervour, their eyes fixed on the large packet of sweets which each of them was about to receive from Her Majesty. When we left, again among cheering crowds, every child was happily chewing.

Back at the camp, we found the king's audience chamber full; we tiptoed in through a side door and sat down to watch. What we were witnessing was the involvement of the Crown in the Panchayat system, and the system itself, at work. The king was seated at a large desk on a dais at one end of the hall, with his secretary and clerk on his right and three high officials, or 'wise men', on his left. Below them, and equally official-looking, sat two elders, the District Panchayat President and his Vice-president.

In the body of the hall, ranged in military files of nine, were the elected representatives of the village assemblies – the village Panchayats. At the head of each file were the spokesman chief and his seconder (*Pradon Pancha* and *Upa Pradhan Pancha*), and behind them the seven other members who could also put in a word if they felt like it (and often did – though they were sometimes shut up if they rambled on too long). The king listened carefully to each case, consulted papers, maps, records, asked questions of both ministers and elders and dictated notes to his secretary with what seemed to me dedicated thoroughness. It was like a British MP's constituency 'surgery', except that here the minister concerned was on the spot, as well as heads of local government and experts, not to mention sovereign power that could, if necessary, over-rule the lot of them.

Yet it was not an awe-inspiring occasion. No doubt His Majesty had met many of the elders many times before, and the atmosphere was convivial as well as respectful, jokes were cracked, and the whole procedure was conducted with good humour – even when requests were refused or schemes changed. He was their king, one felt, and they were enjoying every minute of their joint performance and would talk about it endlessly in the months ahead.

We passed on to the queen's audience hall, where much the same scene was being enacted between Her Majesty and the office-bearers of the women's organisations, the teachers and social workers. It was very impressive to see a queen so totally and personally involved, and when we left the building I saw mountains of books, packaged into nylon sacks for easy transport, being distributed to the women's organisations by Her Majesty's secretariat.

The crowds round the camp were now thinning and many families were wrapping babies more firmly into shawls and gathering children and possessions together in preparation for their long trek back to their mountain homes. We climbed into our comfortable jeep and headed back to Pokhara, thankful there was not a two-day climb ahead of us, but Their Majesties were still hard at it when we left Damauli and Mr Pandi assured us that the debriefing with government officials at the Royal Camp would last for many hours into the night.

The king's doctor paid us a visit that night, armed with a sphygnoman-ometer and a bottle of Marfa, which is the quite exceptionally good local applejack – a lot smoother than the average Calvados and tasting more of fresh apples. After ascertaining that our blood pressure was that of teenagers, he stayed and talked. He told us that if every village or community in Nepal had tap water or enough fuel to boil water and the nous to do it, 'forty per cent of our illness and half of our infant mortality would be eradicated', but that ignorance, lack of fuel, deforestation and the almost insurmountable problem of the Himalayan terrain itself made this a distant goal. We all agreed that hydro-electric schemes would be one answer, but 'they need enormous capital investment, and Nepal is a poor country'.

At six o'clock the next morning, the 'Fish-tail' glowed with all the colours of a rainbow trout, and there were only a few wispy clouds around it by the time we had polished off the delicious eggs and bacon that the Pishti hotel provides at breakfast-time.

King Birendra and Queen Aishwarya were just coming out of their large villa-cum-palace as we drove up, and we walked with them to the helicopter pad on the other side of the garden. That morning the queen was wearing a pale blue sari and a blue silk bandeau with a little jewelled tassel in her very black hair and, of course, the ubiquitous sunglasses. She looked very pretty (except for the shades). Courtiers carried two jumbo duck-down anoraks, and I was glad to see that the army had rustled up two rather more workaday khaki cotton ones for Fitz and me. (Mustang, which is the other side of Annapurna, is nearly 13,000 feet high, with an almost permanent wind blowing straight off the glaciers.)

We passed a line of low-bowing dignitaries, then another of the senior officers of the camp, standing at rigid attention; salutes were exchanged and we climbed into the very comfortable four-seater royal cabin of the Alouette helicopter. The king, taking off his padded anorak, Nepalese topi (and, thank goodness, his dark glasses), exchanged it for a scarlet baseball cap and passed through to the flight deck to take over the controls himself.

The ADC general, the doctor, Mr Pandi, a secretary and a couple of photographers occupied the rear cabin. Soon we were up and away, flying first along a river valley, then across a watershed, and finally towards the great Annapurna Range and the narrow gap between its towering escarpments of sand-coloured rock, here and there powdered with snow. We flew through it and a new and pitiless landscape of high snow peaks and a desert of rocky flat-lands now lay below us. Soon we were approaching our destination, a wide mountain valley which slopes gently towards the east. Yaks and sheep, like tiny clusters of black flies, gathered round feeding stations and scattered wildly as the helicopter's shadow passed over them. Here and there crumbling walls ghosted the outline of an earlier civilisation, but it was impossible to tell whether they were monasteries or sheep-folds or ancient chateaux-forts.

And then we saw it, lying immediately below us, a scarcely believable, tiny, mediaeval toy town, a fortified mini-city, neatly defined by the perfect rectangle of its own high, wine-red walls. Inside these and at the very centre a large, tall building and, at one end, an obvious monastery in the same blackcurrant-fool red; closely packed houses, flat roofs with clusters of people standing on them, waving. But there was no time to observe more. His Majesty was bringing the machine down to a gentle landing on the bull's-eye pad outside the city gate.

There is only one gate into Monthang Lo, which is the ancient name of the country and its capital, and that is still shut at dusk and opened at dawn, originally to keep out the Khampas or Tibetan brigands, but now probably only to deter a few pilgrims and wandering yaks. It was very much open to us, and decorated with floss and tinsel and flags and bunting. A part-religious, part-royal welcoming party poured out of it towards the helicopter, whose passengers were being helped into their various comforters for the temperature was at least 13° cooler than at Pokhara.

Their Majesties were immediately surrounded and swallowed up by the crowd, to be borne away in a cheerful, noisy and only semi-ceremonial procession. The four classes of the Kingdom of Lo – nobles (dukes and barons), lamas, yeomen and serfs – were all, no doubt, well represented in the throng (though it was not easy to tell which was which), while the rest of Monthang poked their heads over the walls or stood on their roof-tops, cheering. The colours and clothes of the crowd were as mind-blasting as the music from the gongs and drums and horns and conches of the monastery band. We followed at a discreet distance and stopped in front of the king's winter palace, a whitewashed and black-beamed edifice, Tibetan in style, walls narrowing towards the roof, windows only starting twenty feet up, whose massive stone base was that of a formidable fortress.

It was the large building we had seen from the air and it stood on one side of a central square. Here dancers and musicians were lining up to entertain the visitors. There was a lot of leaping and twirling and archery movements but when we brought out our cameras the dancers froze – no doubt in well-meant cooperation with our Fuji-chrome 400, which they did not distinguish from the plate photography of their last European visitor.

Their Nepalese Majesties had disappeared up a stone staircase on one side of the palace's wide entrance. This was as steep as a ladder, with each step nearly two feet high. A message came down it to say the Rajah of Mustang/King of Lo would be happy to receive us. The cluster of officials and courtiers around us looked doubtfully at our mountaineering potential and then offered to *carry* us up. 'It's the usual thing,' whispered King Birendra's ADC, 'think nothing of it. Just get up piggy-back on to this man, he can carry *an ox* up Mount Everest.' He indicated a giant Mustangan, possibly a duke, who smiled encouragingly but fell flat on his face when, after the first two steps, he received the full sum of my avoirdupois. Hoping it was bashfulness that had caused the collapse, and suppressing a fit of the giggles, I clambered off him and proceeded on my own, and indeed the next two storeys of ladder-like staircases, which were made of wood, seemed much easier.

Windows only began at the first floor and there was a central courtyard with galleries running round it and small rooms opening off them. The chamber into which we finally staggered was on the top floor (a ladder led up from its gallery to the flat roof) and was much larger. It was lit by a double row of leaded, diamond-paned windows which looked down on the courtyard; the crowds and the dancers (who were still performing) a long, long way below. The room seemed full of people all dressed in exotic and strange Tibetan clothes. We were pushed towards the cushion-covered window seat on which King Birendra and Queen Aish-warya were already sitting, all too conscious that we were not following the correct, courteous Mustang protocol. Are white silk scarves pre-

sented? Should we namaste once or three times? We did not even know
to whom our obeisances should be directed. But once seated and given
an encouraging grin from our twentieth-century king, I began to take in
the surroundings.

The room was roughly divided by four carved wooden pillars which
rose from the wooden floor to the heavily beamed ceilings. In one of the
four corners was an altar, round which hung many *tankas* and on which
lamps burned. I could dimly discern sacred vessels and a gold bas-relief
of the Lord Buddha. There were several lamas in the background but
they seemed to be in a subservient role, perhaps royal chaplains? The
very tall and altogether large man with a flat, smiling and unlined face
was obviously King Angun Tensing Trandul, for he stood on the right
of the seated Birendra, orchestrating the proceedings. He wore a leather
hat, rather like a 1914 RFC airman's, with ear flaps and a bright yellow
silk lining, and a handsome blue silk robe that was lined with curly white
lambskin.

Little chest-like tables were placed in front of us and an elderly lady,
whom I took to be the Queen of Lo – grey hair in neat plaits and a grey
sari and lots of turquoise and gold necklaces – directed a number of
servitors. Tibetan milky tea was brought (the Nepalese royalty were
served in beautiful silver bowls with dunce's-hat-shaped, carved and
chased covers; we simple folk in ordinary cups and saucers). Then came
momos,* little sweet cakes, and other Tibetan delicacies. While this was
going on, speeches of welcome were being made, a long declaration was
read from a scroll by the king's right-hand man, an impressive looking
individual who stood close by him, and presents were exchanged – the
donors kneeling and bowing low as they handed over their gifts.

Discussions followed and a very good-looking, slim young man, who
I later learned was the Crown Prince, the King of Lo's eldest son, took
part in these. I also learned that in the kingdom, when the eldest son
of the family marries his father 'retires'; the second son has usually chosen
a monastic career and become a lama, while the third, fourth and any
other sons move into the paternal house with their eldest brother, who
then takes over the governance of the family and its properties. The
brothers apparently live in perfect amity, sharing *everything* (including
the eldest brother's wife). It is as good a method of preventing a family's
wealth from being dissipated as any I have heard of, and I wondered if
this custom is still upheld and if it had already happened in today's royal

---

* The meat-stuffed dumplings beloved by Tibetans, Chinese, Mongolians and most North Asian
races.

family, for the king did not seem to play a very active role apart from being an attentive host. On the other hand his wishes may have been conveyed through his 'right arm', the councillor-courtier who never left his side.

Both the queen and the crown prince have lived outside the kingdom much more than he has, the queen being a graduate of a Nepalese university and the crown prince, also a graduate, now only spending summers in Mustang. But for the majority of Mustang's inhabitants, the mediaeval institutions, local laws and social pattern have changed very little in the last 600 years since, in 1460, the dynasty was founded, a dynasty of which the present king is the twenty-fifth descendant.

The greater part of the town's population had already moved down to lower and kinder regions of the country, as they always do every winter, partly to trade their animals, but mostly because there simply is not enough fuel, fodder or food to support more than half the population in the wind-swept, desert-surrounded city. But to us there still seemed a great many inhabitants, perhaps swelled by other villagers who had come from afar to greet King Birendra – and the narrow, winding streets, when we emerged from the palace, were crammed.

We caught the tail-end of the religious procession which was wending its way back from the Temple of Thugchen.* The monks were dressed in the same claret red as their monastery walls. As the temple musicians passed I noticed one carried a large and beautiful conch shell decorated with a fine tracery of gold through which he blew long, mournful notes, a homesick, melancholy sound, as if it was calling from its present harsh and land-locked exile to a wave-lapped, sunny homeland in distant southern seas.

The houses are mostly two-storeyed (only nobles are allowed a third and no roof can be higher than the walls of the city – except the king's). The ground floor acts as stable, storehouse or shop, the upper one is for sleeping and living in during the winter; but in summer, rooftop life is the most popular and, anyway, half the population takes to the high passes, herding their animals and leading a near-nomadic life. The Tibetan (which is now the Chinese) border is only six miles away and, where once there was a steady flow of trade, pilgrims and scholars, regular communication has now stopped, owing to the restrictions of the Chinese government and its persecution of the Tibetan monks.

---

* There are two temples in Lo Mustang: Thugchen, with fading eighteenth-century frescoes, and a smaller temple dedicated to Chamba Maitrena, with frescoes and a mandala of Dorge Sempe, neither in very good shape.

There are eighteen passes between the high ranges of Nepal and Tibet, but the comparatively easy route via Mustang contributed to its eminence and riches in the past. Salt from Tibet was exchanged for beasts from Mustang or other goods that came up from the rich lowlands of Nepal. That many pilgrims had passed through its great gate and worshipped at its temples was evident from the stone slabs, carved and inscribed in Tibetan script, that many of the street walls had tucked in to their ledges, like books into bookcases, together with animal skulls and other strange offerings.

While my husband photographed everything within sight, I peered into houses and chatted to the inhabitants in sign language, while they did the same to me, roaring with laughter, for I have seldom met people so cheerful, friendly and merry.

All too soon the procession returned from the temple and headed for the great outer walls and city gate. Her Majesty had told me that the wind never stops blowing in Mustang and that the walls are essential to protect its inhabitants from being blown away. This is certainly true as every day, with clockwork regularity, it builds up in the funnel between Annapurna and Dal and blows fiercely from 12 noon till dusk. But they are also defensive walls that have deflected many assaults throughout the centuries. They are proof against arrow and shot, but would they withstand the tanks and artillery of ruthless modern armies across the border? As we whirled up into the sky, I hoped very much that under the benign protection of King Birendra they will never have to.

That same evening, back in the Royal Camp at Pokhara, we were received in audience by King Birendra – it was as friendly and informal as our first meeting. I told him how impressed we had been by seeing the Panchayat system actually working – grassroot participation in a clearly democratic process – and then added: 'but what would happen if the king who succeeded you was lazy, incompetent and backward-looking?'

He answered that the power of the Prime Minister would then assume greater importance, and that *his* power could also be held in check by that of the Chairman and Vice-Chairman of the Council of Ministers who could, with the consent of the Assembly, vote a Prime Minister out of office. 'The Constitution which my father gave the people of Nepal in 1959 has been amended several times,' he told us, 'and now a series of checks and counter-checks virtually rules out any undemocratic abuse of power. But no system is perfect,' he ended, 'and we are continually reappraising and fining down our own polity.'

I asked him about the Zone of Peace, to which Nepal belongs, having

HM King Birendra of Nepal, with Queen Aishwarya,
Crown Prince Dipendra, Princess Sruti, and Prince Nirajan

reciprocal obligations with 107 other countries to live in peaceful co-existence with each other. India has signed it but China has not. 'If you were invaded by any Asian superpower,' I asked, 'would you fight?' This was perhaps too direct a question and he answered it diplomatically. 'In the ordinary course of events our country's policy is one of non-alignment and neutrality . . . Nepal has always been a free and independent sovereign state . . . The Peace Zone movement and their policy of non-alignment were designed to give security to the smaller nations . . . A decision for any deviation from this policy in a national emergency would be taken by the King and the Prime Minister.' We left it at that.

Though the original cause for the movement was the now-ended antagonism of Eastern and Western superpowers, the economic problems of the Third World still remained. The undeveloped emergent nations, of which Nepal was one, needed more than ever protection against the economic might of the superpowers. The 108 non-aligned countries should stand together so that their voice too could be heard in international debate.

'And what about monarchical power?' I asked him. 'According to your father's 1962 Constitution, which was promulgated after the collapse of parliamentary government, "the sovereignty of Nepal is vested in the King – all powers, executive, legislative and judicial, emanate from him". Thus you are the head of the government and the State, and the Crown in Nepal has a paramount role above all other legislators. You can dismiss a government and its officers or call an election at any time. You appoint the Prime Minister (admittedly in consultation with your ministers and the National Panchayat), and, besides all this, to most of your Hindu subjects you are the incarnation of the Lord Vishnu, a demi-God!'

Birendra had his dark glasses on, and I could not see whether he looked amused or indignant, but he explained in a rather charming self-deprecatory way that monarchs in Nepal have ruled the country for a long time, in harmony with the will and the interests of its people, and that the people have always looked to their kings for leadership, to preserve and protect national independence and sovereignty, and to promote their well-being. His ancestor, King Prithri Narayan Shah, unified its many principalities in the eighteenth century, and since then both the institutions of monarchy and Panchayat – the leadership of the Crown and this form of village democracy – have been deep-rooted in the country's traditions.

He explained that of the twenty-eight parliamentary seats that he nominates, the majority go to women and to intellectuals, who are not always chosen by the National Assembly and who are needed in the

legislature. He smiled when explaining his position in the Hindu pantheon: 'You as a Christian believe in the Trinity and the three persons
in the Godhead. In the Hindu religion the Lord Vishnu has three aspects:
1) the Creator; 2) the Preserver; 3) the Destroyer. Monarchy in Nepal
is simply linked with the visible, earthly role of this second aspect of the
Godhead: Vishnu, the Preserver. My powers are earthly, the Lord
Vishnu's spiritual. This is often misunderstood by Westerners and, of
course, very simple people in my kingdom can also exaggerate and mis-
construe it. But you, too, I think, believe that monarchy has a spiritual
role.'

I hastened to assure him that anyone who had seen a British king or
queen crowned could not fail to appreciate the spiritual and sacramental
aspect of that beautiful and ancient ceremony, which still links our
sovereigns with an earlier, sacerdotal role.

We talked about the character of the Nepalese people, their great
tolerance for other races and religions and, indeed, for any ways of life
that were different from their own, their flexibility and their natural
kindness. The only thing that is forbidden to foreign missionaries in
Nepal, he told me, is forcible conversion, proselytising by threat or by
bribery. He also told me that at that moment there was a Catholic, an
ex-Communist and several ex-members of the Congress Party among his
ministers, 'one of whom is my Minister for Education'. And there are
some women ministers, 'whom we need very badly to help upgrade the
position of women in Nepal'. I asked him about the objective of the
Panchayat Policy – *Mulki Ain* – which aims at eradicating the caste
system in Nepal and the position of the untouchables. He told me that
the constitution did not recognise *any* form of caste, that in law it was
forbidden and that people could appeal against caste discrimination; but
in fact, he added sadly, it still exists. 'What has been a social tradition for
generations cannot be eliminated overnight. Of course its very existence
provides fuel for our system's critics. But it *is* slowly disappearing and we
are continually working at it . . . Education and the Basic Needs and
Social Justice programmes will help speed up the process. For example,
a former untouchable has actually become one of my ministers, I'm
delighted to say.'

When my husband asked King Birendra if he would allow political
parties to be revived in Nepal, the King answered with some asperity
that the Panchayat system was a party-less system and that it had been
chosen in preference to a multi-party one by a majority of his subjects
in the 1981 referendum. To bring back a system which had been proved
to be corrupt and destabilising and that did not suit the majority of his

people would be to betray that majority, and this he would never do.

I had one more question: 'Do you ever have time for leisure, for hobbies, for the family?' and he answered that his work was his hobby, but that he firmly believed in an eight-hour day, 'and Saturdays off!' He also said that the queen was his constant companion and help in all his work and now that the royal children, Crown Prince Dipendra, Prince Nirajan and Princess Sruti were older, they also often accompanied them and shared many of their duties.

We said our goodbyes with genuine gratitude and affection and also a certain amount of sadness, for in our minds there was little doubt that Birendra's stubborn yet honourable adherence to a status quo which was unacceptable to a large and noisy part of the population was going to cause him great trouble in the near future.

We spent another ten days in Nepal, waiting impatiently for our visas for Bhutan, alarmed for King Birendra's sake by the fast deteriorating situation, but visiting as much of the country as was possible. We followed the usual tourist trail: drives into the foothills to look for rhododendrons; Buddhist and Hindu temples; viewpoints for Everest; visits to Patan and Bhaktapur, the most militantly radical town in the valley, with a long history of political unrest. There, child beggars swarm round the tourists like gnats, many are professionals from India and Bangladesh (Nepali children never beg), but it did not need their cultivated piteousness to remind one of the grinding poverty and backwardness of the vast majority of townspeople in Nepal.

Standing on the bridge below the Pashupatinath temple, I watched the bundled remains of burnt corpses turn slowly round in the muddy but sacred waters below. On one bank of the river, along the ghats, pilgrim women were washing clothes and filling brass and plastic jars with water. On the other side, on stone piles of great antiquity, the funeral pyres were glowing. The saddest memory I have is coming face to face with a young Nepali from up-country whose eyes had that bewildered, lost look of a sorrow too great to bear. He was carrying in his arms the tiny wrapped bundle of his baby's corpse, and he didn't know where to go, or who to turn to, to help him start the long and comforting rituals for its soul's salvation. He just stood there, alone in his silent and patient suffering. I doubt if a new constitution or party politics would do anything to help him, or many thousands like him, for many years to come.

Meanwhile, the political situation continued to deteriorate. The very next day, in Kathmandu, 'No taxis today, Sahib,' said the resplendent doorman at the Soaltee Oberoi Hotel, where we had returned from Pokhara to five-star luxury, and he looked rather pleased about it. 'It would be better to visit the bazaar tomorrow, sir,' said the under-manager, and he looked deeply worried. A lightning strike of all workers had been called by the Congress Party (illegal but tolerated). Shops were closed and rioting had broken out down-town. A few bricks were thrown and a few tourists were panicked, but the riot police, mostly conscripted youths from up-country, who until then had never seen, let alone dealt with a riot, kept their heads, and quickly restored order; 700 people were arrested and 200 immediately released, there were no casualties.

You would not have thought so from the headlines in the papers next morning. The situation was blown up out of all proportion and the foreign, especially the Indian, press added fuel to the flames. A 'Movement for Restoration of Democracy' (MRD) was supported in a statement by 1,800 lawyers. The Congress Party, whose strings were pulled by Indian politicians, entered into a coalition with various left-wing and Communist parties.

A statement challenging the government was signed by a third of the parliamentarians, a former Prime Minister, six ex-ministers and, worse still, from the position of the embattled monarchy, a deliberate campaign of slander and vilification was directed at poor Queen Aishwarya. No one, radical politician, agent provocateur or revolutionary, however, dared criticise the king, which they knew would have been counter-productive, but Queen Aishwarya was a member of the unpopular Rana family and therefore was fair game for bazaar gossip and slander, which soon reached the realm of almost comic fantasy.

And then on 6 April, a bungled order precipitated a crisis that nearly brought down the monarchy. An unruly mob, shouting for political reform, marched down the street that leads to the palace. The soldiers guarding it mistakenly believed they were about to be attacked and, panicking, fired directly into the crowd. Figures differ wildly, but in all probability at least fifty people were killed. The media made a meal of it and world opinion hardened against what it was told was a corrupt and absolute monarch's intransigence.

On 16 April, the king, to defuse the crisis, lifted the ban on political parties and promised the country elections and a new constitution, in which his powers would inevitably be greatly reduced. He had no other choice.

Nepal is a country rapidly emerging from a primitive past, but the basic trouble is that it is emerging at two different paces. In the foothills of the Himalaya, which cover 90 per cent of the whole country, there has been enormous progress in the last twenty years: better communication, better medical care, better hygiene and clean water, but most of all, organised education has revolutionised the social fabric of the country. Tourism has become its greatest asset and involves the people of the hills, for trekking is one of its most popular forms. Literacy, which was just about zero among the rural population twenty years ago, has now reached 25 per cent of it and is growing daily with the children of a new generation. Queen Aishwarya, who is actively involved in the drive for it, told me that she hoped it would reach 50 per cent by 1995. Land reform, improved methods of agriculture, technical colleges, re-afforestation, hydro-electric schemes all help, but there is still great poverty and many problems to overcome.

In the cities and the Terai, economic and social change has been even faster. There has been a population explosion and the poverty is more obvious, the difference between poor and rich more acute. A professional and even a middle class has emerged in the last decade, hungry for a share in political power and capable of exploiting the masses to achieve it.

Consensus between the politically minded townsfolk and growing middle-class and the 17 million traditionally-minded rural subjects of a benign but autocratic king, is something that at first sight would seem difficult to achieve unless both sides show tolerance and flexibility. But the Nepalese, unlike the excitable, passionately political people of India, are an extremely tolerant, peace-loving and adaptable race, and I believe that it is not beyond their powers to draft a constitution and find a compromise that will suit everyone.

On our last day in Kathmandu we talked to two people who knew Nepal and the royal families better than anyone else. Lord Camoys, who has acted as Birendra's English tutor and friend since his early schooldays and remains deeply attached to him, and Father Moran, the remarkable ninety-year-old Rector of St Francis Xavier's College, who has probably educated half the educated people in the country. He came to Nepal seventy years ago as a young Canadian Jesuit missionary and founded a small non-denominational school which just grew until it became the biggest and best in Nepal. He still lives a busy, hard-working, prayerful life – but he said Mass for us in his private chapel and sat us down afterwards to a simple breakfast and a flood of amusing, irreverent and well-informed comment delivered in a kind of Mark Twain idiom, with a Canadian accent. Outside, in the well-kept garden, a bee-keeping Father from Brazil tended the College's apiary with the total devotion that is in itself a form of prayer.

Tom Camoys utterly rejected the press hysteria about the king and queen. 'The nicest thing about our life together, when, as a young man only a few years older than Birendra, I lived in Nepal and was seeing him every day, was the simplicity and lack of sophistication of their lives. We swam and played tennis, we went for picnics or on hunting expeditions, we lay about and talked, endlessly; in the evening, sometimes, musicians would come to entertain us or we would dance to old gramophone records. All Nepalis love dancing and singing; there wasn't much more to it than that. No orgies, no ostentation, no great luxury or expenditure. I know for a fact that neither the king nor the queen have foreign bank accounts, and I really wonder if any of these "liberal" journalists have been inside the Royal Palace in Kathmandu. As palaces go, it is really quite small and not very richly furnished – pretty hideous, in fact. I also know that if the referendum in 1981 had gone against the king, he would have suspended the Panchayat system of government and accepted a multi-party one – but it didn't. He is a very honest and serious fellow, and a good and kindly one. He cares deeply about his country's independence and *all* his people's well-being; but if I were to write or say that publicly, I would immediately be accused of partisanship.'

We both agreed that the dark glasses were a mistake and he told me he had teased them about it often enough, 'but they both feel that in some way they protect their privacy'.

'Could it be that among simple people the stare of a king who is also a demi-God is too awesome for his subjects to behold?'

Tom did not think so, and we both laughingly agreed that a whizz-kid PR man and a really good press officer could be one of the palace expenses that would be more than justified. However, in this connection, the Nepalese monarchy is still as 'backward' in its thinking as many of its mountain subjects; it is a major part of their indisputable charm. For Nepal is a country which waves charm over one like a silken net, and once caught in it, it is difficult to escape. Whether Birendra remains a ruling monarch or just a constitutional one, I shall go back to Nepal and visit him whenever His Majesty asks me.

A few months after we had left Nepal, I was sent a cutting from the *New Delhi Times*: 'The new pro-democracy Government has dismantled the remnants of King Birendra's *Panchayat* political system, which governed Nepal for 29 years,' said a spokesman for the Nepali Congress Party. The decision was conveyed to the Nepali Congress by Mr Krishna Prasad Bhattarai, the Prime Minister. 'From now on there is no *Panchayat* from village level to national level in the country,' he said. 'This is a very drastic and swift step towards fulfilling the aspirations of the people.'

One cannot help wondering *which* people.

Pro-democracy?

It was in Nepal that I first began to doubt the meaning of the word 'democracy' or, rather, to realise it meant something different in almost every country I had visited. Etymologically, democracy means 'power of the people' and ideally it means the equal power of *all* the people of a nation. But in practice a nation's people are far from equal – particularly in Third-World countries – and even with a ballot box and the most democratic intentions, some people turn out to be, in George Orwell's immortal phrase, 'more equal than others'.

Nepal had been a blatant example of this and the 'Democracy!' one heard shouted as a buzz-word on the streets of Bhaktapur meant by and large 'Republicanism!' – while to the left-wing agitators it signified a socialist state under the hegemony of the country's land-hungry and powerful neighbour, the Indian sub-continent, a sad future for a freedom-loving people.

We had witnessed personally the traditional form of democracy as exercised by the Panchayat system under King Birendra and his elders, and it seemed to us fair enough, but we had also realised that the pace of economic advance was too slow to be patiently waited for by the desperately poor people of the city slums. We knew that the king was too involved, too compassionate, and not ruthless enough to clamp down on their impatience (and perhaps too stubborn to accelerate the pace) and we saw that, sadly, his position was bound to change and a lot of what was unique in Nepal would disappear.

I found it was the same in many countries where traditional authority struggles to retain an imperfect but improvable and slowly improving system of government against the 'quick-fixes' of emergent and often dangerous politicians who frequently use the word 'democracy' as bait for their own advancement. They all mean something different by it, which is another way of saying that no one knows exactly what it means. Monarchy and democracy are not incompatible, but an absolute monarchy cannot become a democratic one without a certain amount of patience and pain – neither can real democracy be learned by a people overnight.

It must be a process of evolution, what Edmund Burke called 'the habit of compromise' and Prince Charles, 'the ability to adapt to changing circumstances'. We in Great Britain learned it under all those Henrys and Edwards (and more sharply under William of Orange) a long, long time ago. It is a confusing lesson for a country's people to learn quickly and in this impatient age a difficult one for traditional monarchy suddenly to accept.

I was therefore heartened to hear again from Tom Camoys that in Nepal a peaceful compromise had, after all, been reached. The new constitution has certainly reduced King Birendra's powers, but it has also silenced many of his critics (who have the new government to criticise instead). King Birendra is still the country's statesman with the greatest experience in government, and the only one who need not think about being re-elected, for he is still revered by the majority of his subjects. He is often quietly consulted now, and his advice is frequently taken, and although today he keeps a lower political profile, he may well find that in this way he can achieve more of the reforms that he initiated under the Panchayat system. Certainly, many of the programmes he put into place are still being carried out, and this is what he will care about most, for he knows and loves all of his people, and his greatest interest is their welfare. He is a good king, and a most likeable one but, though he explained his demi-God descent to us very lucidly, I am afraid I did not detect any divine–magic–mysterious element in his personality. He just seemed to me, as Charlie put it, 'a thoroughly decent fellow'.

15

BHUTAN

King Jigme Seyen Wangchuk

'Monarchs have a religious sanction that confirms political order.'

WALTER BAGEHOT

Bhutan also lies within the shadow of India, but it is not quite so vulnerable as Nepal. Bhutan is by tradition an oligarchy ruled by kings and lama monks but of late it has become what might be called a monarchical theocracy, or a theocratic monarchy with the accent on the monarch. It has made King Jigme Seyen Wangchuk all the more secure, for a nation's strong religious faith, backed up by a monastic aristocracy, sets a king firmly on his throne as long as he remains at the apex of its hierarchy. Just as it did, I suppose, in earlier, primitive times. Indeed, perhaps Nepal's tolerance of all beliefs, of which King Birendra was so proud, may have worked, in the long run, to his disadvantage.

In the small part of Bhutan that we visited there was such universal loyalty and respect for both monarch and abbot that I cannot believe that the king's position will ever be threatened. Nevertheless, if I were he I would keep the communication system of Bhutan as basic as possible. Roads only lead to trouble, as we will see in the following pages.

B hutan is a country which is very difficult to get into and very hard to leave.

After complaints a year or more ago that tourists were disturbing the monks' meditations, their numbers were severely reduced to about 1,500 a year, for the Bhutanese are one of the few nations in the world who realise that, if you want to keep a country's culture intact and admirable, you must keep *out* the visitors who are queuing to get *in* to admire it. Months before leaving London I had asked for an audience with King Jigme Seyen Wangchuk and we applied repeatedly for visas

through the Bhutanese ambassador in Delhi, via our own High Commissioner in India, protocol being a tortuous affair in the 'Land of the
Thunder Dragon'. We had hoped for an answer before leaving Nepal, as
logistically it is the nearest port of entry to Bhutan, but when we returned
to Kathmandu from Pokhara we learnt that all Bhutanese officialdom
had closed down for at least a fortnight, in celebration of a religious
festival of great significance, 'and answer came there none'.

There are only two flights a week from Kathmandu to Paro, Bhutan's
pocket-handkerchief-sized airport and Fitzroy, my husband, had a deadline in London which loomed ever nearer. For one whole anxious week
we haunted the down-town offices of Druk airline and sent frantic faxes
off to Delhi. At last an incoming pilot from Paro brought with him
deliverance in the shape of a personal invitation from the Bhutanese
Foreign Minister, and, Glory-be-to-God, our visas, but the letter also
delivered a knock-out blow, for it explained that His Majesty, King
Jigme Seyen Wangchuk, had now started on his annual tour of the
remoter provinces of Bhutan and much regretted he would not be able
to receive us in Thimpu.

The aircraft was refuelling, and leaving in an hour. There was just
time to catch it, the visas and invitation were burning holes in our
pockets – something might possibly happen to change the king's itinerary
. . . we had always longed to visit Bhutan . . . it was just too good a
chance to miss. We took it.

Our first intimation that someone important was also flying to Paro
was an official flurry at the airport, but it was not until we had squeezed
ourselves and Fitzroy's cameras into the British Aerospace 146, the pride
of our helpful Himalayan airline, that we realised that it was our old
friend, General Yakub Khan, the evergreen Foreign Secretary of Paki-
stan,* who had caused the commotion. He was as delighted as we were
by such a trick of fate and immediately asked us to dinner that evening
in Thimpu, as his official conversations with the King of Bhutan and
India's latest Trade Minister were scheduled to begin only the next day.

And so, nine hours later, and still hopeful, we stepped gingerly over
a mosaic of flower petals and arabesqued sand that had been laid in
traditional welcome for General Yakub and entered the lofty portals of
the Bhutanese Royal Guest House to find Yakub Khan alone – he had
dismissed his aides – and shivering. We were, after all, 7,000 feet above
sea-level, it was February and the hardy Bhutanese, themselves impervi-
ous to cold, regard central heating as foreign decadence.

* Now retired to his country estates, but still an influence to be reckoned with.

The evening that followed was a memorable one and a splendid introduction to our visit. Yakub Khan is not only the cultured aristocrat of
pre-Partition days, down to his elegant, tapering and well-manicured
fingertips, but he is also soldier, littérateur, statesman and, above all, a
survivor, as well as being one of the best conversationalists (in six languages) in the world today. That he and my husband should choose one
of the more exotic of these, and suddenly break into animated Russian
over the Bhutanese pudding, surprised not only me but also, almost
certainly, anyone else who might have been listening.

In fact, they were up to nothing more sinister than discreetly discussing
whether it was possible for General Yakub to intervene on my behalf
when he saw the king the next morning, but they got a good deal of fun
out of it, as well as showing off rival linguistic skills.

That morning our very first view of Bhutan, as we came in to land at
Paro, had been an exciting experience. Everything, but truly everything,
had looked *different*. Mountains, trees, vegetation, monasteries, houses,
pigs, dogs, children, whatever the eye fell upon produced the thrill of
the new, and unknown. There were Tibetan and Chinese echoes and
nuances no doubt, but this beautiful Bhutanese valley was *Bhutanese*,
with an exotic identity of its own, like nowhere else in the world. And
so it was throughout all our journeys in this wonderful country.

The inhabitants of Bhutan are tall and good-looking, taller than
Sherpas but with the same hardiness and quiet watchfulness of high
mountain people, with clean-shaven, smooth faces and mops of thick
black hair, cropped short. The men wear kilts and battledress 'bomber'
tops of tartans or striped material, or sometimes of plain clerical grey. If
they are government officials, or men of means, their tunics have very
clean white cuffs, which are laundered daily, for the Bhutanese are natty
dressers. Some go bare-kneed and wear homespun and hand-knitted kilt
stockings diced in coloured patterns, while others wear long stockings
and knee-breeches, or a kind of pared-down jodhpur beneath their kilts.
The women's kilts reach to their ankles, but are cut the same way as the
men's, a flat apron in front, two deep inverted pleats at the back. The
smarter ones wear brightly coloured silk blouses under little boxy jackets
of brocade or Chinese patterned silk, sometimes trimmed with fur but
with many different variations. A man's dress is called a *ko* and the
richness (and cleanliness) of its material, as well as the ubiquitous silk
scarf he often carries, denotes his rank, which is all-important in the
hierarchical society of Bhutan.

The official party that met General Yakub Khan all wore national
dress and as we watched from the windows of the little aeroplane a

delegation of lamas in claret-coloured robes and shaven heads came forward and presented him with a long address, then larger men in belted kos with huge straight silver swords slung from them, like the ones depicted in the Bayeux tapestry, advanced ceremoniously and bore him out of our sight. Besides this, presumably, royal bodyguard there was also a party of smart, modern soldiers in red berets and khaki battledress who presented arms as if they had been Sandhurst trained. They looked a bit anachronistic among so much ancient ethnicity, but were probably the drivers and escort of the long line of cars which now took off in front of us for the two-hour drive to Thimpu.

Paro is in a valley shaped like a hand, with three fingers stretching into the foothills of the high Himalayan ranges. An enormous black and white monastery, or *dzong*, dominates the foreground and is echoed, in menacing but magnificent style, by a seven-storeyed stone watch tower, Dzong-Ta, which stands guard on an escarpment above it. Below it the valley was lit by bright green patches of winter wheat and the lighter, more tender green of feathery weeping willows. A swift, shallow river idles through the meadows then races through narrow gorges and wooded glens towards Thimpu, and the road follows it most of the way. The rare houses perched above it look like chalets which are lifting their hats, for there is a gap between house and roof. The roofs are of wooden shingles, held down, surprisingly, by very large round stones.

Our destination lay in another, much broader valley that lies between the wooded foothills of steep and rugged mountains, where the present king's father built his modern capital around the ancient hulk of Tasshi-sudon Dzong, another of the huge Buddhist monastery-forts which dominate the land. It was originally a vast and impregnable complex which housed both the royal family and three thousand monks, as well as the officials, soldiers, servants and slaves who made up the courts of the Deb and Dharma rajahs, the religious and secular dual-rulers of a country that until quite recently was both a theocracy and a mediaeval monarchy. Only fifty years ago Tassiudon had two thousand rooms, thirty chapels, three prayer halls the size of cathedrals, but no plumbing or heating. It was lit at night by butter lamps. A great fire had nearly consumed it, but its massive core survived and was rebuilt by King Jigme Wangchuk in the same style, but this time with the then prevailing mod. cons.

It now houses the Royal Bhutanese Government offices, and though the royal family still has apartments in it, they prefer to live a few miles up the valley in a smaller and more comfortable palace, which looks (from a distance) like a neo-Tudor Edwardian shooting lodge. It is surrounded by beautiful pine woods, and a high metal fence.

Thimpu is a well-planned and pretty town, transected by one main shopping street by which you enter and leave it. In spite of its mushrooming growth, it presents a remarkably homogeneous appearance, for every house has been built in variations of the vernacular Bhutanese style and this has changed remarkably little in the last two hundred years. It was graphically described by the first British traveller to Bhutan, a down-to-earth Scotsman called William Bogle, who had been sent to spy out the land for the East India Company and reported back to Delhi in 1794. 'The houses are built of stone,' he wrote, 'with clay as cement, of a square form, the walls narrowing from the foundations to the top. The roof, supported clear of the walls by stone pillars, has a very low pitch and is composed of fir boards placed lengthways on crossbeams and joists of fir and confined by large stones laid upon the top. The lower part of the house accommodates dogs, cows and other animals. The family occupies the first storey to which they ascend by a ladder, composed of one half of a split fir tree, into which rude holes are cut at proper distances to serve as steps.'

The only difference in the smart houses of today's young Thimpuans is that there are now stone steps leading to their front doors, bathrooms, and possibly a Japanese Honda Estate parked outside where once there munched a cow. The ends of the joists, the carved and painted window frames, the little balconies that some houses have sprouted under their windows are brightly painted in traditional designs which, with the prayer flags that flutter from tall poles in many gardens, give the whole town a festive, happy appearance.

There are only three tourist hotels in Bhutan, two in Thimpu and one in Paro. In other parts of the country travellers are put up in monastery guest houses, or government rest houses, local inns being considered by officialdom too primitive for Europeans. Distances are great: it takes a week to travel by bus to the eastern provinces, perhaps the most beautiful and certainly the least explored in all Bhutan. This limits the scope of 'special interest' tourist groups – the only kind the government now welcomes – while it whets the appetite of any 'serious' traveller. The tourist hotel that we now settled into was grandly built in sumptuous traditional style, well planned and spacious, but almost entirely empty, and very, very cold.

Our status as guests of the government earned us two large and lofty corner rooms, prettily furnished – with hand-painted Bhutanese furniture and brightly coloured portières and hangings in exotic Bhutanese designs – but, better still, a paraffin stove and electric fire in each of them.

Despite the size of our rooms, we were always warm and comfortable, and I sometimes felt a pang of guilt as we came across the occasional blue-rinsed and temporarily blue-nosed American tourist in the arctic passages and lobbies of the building.

We had also been assigned a personal servitor who brought us our food, poured our tea, made our beds, looked after my plant specimens and, like the perfect Jeeves, smoothed every wrinkle from our lives. He also got the plumbing mended when on one alarming occasion there was no hot water in the taps but boiling water in the loo. This, however, did not go entirely to plan for when I walked unclad into the bathroom after a particularly gruelling day's drive, I found two enormous men with sledgehammers still crouched in a hole under the bath with only a candle to light the formidable intricacies of the system.

Our attendant was called Djorje, like half the population of Bhutan, for it derives from the Tibetan word for a thunderbolt (an emblem of Indra, God of War and Weather), the other half being called Rimpache after the Indian saint who brought Buddhism to Bhutan in the eighth century. Djorje always entered our rooms in a bowing crouch with his hands cupped in front of his face, and left them in the same position, only backwards, which at first was a trifle unnerving, but we soon had him laughing at our silly jokes and misunderstandings and we established a mutual rapport which I only wish could have lasted longer.

Our official guide and aide-de-camp was also a Djorje, Chuli Djorje. A small, neat man with immaculate white cuffs, he had been sent by the Foreign Ministry to meet and look after us. He could not have been more willing or anxious to help, but unfortunately he was not of sufficient rank to break through the hierarchical system of ministerial and court protocol, let alone relay messages to His Majesty, who it now seemed, in spite of Yakub Khan's intervention, had resumed his journey into the interior. Rank, status and protocol are still as central to Bhutanese institutions as to a Ming emperor or Japanese tenno's court. Everything in Bhutan, except nature (and perhaps because of it and its awesome unpredictability) is systemised and organised into orderly patterns, including even the colour lines of symbolic rainbows in Buddhist frescoes.

Colour is important in the Tibetan and Bhutanese cosmos. One quickly learns to recognise the smallest dzong by the broad red band painted round its walls. Colour is what tells you to which sect of Buddhism an itinerant monk belongs, and colour is what designates the various grades of officialdom. Long silk scarves are both carried and presented in Bhutan on every possible occasion as marks of respect. White scarves are carried by ordinary citizens and are also laid before deities in the dzongs. A blue scarf designates a delegate of the People's Assembly. A red scarf is given personally by the king to a senior official such as the governor of a small district, who carries it as a badge of office on formal occasions. An orange scarf is the perquisite of very senior officials such as ministers, deputy ministers or governors of major districts, while yellow is the royal colour and is only worn by members of the royal family and by the king.

Our chief difficulty was getting to know the patterns and finding out their perimeters. Because Bhutan has no need or wish to publicise itself, it is very difficult to gather information. There is no tourist office or ministry which dispenses it and the contents of the battered old 'book-bag' that accompanies us on every expedition were hopelessly out of date. Our most recent text-books had been published in the eighteenth and nineteenth centuries. A facsimile edition of *Views of Mediaeval Bhutan*, the topographical sketchbook made by Samuel Davis for the East India Company in 1783, was one of the best. Things have changed so little in Bhutan that with Michael Aris's excellent modern text it is still a reasonably practical guide, as well as being enchantingly pretty. It told us that, though Buddhism may have come to Bhutan from India, in the first or second centuries, it was the Indian saint, the guru Rimpache (meaning 'Precious Teacher') who converted the country in the eighth century by merging his pure Buddhism with local superstition and an obscure demonological religion known as Bonz into Nyingmapa, a hybrid Buddhist sect which still exists and is the oldest in Bhutan today. It could not have been easy, because in those days three different races inhabited Bhutan who spoke mutually unintelligible languages, and clan rivalry and warfare were endemic and rife.

It was not until the seventeenth century that a remarkable and determined holy man fled to Bhutan from Tibet, bringing with him a new version of Buddhism, the Drugka school of Tibetan Lamaism. After many vicissitudes he succeeded in unifying the warring clans and provinces of the country and imposing his sect of Buddhism on all of it. * But when he died, the Shabrang Nagarwan Namgyel left behind him no suitable heir and for a long time (an amazing fifty-four years) the lamas kept his death a secret. At last, in 1705, the problem of succession was neatly solved by the monks adopting the Tibetan system of metempsychosis, and a reincarnation was declared. Unfortunately, there were three

---

* Two Portuguese Jesuits are believed to be the first Westerners to visit Bhutan. In 1627 they spent several months with the Shabdrang Nagarwan Namgyel, whom they reported as being 'both King and Chief Lama'.

contenders for the spirit of the Shabrang and, in the end, it became divided between three lamas who claimed in turn his physical, verbal and mental principles. The most powerful of these was the *Dharma Rajah Lam Sebdo*, who became 'The King who rules according to Divine Law'. His residence was the Tassiudon Dzong in the capital, Thimpu, but in winter his court moved to the monastery-fortress of Punakha, which enjoyed a milder and more agreeable climate. From then to modern times, the country was more or less united and ruled by a monastic theocracy, but it was as closed to foreigners and to all foreign influence as Tibet itself.

A major difficulty the British Raj in India experienced in settling the various border squabbles that occurred during the nineteenth century was the ambiguity of the status and powers of the Bhutanese dignitaries with whom they dealt. Between the *Dharma Rajah*, the *Deb Rajah* and the senior *Penlops* (provincial governors) there was constant shifting of responsibility and protracted decision-making. In theory the Dharma Rajahs, the monastic 'Kings of Religion' delegated civil authority to the Deb Rajahs, their lay counterpart, but in practice Deb Rajahs acted more as Prime Ministers or Grand Viziers than equals. They were often self-made men who had risen from the ranks of courtiers or government officials and eventually aspired to become lamas themselves and join the aristocratic establishment. Thus the system was dominated by the lamas and produced no inheritable wealth or power (there were fifty-five Deb Rajahs between 1651 and 1905).

Ultimate power resided in Lhasa, for the spirit of the late Lamagroo being received by a Tibetan child, whose identity was discovered and announced in Lhasa, gave Tibet enormous influence both in Bhutan and Sikkim and the Chinese areas of Greater Tibet. As a nineteenth-century observer suggested, 'This principle of faith has its rise in political as well as religious motives. To maintain under a proper subjection to the court of the Dalai Lama the different countries where his Faith is professed.'

I had always thought of Tibet as a remote and peaceful country whose population was largely composed of erudite and contemplative monks who lived in complete isolation from the rest of the world. But now I learnt that in the seventeenth and eighteenth centuries the Tibetans were a fairly aggressive nation with acquisitive and expansionist ambitions.

It was largely to discourage a renewal of these ambitions, and to bring Tibet into the British rather than the Russian orbit, that Lord Curzon, in the last years of Queen Victoria's reign, turned his attention to affairs in Bhutan. A shrewd and fearless warrior had recently emerged as one of the most remarkable civilian functionaries in Bhutan. He was Ugyen

Wangchuk, Penlop, or Governor, of Tongsa and a member of a powerful clan. The British decided to court his favours. He was rewarded for the wholehearted help he had given to Colonel Francis Younghusband, whose disastrous expedition to Tibet had passed through Bhutan, by being granted a knighthood and when, by a fortunate coincidence, the Dharma and Deb Rajahs both died within a few months of each other, the insignia of Knight Commander of the Indian Empire (KCIE) was presented to him at a solemn Durbar held at Punakha, the winter capital, by the Empress Queen's representative, Claud White, the Political Officer then resident in Sikkim, who was an old friend of the Penlop. Sir Ugyen was a canny operator and it was not long afterwards that the British gave their blessing to his installation as the country's *Druk Gyelpo*, or 'Dragon King', and the first hereditary ruler of Bhutan. It was the end of Bhutan's dual system of government.

From 1907 onwards the role of the Dharma Rajah became less and less significant and increased prominence was given to the *Je Khempo*, or Chief Abbot, who now officiated as head of the monastic establishment. Sir Ugyen Wangchuk had been elected in 1907 by a constituent assembly made up of the monastic community, civil servants and the people, but he ruled his country as an absolute monarch, with one eye on the still-powerful lamas and another on his powerful sponsor, with whom he signed a treaty in 1910 which prescribed that Bhutan 'agreed to be guided by the advice of the British Government in regard to its external relations'. He died in 1926 and the present ruler of Bhutan, Jigme Seyen, is his grandson.

We woke late the morning after Yakub Khan's dinner-party, for we had talked long into the night. It was a sparkling day and a breakfast of buttered toast and honey and Darjeeling tea was laid out for us in the brightly painted sitting-room of our suite.

Chuli Djorje, our ADC, arrived and announced that a car was laid on to take us to Punakha Dzong, where the last day of the Spring Festival was being celebrated. It was a three-hour drive and we had better hurry. We knew from Samuel Davis's sketchbook that Punakha was one of the four great monasteries of Bhutan and that the drive would take us over the Doehu-Lo Pass and through rhododendron forests, but nothing prepared us for the beauty and drama of that road, or what we found at the end of it. Living in Argyll, as I do, I am surrounded by rhododendron gardens and rhododendron experts and have seen many slides of plants in their natural habitat. But the reality is something else.

At the top of the first and highest pass the road is blocked by a huge

white *chorten* of some bygone saint, which our driver first circumnavi-
gated. Then he stopped, assuring us of 'the finest view in Bhutan' and
we got out of the car to pay both our respects, but a minor blizzard was
blowing and visibility was nil. All around us stood silent pine forests,
wreathed in cloud; below us the feathery crests of strange, unknown trees
loomed out of the mist and everything dripped in a ghostly, twilit world.
The silence was eerie, and the chorten vaguely menacing. I walked to
the edge of the precipice, leaving our Bhutanese companions to com-
mune with its spirit and peered down into what may well have been a
Garden of Eden, but it was wrapped in cotton wool and I could see
nothing. A few hairpin bends lower down the scenery changed dramatically.

Now Spanish moss and lyana swung like dusty cobwebs between the
branches of sad cypress trees and at the bottom of the steep escarpments
the huge-leafed Kings of the Rhododendron family lifted bony arms
towards the light.* Then, farther down still, the pines gave way to a
canopy of broad-leaved trees and the real rhododendron forests began.

It is impossible to describe their glory or the immense variety and
vigour of all the precious plants we saw that day. My neck grew stiff from
craning and my cries of 'Stop! Stop! I see a lily!' grew ever-fainter as we
continued our inexorable descent. Nothing is worse for a botanist than
being locked in a car with a deadline and three uncaring and unhorticul-
tural companions, but on two occasions they took pity on me and I
returned after a few minutes of roadside foraging with seedlings of *Rhododendron Hodgsoni* and *arboreum*, branches of *Daphne Bhofua* and *R. Dal-
housiae* and some primulas like pale mauve primroses with yellow eyes
which I believe to be *P. Deuteronana*.

Finally we emerged into a sunny, pastoral valley and followed the river
at the bottom till it branched into two streams and there, sitting like
some great battleship at their confluence, was the enormous hulk of
Punakha Dzong, the monastery-fortress-city and winter capital of the
first Dharma Rajah, Shabrang Nagarwan Namgyel.

It was the last day of the Spring Festival that had held up our visas,
but holiday crowds were still milling along the embankments of the river
and across the swaying suspension bridges that led to a broad piazza in
front of the dzong. It was easy to distinguish the three orders of the
Bhutanese people: the lama 'noblesse' in saffron robes and with shaven
heads; the *zeen caab* or 'lay servants of the government', as they used to

---

* Some plants of *Rhododendron grande* were fifty feet high, or even more.

be called, in tidy national dress with clean white cuffs and a white silk presentation scarf slung over their shoulders; the brightly dressed peasantry in family parties, with red-cheeked, black-haired toddlers clinging to their mothers' sides and proud fathers holding up sons to see and be seen (and photographed) too.

We were introduced by Chuli to the *Dzongdag* of Punakha District, Dasho Sengay Rinzig, who, though dressed in traditional Bhutanese style, still managed to look like an amiable businessman or well-to-do city councillor. After a formal speech of welcome he handed us over to a good-looking young man who introduced himself to us (in excellent English) as the Assistant Planning Officer for the District, and the Dasho Dzongdag then hurried away to superintend another part of the festivities. Tschewang, the APO, told us we had unfortunately missed most of the dancing and games, but had arrived just in time to witness the main event, the re-enactment of a glorious moment in Punakha's history, when a lama-hero rode out of the monastery on a white horse to scatter his enemies and lift a siege.

Looking up at the almost-vertical pitch of the great double staircase that led to the mighty bronze doors of the dzong, we concluded that no one could possibly ride down them, except symbolically. But ten minutes later strange figures in animal masks and plumed helmets appeared at the top of the steps and the crowd's excitement grew intense. There were repeated appeals to move back, to make room and we swayed this way and that as bands of drum-beating, horn-blowing monks flowed down the staircase. We then watched, in open-mouthed amazement, as the present Je Khempo (Chief Abbot and highest dignitary of the lama establishment), clad in a wondrous mediaeval costume of flowing silks and steely armour and mounted on a rather seedy-looking skewbald pony, suddenly burst out of the monastery portals and half-galloped, half-leapt down the impossible staircase to land with a jarring thud at our very feet. The crowd screamed with joy and scattered in fear as the old man, looking slightly shaken, but immensely dignified, circled twice round the piazza, scattering blessings on us all from a strange kind of pepper-pot-cum-sceptre that he held aloft. Then the stately procession moved off to the banks of the river where some further rituals were about to take place. Most of the crowd followed, while others wandered across to the park-like gardens and orchards of the monastery and settled down to extended-family picnics on the grass, beneath the apple and apricot trees.

One thousand monks and a great many administrators still live and work behind the towering walls of the great monastery. No women or

foreigners are allowed inside but, taking advantage of the general confusion and admirably guided by the Assistant Planning Officer, we heaved
ourselves up the ladder-like staircase and, passing through a kind of
atrium behind the great bronze double doors, we emerged into the first
of a series of courtyards, each the size of a town square. They lead into
each other by a rabbit-warren of passages, shrines, prayer-halls, granaries,
workshops, then past a pile of holy stones that the Shabrang Nagarwan
Namgyel himself is supposed to have brought from Tibet, and in front
of which many butter lamps glowed. Occasionally stopping to ask permission from some aged monk, whose reaction was either benign or
bewildered, we scurried on till we came to the last courtyard and the
object of Tschewang's concern. Several years ago a terrible fire had burnt
down a particularly holy chapel in this part of the monastery (butter
lamps again, but I tactfully suppressed the thought) and now a magnificent new prayer hall, the size of an English cathedral, was rising from
the ashes. Its wooden skeleton had already been built and soared up into
the blue sky above us and, in spite of the festival and feasts, a few
dedicated workers were chipping patiently away with hand-held adzes at
huge pale camphor-wood logs that will one day form the beams of its
roof. A delicious fragrance hung on the air and the scene transported
me straight back to the simple faith and absolute certainties of the Middle
Ages.

It was easy to populate, in one's imagination, this fortress-city with
its former inhabitants, the religious and lay courts of justice presided
over by Trimpons, or Lords of the Law, the zeen caab offices, the Penlop's
private apartments, the granaries of first- and second-class rice and the
Nyerchen, or Quartermaster, who organised them, the soldiers and zaps,
or monastery-slaves, the dancers and musicians, porters and artisans,
contemplative saints and hard-faced tax collectors. They had all lived
and worked here only forty years ago, when the equestrian Je Khempo
was already a middle-aged man . . .

The indefatigable Djorje-Jeeves had followed us in a second car with
suitable provisions and we now found these laid out, complete with
paper napkins and flowers, in a small wooden kiosk in the garden of the
monastery's guest house, a peaceful place with an ancient tulip tree at
its centre which was just coming in to leaf.

There had been no answer to a request I had made for an audience with
the Queen Mother (with whom I shared mutual friends in England) or
with one or other of the princesses, so, *faute de mieux*, the next day we
scouted out the offices of Bhutan's only national newspaper, which we

found among some new factory prefabs on the outskirts of Thimpu. Talking to its bright young editor, who was a graduate of an Indian university, brought modern Bhutan back into focus. At least I think it did. He laughed at, and was frequently puzzled by the terms I used in many of my questions, which had been culled from our antiquated and obsolete reference books. Penlops, zeen caabs and zaps have disappeared from the Bhutanese bureaucracy and language, he told us, admitting they had been replaced by 'ministers', 'governors' (Dasho Dzongdags), 'civil servants' and West Bengali immigrants, which seemed to me practically the same thing. Taxes were no longer paid to the government or the monasteries in kind, but in crisp Bhutanese banknotes – yet the dzongs were still their collection point. Lorries thundered up the Kalimpong–Thimpu road from India, but travel in the remoter parts of the country was still on horseback or by yak.

Of course enormous progress had been made in international relations and Bhutan is now a member of the UN, UNESCO, UNICEF, FAO and the WHO, she has joined the Non-aligned Movement, the South Asia Regional Cooperation, and is a client and also, inevitably, a debtor, of the World Bank. The judiciary has been modernised, schools built, and a system of traditional doctors as well as hospitals organised.

He told us that the immigrant questions was one of the country's worst problems. In the 1970s and 1980s starving families from Nepal, West Bengal and Bangladesh had flooded into the country, which had needed their labour to build roads, houses, the capital's infrastructure. But the Nepalis are polygamous and before long over half of Bhutan's population was non-indigenous. The government took fright and expelled half the alien workforce but, he added with a wry smile, 'this was not altogether sensible, for many immigrants had been the skilled craftsmen and modern technicians that Bhutan so badly needs'. I thought of my burly Bhutanese plumbers and sighed.

We leafed through piles of old newspapers to find some of the photographs I needed. There were pictures of the King squatting among the elders of a village, opening a session of an international conference, handing out prizes at a sports gala, with his four wives in attendance. 'The King and the Queens', is how they are described in the subtitles, and even in blurred, black-and-white newsprint they make a pretty picture for the king is very good-looking, the queens young and attractive.

The editor told us about the monarch's annual spring tour of the country, and of his personal crusade for the emancipation of all Bhutanese women. In the upper ranks of society there is no discrimination, but among the peasantry women are still treated little better

than beasts of burden and are mostly illiterate. The king's four sisters
have all worked for women's causes and for the promotion of cottage
industries. There were photographs of them, but none of the Queen
Mother, who now lives a secluded life on her estates in the Paro Valley.

It was obvious that the Thimpu newspaper was an orthodox publication that followed a conventional and loyalist line where the royal
family is concerned. We found once again that any questions of a personal nature about the royal family were parried and that the respect
shown to the king is tinged with awe.

The reason for this may well be the violence of the events that not
so very long ago shook the Dragon Kingdom to its very foundations, but
are now a taboo subject or one which must only be approached with the
utmost delicacy and caution, yet I believe that to understand the present
monarchy in Bhutan it is a story that must be told.

I shall call it the story of the Two Jigmes, and although I cannot
vouch for its total and unbiased veracity, my main source is an account
written by a distinguished Indian pro-consul, Nuri Rustomji, one of the
tale's own dramatis personae, whose book, published in 1978 by the
Oxford University Press, seems to me authentic, but is now, sadly, out
of print. It was certainly written by an 'insider', an old family friend,
who did not take sides in the drama and though it is now banned in
Bhutan, for obvious reasons, most of its surviving characters have been
reconciled. It reads like a thriller or a fairy story, with rather a sad end.

The king's father, the late King Jigme, and the whole Wangchuk
dynasty, represented the more conservative and traditional element of
Bhutanese society. They were educated in Bhutan, married Bhutanese
wives and rarely left the country. When there was business to transact
outside Bhutan, they entrusted it to their Agent, who resided for most
of the year in Kalimpong, in North Bengal. For three generations this
Agency had been in the care of the Dorji family, Bhutanese aristocrats
whose education, marriages and connections were just as grand as the
Wangchuks', but much more international. Jigmie Palden Dorji, the
hero-victim of the story, had succeeded his father as Agent and was later
entrusted by King Jigme Wangchuk with conducting the foreign affairs
of Bhutan. The two families were doubly related by marriage; the king
having married Jigmie's sister, Kesang, and Jigmie's brother, Ugyen,
having married the king's sister, Princess Choki, a marriage of very brief
duration.

Among Jigmie's large and international circle of friends (his mother
was a sister of the Choysul of Sikkim) was an Indian civil servant,

Nuri Rustomji, whom he had met on an Indian Civil Service course in Calcutta. Nuri rose to be Political Adviser to the Governor of Assam and then (on loan) to be Prime Minister of Sikkim.

When King Jigme Wanchuk suddenly suffered a massive heart attack in Thimpu, he called upon Jigmie Dorji to take over the administration of Bhutan and be his Prime Minister, and Jigmie called upon his old friend Nuri (or 'Uncle', as both families called him) to be Political Adviser – again, on loan from India – to the government of Bhutan. The king, who had slowly begun to recover, approved the choice. There is a wonderful letter notifying the appointment addressed, according to the protocol of the Bhutanese court, 'To the Most Excellent Shri Rustomji, The Incomparable One, who is richly endowed with the glory of meritorious deeds . . .', and it goes on to confer upon him the designation of *Loten Dingpon* and the rank of a noble, with red scarf. A five-year plan for the economic development of Bhutan was devised by Jigmie and Nuri and approved by the king, and the programme was started with enthusiasm, the first step being to tackle the country's non-existent communication system and build roads.

Lhendup, Jigmie's maverick younger brother, who had been educated in the United States, was groomed to take charge of planning, while Tashi Dorji, his brilliant and capable sister, was entrusted to negotiate Bhutan's entry to an international body (the Colombo Plan), which would give the country the economic assistance and the international status it so badly needed. Nuri shared the palace guest-house with Dr Craig, the king's doctor. There were no telephones, electricity, heating or even sanitary fittings in those days and the king was not always an easy patient. One night he complained of acute jabbing pains in his chest and Dr Craig was summoned, only to discover that the cause of the monarch's discomfort was overindulgence in a special Bhutanese delicacy, a dish prepared from local hornets, which was not on his carefully planned regime of invalid foods – one can imagine why!

Before the king left for further treatment in Switzerland, Nuri saw him frequently and he was treated as one of the family by the queen, Jigmie's sister, for whom he had great affection and regard.

Among Jigmie's many reforms was that of the army, and he planned that in future all young officers should be trained at a modern military school such as the Indian Defence Academy. This upset the senior officers in the Bhutanese army, who thought they might be pensioned off and replaced by foreign-trained juniors. The Deputy Commander-in-Chief of the army was *Chabda* (Brigadier) Namgyel Bahadur, an uncle of the king. The lama establishment, who also disapproved of foreign influence and modernisation, suspected Jigmie of Indian bias. Why did the roads he was building all lead south to the sub-continent and not north to Tibet?

The scene was obviously set for a drama, and only one more character is left to be introduced. She came as a surprise to Nuri, as much later she did to the queen, for the king had given orders *under pain of death* that his long-standing affair with the 'lady', as Nuri calls her, should remain a closely guarded secret.

According to Nuri, 'she was a Tibetan by extraction and of only slight education. She was plumpish and did not strike me as the style of woman to launch a thousand ships.' Nevertheless, she launched the rather comic prologue of a drama which was to end in death. Once the king had left for Switzerland, she began throwing her weight about and, encouraged by the disaffected military, abusing her highly questionable position.

Matters came to a climax when Jigmie issued orders that army trucks which he needed and which she had commandeered to bring luxuries from India should off-load her shopping by the wayside, and return to base. He intended no disrespect to his sovereign, but, as Nuri points out, 'in an absolute monarchy the favourites of the king enjoy a position of exclusive privilege and an insult to a favourite is an insult to the king'.

Shortly afterwards, on a return journey from India to Bhutan, Jigmie was shot and killed as he was innocently playing cards in the house of some friends with whom he had stopped for the night. The windows had been left open to let in the cool night air and the assassin escaped through the garden under cover of a moonless night.

On 5 April 1964 Nuri sent a telegram to King Jigme Wangchuk in Switzerland: 'Deeply regret to inform Your Majesty of death at Phuntsholing of your Prime Minister Jigmie Dorji on Sunday night at nine thirty STOP He was apparently shot by some unknown person but no details are yet available STOP I am proceeding at once to Phuntsholing to enquire further STOP My most heartfelt condolences to Your Majesties and children STOP "Uncle" Rustomji.'

It would take too long to tell the rest of the story in detail: Nuri's CIS training, which assured that when the assassin was caught his statement was recorded at once before a magistrate; his confession that it was the Chabda, the Deputy Army Chief, the king's uncle, who had hired him; the rumour that the king himself was involved; the ridiculous Lhendup whose 'triumphs up to now had been in the battlefields of Calcutta's nightlife' assuming his poor brother's mantle and acting Prime Minister in a brief moment of glory, the mutual and very real fear of the two families that each would now try to exterminate the other; the dreadful position of the queen in the middle, who was torn in two ways by the tragedy, the king's return and the arrest of the Chabda – a quick trial processed by an English barrister, Edward St George, and the execution of the king's uncle by firing squad, were only the beginning of it. There was more, far more, to come.

After his friend's funeral, Nuri had left for America on a Ford Foundation fellowship and study tour. On his way back to India he met the king in Zürich and heard from Lawrence Sitling, His Majesty's secretary, the latest developments in Bhutan. The assassin's pistol, it transpired, had been loaned to him by 'the lady', and, worse still, it was a weapon that had been given to her some time previously by the king himself. 'The lady' had borne sons to the king and was thought to be plotting their succession. The Dorji family, outraged, had decided to enlighten the queen about her husband's infidelity and the risk thereby to the future of the crown prince. They urged her to smuggle herself and her children out of Bhutan.

The king, in Zürich, was distressed by what he regarded as mischief being made by meddlesome people between himself and the queen. He had always tried to spare her hurt and to be discreet and could not understand that this was not appreciated by her family. He asked Nuri to await his instructions in Calcutta and do nothing. Not long afterwards a crisis was precipitated by an over-zealous official who arrested 'the lady' on the Bhutanese frontier when, in a fit of panic, she had tried with her entourage to seek asylum in India until the king's return. The order was swiftly countermanded but the damage had been done. The king was enraged by what he considered 'a colossal insult' and Lhendup's days as self-appointed Prime Minister were numbered. This was made abundantly clear in a letter Nuri received from the king: 'I am not going to receive an insult lying down. *Anyone* who insults me in my own kingdom is going to pay for it, and pay many times over . . .'

It is to the eternal playboy's credit that in the middle of such a crisis he should have thought fit to invite Shirley Maclaine for a holiday in Bhutan, 'to relax in the unsullied peace of the mountains and absorb the quintessential spirit of the Holy Buddha'. While Lhendup was whizzing round Bhutan with the film star, the situation was further aggravated by the escape to Nepal of two young colonels, some civilian authorities and a handful of junior officers, all fearful of arrest for their part in the 'insult'. Rumour bred upon rumour and the press ran wild in its fevered imaginings of what lay behind their flight. It was the king himself who dissipated the hysteria. He flew back from Zürich, had successful talks in Calcutta with India's Foreign Secretary about Bhutan's entry into the UN and returned to Thimpu to take charge of his country once more, on his own. Lhendup and Tashi Dorji left quietly for a period of exile in Nepal, Tashi still conducting a wild campaign of accusation and slander against the king and the entire Wangchuk family, which was just too violent to be credible. The queen and her children remained quietly in Calcutta, where the oldest now attended school. The rift between husband and wife had grown wider, but the family nevertheless returned to Bhutan for their holidays every few months and the children, according to Nuri, retained a deep affection for both parents. Nuri continued in his role of adviser to the king for some time but, though much was accomplished, the speed and nature of the reforms that were now carried out had greatly altered since Jigmie's assassination.

The second act of the drama was an attempt on the life of the king. While he was camping one night at Kyichu monastery near Paro, a hand grenade was thrown at the king which missed him by inches. The Dorjis were immediately suspected and several of the queen's household, who had been awaiting her imminent arrival from Kalimpong, were arrested. Tashi, Jigmie's and the queen's sister, was also implicated. According to the accepted Bhutanese code of ethics this sequence of events was but to be expected: Jigmie, the head of the Dorji family, had been assassinated by allegedly pro-king elements. It was only natural for the Dorjis to avenge the assassination by killing the king. But the attempt had failed, and it was this failure that gave the Dorjis reason to suspect that the whole incident had been a charade, cunningly devised by the king's party to blacken their name.

And so the vendetta dragged on. It is a tribute to Nuri's diplomacy and his genuine affection for both families that he managed to remain on good terms with all of them. He knew that the king had not much longer to live and his one desire seems to have been to bring about a reconciliation between the royal couple, whom he remembered twenty years back as 'the King and Queen of a fairy tale, so handsome, so fresh, so attuned to each other and in the flush of youth'. His ambition was nearly achieved when four months before the king's death he announced the appointment of his son as Governor of Tongsa, which was tantamount to declaring him his heir. The last months of the king's life indeed brought reconciliation and peace, and though the king did not discard his mistress, his old love for his queen seems to have been reborn. In Nuri's judgment the king was basically a good man, 'with a lively sense of humour and an essentially kindly nature'. He did not believe that the king had ordered Jigmie's assassination – he did not believe he had even sanctioned it. And afterwards? It could not have been a welcome situation for the king to find himself publicly branded as the murderer of his Prime Minister, and maliciously maligned for 'moral lapses' that were a commonplace both inside and outside Bhutan. He was a man with considerable self-respect and pride and he was not going to be insulted in his own country. Nuri concludes, 'The Bhutanese, better than any people of whom I have had experience, know how to keep a secret . . . it is doubtful whether the whole truth will ever come to light.'

Of the young king who now ascended the throne Nuri wrote: 'Like his father in his early years, he was a lad of high spirits who enjoyed speeding along the hill slopes at breakneck speed on his high-powered motor-cycle. On my latest meeting with him at Thimpu he was sedate and dignified and noticeably conscious of the heavy burden that had suddenly fallen on his youthful shoulders . . . He was surprisingly balanced and composed despite the tensions he must have been subjected to through the family estrangement. It had not been an easy upbringing and it is to the credit of both his parents that they did not allow their own differences and troubles to embitter their children or create psychological conflicts.'

Eighteen years have passed since the death of the old king, twenty-six, or a generation, since the Prime Minister's assassination, but both events were watersheds in the history of modern Bhutan and cannot be ignored.

In the short time they worked together they made enormous changes in the outlook and infrastructures of the country and, though there was a partial reaction against these after Prime Minister Jigmie's death and the family vendetta which followed it, nothing could ever be the same again. Bhutan has made steady progress in modernisation ever since, but it proceeds at a leisurely pace, the traditional suspicion of foreigners, the conviction that a religious state must have different priorities to a secular one acting as brakes to a headlong rush into the 1990s. There is an enormous divide between the educated few and the illiterate peasants who still live in mediaeval conditions in many parts of the country where communication remains at the pace of the ox-cart.

It was impossible for us to find out how much the king really contributes to this progress and how much is the work of his able administrators and the excellent foundation that Nuri and Jigmie and the king's father set up twenty-six years ago, but there is no doubt at all that the royal family is popular and deeply respected. At the moment, anyway, the institution is secure. In twenty years' time will it still be?

The destiny of Bhutan is not of its own making, but lies in the hands of other nations. It may at present still act as a buffer state between India and China, but China has consumed Tibet and India has eaten Sikkim and looks like eating Nepal. The chief danger to Bhutan and its monarch, I would have thought, is not revolution or economic collapse, but its slow, steady absorption by one of its two powerful neighbours.

Before we left Thimpu we were visited by the Deputy Foreign Minister, who breezed into our hotel sitting-room one evening. He apologised for his ministers' and his king's elusiveness: 'They really are tremendously tied up just now, you know, with the Assembly about to meet – it only does twice a year – and His Majesty's spring tour . . . logistically he's a five-day journey away at the moment. Why not put some of your questions down on paper and I will see that he gets them when he returns? We can always send on the answers.' (If given, the answers were certainly never received!)

He talked very knowledgeably about the monasteries and their aesthetic interest and told us to be sure to visit the museum at Paro. He explained the intricacies of the constitution and the Assembly. He believed the country was adequately protected from any outside intervention or threat and felt its future lay in fruit-growing, mineral exploration and the development of its hydro-electric potential, which was enormous and could be exported to India or to China. He was relaxed, charming, debonair, with a sophisticated sense of humour and a nice sense of the absurd. His realistic but affectionate view of his country's strengths and shortcomings was tempered by a pride in its uniqueness, with which we thoroughly sympathised. He invited us to return whenever we wanted to and left us convinced that all was well in the best of possible worlds. He would make a very good ambassador for his country in London or Washington, and everyone would love him, I thought as we said goodbye.

Our second encounter with the Bhutanese establishment came when we visited Ta Dzong, the seven-storey watch tower that looks down on the golden hats of the Paro Monastery in the valley below it. It now houses the Bhutanese National Museum and a magnificent collection of Bhutanese and Tibetan art and artefacts and here at last I found in its Director the holy and learned lama of my expectations.

Dr Mynak R. Tulku is only approaching middle-age, but he is a scholar of international reputation and it was an education to listen to him enthuse and explain and expound, and to share his delight in the beautiful things we saw together that day.

The side valleys around Paro are enchantingly beautiful and this is where the majority of tourists come to trek or to relax in the chalets of the Paro Hotel. It is a large complex built on one side of the valley opposite the watch tower on the other; both look down on the little town, the great dzong and the airport apron spread out like a green and grey handkerchief alongside the river's weeping willows. It was here that we parted company with the two Djorjes. We promised to visit our faithful attendant's home when we returned. He told us it was in eastern Bhutan, a week's journey by bus across the country, 'but there are Rest Houses on the way' and his family would meet us with horses for the final lap. He was such a dear man that I felt like crying.

Our pilot came over and introduced himself. He was a Scotsman from Pitlochry, who had been flying the Himalayan air-routes for half a dozen years and had so fallen in love with Bhutan that he had made his home among the peach orchards of the Paro valley. But he was pessimistic about the country's future. At the moment, he told us, 'I fly over the frontiers of four countries: Bhutan, Sikkim, India and Nepal. Tibet is already Chinese and by the year 2000 there will be just one straight line of frontier, that between it and the sub-continent.' I said, 'Surely Bhutan is impregnable against any military attack and what about its collective guarantees of security from organisations like ASEAN (Association of Southeast Asian Nations). But he shook his head gloomily. 'There would be no need for invasion, with infiltration and economic usury [i.e. loans which cannot be serviced and are called in and their guarantees re-possessed]. A country as unsophisticated as Bhutan is easily undermined. The Bhutanese are an over-tolerant race with barely developed political awareness – the Indians and Nepalese who work here are political by nature. They will soon start shouting for "democracy", which means overthrowing the orderliness of this tightly governed little kingdom for the multi-party factional chaos of their own politics.' He also told us that the gifts in kind that various international agencies made to Bhutan were never followed up by maintenance. 'There must be more out-of-order photocopiers in Bhutan than anywhere else in the world, with no one who has a clue how to mend them.'

The Queen Mother lived quite near him in a small palace close to the oldest and most sacred monasteries of the land, which she was heavily involved in supporting. She was much respected and loved in the valley. He also said that he often flew Lhendup Djorji in and out of Bhutan. 'He comes in from India or London with his leather jackets and gold chains – a real joker, but very good company all the same,' and Tashi Djorji is also now a frequent visitor, so the vendetta, I was relieved to hear, must now have finally ceased. Bhutan, it would seem, is very like Scotland. Everyone knows what everyone else is up to.

Soon we were flying back to Kathmandu, not exactly triumphant, but certainly satisfied with our Bhutanese adventure. The great mountains marched beside us. This time I scarcely gave Everest a second glance, so used was I by now to great mountain kingdoms, but it had more snow on it than on our outward journey.

The palace of Tassiudon, engraving based on Samuel Davis, 1783, from *Views of Medieval Bhutan*

Part Four

THE MIDDLE EAST

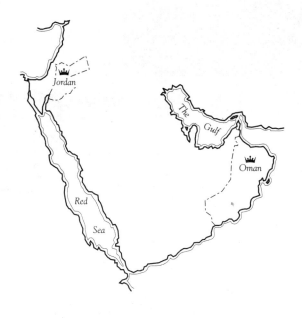

HM Sultan Qaboos of Oman;
and the Sultan in conversation
with the author.

16

OMAN

Sultan Qaboos

'We cannot live without an elite, and there is no elite if the mass rules. God's law, what you call "the natural law", is elitist. It exists in nature and also in our higher natures.'

ABDUL AZIZ BIN MOHAMMAD AL ROWAS

Two Arab countries came next – and again I was lucky in finding friends who knew their sovereigns.

My son had served in Oman as a young army captain when British troops were sent there in 1970. After two happy and eventful years he missed being presented with a gold watch by Sultan Qaboos because he was climbing a mountain at the wrong time – but that is his only regret. He had fallen in love with the country – who doesn't? – and before I started out he gave me a lecture and a long list of places that it was 'absolutely imperative' I should visit.

An Arab country, especially one as little spoilt by tourism as Oman (there is very strict control of entry visas into Oman and they are only issued for specific purposes and have to be approved by the sultan), casts a long and lasting spell, and I find it difficult to disentangle objective observation from romanticism when I think about the country and its ruler, a weakness that many better travellers and more informed writers before me seem, without exception, to have shared.

Sultan Qaboos is an absolute monarch. He can throw anyone he likes into gaol, cut off his head and pickle it for all the world knows, or cares, or can do about it. But he is an enlightened autocrat and, provided that everyone does what he tells them to, his rule, though strict, is benign. Most of the Omani seem to like it that way and count themselves fortunate to be his subjects. He was certainly the greatest contrast one could imagine to the business-school-type monarchs of Central Europe and Scandinavia.

Sultan Qaboos is not a desert-hawk-type sheikh; his childhood was

spent on the soft, languorous Incense Coast of southern Oman, and
though his parent may have been a hard task-master who raised him
under the strict tenets of Islam, there is something soft and languorous
about Sultan Qaboos too, which is infinitely attractive to women,
though I believe many have sighed for him in vain. *

 I had already discovered in Nepal and Bhutan that the questions
one can ask European monarchs, such as, 'How does Your Majesty
see your role in . . . today?' or 'Does Your Highness feel you can
still influence events?', etc., do not apply in other parts of the world.
Absolute kings shape events; they only happen with their permission.

 There is little chance of this Sultan of Oman allowing himself to be
deposed.

My plane landed at Muscat at 1.00 a.m. and, still half-asleep, I stepped out of the airport blaze and bustle into the scented warmth and darkness of a tropical night, and all the excitement of a completely new experience. Arabs in the long snow-white *dishdashas*, which all Omani civil servants wear, moved in on me and my luggage and, having been welcomed by their leader on behalf of His Excellency Abdul Aziz, I was whisked into a waiting limo by two of his minions as smoothly and as swiftly as if I had been kidnapped.

'We are taking you to Al Bustan Palace Hotel. It is very comfortable. It is a personal project of His Majesty's,' said my chief captor. 'He wanted a suitable dwelling for foreign VIPs and he wanted accommodation for international conferences, an auditorium and a concert hall. The Al Bustan Palace fulfils all these roles and in between it makes a great deal of money as a hotel. That is clever, is it not?'

I agreed that it was very clever, even crafty, but my attention was focused on a strange new landscape that was flashing past on either side of the neon-lit road: flat sandy scrub, aloes like buried daggers, feather-duster palm trees in the distance, then, reaching out into the desert like the fingers of a clawing hand, the huddled shapes of a modern city, intersected every now and then by the graceful white pencil of a floodlit minaret.

'Muscat is growing all the time. It covers forty-five square kilometers, so be patient,' warned Osama, whose English was perfect and only faintly overlaid by the influence of his Princeton graduation. 'Now I work for the Minister of Information, looking after foreign guests. I am married

---

* Sultan Qaboos has two wives, one of whom is a Bedouin, but they are practically never seen in public, and, as yet, there is no designated heir apparent.

to a young wife, we are expecting our first child, Inshallah it will be a boy. I have a fine house in a smart part of our town, and life is good.'

He took off his superfluous tinted glasses and polished them, at the same time flashing me a winning and self-congratulatory smile. We were climbing through cement-coloured hills as he spoke. 'There used to be a fishing village here, and a fort, but now . . .' and then, blazing with light, and almost visibly vibrating in oriental splendour, Sultan Qaboos' personal project burst into view.

It is everyone's dream of an 'Arabian Night' palace: *enormous*, turreted, crenellated and golden-domed; its floodlit, Mogul-style windows stand high up in fortress-like walls, reminding one of Fathipur Sikri or Granada – take your pick. But that is nothing to the shock that awaits behind its imposing bronze and glass peristyle. The foyer covers at least an acre of marble floor. Its walls, around which run intricately carved, marble-screened balconies, are a mosaic of beautiful, softly coloured ceramic tiles. Its centre is an octagon of immense green pillars soaring three storeys upwards to support the golden cupola of its roof. Fat, creamy leather armchairs with, here and there, a similar occupant, surround a central fountain fringed with exotic greenery, the only discordant note in an oriental fantasia.

There were no discordant notes in my ravishing bedroom, tiled and curtained in blue and white with custom-built white furniture of classical Moorish style. I remembered Julian Amery's *envoi*: 'I hope he will put you up at the Al Bustan. It's the best hotel in the world,' as I sank gratefully into my long-desired, super-luxurious, down-pillowed and linen-sheeted treble bed.

My audience with Sultan Qaboos was three days ahead and, in the interval, it had been decided that I should see as much as possible of the country. Consequently I was picked up early next morning by a rather ruffianly-looking Arab in a duster-check *gutra* headdress and a striped dishdasha, over which he wore a grubby Western jacket. He was called Selim and was to be our driver for the rest of my visit. To begin with he treated me with the scant courtesy that I imagined was women's lot in this male-dominated society. It was only later I learnt that taxis and hired cars are driven exclusively by Omanis of the interior, whose fore-fathers led camel trains across the desert (and who no doubt enjoyed a long tradition of treating women badly), but by that time Selim and I had made friends to the extent that, on the last day, he actually carried my luggage for me and enthusiastically participated in the famous spec-tacle stakes, of which more later.

We drove out to Osama's fine house in the 'very smart quarter' where

pale pink, white and rose-red bougainvillaea and fat crimson roses spilt
over white walls, while elegant villas and apartments, in every possible
variation of traditional Omani style, rose proudly above immaculate
boulevards whose centres were planted with flowers and shrubs (automatically watered three times a day). Signposts sparkled with fresh paint
and roundabouts were embellished by statues or monuments of cultural
significance.

Money talks, and oil money in the two ancient and newly rebuilt
cities of Muscat and Mutrah is not only overheard but is also seen.
Fortunately, Oman is different from the other oil-rich Arab countries.
Different from Saudi Arabia and the Gulf Emirates,* for though it has
enough oil money to improve, it has not quite enough to corrupt. Its
people still work and aspire to better themselves, and one can still find
a man who will dig a hole – Oman does not depend solely on its oil
revenues. It has water and minerals and good farming land on the northern coast of the Batina, and in the valleys of the interior. It has a
sea-faring history and a civilisation as ancient as the pyramids; it has a
clever king, a controlled economy, strictly controlled development, and
a contented population with an average per capita income of 350 Omani
reales a month (approximately £600); and it has lots of room for further
improvements – most of which have already been planned for – with
and without oil.

The dramatic change in scenery between the low, fertile plain around
Muscat and the abrupt mountain ranges of the interior is startling. They
rose before us as soon as the road turned inland – high concrete-grey
hog-back mountains powdered with tumbled stone; grim by day, but
turning delicate colours, rose-pink, then lilac, and violet, as dusk falls.
It is a beautiful country and a splendid modern highway runs smoothly
through its rich valleys which are watered by wadis, fierce mountain
streams that carve their torrential way downhill in winter and spring,
and by the *Falaj*, the elaborate system of underground irrigation, which
was brought to the Omanis by their Persian conqueror, Cyrus the Great,
in the sixth century BC. Here and there, at the confluence of two wadis
or the head of a valley, lies a date palm oasis, very green and luxuriant
in contrast with the bare hills all round, with a brash-new house or some
palm-frond huts peeping out of its edges.

In the valley, fiercely independent farming and pastoral communities
flourished from as early as the eighth century BC, when the first of the

---

* I was visiting two months before the Gulf War began.

Arab tribes, the Yarubi, came to Oman from that part of southern Arabia
which is now called the Yemen. The Arabs came in successive waves
but the Azd, the tribal family from which Sultan Qaboos descends,
probably arrived at the end of the third century BC after the bursting of
the great Mariba Dam, a catastrophe which changed the whole ecology
of southern Arabia, turning fertile lands into desert and causing a
diaspora which is not yet fully researched or understood.

By the first century BC the Azd, the Yarubi and other nomad tribes
had spread their rule to all parts of Oman, but it was not until the sixth
or seventh centuries of our millennium that they finally drove out the
Persians, and that only in a manner of speaking, for throughout the two
countries' histories there has been so much coming and going between
the northern and southern shores of the Gulf that Omani and Arab
influence was as much felt in southern Persia as Persian influence was
on the Arabian shore.

The imams and sultans of Oman's Islamic past were forever moving
their capital as the tide of power shifted from one group of adherents
to another, and the country is littered with the defensive forts they
built to substantiate their claims. Our first stop was al Hazm, the
great fort that Sultan ibn Saif II al Yarubi built when he moved his
capital from Rostaq in 1711. In its solid, unadorned style, square keep,
round tower, high crenellated walls, fluttering flag, it is the archetypal
model for all of them and for all 'traditional' building in Oman today.
The present sultan feels strongly about architecture and planning
and he personally ensures that all buildings, however modern, large
or small, are in harmony with this indigenous tradition, a pleasing
self-imposed duty that Prince Charles might envy and that gives
Muscat and other Omani cities today their remarkably homogeneous
and stylish appearance. (It is rumoured that once, on returning from
a journey abroad, he found a large new edifice three-quarters built
which did not conform to his rules: 'Pull it down,' he ordered. 'But, Sir,
it is the new house of Your Majesty's . . . [one of Qaboos's closest re-
lations].' 'Pull it down, I said.' And it was demolished the very next
day.)

Alongside the fort lies an oasis of feathery date palms and from this,
in a beautifully constructed stone watercourse, runs the sparklingly clear
waters of the Falaj. Little girls from the local school inside the fort
hopped across it to talk to me and showed me where it disappeared under
the ground to emerge once more in cultivated fields beyond the village.
I sat on a stone seat and wondered if they had been taught about the sad
end of the Imam Saif ibn Sultan who, victorious but despairing, had

crept away from the camp of his Persian allies, who had cruelly betrayed him, and died here of a broken heart.

The Yaruba dynasty, which gave Oman ten imams (sultans only came later) were a remarkable race. They are one of the oldest of all Arab tribes whose antecedents go back, at least traditionally, to Abdul Shams and the Himyarids and further back still to the Sabeans and their Queen of 'Sheba', whose state visit to King Solomon in the year 1000 BC is recorded in the Bible with amazement and awe. In later times it was the first two Yaruba imams, Nasir ibn Murshid and his successor, Sultan ibn Saif, who built up the powerful fleet and armies that in 1650 recaptured Muscat from the Portuguese, who had conquered and sacked it a century and a half earlier. They eventually chased the Persians out of the entire Indian Ocean and created for Oman a small but wealthy maritime empire with possessions in Persia, India, and far down the coast of East Africa. There, Zanzibar, Mombasa and many other African ports were captured and became centres of valuable trade. It was Oman's finest period, and in the seventeenth and early eighteenth centuries the fame of the Incense Coast and its rulers spread far and wide. But frankincense and myrrh, copper and gold were not the only cargo that Omani ships carried.

The slave trade – which flourished between the African interior, Dhofar and Muscat until it was abolished by Franco–British endeavour in the late nineteenth century – had been for many centuries a considerable source of revenue to the sultans. The slave traders re-routed their pitiful merchandise to all parts of the Middle East by caravan or slave ship 'from the coast'.* Slaves, however, who remained in Oman were rarely treated harshly, occupying the position of trusted servants and even sometimes inheriting money and property from their masters.

Sultan Qaboos's father had his own household slaves at Salala as late as the 1950s, but according to James Morris in his book *Sultan in Oman*

---

* It was a dreadful trade, which the following extract brings vividly to life: 'Old Mbarak, a retired slave trader, came round to my house one evening – after supper – I gave him a sheep for which he was most thankful. I tried to get more information from him about the Quitale slave market, how the slaves were taken to the Coast, their casualties and the route taken, but he remembered very little. 'The only definite statements he made were that the castrated boys were the best looked after as they were the most valuable, but that 50% died before reaching the Coast. The girls were not shackled but went free and were raped both at night and through the day when the caravan halted. About 10% of the men died from fatigue or undernourishment; if a man showed fatigue he was shot and left. Mbarak had originally worked under Emir Pasha, but deserted with his rifle and joined up with the slave raiders under Arab leadership . . . Slave caravans went down the coast, always avoiding the Masai . . . he thought Lamu or Bagomoyo did most of the export trade in Zanzibar.

'I asked him if he enjoyed it all. He said: "Plenty good, plenty women; very lovely."'
from Richard Meinertzhagen's diaries (1905).

(1957): 'They were not only well-fed and generally kindly treated, but even (in some cases) went home in the evening like commuters. Slaves serving in his private army were given weekend leave, some were paid wages, and old men were often pensioned. Some, granted manumission, preferred to remain in the Sultan's service anyway. They had all the advantages of the welfare state, with one exception: they had to work.'

Osama told me proudly that his father had had a hundred slaves, but whether there are still slaves in the Royal Palace in Muscat I did not find out. There are certainly plenty of large jolly-looking black people, freed men or their descendants, walking around Muscat today who seem to be enjoying life in Oman as much as their Arab compatriots. As to the dark and illicit purveyance of African children to the Saudi Arabian interior, it *may* still happen but the Omani police and various international organisations certainly make strenuous efforts to see that it doesn't.

The immense fort at Rostaq, which now dominates a town of considerable size, was our next stop. It is pre-Islamic, originally built during the Sassanid period of Persian occupation either to keep the Arab tribes of the interior safely *in* and the Persians safely *out*, or vice-versa. No one seemed to know exactly which. Rostaq has a long history.

It was from here that the national hero Nasir ibn Murshid was elected Imam in 1624, to bring peace 'and to make the sun of salvation' shine on a warring, divided nation, and he and most of his successors made it their capital. Indeed, peace under the Yarubi imams lasted for nearly one hundred years, but after the death of Sultan ibn Saif II in 1718 a period of civil war, similar to the Wars of the Roses in pre-Tudor England, followed and it was then that one of the contestants, Imam Saif ibn Sultan of Hazm, he of the broken heart, disastrously enlisted the help of the Persian, Prince Nadir Shah, to overthrow his rivals.

It is said that the shah's first answer was that he was not interested. His second was to send a splendid Arab stallion back to Oman with the message that if the Imam Saif could ride it he would send as many troops as were desired. Saif mounted and rode the horse furiously through a Muscat wadi. On reaching a dead end the horse leapt a high city wall, on the top of which Saif landed safely on his feet. This prowess so impressed the shah that he sent his support – but the horse broke its legs and was killed, much to the distress of its rider.

The Persians, moreover, stayed on in Muscat, settling in and levying taxes on the unfortunate imam and his people. It was only the courage and cunning of the Governor of Sohar, Ahmad ibn Said, who was later to become the first Imam of the Al bin Said dynasty and the ancestor of the present sultan, that finally dislodged them. He invited the Persians to a great gathering outside Barka and fifty Persian officers were summoned to a banquet in the city, hosted by Ahmad. When everyone was gorged with wine and roasted meats the drum of the fort was sounded and the crier proclaimed: 'Anyone who owes the Persians a grudge may now take his revenge.' The Omanis fell upon the Persians and massacred the lot.

It was a cruel age, and the slits above the doors of Rostaq Fort, through which boiling honey (better than oil, it sticks) was poured on would-be attackers, showed as much.

The next day we set out for Nizwa on a road which skirts the foothills of the Jebel Akdhar (or Green Mountain) and joins the main north–south highway just before you get there. This is the newly built overland trade route which runs across some six hundred miles of gravel desert before turning south through the highlands of Dhofar to reach the ancient ports of the frankincense trade, Salalah and Mirbat, thus joining together the two halves of the kingdom and their very disparate peoples.

To the west of it lies the 'Empty Quarter' of the great Arabian Desert, the Rub al Khali, where nothing except sand and rock exists between it and Mecca. Here a few Bedouin, or desert-dwelling tribes, still lead their pastoral and nomadic life and their red and black striped tents can sometimes be seen from a car or lorry window, though many Bedouin now live on the fringe of oases, their men working in the oil industry and their children going regularly to local schools. Modern transport has destroyed the livelihood of the desert tribes, for thundering lorries and an asphalt highway have replaced the camel trains which once set out from Salalah and Mirbat on the Incense Coast, following caravan routes that ended many weeks later on the shores of the Mediterranean or the Gulf. But it is in the desert, and among the few remaining desert tribes, that the virtues of Arab life can still be found. As Wilfred Thesiger, who crossed the Empty Quarter starting from Salalah in 1946–7, wrote: 'All that is best in the Arabs has come to them from the desert: their deep religious instinct, which has found expression in Islam; their sense of fellowship which binds them as members of one faith; their pride of race; their generosity and sense of hospitality; their dignity and the regard they have for the dignity of others as fellow human beings; their humour, their courage and patience, the language which they speak and their passionate love for poetry.'

Sultan Qaboos understands this and has a particularly close tie with the tribes of Dhofar, for his mother came from a Dhofar Bedouin tribe. He makes annual tours into the interior and upholds age-old traditions whereby every tribesman has the right of access to his ruler and imam.

Islam came to Oman while the Prophet Mohammed was still living and it came 'by the spirit and not the sword', for a council of the Azd tribe agreed to accept a direct invitation from Mohammed himself to embrace the new religion in a letter which he sent by a rich Medina merchant to Jaifur and Abd, the two brothers who then ruled the Arab part of Oman. This early conversion meant that the Omani played a leading part when, later on, Basra became the main base camp for Muslim jihads and it was here that the Ibadhi doctrine, which still predominates in Oman, evolved, although it is founded on the teaching of a learned Azdi of the Yahmed clan who was born at Firq, near Nizwa.

The Ibadhi doctrine believed in restoring the pure Islamic state as it had been during the time of the Prophet and the first two caliphs. It also believed that the caliphate was not necessarily hereditary but should go to the best man available to lead the people. As a result, the position of the imams has always been a powerful one in Oman and it is this dichotomy between the power of the imam and that of the sultan (as well as that between the puritanical Ibadhi interior and the more lax and outward-looking coastal lands, whose people are mostly Sunni or Shi-ite Muslims) that has been the root trouble of the dynastic and tribal squabbles of the country.

The earliest imams were elected by 'four eminent men of virtue and probity' under the presidency of the local sheikh who, having given him allegiance, then presented him to the great crowds of the faithful gathered on the plain of Nizwa, which was frequently the capital, and very much the stronghold of the Imams of the Ibadhis.

The present fort's enormous round tower was built by the second ruler of the Yaruba dynasty. It took twelve years to build and played an important part in the hereditary squabbles and civil war that soon followed the imam's death. On the day we visited it was closed but we spent an agreeable hour in the *suq* below it and drove on to Jabrin, which I thought the most beautiful and intimate of all the forts I had seen, having a little suite for the Imam and his family on top of the highest tower, with rooms to pray and read and relax in or simply gaze out at the mountains on the far horizon.

The last day of my Omani reconnaissance took us along the Muscat coast to Sur, a sleepy little port on the Indian ocean that had once been famous for the beautiful, high-prowed *baghalas* it built to sweep the seven seas and for being, with Sohar, one of the chief entrepots for trade in the ancient Arab world. Oman lies along the sea-routes between East and West and for thousands of years her sailors were the link between the two. They were known in every port of the Indian Ocean and her merchants did business with all the seafarers of the ancient world. Frankincense* and myrrh, copper and gold, indigo, dates, limes and coconut, cattle, carnations, arms and ostrich feathers, silks and slaves, the seafaring peoples of the Omani coast transported them all to Mesopotamia, Egypt, Rome and Byzantium, unloading them on to Bedouin camel trains for their long and stately march across the deserts or sending them up or across the Gulf to their other entrepots at Basra or Hormuz.

For a long time the ports of Muscat, Sohar and Sur had a near monopoly of the Far Eastern–European trade, but this was to change almost overnight when Vasco da Gama rounded the Cape of Good Hope in 1498 and discovered the road to the Indies (by some special irony his navigator was an Omani seaman). Soon afterwards a powerful Portuguese fleet under Admiral Albuquerque sailed into Muscat harbour and destroyed its installations and merchant fleet, slaughtering most of its inhabitants in the process (the old men who were not killed had their ears and noses cut off).† The aggressive and cruel conquest of the African and eastern sea trade by the Portuguese endeared them to no one. They built forts everywhere to protect their interests and the twin forts of Mirani and Jhali in old Muscat harbour still stand witness to their occupation of the town, although one now contains a police college and the other, up till just lately, was a prison.

The Portuguese in Oman were soon followed by the Dutch and the British and then the French, who, realising the commercial and strategic value of the Omani ports, all sought concessions or treaties with the Omani imams, sending representatives on more or less successful missions to Muscat. John Newberry and Ralph Fitch were the first Englishmen to parley in 1588 and it was their travellers' tales (and the fact that the Dutch raised the price of pepper from three shillings a pound to eight shillings) that spurred the merchants of London to form their own company in the year 1600. It was to be called the East India Company and it was destined to have a long and influential future.

The Imam Nasir and his cousin, the Imam Sultan ibn Saif, finally evicted the Portuguese, and the friendship and interdependence of the British and Omani began in earnest in 1645 when the Imam Nasir wrote to the East India Company, offering them sole trading facilities at Sohar.

---

* The resin or gum of the frankincense tree which is still widely grown on the south Omani coast.

† This was the same admiral who commanded the Portuguese war fleet that captured Malacca in 1509, with the result that both ends of the spice trade were secured and it became a Portuguese monopoly for nearly two hundred years.

A century and a half later, as Napoleon's ambitions in the East grew, so did the rivalry of the French and British. It was a coup for the British when Sir Arthur Wellesley (later the Duke of Wellington), then Governor of Bombay, sent an impressive mission under an able young Scotsman, Captain 'Boy' Malcolm, to conclude treaties with both the Shah of Persia and the Sultan of Muscat. The latter, reaffirming an earlier treaty, provided that 'an English gentleman of respectability should always reside in the port of Muscat', and that the friendship of the two countries 'should endure till the end of time or the sun and moon cease in their revolving careers'. The British indeed helped the Omanis on several occasions with advice, and even occasionally with a little 'gun-boat' diplomacy. But Britain's nineteenth-century policy consisted chiefly in protecting the approaches to India, and she conducted her relations with the Sultans of Muscat and Oman from the subcontinent with this in view.

Friendship and collaboration continued during the long and prosperous reign of Sultan Sajid Said; Queen Victoria and the sultan (though they never met) exchanging wonderfully unsuitable gifts – a state carriage and harness from Queen Victoria (for which no suitable road could be found in Zanzibar, to which he had by then retired) and a group of islands in perpetuity from Sultan Said, which there was no possibility of administering, and to which the Foreign Secretary rather meanly responded with a gift of a small engraved snuff-box.

Oman's fortunes went into a steep decline after the death of the 'good Sailor Said' of whom his biographer, Salil, wrote: 'Praise be to God, through whom Said, the happiest of rulers, attained quiet prosperity and perennial glory, decreeing to him sublime eminence in the sphere of happiness and renown, in so much that by the divine aid vouchsafed to him he subdued the sovereigns of his time, acquired dignity by the battles which he fought with his enemies, conquered with the sword hitherto unknown countries and made a straight road over the dissevered necks of the rebellious.' Quite a record – and quite a sentence!

The sultanate was divided between his sons, Majid taking over Zanzibar, and Thuwaini, who had been Wali of Muscat, the whole of Oman; but another brother, Turki, who had been Wali of Sohar, disputed this with armed threats. Their quarrel nearly led to civil war. The British, from India, intervened and suggested arbitration. The Viceroy, Lord Canning's eventual solution was that Majid should continue as Sultan of Zanzibar but pay his brother as Sultan of Oman 40,000 crowns a year, for by this time Zanzibar was by far the richest part of their inheritance.

Thuwaini's reign was short and troubled. He had lost Oman's navy to

Zanzibar and his mercantile fleet was superseded by new European steam-ship lines, whose speed soon eclipsed the traditional baghalas of the coast. Thuwaini's brother, Turki, and his cousin, Azzan of Rostaq, were mounting separate rebellions against him when his earthly troubles ceased abruptly in 1866 for he was assassinated by his own son, Salim, who shot him through the head at his palace at Sohar while he was enjoying a post-prandial siesta. There followed some sixty years of family and tribal division, strife and the steady decline of Oman's position in the civilised world.

Turki's son, Sultan Faisal, died in 1913 and his son, Taimur ibn Faisal, succeeded him at the age of twenty-three. By this time the Ibadhi tribes of the interior, led by an elected imam, Sultan ibn Rashid al Kharusi, were getting disenchanted by the weak government and family quarrels of the Said dynasty. They refused to acknowledge Taimur, captured some coastal forts and in 1915 launched a full-scale rebellion against him. British troops from India intervened and after several small battles man-aged to quell the rising and reach an accommodation with the rebels, by which Taimur agreed not to interfere in the internal affairs of central Oman nor to overtax or prevent the rebel tribes from visiting Muscat, in return for being left in peace to administer the coastal states of Muscat and Dhofar. This rather nebulous arrangement, which divided the country in two, became known as the 'Treaty of Sib' though few people in the outside world, convulsed by the Great War and its aftermath, knew where Sib was or, for that matter, cared.

The agreement and the peace only lasted some dozen years and in 1932 Sultan Taimur, weary of the struggle, abdicated in favour of his son, Sajid Said. Sajid, Qaboos's father, took over a country that was heavily in debt and seemed to have been forgotten by the rest of the world. By long and patient effort he restored Oman's finances, re-united, at least temporarily, the country's two warring halves, and laid the foun-dations for its renaissance, though, sadly, he could not himself adjust to the changes this would inevitably bring. He had been educated in India, and though he spent much of his youth and all his old age in the southern capital of Salalah – where the royal palace, a kind of southern-hemisphere Balmoral, stands directly on the shores of the Incense Coast, with a second, more romantic 'garden palace' only a few miles further along it – he was adequately travelled, intelligent, and seemed at first more Westernised, or at least cosmopolitan, than any of his predecessors.

Sajid, when he succeeded his father, was only twenty-one but he was already astute enough to realise that the rapid economic and cultural developments, which were happening all over the Middle East, had transformed the Arab world and that the discovery of oil in Arabia and the Trucial States, and the growing ambitions of the Saudis and the American oil companies, had made it imperative for him to reunite the two halves of his country and to regain control of the Interior, which was rapidly drifting into the position of a separate state. This achieved, he intended to rebuild the nation's fortunes by careful stewardship and cautious development. But this was easier said than done.

Although he had no doubts that it was part of his heritage, Sajid had never actually set foot in Oman, as the mountainous Interior had come to be called. More peaceful imams had succeeded the fiery Salim, who had led the quarrelsome Ibadhi tribes to open rebellion against Thuwaini and Taimur, and they had no wish to stir up trouble unnecessarily.

By 1937 two efforts to discover oil in southern Muscat had been made. Both had been unsuccessful, the second by P.D.(O), an international company, was interrupted by the Second World War and, after it ended, drilling had not been resumed. It did not look as if oil would restore the fortunes of his country, so Sajid Said, with the help of the British, built up his country's forces into a small but efficient private army and bided his time. It nearly came in 1950 when a Saudi Arabian force crossed into Oman territory, occupying a village at Buraimi, an oasis of scattered villages on the borders of Abu Dhabi and Muscat, where the frontiers between the three countries had never been clearly defined. American oil companies had expressed a desire to prospect in the region, and the Saudis were not slow to pre-empt this and stake their own claim. Sajid Said had rallied his tribes and his fighting men and a considerable army had gathered on the shore at Sohar, ready to march on Buraimi and repulse the invader, when the British government intervened, maintaining in Foreign-office speak that it would be 'distinctly awkward' if an American oil-man got himself killed.

The Foreign Office urged arbitration rather than confrontation, the case dragged on, and it was only five years later that the Trucial Oman scouts, together with the sultanate troops, finally settled it, forcefully ejecting the Saudis in October 1955. But the story does not end there.

In 1954 the peaceful Imam Abdullah had died and a new imam, Ghalib ibn Ali had been elected. No doubt dreaming of a possible oil bonanza and supported by Saudi money and Egyptian encouragement (Nasser wishing to eliminate British influence in the peninsula), Ghalib now declared central Oman to be a separate principality, issued edicts and began printing his own banknotes. For Sultan Said it was time to act.

Driving north from Dhofar across the gravel desert with flags flying

and drums beating, Sultan Sajid Said's troops captured first Nizwa and
then Firq, with only a single shot being fired (which narrowly missed
Peter Fleming, Special Correspondent of *The Times*, who, scenting
trouble, had attached himself to another of the Sultan's private armies).

A delightful account of this memorable *coup de main* is given in *Sultan
in Oman* (1957) by James Morris, then Middle East Correspondent to
the same newspaper, who accompanied the Sultan all the way:

'One fine Arabian morning in the middle of December, 1955,' he
wrote, 'I walked into the palace of the Sultan of Muscat and Oman, on
the shore of the Indian Ocean in Dhufar. Through the great gate of the
outer courtyard I passed, and the slaves bowed low; through the gate of
the inner courtyard, with the sea glistening beyond the wall; into the
polished hall of the palace, lined with bearded and begowned retainers,
their rifles in their hands; until there approached me from the darkened
recesses of the building a small dignified figure in a brown and gold aba,
a turban on his head, a sword by his side, a soft scent of frankincense
emanating from his person.

'"Good morning, Mr Morris," said his Highness the Sultan Said bin
Taimur. "I wonder how familiar you are with the map of south-east
Arabia?"'

As one can imagine, with such an opening paragraph it is impossible
not to read on . . .

But though the Iman Ghalib fled and his brother, Talib, perhaps the
more ambitious of the two, escaped to Cairo, there was yet more trouble
to come. In 1957 Talib returned and continued to stir up the dissident
tribes of the Interior. This time he was supported by more sinister allies,
the Chinese Communist 'advisers' in the Yemen, who aimed at not only
threatening the interests of the sultan and his allies, the British, but also
destabilising peace in the Middle East.

British involvement in what happened next is now history, and I have
the following interesting, if rather terse, account of it on the best military
authority. In the summer of 1957, a composite Sultan's Armed Forces
unit, known as the Muscat and Oman Field Force, tried to dislodge the
rebel forces of the Imam Ghalib and his brother, Talib, from the foothills
above Firq, and Ghalib's own home village of Balat Saif. The sultanate
force fared badly, sustaining many casualties and, what is more, signally
failing to take any of their objectives.

The SAS (Special Air Service), under the command of Lieutenant-
Colonel (later Major-General) Tony Deane-Drummond, arrived in
Oman from Malaya in November 1958 and, on the fully moonlit night
of 25 January 1959, two squadrons of 22 SAS climbed and stormed the

Green Mountain, capturing the whole plateau summit within three days. The rebel leaders fled from their mountain lairs and Sultan Said bin Taimur regained control of his whole country.

Oil was finally discovered in Oman in 1967, and when oil revenues began to pour into the country it was Sajid's tragedy that he did not know how to pass on their benefit to his poor and disadvantaged subjects. He seemed stuck in a time-warp of his early struggles when careful and prudent economy had been the first priority, for he had inherited a nearly bankrupt country. He retired to his palace in Salalah in 1958, steadfastly refusing to join the United Nations or to have dealings with any of the respectable international organisations that could have helped him develop the country. Instead he ceased travelling abroad or visiting his northern capital of Muscat. The nation stagnated and discontent festered. It was not surprising that many talented but frustrated young Omanis left the country or that, in 1965, a rebellion broke out in his own province of Dhofar, which rumbled on until finally in 1970 'eminent men of value and probity', supported by international pressure and the mounting military and political crises in the south, forced the Sultan Sajid Said to abdicate in favour of his only child, Qaboos, who took over the reins of government in July 1970 and immediately flew to Muscat to be greeted and acclaimed by the people as their new sultan and saviour. He promised to abolish out-of-date laws and restrictions, to develop education and health care and international contacts. He was wildly applauded, but the coup and the manner of its making caused both father and son great distress, and even today Qaboos will not talk about it.

I had been groomed for my audience with Sultan Qaboos by two visits to Tony Ashworth, ex-cavalry officer and diplomat who now has the resounding title of Personal Adviser to His Majesty and is a kind of one-man liaison officer, cultural attaché, press officer and propagandist for the sultan. In the tradition of so many British, and quite apart from the privileges such a position brings, Tony Ashworth is clearly devoted to his royal master and also to the country that for so many years has been his home.

   The second visit, also in the labyrinthine corridors of the Ministry of Information, ended with an introduction to the minister himself, His Excellency Abdul Aziz bin Mohammad Al Rowas. It was my first experience of the Arab Establishment in an Arab country and it was not at all what I had expected.

The minister is tall, elegant, austere yet urbane and exquisitely polite. He wore a simple snow-white dishdasha and tucked into the sash at his waist was the most beautiful *khanjar* (a curved and sheathed ceremonial dagger which all Omanis wear as part of national dress) I had yet seen, richly chased in silver and gold and studded with the odd diamond. I remembered not to cross my legs or show the soles of my feet, for his is a presence which naturally commands respect and circumspection. Until the conversation got too interesting I sat on the very edge of my chair, sipped mineral water carefully and acted prim. We talked about monarchy, elitism, the media, poetry and religion and it is surprising that, carried away by such a flood of eloquence, conviction and charm, I remembered to ask any practical questions at all. My notebook is full of such phrases as 'the breath of history', 'God's law', 'corruption which endangers the soul'.

'A monarch's position,' he told me, 'is unique. He is above all and everyone in his country, and yet he is part of his country as his country is part of him. He is the breath of history. And history consists of change. It is essential to have a point of reference in that change. How can an ordinary man be linked with the past, with his grandfather, his great-grandfather, without one? Now we have photographs, but you *still* say an Elizabethan poet, a Georgian house, a Victorian attitude.' I nodded dumbly, overwhelmed by the eloquence and his perfect command of my mother-tongue. 'His Majesty is very conscious of this – of the historical factor. Monarchs have a particular sense of history, a stake in it, if you like; they *wish* to be remembered. They are attached to the tradition of their country for they are part of it. They do not change like rulers chosen by a non-elite group. Monarchic rule means constancy and continuity. A king is always there and "sees it through" to the end. Party politics are expensive and wasteful. His Majesty has achieved unity in our country by his courage and by his devotion. These are the qualities that mark a good king. Those, and knowing his people (shades of King Juan Carlos!). The Sultan has often said to me, "You can tell me what *you* want, but I tell you what I know *my people* want, because I know my people." We can't live without an elite, and there is no elite if the mass rules – God's law, what you call the "natural law", is elitist. It exists in nature and also in our higher nature. And who but the elite can supervise the noble role of the artists?'

Here the minister paused dramatically, or ran out of breath, and I shuffled my feet, for I know more than a few non-elitists who jolly well think they can – including several who paint, but I didn't dare say so, and then perhaps he may be right and that's why I like the Renaissance and the eighteenth century better than modern art? But he had started off again. . . .

'Democracy is demotion – government should see to the needs of the people but be watched, supervised by the monarch. His view is always the balanced one for he has nothing to gain. He is both the sultan of our country and the imam, but he does not adjudicate. Civil law cases are dealt with by the Minister of Justice and the Court, and Islamic laws by the Mufti,' he finished, coming down to earth a little.

His Excellency told me that Oman is governed by a cabinet that is appointed by the sultan by totally elitist methods – simply the best in the country – and a consultative committee whose terms of reference have been drafted by Sultan Qaboos. They are nominated by a government committee who send their list to His Majesty who chooses from it, but who usually follows their recommendations – everyone aims at a good tribal balance. The tribes are important, their very intimacy is invaluable. 'In a tribe, everyone knows the capabilities of everyone else. They do not lie because this would scandalise their fellow-tribesmen and bring shame to the whole tribe, so they have a *double* conscience: their own, which is part of their family's, and their tribe's, which is part of their country's.'

I asked him if there were problems about tribal lands and he said all traditional grazing and agricultural rights were respected. In government-owned lands, priority was given to tribal members of that area, but even-handedly, so that all would benefit.

'Omanis,' he told me, 'are different from other oil-rich Arabs. They have had traditional occupations for thousands of years, farming their lands has taught them patience. The sea and seafaring have taught them courage, judgment, certainly tolerance, and maybe fantasy,' he added thoughtfully, and embarked on a metaphysical discourse which he finally interrupted to tell me that his own ministry appointed the walis who govern the different districts of Oman and that the Central Bank was the instrument of financial control – of other banks and the government's economic programme.

Lastly we talked about foreign affairs. He told me severely that European unity was based on making money and not on spiritual needs and that, since the Second World War, the superpowers have harnessed all their talent and know-how to consumerism and have produced too much. This had widened the gap between the haves and the have-nots. Not understanding much about world economics, I instinctively agreed, felt guilty on behalf of the superpowers, thanked him for the wonderful hospitality I had been shown and took my leave – a born-again, at least temporarily, Arabist, much impressed by the high moral tone and alarming efficiency of it all but a bit uncertain about artistic patronage, all the same.

The next day, as I sat with Mr Ashworth in an ante-chamber of the royal palace in old Muscat, I was reassured. The room was hung with charming orientalist paintings of the early nineteenth century – European, mostly French – and there were beautiful old Persian carpets on the floor. Someone, somewhere in the Omani Establishment, knew a bit about art and had good taste. I hoped it might be Sultan Qaboos.

We had driven to the palace in best bib and tucker in the 'adviser's' handsome car, but had left it at the postern gate between the two forts because the courtyard was occupied by the brass band of the Royal Guard which was smartly marching and counter-marching up and down it in the impressive finale of their afternoon performance. We edged past them to the steps leading into the seventeenth-century building – a great square edifice that had once been the Portuguese governor's residence, as well as factory, chapel, warehouse and barracks. It looked as if it could have easily coped with every one of these activities.

Askaris saluted and ADCs in the uniform of the King's Royal Guard, almost certainly ex-Sandhurst cadets, led us up a noble staircase to passages where men in uniform, or white dishdashas, scurried about their business. It was a long wait, but relieved by several courteous officials dropping in to chat with us. At last the Grand Vizier of the Divan appeared and, after courtesies had been exchanged and it was intimated that a cabinet meeting would follow on the heels of my audience and must not be kept waiting, he inclined his head graciously and led us into the audience chamber.

It is a large room, elaborately decorated and brilliantly lit in a sumptuous Middle East middle-class style that dazzles and defies description, but the small, quiet figure in a filmy dark *bisht* edged with gold who stood at one end of it, his hand on the golden dagger at his waist, his expression remote and unsmiling, completely dominated the scene. We walked up to him – a long way – and I curtsied. Mr Ashworth bowed. We were motioned into two throne-like chairs. Soft drinks were offered and declined.

Mr Ashworth's business was soon over, but while it lasted I covertly observed His Majesty's blend of grave dignity and charm. He has a rather sad young face, younger than his years, and it is framed in a carefully trimmed beard that is frosted a surprising white in its lower dimensions, but is still dark around the full mouth and upper lip. The eyes, beneath an elaborately wound turban, are enormous, as softly brown as a gazelle's, with long dark lashes. The features are regular, perfectly proportioned, with a strong, aristocratic nose. Despite these almost feminine good-looks there is a resolute strength about his face and a gravity that is almost stern. He rarely smiles, but when he does it really is sunshine breaking out all over. He has strong, white, beautifully even teeth and I thought, but it may have been wishful thinking, that I detected a whiff of incense about his person. (A generation ago it was wafted around by the sultan's special incense slave 'to sweeten the beards' of distinguished guests.) His golden khanjar was finely chased but not quite so beautiful as the minister's.

I asked him if he ever had time to rest or relax and it touched a raw nerve. 'Papers, papers, papers! They even bring me papers after dinner. I delegate, but they still want my comments. It gets worse all the time. In the beginning there was only one ministry, that of the Interior – but now . . .' and he shrugged his shoulders and smiled a deprecatory and devastatingly attractive smile. I asked him if he would ever introduce a system of government which would give the Omanis greater political responsibility. And he answered that, though they were still politically a backward country by Western standards, enormous strides forward had been made in the last two decades. 'The process is a natural one.' Young Omanis were being sent abroad to Arab and foreign universities. It would all take time, but if I meant a parliamentary democracy I must remember that the traditions of kings in Oman are two thousand years old.

I asked him if there were still tribal and religious divisions in Oman that could endanger the present system, or was that all in the past? He replied that he had personally brought about 'a happy marriage' – he was both sultan *and* imam to the people of Muscat and the Interior and when I raised enquiring eyebrows he told me his father had insisted on his receiving a religious education after his secular one and that it had been long and arduous. He remembers poring over large *photographs* (photostats had not yet been invented) of Koranic and Islamic texts on the floor of the palace at Salalah. They had come from a Cambridge college and the next time he saw them – the originals – was when he visited the college one day from Sandhurst. 'We have our own fine library of Islamic literature now, but in those days . . .' and he again rewarded me with a beautiful smile.

We talked about land tenure, the tribes, housing, agriculture. I asked him if I could take my hat off, we forgot about the agenda and talked about Britain, about Arab solidarity, which he did not seem too interested in – 'We look after our corner' – about foreign concessions – 'International companies have built our road systems and our oil and mineral industries have been developed jointly with foreign investment and foreign know-how. France, Britain, America, Holland, Japan have all invested in my country and contributed to its technical advances and social development. Our oil, incidentally, is mostly bought by Japan.'

Here the Grand Vizier poked his head through the door and I could see a row of stately looking gentlemen in turbans behind him. His Majesty shooed him away with an imperious wave of the hand and we settled down to discuss the Vietnamese boat people. Immigration? 'None, we have very tight security.' The shifting centres of economic power, religion, monarchy. Again the Vizier opened the door and there was an unmistakable buzz of protest from the cabinet ministers, like a hive of bees ready to swarm, but the Sultan ignored it. He was telling me what it was like to be a king.

'I feel responsible for all my people. A monarch should see himself as a father, his people as his children. A monarch is a mirror. He reflects his people's religion, their history, their culture. They can understand their collective identity much better through him. He must understand them all the time, inform himself of their needs. He should do things in their interest *before* they ask him to' (again I was reminded of King Juan Carlos. Could Islamic ideas have percolated through Moorish culture? But there I stopped and concentrated on what Sultan Qaboos was telling me). 'Young people get bored with old kings, they think they know better, so the system cannot stand still; it must improve all the time and you must never allow any *cracks* to develop. Never.' He brought out the word 'cracks' like a pistol shot and that, I thought, is probably what any saboteur of the system would hear, and pretty quick too, for suddenly there was a look of tremendous hauteur and authority on the sultan's face and the gleam in his eye was more that of the eagle than the gazelle.

The door opened a third time and the Vizier looked at me imploringly. In some confusion I picked up my hat, my notebook and my camera and, curtsying hastily, removed myself from His Majesty's presence, who was immediately re-engulfed in papers, plans, discussions and more papers . . .

It was only later that evening that I realised I had left my spectacles behind (I *always* leave my spectacles behind and it maddens friends and relatives alike). But this time it was serious. I was flying out early the next morning to another interview and was lost without them. I rang Osama. He rang the palace. It was closed for the night. I sat on my bed and rang every official in the book. Eventually someone took pity and promised to deliver them to Osama in the morning.

But he did not.

We reached the airport an hour ahead of flight time and Osama and Selim went to work on it, while I sat biting my nails. My flight was called. Osama had disappeared and Selim restrained me from joining the other passengers, who were already embarking. Another ten minutes ticked on and still no news. Sympathetic airport officials concluded ruefully that we could delay no longer and I was walking out on to the apron when I heard behind me a siren, a screech of brakes and a shout; then Selim and an official came running on to the tarmac, waving a small packet and yelling.

We had won the great spectacle stakes by a whisker and, as we circled over the airport, I could see two tiny figures below me, a white and a parti-coloured one, waving triumphantly.

17

JORDAN

King Hussein

'Until my time comes no-one can harm me; and when my time comes no-one can guard me.'

KING ABDULLAH OF JORDAN a few days before his assassination

Oman is an ancient kingdom, converted to Islam in the lifetime of the Prophet 'by the Spirit and not the Sword', with an identity and a long and proud history of its own that has little to do with European meddling.

Jordan is the makeshift solution of an awkward problem: the carve-up by Europeans of conquered spoil; it is a disaster waiting to happen, for economically and logically it can never work. There could be no greater dissimilarity than that between these two desert countries – or their two Arab rulers.

King Hussein of Jordan is probably more 'Western' than any other Arab king, but he is also a son of the desert who has kept one foot in the black tents of his beloved Bedouin tribes, while the other is at the very centre of international politics. He is a dreamer obsessed with an impossibly ambitious dream, and a very small chance of surviving to see it realised.

Qaboos's mission is to keep Oman out of Middle Eastern politics and crises and to get on with raising its already very high standards of living. Hussein's is to make the rest of the world understand his country's impossible situation, the full extent of its suffering and deprivation; and then, after some miraculous solution of the Palestine question, to lead the entire Arab world back to its former unity and glory. Qaboos sits securely on a golden throne. Hussein's is neither golden nor secure and it is a small miracle that he has been able to cling on to it at all.

European value judgments and forecasts make little sense in the terrible Arab–Israeli dilemma, and I do not take sides for my sympathies lie with both. I only know that there will be no peace in the

*Middle East until the Palestine question is resolved – and anything
could happen to Jordan's king in the process. His courage is the only
constant in the shifting elements of a crisis that merely seems to change
gear and to be headed, inevitably, towards a final showdown.*

I visited Jordan in mid-May 1990, ten weeks before Saddam Hussein
invaded Kuwait. I was received in audience by King Hussein, which
was in itself a small miracle of pro-British courtesy as his country was
already poised on the brink of inevitable crisis, a crisis for which the
incoherent policies of America and the West must have seemed to him
at least partly responsible.

Jordan is a poor country of mountain and desert which, ever since its
lop-sided creation by the British in 1921, has needed a superpower
backer, or an alliance with one of its richer Arab neighbours to sustain
its economy. At the time of my visit US aid had been drastically reduced
and his oil-rich and arrogant neighbours were, in Hussein's own words,
'dilatory and uncaring'; they had not, with the exception of Iraq's dic-
tator-president, exactly rushed in to fill the gap. Worse, Hussein's perennial problem, that of the Palestinian refugees, was growing daily more
acute as new waves of dispossessed Arabs flooded into the West Bank,
pushed out from Israel by an influx of Soviet Jews and the growing
opinion there that Jordan was already the Palestinian state-in-waiting.

America's newly defined 'strategic relationship' with Israel, Congress's
acceptance of Jerusalem as its undisputed capital and the breaking-off of
USA–PLO dialogue has also increased tension and anti-Western feeling
in Amman. Two days after I left, the school bus incident on the West
Bank inflamed the situation still further – flags were burnt, mobs rioted
and the Jordanian police only just managed to restore order without
calling out the army. But passions had only been dampened down. The
seething discontent of the Palestinian refugees, who make up over sixty
per cent of Jordan's population, was growing and there were plenty of
radical and revolutionary elements among them to exploit it.

The Arab summit, which Hussein was trying desperately to arrange
when we talked together, led to no positive or immediate result; the
West, occupied by the pressing question of the Soviet empire's collapse,
the re-unification of Germany and the Common Market agricultural
policy, turned its blind eye on the ever-growing crisis in the Middle East;
Jordan drifted ever-nearer to bankruptcy, the Palestinians to despair, and
Hussein, whether by necessity or choice, into the arms of the Iraqi
dictator, a dangerous and unpredictable ally. 'He even seems to enjoy

going fishing with him,' our nice and intelligent ambassador in Amman had told me despairingly. On my last day in Amman there was a front-line atmosphere on the streets and doom seemed to loom in every direction.

Nevertheless, Saddam Hussein's invasion of Kuwait on 2 August, only two months later, surprised and shocked me as much as almost anyone else in the Western world.

It had not been difficult to organise my visit to Jordan, for I had met Crown Prince Hassan, his younger brother and right-hand man, and his graceful Pakistani wife, Princess Sarvath; they came over to tea with the Queen Mother at Royal Lodge, and when I told him I wanted to come to Jordan and be granted an audience by its king, he immediately invited me to come any time, and to be their guest.

The following summer it was all arranged, and before leaving London I talked to Julian Amery about King Hussein. 'Of course you will fall in love with him,' Julian told me. 'Girls all do.' Julian has a nice way of discounting an old friend's advancing years.

My arrival in Jordan was not quite what I had expected. 'Don't worry, someone will meet you and give you your visa at Immigration, then take you to your hotel,' I had been promised by the king's secretary in England, a pleasant young voice at the end of a telephone, and I had been foolish enough to confide this to a British couple from Kenya on my flight, who had offered me a lift into Amman. But when I presented my visa-less passport I was sternly told to stand aside, and no one turned up to rescue me. The Kenyan couple gave each other a knowing look, then avoided catching my eye as I was smartly marched past them by two fierce-looking guards. But once inside the guards' little office it was Jordanian hospitality at its best. No interrogation or body search, but cups of cardamom tea and reassuring smiles, plus a lot of yelling down a telephone and enough English to make me believe: 'It is always happening . . . just a local hiccup . . . no problem . . . just wait'. I immediately felt at ease and throughout my visit this hospitable, disorganised and slightly scatty kindness and friendliness prevailed. I really liked Jordan – it was very like home.

The young lady from the Protocol Department, who called round to see me at the Intercontinental Hotel, where I finally landed, was equally friendly and hoped I would see as much of the country as possible during my visit. Regrettably there was no word as yet from the palace about my audience. King Hussein was very busy with the forthcoming summit, but still hoped he would somehow find time to see me . . .

And so, courtesy of the Hashemite brothers, an army car and a

Bedouin corporal driver appeared every morning at the hotel and for the next three days we visited the sights around Amman, but always with an anxious ear cocked towards its radio telephone, which sometimes crackled ominously but never delivered the royal summons. We drove out to Petra, the secret 'rose-red city, half as old as time' where I joined a party of Prince Hassan's other guests, six super-fit young Austrian mountaineers, and nearly killed myself keeping up with them; to Jerash, or ancient Philadelphia, the Roman city that had once been part of the Empire's Decapolis; to Qalat al Rabun, an Arab fortress, near Aljun, of immense size and beautiful proportions. It had been built by Saladin in the twelfth century in response to the Crusader castles with which the Christians had ringed the coast. It was captured by Tamerlane after a battle between Mamelukes and Mongols, for the Mamelukes had occupied that part of the country until the Ottoman Turks drove them out. From the top of its great tower, one could see on a clear night the lights of Jerusalem across the River Jordan and by day the hills of the West Bank, while away to the north, the mountains of Syria towered on the horizon. From here beacons were once lit which sent dreadful warnings to armed men across the land and in peacetime it was a stage of the pigeon post between Damascus and Cairo, which only took between sunset and sunrise to deliver, and never failed.

As we started on our descent from its summit I noticed my Bedouin driver gazing out across the plain with such an expression of yearning that I asked him what he was looking at. 'Jerusalem,' he answered simply, 'my home.' Driving back to Amman, where another 'Perhaps tomorrow' message was waiting for me, I decided that it was no good writing about an Arab king unless one could understand what he felt about Arab land and the Arab cause and to do that one had to go back – back to Jerusalem and to where its story and Hussein's own troubles began.

The first war between the Arabs and Israel was fought in 1948. Its immediate cause was the partitioning of Palestine by a vote in the United Nations General Assembly on 29 November 1947, but the roots of the two nations' antagonism go back to the First World War and beyond it. Turkey had declared war on the Allies in 1914 and King Hussein's great-grandfather, Sharif Hussein bin Ali, Sultan-Caliph and Prince of Mecca, was living in temporary exile from his Hashemite kingdom in Istanbul, as were Abdullah, Feisal and Ali, his sons. They had been suspected of Arab nationalism by Abdul Hamid, the last Turkish sultan, and rightly so, for it was Sharif Hussein and the Hashemites who, in June 1916, fired the first shot that led to the great Arab Revolt, a revolt which broke up the once mighty Ottoman Empire of the Middle East and freed the Arabs from a subjugation that had lasted for four hundred years. Abdullah and Feisal raised Arab armies and had fought side by side with the British in the First World War. The Arab Legion, with Colonel Lawrence of Arabia as its inspiration, distinguished itself in the desert, while Feisal's Arab army had ridden in triumph into Jerusalem with General Allenby in 1918. It was a resounding victory and Sharif Hussein felt certain they would be rewarded by the liberated Palestine and Greater Syria (which included Iraq and Kuwait) becoming Arab and Hashemite kingdoms. Indeed, the British had made extravagant promises to the Arab leaders when they needed their help to win the war, but they failed to keep them in the uneasy peace that followed. In a secret plan, known as the Sykes–Picot Agreement, which was signed in 1916, Britain and France had already carved up Turkey's former provinces between themselves, the French taking over Syria and the Lebanon, the British Palestine and Iraq, which was then called Mesopotamia. Their excuse and justification was that the Arabs were not yet fit to rule themselves and the countries were only under *mandate* to the European powers until such a time (undated) when they would be handed back. Quite arbitrarily and without consulting the countries' inhabitants, they then nominated the Arab rulers (under their tutelage) of their choice.

The French made Feisal titular king of the newly created Syria but then, after a nationalist revolt, they expelled him. The British had promised Abdullah Iraq, but then, fearing the same thing would happen, they reneged on their promise. But, worse still, from the Arab point of view, was the promise made by the British Foreign Secretary, Arthur Balfour, in 1917 to the Jews of the Diaspora. The Balfour Declaration guaranteed British support 'for the establishment in Palestine of a national home for the Jewish people'.* This, of course, could only be achieved at the expense of the Palestine Arabs, many of whom had fought in the Arab Legion, and who had conquered Palestine, and then lived there for the last one thousand four hundred years.

The Sykes–Picot Agreement had specifically left out the wild and desert country to the south of the newly created Syria so that it would act as a buffer between the possibly expansionist ambitions of the French and British interests in Palestine. This the British called Transjordan. It was almost entirely inhabited by Bedouin tribes, the camel-breeding

---

* After signing the Declaration, Arthur Balfour wrote to a friend: 'I have no idea what the result will be, but I am certain that it will lead to a very interesting situation.'

nomads who had burst out of Arabia in the seventh century to become the vanguard of Islam, and who had fought equally fiercely for their freedom in the recent war. Ethnically and economically identical to their neighbours in Palestine, the Arabs in this part of the previous 'province of Syria' were now in a state of turmoil, without leaders or government.

In early March 1928 the Emir Abdullah, Sharif Hussein's second son, left his father's palace in Mecca to carry out a 'tour of inspection' in the northern Hejaz, the Hashemite emirate. He was accompanied by a small army of regular troops and tribal levies. In Amman his arrival was greeted with wild enthusiasm. He was, after all, a Hashemite prince and the direct descendant of the Prophet. He sent a message to the British Governor in Jerusalem that he had come to restore law and order, but let it be known locally that he wished to recover Syria for his brother, Feisal. This put Britain in a fix. Fortunately, the new Colonial Secretary was Winston Churchill and he was at that moment in Cairo, debating the Middle Eastern 'problem', the nub of which was that an exhausted and impoverished Britain had over-extended herself, and could no longer safeguard her commitments in that part of the world.

Abdullah and Churchill met in Jerusalem to thrash out a deal. Churchill turned down Abdullah's request that Palestine and Transjordan or Iraq and Transjordan should be joined together under an Arab king, which would have made economic sense. Instead he proposed that Transjordan should become a Hashemite principality and offered it to Abdullah. Abdullah, who had expected to be re-offered Iraq, felt that the deserts of Transjordan were a very poor substitute, indeed hardly viable economically, but when Churchill promised him a British subsidy and agreed to exclude the country from the Balfour Declaration and hinted that Transjordan might well be the springboard to the Syrian throne in Damascus, he accepted, albeit with reluctance, keeping always at the back of his mind the dream of restoring one day Greater Syria and Jerusalem to Hashemite rule. As the exiled Feisal wrote to his brother Said in 1921, 'The wisest course is to take everything we can take and wait for tomorrow, because nights are pregnant and might give way to miracles . . .'

And so Abdullah ruled Transjordan under British tutelage and a League of Nations mandate for nineteen years spanning the war. His chief difficulty in doing so was an endemic lack of money and a paucity of arms, which were greatly needed now as a new threat to the stability of the Arab world had arisen. A fanatical Muslim sect, the Wahabis, who called themselves Al Ikhwan (the Brotherhood), had emerged in Central Arabia at the end of the war and were causing mayhem throughout the deserts of the Middle East. They had been skilfully exploited and led by Abdul Aziz bin Saud, the Emir of the Nejd, to support his claim of being 'King of the Bedouins' and would-be ruler of the entire Arabian peninsula. Their murderous raids terrorised the desert tribes from Kuwait to Iraq, from Palestine to Transjordan. It was only in 1930, after King Abdullah had asked for and secured the services of Captain John Bagot Glubb (who built up an extremely efficient Bedouin army in Iraq and defeated their warriors there), that Abdullah finally managed to pacify the Transjordan deserts.

During the Second World War Glubb's Arab Legion was transformed into a small but very efficient army which fought with the British (once again) in the 1941 campaigns in Iraq and Syria. Churchill, in spite of everything, had remained on good terms with Abdullah and now he was to find him his staunchest ally during the early days of Britain's lonely stand against the Axis powers. Indeed, at one moment tiny Transjordan was Britain's only ally in the Middle East.

But once again the Arabs were to lose out in the ensuing peace. First came the 1947 United Nations bombshell: the vote in favour of the Partition of Palestine; and then, six months later, after three years of policing Jewish-occupied Palestine and being shot at and bombed by the Zionists, the British government's decision to give up its mandate. It announced its intention of pulling out in May 1948 and made it clear that it had no intention of acting as referee when Jews and Arabs took over that part of Palestine which Partition had allocated to each of them.

The story of the first Israeli–Arab war, which was the inevitable result of Partition is too long to go into here. Suffice it to state that the Jordanians were let down by their Arab allies, but that their Arab Legion secured for them the Old City in Jerusalem, the part that all Muslims venerate, and the 'West Bank' of the River Jordan, while the Jewish nation learnt a valuable lesson in *Realpolitik* which led to a re-thinking of their ideas and of their defences, the birth of a formidable new army and a more determined and aggressive form of Zionism.

People's opinions vary about Abdullah. 'He was the most impatient man I ever met'; he was 'The King with a twinkle'; 'he was forever plotting the aggrandisement of his country and his family'; he was 'the sworn enemy of the Jews', etc. But few can deny that Abdullah was one of the outstanding Arab figures of his day. He was also undeniably an Arab aristocrat of the old school. A grand seigneur who exemplified the Arab traditions of generosity and magnanimity, he inspired loyalty and love in the people around him, and he never lost touch with the Bedu, his people, frequently spending long periods in the desert with them. His grandson, Hussein, was one of his closest companions and the affection between grandfather and grandson was mutual. 'He is the elite of the elite. He is the continuity of my dynasty,' Abdullah told Nasser Nashabishi, the night before he died.

Abdullah's obsessive love of Jerusalem and his habit of attending Friday prayers in the holy places there was a constant worry to his family and advisers. Assassination is the occupational hazard of monarchs, especially Middle Eastern ones. But King Abdullah, like his grandson, Hussein, was a fervent Muslim, and a fatalist. 'I believe in God – my life is in His hands,' he would tell his grandson, and, 'Until my time comes, no one can harm me; and when my time comes, no one can guard me.'

He was well guarded that Friday, 20 July 1951. In fact, because of several warnings that a coup might be attempted, the presence of troops in the Haram es Sharif, the holy centre of Muslim Jerusalem, and in front of the Al Asqa Mosque itself, where he was about to pray, was very noticeable. 'Don't imprison me, Habis!' he said to his Chief of Staff, Habis Majali, and told him that so many soldiers in a holy place was not suitable.

'Then he entered the Mosque to be greeted by the Shaikh, who bent to kiss his hand. Simultaneously a man appeared behind the great door. There was a pistol in his hand and a shot rang out. Abdullah never saw his assassin, although he was less than six feet away. He fell instantly, his turban rolling away across the floor. He was dead. Hussein, only a few paces behind his grandfather, was stunned. Then shooting broke out all around him. He saw the assassin with glazed eyes pointing the pistol at him. There was a shot, but fortunately the bullet was deflected by a medal the prince was wearing over his heart. The assassin then fell to the ground, riddled by bullets from the escort. In the meantime, Abdullah's companions had scrambled helter-skelter for cover, their one desire to save their own lives. It was a pitiful exhibition of human weakness which Hussein was never to forget.'

Some hours later, after being treated for shock, Hussein, in crumpled uniform and shaken by grief – he was fifteen, still only a boy – stood by the airport outside Jerusalem, scarcely knowing what to do next. A British officer in Arab Legion uniform came up and saluted. He was Squadron Leader Jock Dalgleish, Second-in-Command of the fledgling Arab Legion Air Force. 'Come with me, Sir,' he said, 'I'll look after you,' and he flew Hussein back to Amman. *

* I have taken this account of Abdullah's assassination from Major-General James Lunt's biography, *Hussein in Jordan* (1989), as well as much else.

It was the beginning of a friendship which has lasted down the years. It was also the first time that someone had tried to kill Hussein – but not the last.

Abdullah had married three times, and his eldest son, Tallal, succeeded him. But Tallal's life had been blighted by an incurable (in those days) mental illness and the strains of ruling a country plunged into crisis by the murder of his father would soon prove more than his fragile health could stand. During the three years that followed, his illness grew worse and, after a meeting in August 1952 of the Divan and his close relatives, it was decided that he should abdicate in favour of his eldest son, Hussein.

It was about a year after this that my husband and I stayed at the British embassy in Paris, in the Faubourg St Honoré, and Maudie Harvey, the ambassadress, told me the following curious story; but as she and Sir Oliver (later Lord) Harvey are now both dead I have corroborated it through their private secretary of that time, Walter Lees.

Not very long after the Harveys had arrived in Paris, the following dramatic events took place: the Harveys were coming down the grand staircase of the embassy one day preparatory to lunching out, when there was a shout and a scuffle in the hall below them and a veiled but well-dressed woman shot past the startled secretary, who was also going out, and the maître d'hotel, who was holding the front door open for Their Excellencies, and precipitated herself at Sir Oliver's feet. 'Save me, save me!' she cried, 'shut them out or I shall be killed.' Faced by a couple of wild-looking Arabs who were brandishing revolvers, the maître d'hotel had already come to the same conclusion and closed the heavy embassy doors in her pursuers' faces. 'Lock them,' ordered Sir Oliver and took the distraught lady into an ante-room where he sat her down and listened to her story.

It soon emerged that the British ambassador had given asylum to a run-away queen, the wife of a reigning monarch who at the time was undergoing psychiatric treatment by doctors in Paris. According to poor Queen Zein's story he suffered terribly from the delusions of his mania and every now and then believed she was conspiring with courtiers to poison him, at which times he would order his palace guard to do away with her. The queen, though she loved her husband, feared for her life and she had escaped the close supervision she had been put under on the excuse of going shopping. She had then ordered the royal car to turn in at the embassy gate, but she had been followed and she now begged the Harveys to hide her and to resist all attempts to hand her back.

It was a delicate situation. The Harveys had no previous knowledge or confirmation of Queen Zein's story, but they believed her and in spite of dismayed and excitable telegrams from the Foreign Office urging the utmost caution, they stuck to their decision. The queen was given a bedroom and a sitting-room that could be discreetly guarded, a nightie and a toothbrush from Maudie, and all the sympathy she needed until her dilemma could be sorted out.

It took many days and bristled with national and international complications. Finally, Sir Oliver devised a master-plan. A decoy car with a brave volunteer, veiled like an Arab lady, left the embassy one morning in the ambassador's Rolls-Royce. It was immediately seen and followed by the king's 'heavies' who had been waiting in the St Honoré Faubourg for just such an event, while the real queen escaped by the garden exit where another car was waiting which whisked her through Paris to a private aeroplane which flew her out of the country.

Hussein, after attending a variety of schools in Jordan and Victoria College in Alexandria, had been sent to Harrow School, where he worked moderately hard and excelled at games. The trauma of his grandfather's assassination had left its mark and his house matron, in whom he confided, found him 'highly strung' and 'sometimes lonely'. His best friend at school was his cousin Feisal and the two boys shared a passion for cars and driving them at outrageous speeds. Hussein kept a secret Rover with Maurice Raynor, a local garage owner. Raynor soon became a trusted ally of the boys and eventually he and his family moved to Jordan to become the king's chief mechanic and close friend. At weekends Hussein would escape to London, where there were parties and dances and fun organised for him by the Jordanian ambassador, Fawzi al-Mulki, which his housemaster and teachers no doubt deplored.

Hussein was barely seventeen when his father abdicated and there was a year to wait before he could assume his Royal Prerogative. His mother's brother, Sharif Nasser, who was to be one of the young king's wisest counsellors and his most faithful friend, suggested a short course at Sandhurst and to Hussein's delight this was decided on. Officer Cadet King Hussein was taken on the Sandhurst strength on 9 September 1952 and for the next nine months he was put through that rigorous but admirable training that has been the foundation of so many great soldiers' careers. Hussein was a born soldier, and the discipline at Sandhurst did not irk him. He excelled at field exercises, became a marksman and was soon promoted to Corporal Cadet. Colonel David Sutherland, Black Watch and SAS, was one of his instructors and Sergeant-Major 'Jacky' Lord was his Drill Sergeant. It was typical of Hussein that when a *This is Your Life* TV programme was made years later about Sergeant-Major Lord, he agreed to take part and was smuggled into the studio to appear before the delighted 'Jacky' as one of his most successful cadets. When his Sandhurst course ended, Hussein returned to Jordan to take up his constitutional powers and begin his reign. He had inherited formidable problems and he had to deal with them immediately. There was to be no respite.

The climate of opinion in Jordan had very much changed since Abdullah's murder. With the revolution and overthrow of King Farouk in Egypt in 1952, a wave of republican anti-colonial (and therefore anti-French and anti-British) left-wing socialism swept over the Arab world. It was fostered and fed by Egypt's new ruler, Gamal Abdel Nasser, who had come to power by a military coup which had ended years of British occupation. Nasser was a republican pan-Arab who aspired to the leadership of the Arab world, but always to the advantage of Egyptian interests.

Abdullah's assassination had been the result of a Palestinian plot. Many Palestinian Arabs disliked and distrusted the Hashemite dynasty. They had wanted confrontation with Israel, not Abdullah's canny diplomacy. They thought that Jordan, despite her newly acquired freedom, was still far too closely influenced by Britain and that the Arab Legion, with its British officers commanded by Glubb Pasha, was not truly an Arab force. After the disastrous 1948 war, in which so many of them had lost their prosperity and homes, they felt humiliated and bitter and they resented Jordan's take-over of the West Bank, which had once been their own country. Six hundred thousand refugees from Palestine had fled into Jordan after the war, and had to be accommodated in camps in a desert country whose economy could scarcely support its own inhabitants, let alone this tragic and terrifying influx. Their overriding desire was to return to the land of their fathers and they implacably denied, and would always deny, Israel's very right to exist.

As Hussein's reign progressed, the Palestinians, and the many thousand others who joined them, would prove to be the most politically active and radical of all King Hussein's subjects, eventually dominating the nation's politics and, like some latter-day Trojan horse, their outcome.

For the next seven years the monarchy in Jordan stumbled from crisis to crisis. At one moment the British ambassador, Charles Johnston, wrote: 'Not a single foreign observer in Amman outside the British embassy believed that, even with British and American help, the Jordanian monarchy had a chance of surviving.' That it did so was due entirely to the king's personal courage and determination.

Of courage the 'plucky little king', as the newspapers called him, certainly had plenty. But it is debatable, during this period, whether he had a sufficiency of common sense.

The British embassy garden at that time was in the royal compound, and Sir Charles Johnston has told me how the young king would often turn up in his office, or drawing-room, with some wonderful new plan he had dreamt up which would solve all Jordan's problems and how he had frequently to bring him down to earth by a cold douche of not-always-welcome reality.

That he made mistakes is certain – who wouldn't at his age? His impetuous and abrupt dismissal of Glubb Pasha was probably one of them, although the political need to distance himself from British influence and to arabise and modernise his army was without doubt real.

He already had one (arranged) failed marriage behind him, and in politics he also showed lack of experience and judgment. The appointment of the unreliable Ali abu Nowar in Glubb's place as Commander-in-Chief was certainly unwise and, after the free elections of 1956, in which a left-wing majority was returned, the choice of Suluman Naboulsi, a West Bank lawyer with Marxist tendencies, as Premier was plainly disastrous. So was Hussein's decision to allow Naboulsi to choose his own cabinet, a cabinet which was responsible to parliament instead of, as previously, to the king. This deliberate policy of Hussein's of allowing younger men in politics to 'show their mettle' led to some extraordinary results.

When Hussein ordered his army to advance into Israel at the time of the Suez confrontation in 1956, the cabinet countermanded his order; shortly afterwards his Prime Minister made several fiery pro-Communist speeches and opened diplomatic relations with the Soviet Union and Red China; shortly after that, General Ali and his newly appointed non-Bedouin officers hatched a plot (encouraged by Nasser) to overthrow the monarchy by a military coup, which was only just aborted by the loyalty to Hussein of an elite regiment and the mutiny of Bedouin soldiers at Zerqa, who thought their king had been killed. Hussein, who had proof of the government's involvement in the plot, demanded its resignation, but he was isolated and marooned in his palace in Amman by roadblocks set up by the army. That evening he sent for Ali to demand explanations.

At the height of their heated conversation the telephone rang. It was the Brigade Commander at Zerqa. 'The situation is out of control here,' the Brigadier told Ali. 'The whole Brigade believe their king is dead or will be tonight. Their officers cannot control them. They are trying to move to Amman. Nothing will save the situation except the immediate presence of His Majesty.' Hussein seized the telephone and shouted down it that he was very much alive and would come at once. He ordered his car to be brought round and quickly changed into uniform. The account of his dramatic drive through the night to Zerqa, not knowing what kind of reception awaited him, is told by the king himself in his autobiography, *Uneasy Lies the Head.* He has said that he never felt so angry in his life, but the milling mass of shouting and excited men he found at Zerqa, who went berserk when they saw their king, mobbing him, kissing him and swearing that they were his men, firing shots in the air and calling for the execution of all traitors, reassured him completely, just as he was to reassure and calm the mutinous soldiery by his very presence. Having persuaded them to return to barracks he drove back to Amman to find the palace ringed by the faithful 1st Armoured Car Regiment and the wretched Ali abu Nowar cowering in his study, where he had taken refuge from the soldiers outside.

In the aftermath of the coup and the Zerqa mutiny, Hussein showed a magnanimity which astonishes. Ali was flown out to Egypt and eventually granted a free pardon. His cousin, Brigadier Ma'an, and many other officers were court-martialled, sentenced to death and then either reprieved or given not very long terms of imprisonment. Naboulsi survived to become Foreign Secretary in the cabinet which was then formed by the next Prime Minister. It was still Communist-orientated and by the end of April Hussein, finally convinced that Jordan would go Communist if he did not act swiftly, dismissed the government and returned to a period of direct rule. He appointed two dependable elder statesmen, Ibrahim Hashim and Samir Rifai, as Prime Minister and Foreign Secretary, and his grandfather's old friend, Major-General Habis Majali, as Commander-in-Chief. Majali was a tough but likeable man, an Arab aristocrat from the Kerak, who had been Abdullah's Chief-of-Staff at the time of his murder. He told Charles Johnston one night over dinner at the British embassy, as he passed the butter, 'We Majalis are used to killing and being killed.' Martial law was declared and political parties were banned. Curfews kept down demonstrations, the army was quietly purged and Hussein breathed a sigh of relief.

But not for long. Iraq, Jordan's neighbour and partner under a rather airy-fairy pact which Feisal and Hussein signed in February 1958, joining them still more closely in 'political union', was also suffering from the nationalist-socialist ideas that, encouraged by Nasser, were sweeping through the Arab world, and its young army officers held strongly radical views. Two of them, Colonel Abdul Karim Kassem and Colonel Abdul Salam Arif, carried out a coup in which Hussein's Hashemite cousin

Feisal, the women in his family, his uncle, the Regent and even two baby princes were gunned down and brutally murdered in the garden of the royal palace. General Nuri es Said, the unpopular and corrupt army chief, fled disguised in a woman's *burqua* but was captured and shot, his body being dismembered and dragged through the streets by a howling mob. One of those who took part in Colonel Kassem's coup and the massacres of the royal family was an ambitious young officer of whom more, much more, was to be heard – a certain Lieutenant Saddam Hussein.

At first King Hussein thought wildly of avenging his cousin's death and even of claiming the vacant throne – the Union had, after all, made him deputy head of state, but wiser counsels prevailed and soon, one after another, first Turkey, then Britain, then America recognised the bloodstained regime of Colonel Kassem, Iraq's new president.

King Hussein was shattered by the massacre. Not only had he lost a much-loved cousin, whose friendship he had enjoyed since their school-days at Harrow, but the end of Hashemite rule in Iraq brought new dangers to his own frail and now totally isolated country and its monarchy.

President Nasser was quick to exploit them. Having already established a tight embargo of goods reaching Jordan, he now prevented Jordan's oil tankers from sailing from Baghdad. An oil blockade would inevitably bring Jordan's economy to a grinding halt.

Hussein had shown great physical courage during the failed revolution-ary coup and the Zerqa mutiny in April. He now showed his countrymen he was capable of moral courage, too. His cabinet, chosen by him, supported his decisions and, after he had explained the crisis to a hastily reconvened parliament and senate, Hussein formally requested from Britain and America the immediate support of British or American troops. 'I look upon this move,' he told them, 'as a symbol of the ties that bind free peoples in times of crisis.'

It may have been lucky for King Hussein that Harold Macmillan was Prime Minister and Julian Amery, Macmillan's son-in-law, Minister of State at the Foreign Office, both of whom held him in high regard, but, in all conscience, he deserved a little luck. After an all-night session of the British cabinet, the Parachute Brigade was ordered to fly to Jordan via Cyprus, where Wing-Commander Jock Dalgleish happened to be in transit and would join them to command the RAF support. They would fly over Israel, with or without permission, their objective being to reach Amman, secure the airfield there and protect King Hussein and his government. It was a calculated risk, but to Macmillan's credit and thanks to his courage it came off and 'Operation Fortitude' did much to restore good relations between Britain and Jordan, which had been shaken by Suez and by Glubb's abrupt dismissal. *

The British stayed till November and normality seemed to return to Jordan. Hussein visited every unit of his army by day and consolidated his popularity with the soldiers. He began again to give the occasional palace party at night. After all, he was still only twenty-two. World opinion was also changing in favour of Jordan's anti-Communist stand. The USA, which had already announced its Eisenhower Doctrine of support for countries who would stand up to the Communist threat, produced $50 million in aid and the United Nations passed a resolution – the first of many – calling on all member nations to respect the sovereignty of others, which was unanimously adopted by all the Arab nations, though it did not stop Cairo and Damascus radios pouring out their messages of hate and invective, and even open sedition, against Jordan.

It also seemed that the political skill and firmness of Samir Rifai and the tough army discipline of General Habis Majali had brought Jordan once more under firm government. Plots, and there were many, were discovered before they could be implemented and the perpetrators were punished. By October Hussein felt he deserved a holiday. He decided to fly to Switzerland with Sharif Nasser, his uncle, Jock Dalgleish, Maurice Raynor and a couple of RJAF officers, who would bring their small RJAF Dove plane back to Jordan. That was the plan but things turned out differently. Once over Syria, and despite all normal clearances, they were suddenly, and peremptorily, ordered by radio to land at Damascus. Scenting a plot, Hussein turned the little plane round and began flying back to Jordan. They switched their radio off and dropped almost to ground level to avoid detection. Dalgleish had just taken over the controls when two Syrian MIG 17 fighters appeared from nowhere and went into attack. Had they fired the Jordanians would all have been killed, but it soon appeared that the MIGs were bent on a more subtle form of murder: they were forcing them instead to crash. By now they were only thirty miles from the Jordanian frontier, but the Syrians continued diving at them in concerted attacks until they were well into Jordanian territory. It was entirely due to Jock Dalgleish's flying skill and experience, and his ability to turn in much closer circles than his attackers, that Hussein's and all their lives were saved.

---

* It would not be amiss here to acknowledge Hussein's personal generosity to Glubb in his retirement – a generosity not matched by the British government's initial pension award.

Landing in triumph to a hero's welcome (the crowds had heard about it on Amman Radio) he decided not to go on holiday after all. East, West, home's best. But he has written: 'The scrape with the Syrian MIGs was the narrowest escape from death I have ever had and I must admit that at one time I felt, to use the Air Force jargon, that I had "bought it" . . . the incident was an attack on a Head of State as yet unparalleled in history and it will take me longer to forget it than it has taken me to forgive those responsible.' Dalgleish, after praising the king's coolness and quiet courage, wrote: 'Drenched in perspiration from the exertions and nervous tensions of the last twenty minutes, I suggested we have breakfast. This, however, proved impossible. The manoeuvres we had subjected our aircraft to had smashed all the crockery on board. But Maurice Raynor, like a true Brit, came to the rescue. He had nursed a thermos of tea throughout all the buffeting and, using some plastic cups . . . poured out a nice cup of tea . . .'

What else would you expect from a Londoner?

There were other attempts on Hussein's life during the next two or three years, and on 29 August 1960 his Prime Minister, Hazza Majali, one of his closest friends, was blown up by a bomb, and a short time afterwards a particularly nasty attempt was made on his own life by a member of his household. Who it was, was never discovered.

After Majalis' murder, Hussein felt it prudent not to sleep in the palace for a night or two. He decided to stay with the Raynors in their small bungalow in the palace grounds. Mrs Raynor unpacked for him and he asked her to throw away his old bottle of eye-drops as he had just bought a new and fresh one. When she poured it into the sink she watched in horror as the 'eye-drops' frothed and bubbled wherever they splashed, peeling off the chromium from the sink's fittings. Even the king blanched at the thought of what would have happened, had he used them.

Hussein was so outraged by the murder of his Prime Minister that he thought at first of attacking Syria who, without doubt, egged on by Nasser, was behind the assassination. He felt he could not go on for ever being the victim of Syrian and Egyptian plots. He no longer believed in Nasser's role as 'spokesman for the whole Arab world' or 'defender of their faith'. He himself was a fervent Muslim who, from religious just as much as political reasons, was strongly opposed to Communism, and he himself felt equally capable of defending and explaining the Arab position to the world.

In October 1960 he decided to fly to Washington and address the General Assembly of the United Nations. His speech followed immediately that of Nikita Khrushchev's famous shoe-banging one. When

Hussein stepped up to the rostrum Khrushchev and the entire UAR delegation left their seats and walked out. Such calculated rudeness won him immediate sympathy and when he sat down it was obvious that the young king, fresh from his near-miss escapes from assassination, ringed round by enemies in a small country that was fighting for its physical, let alone economic, survival, yet bravely proclaiming its stance in the conflict of ideologies that was threatening the peace of the world, had deeply moved and won over many of his audience. 'In the great struggle between Communism and freedom, there can be no neutrality,' he had told them, and he had warned that the growing tension between Jordan and the United Arab Republic, the long-delayed independence of Algeria and the unanswered problems of Palestine were three vital flash-points in the Middle East that would affect the peace of the whole world. President Eisenhower, Prime Minister Harold Macmillan and Secretary-General Dag Hammarskjöld all personally congratulated Hussein on his speech and he left America feeling that at long last he had truly put Jordan on the map.

In the next seven years Jordan achieved a much greater stability and prosperity than it had ever known. It was due, to a large extent, to the resilience of the Jordanian people themselves and to a certain extent to the refugees, not only Palestinians, who had flooded into the country and whose education and trading instincts, as well as skills in engineering and in constructional work, were often of a high degree. Amman became a modern capital city, unrecognisable from the small provincial town of Hussein's childhood. But social life was still quite formal and circumspect and the young RAF officer stationed at Amman who wanted to bring a pretty English girl with him to one of Hussein's Scottish reel parties at the palace needed to ask a diplomat's wife to chaperone her. She was Miss 'Toni' Gardiner, the daughter of Colonel Walker Gardiner, who was helping Jordan solve their water supply problems.

As the king, by convention, could not ask a lady to dance, the blonde and petite Miss Gardiner was taken across the floor by her chaperone to be introduced. She was struck dumb by shyness, but somehow it was managed. They danced, courted, got engaged and were married in a remarkably short time. He called her Muna al Hussein, which means 'Hussein's wish' and Princess Muna, as she insisted on being called, was well liked in Jordan. She made him a good queen and for many years a happy man, bearing him four children, the eldest of whom was called Abdullah, after his great-grandfather.

But in 1972 Hussein met Alia Toukan, the beautiful tawny-haired daughter of a Jordanian diplomat. She was well-educated and intelligent and was equally at ease in Arab and Western society, among politicians and generals, artists and diplomats; altogether she was a more sophisticated lady. Hussein was 'bowled over' and, soon after his divorce from Princess Muna, they were married. But the happiness of this third marriage was short-lived. Only five years later Queen Alia was killed in a helicopter crash as she was returning to Amman from visiting a hospital in South Jordan. Hussein, for a time, was inconsolable and seemed plunged in melancholy. He retreated from all social life and not even his large and lively young family (there were by now eight children) could cheer him up. But then, almost miraculously, he fell in love again. As one of his courtiers said with a heart-felt sigh: 'It was a great relief'.

Jordan's independence and stability and the welfare of all its people have been Hussein's primary concern throughout his reign. He has also dreamed of the eventual unity of the Arab world, of a pan-Arab renaissance, of the restoration by Israel of the Occupied Territories and perhaps even, one day, of Jerusalem itself, but it was the practical problem of Palestine and the fate of the Palestinian refugees that dominated the policy of Jordan in the years that were to follow.

The Palestine Liberation Organisation, or PLO, accommodates a number of organisations with differing objectives, tactics and philosophies. The largest and most effective of these undoubtedly is Fatah, which was founded in 1957 by Yasser Arafat as an underground resistance movement, but which came out into the open in 1965 and took control of the PLO, with Arafat as its Chairman. Arafat was born in Cairo in 1929 and is a distant relative of the once pro-Nazi Mufti of Jerusalem. He was trained as an engineer and he made a considerable fortune working in Kuwait, a fortune which he dedicated to the Palestinian cause.

It has been the turns and twists of PLO policies, their internecine quarrels and the fundamentally flawed nature of Arafat's leadership that have compounded the Palestinian problem.

King Hussein took part in the 1967 or 'Six-Day War' with Israel, as a matter of honour and Arab solidarity, only to be let down by Nasser's dishonest politics and Egypt's abysmal military performance. As a result, the loss of the West Bank and Jerusalem, the new wave of refugees into Jordan, the Fedayeen insurrection, the emergence in Israel of expansionist Zionism, the Black Septembrists and the rise of Palestinian terrorism, the expulsion of the PLO from Jordan, have all been part of the Palestine story. The countless American, United Nations and Jordanian peace initiatives, the withdrawal of American support and finally, at the time of my visit, the Intifada and the breaking of Jordanian relations with thè PLO are only further developments in the Middle East problem. It is a problem that is still a long way from being solved, but no one can say that Hussein has not tried, over and over again, to do so.

Word finally came through that King Hussein would see me, but that my audience had been postponed to my very last morning in Jordan, hour unknown. So, packed and organised for an early afternoon flight to Bangkok, I sat biting my nails in the hotel lobby, waiting for the summons. At last the telephone rang and the manager came over to tell me: the Basmani palace. Twelve noon. My car and Bedouin driver were waiting outside. There was just time to get there.

The Basmani palace nestles into a hillside on the outskirts of Amman, with splendid views of the city which, like Rome, is built on at least seven hills. It is of solid works-department Middle Eastern style, with a couple of cupolas thrown in for luck, and its bleak undeveloped grounds are surrounded by high metal-mesh fencing. Guards challenged then saluted us, but the security appeared to be no more than is normal in most palaces today. A tall Arab in an impeccable Savile Row suit, whom I took to be a court minister or head of protocol, received me. He bore an uncanny resemblance to my late cousin Peter Wilson, Chairman of Sotheby's, as, with exquisite courtesy, he apologised for the delays, explaining that the king might even now be a little late as he was embroiled in meetings and arrangements for an emergency meeting of the Arab heads of state.

The room I was shown into was a cool and comfortable Western-style drawing-room. White silk damask covered the walls, a wonderful Persian carpet lay underfoot, three huge white sofas with scarlet and white silk cushions looked after comfort, and there were some good bits of antique furniture and lots of marble-topped little tables with flowers and family objects on them. On a table desk at one end of the room were off-duty photographs of Their Majesties' friends: King Juan Carlos and Queen Sofia of Spain, signed with love; the Swedish royal family; as well as many of their own and very extended Hashemite one. Pride of place was given to a faded photograph of an old man whom I took to be Hussein's grandfather, King Abdullah.

I sat on one of the large sofas and waited. Behind my head silver daggers made a pattern on the wall and on perspex shelves small antiquities; Roman glass and Nabataean pots were displayed. In front of me hung two large Molly Bishop-style portraits of Their Majesties; Queen Noor's white dress and the scarlet sash of some royal Jordanian order giving the keynote to the room's decoration. She is very pretty and, despite the picture's formality, very natural. A mane of fair hair hangs round her shoulders and her finely chiselled features are somehow un-American. In fact her father, Najeeb J. Halaby, one-time government official and president of Pan-Am airways, is of Syrian origin, while her mother is Swedish, though both settled in the United States a long time ago. Lisa Halaby was an American citizen when she arrived in Jordan in 1976, having studied architecture and urban planning at Princeton University prior to taking up work on a new university that was being built in Jordan.

Although Lisa Halaby had fallen as much in love with the king as he with her, she did not accept his proposal of marriage at once. There were many difficulties. It would not be easy taking on a family of eight children, some of whom were teenagers; America was far from popular in the Arab world of the 1970s; Hussein had already been married three times and there was his enormous extended family, to all of whom he was devoted, to take on board. Jordan was still a male-dominated country. There was also the question of her religion, her language, and her American culture; but in the end love triumphed and the marriage has been a very happy and successful one. Hussein named his bride Lisa Noor al Hussein, which means 'The Light of Hussein'. Queen Noor and he have had four more children, two boys and two girls, and she now plays a very active part in Jordan's public life, specifically in the cultural and academic development of the country, and the Jordanian Red Cross. I was thinking how fortunate Hussein had been in his marriages when the door opened and he walked in.

Hussein has the gift of putting people at their ease, of talking naturally and spontaneously and of making it seem as if you are the one person in the world that he wishes to converse with, and that day, when I knew perfectly well he was aching to get away and snatch a quick sandwich in between serious political meetings, he exercised it to the full.

He told me the Arab world was deeply worried by the mass exodus of Russian Jews into Israel. It was thought as many as half a million were to be granted exit visas by Gorbachev and it was feared they would mostly be settled on the West Bank by the Israelis, in the Occupied Territories. He hoped to arrange talks in the next few days that would thrash out a united Arab stance on this emergency before the summit meeting of Gorbachev and President Bush in Washington, but as always there were serious difficulties. I asked him if he did not sometimes despair of the Arab League's ever *not* making difficulties, or *ever* acting in unison, and he firmly disagreed: the pressures from their own people, as well as international opinion, were greater today than they had ever been before.

People are better educated, they think for themselves, they see what is happening, what other nations think, through the media and on TV, and then he stopped, and paused. All the same, he admitted, the Arab world has not yet understood the political earthquake that has taken place in the West, nor what the collapse of Soviet Communism and Marxist ideology really means.

He told me that his richer Arab neighbours now produced 65 per cent of the world's oil and that had made them arrogant, uncaring. This had a bearing on their complacent and dilatory approach to other nations' problems. They simply believed that because of their economic clout their own confrontation with Israel had diminished. 'But the refugee camps are still there,' he added passionately, 'and no one has resolved the human rights problem of the Palestinian people. It still exists and while it exists extremists are a grave danger to both sides.'

I asked him what would happen if Israel pushed all the West Bank Palestinians over the Jordan to make room for the new influx of Soviet Jews. 'You could not, after all, fight or kill your own race, and would any other Arab country come to your help?'

'Yes,' he answered, 'that would indeed be terrible. We have already received more than a million refugees. There simply wouldn't be enough land or water to sustain any more.' He did not answer the last part of my question, nor could he know that before long a million more refugees would indeed pour into Jordan, but from Kuwait and Iraq, and that he would turn none of them back.

We talked then about his recent shock tactics with the PLO, and how, having lost patience with their intransigence and intrigues, he had cut all administrative links and aid to the Palestinians of the West Bank. 'They are on their own now,' he told me, and when I asked him whether making the PLO stand on its own two feet had made them more responsible, he answered, 'On the whole, yes.' But eventually, he thought, they were bound to need help from Jordan and he still hoped one day that some kind of federation between Palestine and Jordan would come about. He believed that the Intifada – or spontaneous uprising of the Palestinians in the Occupied Territories – had had much more effect on world opinion than any amount of PLO terrorism, which he had always strongly condemned.

He did not seem to think much of Arafat as a statesman, but he admired his gifts as a public relations man and propagandist. His greatest fear was that extremism, born of despair, might take over on both sides of the Jordan and he felt there was urgent need for a new pan-Arabic assessment.

I asked him if he thought Arafat had the wisdom or judgment to lead the Palestinians now that they were on their own. 'Could anyone else, a stronger man, perhaps emerge?'

The King stalled on a direct answer, but thought anything was possible if only the PLO 'could agree among themselves'.

Although he was sitting quietly beside me, a short, compact man in a neat city suit and talking gently in a surprisingly deep voice about his country's politics and its future, I was very conscious of the restless urgency, the energy and dynamism of a man of action behind his calm. It is immediately apparent that he is still a soldier, a leader – possibly still an over-impulsive one? – and that, behind the courtesy and the charm, lies the strength of instinctive authority, born perhaps of heredity, and a long line of autocratic kings.

When I asked how he could forgive those individuals and countries who had so often plotted to overthrow and murder him and who never ceased to blacken his name, he thought for a bit, then turned on me a very innocent, youthful smile: 'One must be realistic, one must always take the pragmatic view, never the personal one. One must try and see what will be good for one's country in the long run.' Never take an assassination attempt personally? My mouth fell open and words failed me, but it was quite obvious that he meant it.

We talked about American policies on the Middle East, or rather, as he put it, its lack of a policy other than the support of Israel, and occasional 'crisis-management'; of the strength of the Jewish vote and media; of the difficulty of any initiative moving forward, or in any direction whatever, during election time in the USA.

He felt the Middle East was entering a period of exceptional instability. The end of the Cold War and the Great Powers' preoccupation with events in Europe had distracted the world's attention from the area and the extreme frustrations that were building up in the Arab world.

He saw that world and his own country at a crossroads. There were great opportunities, but also very great dangers. His duty lay in steering his country safely through those dangers. 'My role, my fight, is to bring dignity and peace to all my people,' he told me as I rose to say goodbye. 'Just now it is a heavy fight.'

Six weeks after I left Jordan, Saddam Hussein invaded Kuwait and King Hussein faced the ultimate crisis of his reign. He found himself between a hammer and an anvil, the devil and the deep blue sea. Jordan was a close ally of Iraq during its eight-year-long war with fundamentalist Iran. Many Jordanians and Palestinians fought in it, and food and war

materials were brought through Jordan to its fronts. The country's economic stability – through other Arab countries' and the West's default –
was now heavily dependent on Iraq. Ninety thousand Jordanians worked
there and repatriated their earnings in valuable foreign currency. Saddam
Hussein paid Jordan at least $125 million a year in subsidies and loans.
Iraq was Jordan's largest market and Jordan's port of Aqaba had enormously benefited from the bulk of Iraqi trade. Furthermore, the waters
of the Euphrates had been diverted to supplement Jordan's own irrigation
schemes and its food production now largely depends on this new source.

The rupture of their alliance would probably bring economic ruin and
possibly starvation to Jordan, who already had a million Palestinian
refugees to accommodate (and now half a million more, who have
flooded across the deserts from Kuwait and Iraq). Yet no one who knows
King Hussein or any member of the Hashemite royal family can doubt
their personal sympathy and involvement with the West, their loyalty
to the United Nations and to the rule of international law, their horror of
inter-Arab aggression and the violation of national boundaries. Jordan's
whole case in the Arab–Israeli conflict has rested on this. But again,
those who know Hussein of Jordan and the story of his past will also
understand his fierce family pride, his innate and committed Arabism.
Until the Saudis deprived them of it, were not the Hashemites Princes
of Mecca, hereditary keepers and defenders of the Holy Places? And
were they not direct descendants of the Prophet, the noblest of all
the Arab dynasties? 'Sharif' means both those things and it is perhaps
significant when Saddam Hussein formally annexed Kuwait and declared
a jihad against the West, and thousands of Jordanian and Palestinian
volunteers rushed to join it, that King Hussein revived his great-
grandfather's title, Sharif Hussein – or had it thrust upon him.

The end of the Gulf War has produced no miracle for King Hussein,
only more problems. Whether the adventurism of a ruthless, inhuman
and power-crazed dictator has finally been crushed remains to be seen,
and whether the rising tide of Arab nationalism in the Middle East will
now change direction is also uncertain. To my mind it is the Palestinian
question which is still the acute one, the one which will ultimately
decide King Hussein's fate, and I somehow doubt that international
conferences will resolve it. If one turns the pages of history one will find
not only the sad story of the Crusaders, but also those of the Dardanelles,
Kut-al Amara, Suez. Fate or history in the Middle East rarely rewards
the just. It never favours the foreigner, 'the infidel', and it always takes
its revenge upon those who see the region through their own eyes.

Most Arabs believe that the West's Middle Eastern policies have been entirely dictated by self-interest and by their greed for Arab oil, and most Arabs refuse to forget the past.

Through Arab eyes it was the Western allies who led them into the 1914–18 war, promised them independence and instead carved their land up into colonial mandates and created the state of Israel in Palestine. They believe that it is the West that has created Arab disunity from that day to this. Since 1945 they have struggled to recover it and to shake off the humiliations of the past, but there have been new humiliations . . . Millions of Arabs still believe that only another great Arab leader can avenge their successive defeats by Israel, return their people to Palestine and undo the shame of their Westernised corruption, their dependence on foreign powers, their falling away from the ideals of Islam.

I recall standing on the tower of Qalat al Rabun, the tower that was built by Saladin, and looking towards the Jordan and Jerusalem, where all King Hussein's troubles began. They are far from over yet.

In the last year King Hussein has taken on another battle, a personal one this time, which he will fight with his usual courage until the end. He has returned to his beloved country from the United States where he had undergone an operation from which there is little hope he will recover. He has made Prince Hassan his heir and has told his people what to expect.

Like his grandfather, King Abdullah, he is a fervent Muslim and fatalist. As the old man had told him, 'I believe in God – my life is in His hands. Until my time comes, no one can harm me and when my time comes no one can guard me.'

Part Five

EASTERN ASIA AND THE PACIFIC

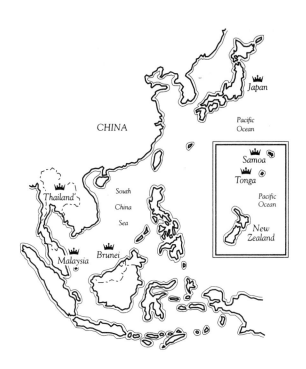

18

JAPAN

Emperor Akihito

'Life must be lived forwards. But it can only be understood backwards.'
SØREN KIERKEGAARD

Japan is different. It stands alone as the only country in the world which still has an emperor. He is an emperor without an empire, without a proper name, who does not rule, is rarely seen, lives in a kind of glorified bungalow (albeit temporarily) and yet is believed to descend from the Gods, and possibly be a God himself, by more than a million of his subjects. It is all very strange, but fits in with the strangeness, to a European, of the country itself.

I belong to a generation that lived through the cruelties and excesses of the last World War, and what I found perhaps strangest of all in Japan is how little a new generation – even students and graduates – know about their country's contribution to some of its darkest moments. Neither the rape of Nanking, Korean slave labour, the brutal 'comfort stations', or brothels, of its Imperial Forces, nor the appalling suffering of the prisoners-of-war who built the Burma Road or who were held in prison camps all over south-east Asia, are mentioned or acknowledged in official Japanese histories or schoolbooks today, not even as a counterpoise for the horrors of Hiroshima and Nagasaki. This obfuscation creates, I think, an unnecessary psychological barrier, fifty years later, to understanding between our two nations.

The stiff court protocol, with the Imperial Household Agency's own standard of exact 'correctness' and good form, also unwittingly contributes to the barrier by censoring any kind of criticism or even unwelcome fact about their imperial masters – even those long since dead!

Although I did not feel that the breath of Heaven emanated from the new Emperor Akihito, or his pretty, dutiful wife, it was paradoxically their very human-ness, quite unlike the web of convention which

surrounds them, that I found warming and sympathetic and which
created an immediate empathy between us. They seemed to me to be
two gentle and civilised, courteous and kind human beings who had
suffered greatly, and perhaps were still suffering from a past that was
not of their making, and it was evident that they had taken on the
burden of that past with courage and dignity, and a kind of philosophi-
cal detachment that was admirable, and also made a lot of sense.

My visit to Japan was perhaps the most humbling of all my
journeys of discovery. I had already encountered countries and
people more backward, more exotic, more xenophobic, more
unique. But I had never before felt so baffled or so constitutionally
incapable of understanding a nation; its esoteric cults and traditions, its
teeming copy-cat cities and its strangely alien people. I did not at first
believe I would ever find a key that would unlock their mystery or a
bridge that would establish a rapport between us. That the Emperor and
Empress themselves should prove to be the key and the bridge came as
a great surprise. But, of course, it should not have done so. For in Japan,
even in today's less rigidly structured society, the Emperor, or *Tenno*, is
still both the apex and the heart of the pyramid; he, or rather his
mystique, is still, in Robert Guillaume's words: 'the reflection of 75
million people's dream . . . he is the man who has no right to be a man,
first, because he is kept at a distance behind a wall insurmountable by
ordinary people and then because he *is* in some way Japan, its living
history, its aspirations, its beliefs'. That I was able to surmount that wall
and talk to the surprisingly simple and gentle couple behind it made all
the difference in the world. It was one more paradox. But then Japan is
made up of paradoxes.

People say you really have to be Japanese to understand the position
and office of the Emperor, and there is no doubt that in the past Westerners have nearly always projected their own cultural image on to this
enigmatic personage – from Gilbert and Sullivan's delightfully pompous
and ridiculously inaccurate *Mikado* to the Australian judge's description
in 1948 of the sad Showa Emperor as 'the leader in Crime'. But since
then, many scholarly works on 'the patterns of Japanese culture' have
appeared which have made his position much more understandable to
foreigners: *The Chrysanthemum and the Sword* by the anthropologist Ruth
Benedict and the much more recent (and readable) *Death of an Emperor*
by Professor Thomas Crump, works which even the Japanese recognise
as an approximation, at least, to their own viewpoint.

In my own mind there were so many misapprehensions to be got rid of that, in the days leading up to our meeting, I felt like Peer Gynt and his onion, peeling away layer upon layer until I reached . . . I had yet to learn exactly what.

For even the English word 'emperor', by which we translate *tenno* or 'mikado', is only an approximation. (*Tenno* literally means Prince of Heaven.) In the past, Tennos have always been more like non-proselytising Popes or Pope-Kings than Napoleon or Peter the Great, their powers more religious and central to their country's Shinto ritual than to its politics. Their descent, through an unbroken bloodline, is more ancient than any other in the world; their lives, isolated by a stifling web of court protocol, more lonely than any other sovereigns'.

There have been over one hundred emperors, and few of them were ever seen by ordinary mortals except for a rare glimpse behind the curtain of the Phoenix Palanquin, as it passed in the court's stately procession from Kyoto to Edo, the Japanese name for what is now Tokyo. There was even no need to give the actual incumbent a name. For the people of Japan there was always one Tenno, *The* Tenno, at any given time, and his reign-name was never used until *after* his death.

The emperor the West knew as 'Hirohito' was only called so (it was his name when crown prince) because of the Second World War, and the people of Japan would not have known him by this name. He became the Showa Emperor on his death in January 1989, after a reign of sixty-three years.

As soon as an emperor dies, his successor (the nearest in the bloodline) accedes. But the accession or initiation of the new emperor is vastly different from coronation ceremonies in the West. It happens in three stages: *Senso*, *Sokui-rei* and *Daijosai* – approximately: 'accession', 'ascending the throne' and the 'great thanksgiving feast'. The accession part of it takes place immediately after the death of the previous emperor. In the case of the present emperor, the former Crown Prince Akihito, the first ceremony was televised and the people of Japan were able to see for the very first time their new emperor receive the sacred sword and jewel which, with a copy of the sacred mirror, have been the imperial regalia since the time of Jimmu, great-grandson of the Gods and the Tenno's mythical ancestor who, on 11 February 660 BC, according to imperial chronology, established himself as the first Emperor of Yamato, as Japan was then called.

At the Senso, too, he is presented with the state and imperial seals that he will use in the limited acts of state in which, under the present (1947) constitution, he now participates. In the past there was often a

long gap between Senso and the Sokui-rei and Daijosai ceremonies, but
it was only after the solemn and ancient rituals of the Daijosai, which
go back to the seventh century and were central to state Shinto theology
during the Meiji period, that the new emperor's status as *Arahitogami* was
established, which made him not just a priest, but a unique sort of priest,
the 'Divine Present Emperor', the living God upon whom the welfare of
the whole country ultimately depended. It was this status which enabled
him to perform every year, on 23 November, the rituals of the 'First
Fruits Festival' or *Niiname Matsuri* which no Japanese, even in modern
Tokyo today, could ever imagine not taking place. It would be as if the
Pope dropped the celebration of Easter Mass or Christmas from the
Catholic Church's calendar.

During this ceremony, the emperor solemnly offers the newly harvested rice to the *Kami*, or Gods of the Shinto pantheon, in a kind of
harvest-home service, a feast of thanksgiving and renewal which, to the
Japanese people, seems immemorial and immutable. For rice is the basic
food of the people and 'wet-rice' cultivation is a very difficult and complicated process in the Japanese climate. It is governed by a traditionally
established order and an exact calendar which is codified down to the
last detail. Many peasants who plant and harvest the rice still do so
according to Shinto ritual.

The Daijosai, which the emperor takes part in only once in his lifetime
– usually, but not necessarily, at the beginning of his reign – is also a
first fruits ceremony, but a much more sacred and solemn one. According
to the Imperial Household Agency, in this ritual 'the new emperor, for
the first time after his enthronement, offers newly harvested rice to the
Imperial Ancestor and the deities of heaven and earth, and then partakes
of the rice himself, expresses gratitude to the Imperial Ancestor and
these deities for peace and abundant harvests, and prays for the same on
behalf of the country and people'.

The present emperor's grandfather, the Taisho Emperor, died in 1926
and his father, the Showa Emperor's Sokui-rei and Daijosai took place
in November 1928, though the ceremonies leading up to them had
started in January of that same year. The rites performed in a traditional
Daijosai are Japanese Shinto rites of enormous antiquity. They are mostly
performed in private, in temporary buildings which are later dismantled,
and concern only the emperor, who is not only chief performer, but also
the object of the rites.

Their object was to establish his temporal powers and also to bestow
upon him the supernatural powers of an Arahitogami, or living God. In
the most sacred part of the ceremonies (which were performed at night

in the inner chamber of a specially built pavilion, to which he has been led), the first fruits of the season were, after ritual purifications, both offered to the Gods and eaten with them, the emperor then becoming the repository of the Rice-Gods. Afterwards he was no longer an ordinary man, but a supernatural being who could intervene on his people's behalf with all the Kami. There was also a fertility aspect of the rituals which was so private and secret that no one seems to know exactly what was supposed to occur, or, if they do know, they certainly are not telling.

Whether Hirohito really believed in what is essentially a combined transfiguration and a eucharistic celebration is open to doubt, but that did not really matter. To Shinto's 55 million believers, it was correct *performance* of ritual rather than any deep religious conviction that counted – the reward being the goodwill of the Kami for whom the ritual is performed. He knew that what was expected of him was for the good of his people and, in 1928, the ritual was, as far as the outside world can tell, performed exactly according to Tokyokurei, a government ordinance which embodies the Imperial family tradition.

Shinto has often been described as the religious dimension of being Japanese. It has nothing to do with politics and not much to do with morals or ethical judgments, but largely concerns ritual, tradition, status, and the ritual of Daijosai is of central importance to an emperor's status. Yet eighteen years after the Showa Emperor's traditional Daijosai, eighteen terrible years of military adventurism, corrupt politics and a disastrous war, a defeated and occupied Japan, still stunned and smouldering from the devastating effect of the bombing of Hiroshima and Nagasaki, accepted the imposed dismantlement of these same traditions and beliefs. They had lasted for nearly two thousand years but, in August 1945, the world had turned over and nothing in Japan was to be the same again.

The Showa Emperor formally renounced all claims to being Arahito-gami, or 'Divine Present Emperor', on 1 January 1946, and in 1947 a new constitution was drawn up and promulgated, at the instigation of General Douglas MacArthur and the occupying forces of America. It removed much of the temporal powers and status of the Tenno, handing them over to a democratically elected government, and in essence it is by this constitution that Japan is ruled today. It replaced that of the Meiji Emperor which, in the constitution of 1889, the first that Japan had ever known, declared: 'The Empire of Japan shall be reigned over and governed by a line of Emperors unbroken for ages eternal,' and again (in the Imperial Rescript on Education): 'Our Imperial Throne is coeval with Heaven and Earth.' General MacArthur refused to have any of *that*, and the Imperial Rescript was also rescinded. State Shintoism ceased to exist.

But in Japan today there are still tens of millions of believers in Shinto, including, obviously, the imperial family and most of the rural population who feed the 100 million rice-eaters of the country. Before the Daijosai of the new emperor, the imperial household and their political advisers had therefore to face a delicate situation in planning the ceremonies that were to take place in November 1990. The modernisation of the imperial institution, the post-war constitution, the nervous politicians, anxious at all costs not to offend any section of the population, the new emperor's and his family's own wishes and beliefs, the traditionalism of Shinto priests and old courtiers, were all bound at one point or another to come into collision with each other and with some aspects of the ancient ceremonies. So when I arrived in Tokyo in late September for my audience, there was still a good deal of ambiguity, bordering on obfuscation, in the Imperial Household Agency, about the actual ceremony and the exact form it would take.

From my point of view, this did not matter. It was going to be all the more interesting to hear what Emperor Akihito had to say about it himself. But meanwhile there was much, much more I had to learn about the Japanese people, their customs and history, before I could understand the complexities of the situation.

One of the first things I had observed when I arrived at Tokyo airport was the Japanese obsession for order and tidiness. Everyone seems to walk the same way. At Immigration there are just as many forms to fill in and queues to follow as in the Soviet Union, but here everyone does so quickly and correctly, mechanically dropping torn-up forms into torn-up-form bins, and producing the right documents for the right people at the right time. Things work. The telephone actually rejects your coins when you want it to; once you have mastered the system, the automatic ticket wall on the Metro produces the right ticket. People are kind to bewildered foreigners but, surprisingly, outside the academic or business or tourist world I found that *no one* speaks English (even on the counters marked 'Information'), which seems odd when nearly every shop, street sign, advertisement and public instruction is written in English (or American) and the visible veneer of Tokyo is so horribly Western and mega-modern.

It was the paradox of Japan's extreme foreign-ness beneath an all too familiar copy-cat sameness that intrigued and mystified me: the grim skyscrapers and the cheerful shrines, the bullet trains and *matsuri* (festivals), the traditional simplicities of domestic life and the awesome complexities of modern technology in which the whole population seems to be involved, making money not just for themselves, but for giant corporations which can be as ruthless and demanding as the Shoguns of old and who ask, and seem to receive, lifelong loyalty and devotion from their employees.

And so I read and visited and looked and listened. I travelled by underground, and noticed that most people cat-nap between stations. I asked, 'Why?' and was told: 'sheer exhaustion'. 'Karoshi', or death from overwork and pressure, claimed 10,000 lives last year (it is not uncommon for people to work twelve hours a day, spend a couple of hours commuting and put in one hundred hours' overtime a month) and there is a National Network to defend Victims of Karoshi.

I caught the bullet train to Kyoto. I walked in the gardens of the Gold and Silver Pavilions and was shown round the Shugaku-In Imperial Villa by its curator. I sat as sedately as possible, with the soles of my feet tucked primly 'under', in strange sticky-cake houses and drank delicious *matcha*, or frothy green tea, bright as spinach juice, from delicate porcelain bowls. I found a *ryokan*, or simple Japanese inn, down-town, where I was beautifully looked after by a delightful Kyotan and his wife, and where I was allocated a room stripped down to the barest essentials, beautiful only in its simplicity – it had sliding paper walls, one low table, a futon or palliasse on a floor that was covered by woven tatami mats the colour of ripe corn. Strange but delicious meals were brought, in lacquered and china bowls, and placed around my bedside. I bathed in the tiled communal bathroom with showers, brushes, jugs, bowls (everything to assist the cleansing and purifying process) and a huge tank bath. I avoided the Japanese lavatories, which necessitate excellent balance and strong thigh muscles, and found – thank goodness – one European one. Everything was spotlessly clean, beautifully ordered, 'a place for everything, and everything in its place', as we learned in our Western nurseries, but rarely practise in our homes.

I returned to Tokyo just a little wiser, and stayed in supreme Western comfort at the Palace Hotel, where it costs ten dollars to sneeze, and visited a few of the countless suburbs, their great Buddhist shrines and entertainment districts which, I imagine, are now but a pale shadow of what they used to be in the days of Meiji. There were no major matsuri while I was in Tokyo, which was a pity, as I am told foreigners then see an entirely different people, happy, carefree, full of imaginative fun and merry-making. Matsuri are both religious and secular feast days – they are the people's theatre, and a happy mixture of Buddhist and Shinto cults, which seem to meld without any problems in Japan, and they keep the population in touch with its ancient traditions. There is one for every day of the year (you can look them up like a radio programme in your local paper) and for every kind and category of person. On the day I flew out of Tokyo it was, very suitably, Respect-For-The-Aged Day, but I was unable to stay and see if it was a proper matsuri or just a 'Bunch-a-Grandmother' American importation.

In between my comings and goings there were several meetings with the two representatives of the Imperial Household Agency, who had greeted me on my arrival, and with whom I had held a lengthy correspondence from London and Scotland. Mr Teiji Yagi, one of the many chamberlains to the Emperor of Japan, turned out to be a representative of the old and traditional court: a thin, gentle, worried-looking Japanese, with the deprecatory half-smile and quivering antennae of the born courtier. Mr Yoshio Karita, whose card bore the resounding title of 'Deputy Grand Master of Ceremonies', was an entirely different type and represented the new look that Akihito and his sons were, I guessed, gradually introducing to the Imperial Court.

Just down from Oxford, where he had read PPE at Christ Church, he spoke perfect English and had the positive, smooth approach of a young city high-flyer. Both seemed desperately anxious that everything should go well and according to protocol on the day of 'The Meeting' and that I should avoid sensitive areas of conversation, of which there seemed to be many. Even though I dressed formally for each meeting with the courtiers, and acted as primly as I knew how, I think they found me something of a wild card, unable to be tidily assessed, docketed and assigned its proper place in their hierarchical world, and this made them more anxious than ever. But they answered all my questions most readily, kindly and courteously, producing an avalanche of reading material, and also organised my access to the Imperial Palace in Tokyo and the Imperial Villa gardens in Kyoto, both of which come under the court's jurisdiction.

I do not believe I shall ever penetrate the complexities of Japanese thought, even after brooding on it for hours in the pavilion of a strolling or meditation garden in Kyoto – gai and nai, soto and uchi. After all, I am a gaijin (an outsider) and the concept of everything being either outside (gai) or inside (nai), chaotic and uncontrollable (soto) or tidy and ordered and manageable (uchi), and having to be categorised as one or the other was quite new to me, as was the whole idea of ancestor worship.

In Japan, I now learnt, ancestor worship originated in the ie, or household unit, of a village community and had nothing to do with imported

Chinese Buddhism or other Sino-social customs. The communal prosperity of the village has always depended in Japan on communal rice cultivation. It is therefore of the greatest importance that every household should be a self-perpetuating economic unit, which does not depend on individuals to endure, but must always provide successors to the *ie*'s long line of predecessors. So rice cultivation is carried out in practice by a kind of community conveyor belt. These deceased predecessors are honoured by their names being inscribed on tablets kept on the domestic altars of most rural homes, whether Shinto or Buddhist, until the prescribed funeral rites, which secure their eternal destiny, have been performed – a duty which may take several decades to accomplish. Meanwhile, honour and love, which are the corollaries of *on* (indebtedness) are due to them and dutifully observed.

Then there is *chu*, which means loyalty, and *ko*, filial piety; *senpai*, meaning senior, and *kohai*, junior – two Japanese principles which are the basis for their country's obsession with hierarchy and with status. The Buddhist concept of *ho-on*, or indebtedness, and *on*, unrepayable indebtedness due in return for kindness, have perhaps the most profound effect of all on Japanese society, their relationships with each other and, at least until quite recent times, with their emperors. During the war, it was that sense of *on* towards the Showa Emperor that drove kamikaze pilots to suicide missions and Japanese soldiers to prefer death to surrender, and it is the *on* which factory workers today feel towards their corporate employers (who look after them from the cradle to the grave) that makes the wheels of Japanese industry turn so smoothly. And, sadly, it is perhaps a sense of *on* towards their parents and teachers that make pupils who have failed exams sometimes commit suicide. *On* is tabulated, like everything else in Japan, into enormously complicated (to the foreigner) varieties of obligations and rules of reciprocity. There are *gimu* and *giri* and many more categories, which take up much time in most people's lives. All demand enormous self-discipline and effort. Only small children and old people are exempted from this self-inflicted burden and responsibility, and here we have another paradox. While the concept of 'honour', of 'doing the honourable thing' (which my Webster's dictionary defines as 'principles, probity, a sense of duty, tender conscience, etc.' which we once believed to be part of a Western gentleman's behaviour, as well as a central Christian ethic) is rapidly disappearing in our own materialistic world, it is very much alive in 100 million homes of industrial, technologically advanced, 'democratic' and supposedly materialistic Japan.

Though they would not suit a West Highlander like myself at all, I was beginning at last to understand some of the strange patterns of Japanese behaviour and their origins and, though I still felt I could never sympathise with them, my interest was by now more than hooked – I was fascinated, and I suddenly wanted to know more, and to understand better.

One is always advised to explore the roots of a problem, and with a country so hierarchically structured as Japan it would seem necessary more than ever to begin at the beginning. Much of it, I was told, is pure myth, but this mythical beginning, the genesis of Japan's history, still echoes in the country's habits and daily life. It is bound up in the history of its emperors and in the Shinto cult and it is possibly these religio-magic roots which make Japanese people different from any other race in the world. They are roots that go back to the time of the Gods.

In the dawn of time, two Gods appeared, the female, Izanami, and the male, Izanagi. They were given a long spear with which they stirred the primordial mud, causing the islands of Japan to form, on to which they then cautiously descended. Izanami complained that her body was deficient in one place. Izanagi observed that he had an excess in the same place. So they neatly joined the parts together and begat various other islands and Kami to populate Japan. When Izanami gave birth to Fire she was terribly burnt and went into the Land of Death. Her body was covered with maggots and the grief-stricken and horrified Izanagi fled from her presence. He came to a river where he washed and from his purification were born three mighty Kami: Amaterasu (the Sun Goddess), Susano (God of the Oceans and Storm) and Tsukuyomi (God of Darkness and the Moon). Amaterasu ruled the High Plain of Heaven (perhaps the flat fields in which rice was grown from earliest times?) and Susano the Ocean. But one day the wild, unruly Susano went on a rampage, trampling his sister's rice fields, smearing excrement on her palace walls and killing one of her sacred weavers. Amaterasu was furious and retired in a huff to a cave and the world was plunged into darkness. The Gods assembled (like a meeting of the Security Council?) to woo her back with various ploys. Finally a lady Kami performed a ribald dance, causing roars of laughter from the other dignitaries. Amaterasu, wearing a beautiful necklace, peered out to investigate its cause and saw her own reflection in a mirror that the Kami had set up. As she stepped closer to admire herself she was seized, a rope was thrown across the entrance to her cave and light was restored to the world.

Later, Amaterasu's grandson, Ninigi, ruled from her palace above the cave and she handed over to him the magic mirror, sword and jewel.

He, in his turn, bequeathed them to his successor and great-grandson, the Emperor Jimmu, who (owing to a remarkable Chinese feat of counting backwards) became the first Emperor of Japan on 11 February 660 BC. The story goes on to include Susano's slaying of a dragon with eight heads and the making of a magic sword out of its tail. But already it has all the elements of Shinto and imperial culture: the imperial regalia, bronze mirror, sword and jewel; the inviolate and primary importance of rice cultivation; the Japanese horror of putrefaction and obsession with ritual purification; their fear of chaos and delight in order.

For the next dozen or so centuries, Japan grew rice and prospered and, by the time historical certainties first made their appearance, it already had a military foothold in southern Korea and was receiving Korean scribes at the Imperial Court. The country was organised into clans, or clusters of clans (*uji*), with subordinate guilds of farmers, fishermen, weavers and potters, all subject to the dominant uji of the imperial family.

It was from Korea that Buddhism came to Yamato in the sixth century and with it came Chinese culture. It was a revelation to the Japanese and soon, under the regency of Prince Shotoku, the court developed Chinese patterns of centralised government and protocol, basic laws and a burgeoning interest in the arts. But even in those early times, Japan was only nominally ruled by the emperor. *De facto* power was held by the militarily and economically strongest in the land. The emperor's position could be summed up as: *Yumei Mujitsu*, literally 'having a name [but] no substance'. He may have reigned, but it was the Shoguns who ruled.

The Fujiwara family were perhaps the longest lasting and most powerful of these clans; by cunning diplomacy, careful marriages and artificial regencies, they manipulated the imperial family for several hundred years. They borrowed much that was good from the Tang emperors of China, but adapted their ideas to specifically Japanese traditions. The court moved from Nara, where the Buddhist monks had great influence, to Kyoto, or Heian-Kyo as it was then called. It was here, among the most powerful families, that while Chinese influence dwindled and purely Japanese values grew, a form of hierarchical and structured feudalism evolved that lasted right into the nineteenth century – indeed, if by a stretch of your imagination you count government ministries as court patrons, conglomerates as Shoguns, company directors as estate managers and so on, right up to the present day.

Towards the end of the tenth century, Heian court life reached aesthetic heights of exquisite sensibility that have never been surpassed.

'Literary party-games held in ornate palace gardens required each guest to compose a small poem as his wine cup floated towards him along a miniature winding channel of scented water. Expeditions were organised to the best vantage point for the first spring cherry blossom and special pavilions were built to watch the rising of the full moon. Every gesture, from the opening of an umbrella to the sublime act of love-making, had its appropriate ceremonial and conversation often took the form of elegant exchanges of improvised verse.'

What we foreign 'barbarians' think of as particularly Japanese today – the disciplined moulding of nature through bonsai, the austere but beautiful *ikebana* flower arrangements, the graceful patterns of *kaiseki* haute cuisine, even the elaborate courtesies of twentieth-century company directors can all be traced back to the exquisitely mannered behaviour and style of the Heian court. Although its scholars had, by this time, adopted Chinese ideograms (with enormous difficulty, as Chinese is monosyllabic and they did not fit polysyllabic Japanese) into a simplified set of *kana* characters, the cultivated gentlemen of the Imperial Court continued to write in Chinese in the same way that mediaeval scholars used Latin in the West. It was only women who wrote in the more frivolous native language and it is a bull's-eye for feminists that the first two masterpieces of Japanese literature – *The Tale of Genji*, the world's first real novel, and *Pillow Book*, a lady-in-waiting's account of court life – were both written by women, in Japanese, during the first decade of the eleventh century.

The end of Japan's classical period came with the waning of Fujiwara power and the rise of other clans. The austere and ruthless Yoritomo Minamoto was the first of the national rulers to call himself *Sei-i-tai-shogun*, which means literally: 'Barbarian-subduing Great General'. His army consisted of local militia originally enlisted to ward off brigands, but it rapidly became part of the feudal structure as *samurai* (retainers) and *bushi* (warriors), whose loyalty to their overlord was total and whose code of *Bushido* became legendary.

The Middle Ages were a period of endless struggle between the *daimyo* (feudal war-lords) and the ruling shogunate. When the Mongol armies of Kubla Khan overran China, it looked as if the Khan would turn his attention next to Japan, but a providential typhoon helped the Japanese repel two separate Mongol attacks, and a third never materialised. Chinese Zen priests had escaped to Japan and for a time became the religious and aesthetic advisers to the powerful Shoguns; they are said to have invented the meditation gardens of Japan, which carried Sung paintings and abstract ideas into garden design.

Takauji Ashikaga had risen to power after defeating the Minamoto Shoguns in 1333 and had introduced a golden age of elegance and artistic creativity to Kyoto, his power base. His grandson built the Golden Pavilion in Kyoto, patronised *noh* drama and, despite the various feuding factions, which were forever at each other's throats, managed to introduce a second age of elegance and artistic achievement. In 1543 the Portuguese established a trading base at Nagasaki and brought firearms into Japan, as well as tobacco, bread, potatoes, clocks, pantaloons and eyeglasses. St Frances Xavier and Jesuit missionaries followed soon after and, by 1582, there were about one hundred and fifty thousand converts to Christianity.

When the Ashikaga shogunate was overthrown, fighting among the clans continued until the most intelligent of three rival war-lords came out on top, and a century or more of civil war ended. Ieyasu Tokugawa (1543–1616) established effective rule over the whole country by organising a tightly controlled coalition of some 260 daimyo and skilfully appointing his own family members and trusted Samurai vassals to positions of authority. He curbed the powers of the Samurai and created a much stricter school of Bushido: 'loyalty to one's master, defence of one's status and honour, fulfilment of all obligations'. Long before Louis XIV thought of it, the Tokugawa regime contained an unruly aristocracy by making crippling financial demands on their loyalty, forcing them to attend (and provide services to) the Shogun's court, which he had moved to Edo.* They also had to finance the building of his huge new castle there. For now that the Spanish and Portuguese arquebus played a significant part in warfare, defences had to be modernised.

The castles of Japan exemplify a unique form of showing off and looking out for yourself which was entirely characteristic of the Tokugawa Shoguns. Before long, cities were built around the castles and commerce thrived – urban populations grew large (over a million people lived in Edo by the end of the eighteenth century). The Tokugawa Peace was the formative period of Japan's great industrial development. For example, the Mitsui family, who owned a small *sake* brewery at Ise in the seventeenth century, turned first pawnbroker, then money-lenders and then dry-goods storemen, which eventually led to the huge economic conglomerate which the world knows today. *Petit à petit, l'oiseau bâtit son nid.*

During this period, although Shinto and Buddhism still coexisted in

---

* Edo – the original name for the city that was to become Tokyo.

harmony, the Tokugawa shogunate revered Confucian ideals of filial
piety and ancestor worship, which included the unseen and powerless
emperor, and obedience to authority, for it bolstered their centralised
government and helped them maintain power and create order in a
stratified society. The country was closed to all foreigners' influence, the
Jesuits were expelled and their Christian converts cruelly persecuted: at
least 30,000 Japanese converts were burnt alive or killed in battle during
the tragic and abortive Shimabara Rebellion (1637) which sealed the
fate of all Christians in Japan for several generations. Yet Ieyasu Tokugawa founded a dynasty which ruled a united and peaceful Japan for the
next 250 years.

It was the very strength and rigidity of the Tokugawas' unshared control of the country that brought about their downfall, and it happened
very quickly. Towards the end of the eighteenth century, a rash of
catastrophes – plague, drought, floods, famine, uprisings in towns and
countryside – destabilised the population and threatened the Shogun's
authority. Sensing panic, the Samurai turned their loyalties to the
Emperor of Japan, the silent but enduring symbol of national unity.
Soon alienation from the Shogunate was complete and the feeling grew,
especially among the educated, that it was imperative for Japan to open
her ports once more to foreign trade and to new ideas. So little did
the mid-nineteenth-century Japanese know of the world outside that all
Western knowledge was called 'Dutch learning', a reference to the minimal contact that some scholars had kept with the Dutch trading company
in Nagasaki Bay. Incidentally, it was the Dutch whalers who operated
from this port who were the first to start its infamous annual slaughter.

A few American ships had tried to open negotiations but had been
repulsed, and it was only the stubbornness of Commodore Mathew Perry
which finally succeeded in establishing commercial and diplomatic
relations in 1853. In 1854, he negotiated the Treaty of Kanagawa, which
opened two Japanese ports to Western trade. Before the Treaty was
signed, there was an exchange of hospitality and gifts. The good Commodore Perry, who wanted to bring the 'nobler principles' and 'higher
civilisation' of his country to Japan, laid on as entertainment for the
amazed Japanese delegation a Negro minstrel show, while the Japanese
responded – to the equal amazement of the Americans – with a Sumo
wrestling match. The gifts were equally incongruous, the Americans
bringing rifles, pistols, telegraph apparatus, Webster's dictionary, cherry
brandy, bourbon whisky and a miniature railway (on which the delegates
had great fun riding up and down). The Japanese presented silks, golden
lacquer bowls, porcelain, and what the Commodore described as 'a box

of obscene paintings of naked men and women, another proof of the lewdness of this exclusive people'.

But Kanagawa was the thin end of a very large wedge. In 1857, the 'Institute for the Study of Barbarian Writing' was established and soon the floodgates were opened and European culture overwhelmed Japan. It produced a violent counter-reaction, especially among the Samurai, who felt Japanese values were being betrayed and rallied under the slogan *sonno joi* (Honour the Emperor, expel the barbarians). Bands of Samurai assassinated British and Dutch representatives and some reactionary but foolhardy daimyo fired on foreign ships in the Shimonoseki Straits. There was an immediate and devastating response from a combined fleet of American, British, Dutch and French forces, which swiftly put an end to all resistance. In January 1868, the Tokugawa Shogun was overthrown and the authority of the emperor restored. Edo was renamed Tokyo (Eastern Capital) and the Fujiwara family once more emerged as the close friends and advisers of the fourteen-year-old emperor. His restoration, known as Meiji (enlightened rule), saw a stupendous release of the energies and dynamism that had been locked up in Japan during the 250 years of Tokugawa isolation.

Remarkable statesmen such as Toshimichi Okubo and Hirobumi Ito set about dismantling the entire feudal framework of the country and replacing it by a modern, Western-style, and if not exactly democratic, at least representative form of government. Two hundred and sixty-six feudal domains were abolished and transformed into forty-five prefectures. The private armies of the daimyo were disbanded to form the core of the imperial armed forces, augmented by universal conscription. The Samurai lost their traditional swords, their distinctive top-knot hair-do and feudal privileges at one blow and were for the most part pensioned off. At first they were in a state of shock, but recovered enough for (in 1877) a short-lived rebellion in Kyushu where Takamori Saigo led 40,000 sword-swinging Samurai in a suicidal assault on to the guns and cannon of the imperial army, a heroic but finally futile gesture that marked the end of an era.

The next decade saw the country rush headlong into Westernisation, handshaking became popular and was sometimes seen to replace the complicated procedures of bowing, city suits superseded graceful kimonos and *moningu* (morning coats) were worn by some bold spirits at Imperial Court ceremonies. Any new Western fashion was known as *haikara* (high collar), ballroom dancing became so popular that in the 1880s the government built a special dance hall for ministers to cavort in with the wives of foreign diplomats, till the conservative opposition created an uproar and it was hastily closed. But by the 1920s, young bloods, known as *modan bois* (modern boys), were swaggering down the main shopping street in Tokyo *hand-in-hand* with their *modan garus* (modern girls), smoking cigarettes and wearing – what had become all the rage – large horn-rimmed spectacles, inspired by their latest American film-idol, Harold Lloyd.

With hindsight one realises that it all happened too quickly, that the new ideas, the rejection of their own past for an alien 'modern' and possibly flawed culture were imposed on the people from above. It was not a true revolution, a popular democratic revolution, neither was it a change of direction wished for by the people themselves.

The sensibilities of the ordinary Japanese must have been deeply offended by the Meiji 'reforms', and perhaps that is why they clung to the few things that were still familiar in a frighteningly changing world: hierarchical order in all things (it is now called 'seniority'); an obsessive desire for 'correctness'; blind obedience to authority; pride in the valour and discipline of their own race and contempt for all others; and veneration of their emperors. These were sentiments that belonged to the previous era but they certainly existed in the two wars that inevitably followed, and may perhaps explain the inhumanity of the imperial armed forces in their invasions of Korea and China in 1937 and of south-east Asia and the Pacific in 1942.

The Meiji Restoration was both an end and a beginning, and a beginning and an end. It put an end to mediaevalism and imperial seclusion, it jerked the country forward in less than thirty years into matching and even surpassing Western economic progress. It introduced state Shintoism which underlined traditionalism and the emperor's divine status (as a sort of counterbalance to modernism?) without increasing in any way his political influence, and it started the militaristic adventurism which was to lead to final disaster, the country's defeat, occupation by a foreign power and the Tenno's demotion to the ranks of common humanity.

Or not so common? The evening after my return from Kyoto, I had been briefed and re-briefed by my two kind advisers from the Imperial Household Agency and set out the following morning, suitably behatted and gloved, clutching a bag with presents, notebook, camera and pencil and feeling distinctly nervous. A car and a young man from the Japanese Foreign Office had been sent to escort me to the Akasaka Palace, a temporary residence where the Emperor Akihito and the Empress Michiko were living while their new palace was being built nearby within the Imperial Palace compound. When this is finished they will move into it and hand over what is really just a large villa to the crown prince.

The vast and formidable Imperial Palace compound, the site of the Tokugawa Shogun's original castle, now stands in the centre of Tokyo's banking district. It was taken over by the Meiji emperors in the nineteenth century and a new wooden structure was built in 1888 but this was bombed by the Americans during the war and, like most of Tokyo, was almost completely destroyed, but has now been partially rebuilt. It is rarely lived in by the emperor, who uses it for his offices and receptions (and entertaining foreign guests), preferring more modest and comfortable quarters in its park. The outer walls of the compound originally measured sixteen kilometres in circumference and they were surrounded by a deep moat. In Ieyasu Tokugawa's day it was virtually impregnable.

It was a misty day, not quite raining, and the civilian guards at the palace gates wore black mackintosh capes. There was a short drive through a leafy wood and then the car stopped in front of a two-storeyed building of modest proportions and very modern design. Inside its large, split-level hall, my two friends, Mr Teigi Yagi and Mr Karita, were waiting to greet me and we proceeded up a steep open staircase from the vestibule to the upper level, which was a bare and almost empty waiting area, lit from the roof and furnished with a few low tables and square modern chairs. The very high ceiling above us had open beams of some gleaming silver substance, like aluminium. There was a large four-panelled golden screen with flying cranes on it against one wall. The ambience was severe and rather like a very grand bank's outer office.

Before long, two of the empress's ladies-in-waiting joined us. They immediately put everyone at ease. Charming, quietly elegant women of the world, they both spoke perfect English (though one had learnt it in America). They told me they were both married, with busy lives outside their palace duties, 'But we come when we are needed, and it is always a joy to serve Her Majesty.' They led us down a long passage which emerged on another split-level arrangement, but this time a musical one. On the top half stood a grand piano, a beautiful harp, a stool, music stand and cabinet, forming a kind of platform/music room. The bottom half, except for a chair or two, was bare. We bypassed it and proceeded down a wider passage with several closed doors. On one of these Mr Karita tapped, and we entered.

This was a large and pleasant drawing-room, with light pouring through a long window-wall which brought the informal woodland garden outside almost into the room. The emperor and empress stood side by side in the middle of it, posed as if for a photograph, and I went up to them, curtsied and shook hands, silently. The emperor then gestured to the usual Western seating arrangement at one end of the room and we settled down on comfortable white sofas and armchairs drawn round a large low table. The imperial couple sat opposite me with Mr Karita and one of the empress's delightful ladies on either side of them. A tiny white porcelain cup of some delicious golden liquid, which I took to be an unknown kind of imperial tea, lay on the table in front of each of us. Nervously sipping it, I started by extolling the virtues of green tea and how my husband could never write his books without it.

We then got on to my own book and its *raison d'être*, my gratitude for the unique honour they were showing me, and mutual friends. I happened to have had both an aunt and a first cousin,* her daughter, who had married diplomats and ended up as ambassadresses in Japan. The empress remembered Alice Morland well as being kind to her and sometimes helping out with her early struggles with the English language, for she went to some of the same classes as young Martin Morland and often played with him and his brothers. We were off! From then on our conversation was altogether relaxed and happy. The emperor has a charming, mobile face, a furrowed brow when he is concentrating, and happy smile lines when he is amused. He has thick hair streaked with grey and kind eyes. He understands English perfectly and answered many questions in it, but for the ones he wanted to get absolutely clear, he used Mr Karita as interpreter.

He was a good deal taller than I had expected and wore a very well-cut light grey suit and narrow dark tie. Somehow General MacArthur's words about his father's dignity in defeat floated back into my mind for, at his own request, the Emperor Hirohito had visited MacArthur at the American embassy on 27 September 1945, three weeks after his country's surrender and, accepting his historic role as head of state, had told him he himself was ready to accept full responsibility for the Pacific War. 'I come to you, General MacArthur, to offer myself to the judgment of the powers you represent as the one to bear sole responsibility for every political and military decision made and action taken by my people in the conduct of the War.' It was what one can only call a noble act, and one which was finely appreciated by the general. 'He was an Emperor by inherent birth,' MacArthur was to write much later, 'but, in that instant, I knew I faced the First Gentleman of Japan in his own right.'

Emperor Akihito, however simply and quietly he now lives, and whatever tragedies lie behind him, conveys much the same impression.

---

* Ethel Lindley, wife of HE Sir Francis Lindley, and her daughter, Alice Morland, wife of HE Sir Oscar Morland.

HM Emperor Akihito of Japan
and HM Empress Michiko.

Empress Michiko is small and soignée and pretty in the wonderfully composed way that Japanese women have, which makes foreigners think of them as china dolls. She wore unadorned white, a simple Courrèges-type dress, with a black half-belt and a single row of pearls. She made me feel like a latter-day barbarian with large feet and fussy clothes, but the warmth of her sympathy soon made one forget such unfortunate disadvantages.

Although the list of suitable subjects for us to talk about had been discussed and agreed with the Imperial Household Agency before my visit, I found that, as on other occasions with other monarchs, no one stuck to them. The emperor, for his part, talked to me about the role he sees for himself in modern Japan and summed it up by 'meeting the expectations of my people'. Historically speaking, he reminded me, Japanese emperors have never led the people politically, but have always been the symbol of the state and of the unity of the Japanese people. Among his 100 emperor ancestors, he particularly admired the Emperor Gonara who, in the sixteenth century, during a particularly bad period of flood, famine and plague, had beautiful copies made of the great Buddhist precepts, a sort of Bible of ideals, which he sent to twenty temples, asking the priests to pray that his people should be saved from their misery. It was also a subtle way of gently rebuking their unholy behaviour, which had latterly been the cause of his anxiety. The Emperor went on to tell me, quite movingly, that, like his ancestor, he wished his own virtue was big enough to embrace all his people as a parent embraces his child, but his powers were limited. This was said with the utmost sincerity and might have come straight from Portia's speech in *The Merchant of Venice*.

A second model, for him, he told me, was the Emperor Saga, who when he saw members of the government leading over-luxurious, extravagant lives, sent them a Chinese poem he had written of the greatest delicacy, which hoped, in exquisite verse, that the situation would change. In spite of the new constitution's assertion that he 'derives his position from the will of the people with whom resides sovereign power', the emperor does not feel that, in practice, his role has changed very much from that of his ancestors before the Meiji reform and State Shintoism. He is still the guardian of the spiritual well-being of the nation and his prayers are always that his people should be governed well and that the spirit of the constitution should be enhanced.

I asked whether he would modernise the court protocol and institutions, either gradually or after his enthronement, and he reminded me that he had been Emperor since January 1989, the accession of one emperor following automatically the death of another. He agreed that time always brought change and said there had already been enormous changes in the courts of emperors between the reigns of the Emperor Komei and the Emperor Meiji, and again, after the war, during the lifetime of the Showa Emperor, his father.

There would be major changes, too, in the ceremonies of his enthronement. His father, the late emperor, had asked no foreigners to his enthronement, while he himself had asked every sovereign country in the world to attend, and the first ritual of his accession, what had always been called the Senso, had been televised and seen by the entire Japanese population. Two thousand five hundred people had been invited to the enthronement ceremony, which would take place in the Imperial Palace in Tokyo, followed by a series of court banquets for 3,000 people. This would be attended by the imperial family, friends, politicians and dignitaries, foreign guests and the Diplomatic Corps. The ceremony itself would be a traditional ceremony, but not a religious one, a secular Act of State.

We were now on delicate ground and I had promised Mr Karita I would not press the emperor too far, but I had been told that the religious or Shinto ceremony, known as Daijosai, would take place a few days later in a temporary hall or pavilion in the palace grounds. I asked him about the Shinto rites and the Daijosai which traditionally conferred upon the emperor the status of 'Divine Present Emperor'. Would they be carried out as they were at his father's enthronement? In the rather fragmented conversation that followed, I gathered that there would be a Daijosai Shinto ceremony, but that it would follow the pattern of his grandfather's, the Emperor Taisho's Daijosai, and would concentrate more on the First Fruits rituals and rice ceremonies than the more esoteric ones of deification; that various emperors had followed various forms of Daijosai and that some had waited months, even years, before it could take place, including the good Emperor Gonara, who was too poor and modest to afford even an enthronement ceremony until ten years after his succession; that his own Daijosai would be a private not a formal state ceremony and would take place some time later.

He also told me firmly that, though he and his family adhered to the Shinto cult, state Shintoism was dead and could never be revived.

And then I went a little too far: 'I know that the late emperor renounced his status of Arahitogami in 1946 and was reported even before the war to have doubts about it, but do *you* believe in this part of Shinto ritual? And does the crown prince, who one day will succeed you?' I gathered they did not, but the question was politely turned and it would have been discourteous to probe any further.

At this stage the Empress Michiko took over and we talked about her family and how she had first met the emperor: 'It was at the quarter-finals of a tournament at a tennis club we both belonged to. He and his fellow-student partner looked very tall and strong and were confident of winning. I was much smaller and younger and, what was worse, my partner was only an eleven-year-old American boy but, somehow or other, by sheer determination, we won! And after that we just went on seeing each other, and fell in love.'

What is delightful about the emperor and empress is that they still seem to be in love, or at the very least, sensitive, courteous and protective towards each other. Michiko must be every Japanese man's idea of the perfect wife. She hangs on her husband's words with a beguilingly modest expression of interest (feminists, take note) and once, when they both began answering simultaneously, she gave way to the emperor with the most charming and graceful and intensely feminine gesture. Yet she holds her own corner perfectly well and talked at length of the family's love of music and nature. She plays the piano and harp herself, the emperor plays the cello and the crown prince the viola and they often play classical chamber music together, both for their own pleasure and sometimes for that of the imperial household.

She brightened when I told her how much I had enjoyed Seiji Ozawa's conducting at a London Prom, and then we discussed the Suzuki method of teaching music, which had produced so many fine professional musicians in Japan.

She told me she loved gardening and had at one time a secret garden of her own which she looked after herself, but when the children were growing up there was too much to do and it 'got away' from her. She likes digging up wild lilies and small anemones from the woods in Karuizawa, where the Imperial family goes for their summer holidays when it gets too hot in Tokyo, and she brings them south to plant here. But sometimes she felt guilty at depriving nature in the north, so she would ask her Tokyo gardeners to grow more plants from their seed to give back what she had taken. (My gardener, in Scotland, would have thought her slightly, but charmingly, unhinged!)

We talked about the Imperial Villa garden at Kyoto and how I had been so inspired by its beauty that I would like to 'Japanify' our own woodland garden at Strachur. 'But it takes fifty years to get results,' I said sadly, 'and I shall be dead long before then.'

The Emperor pointed to the sturdy birches outside the window, whose white trunks and golden leaves stood out against the darker greens, and told me proudly: 'We planted those thirty years ago to remind us of Karuizawa, and look how they have grown.' But, fine though they were, the emperor's garden, or as much as I could see of it, did not remotely look like the exquisitely manicured tenth-century stroll and meditation gardens of Kyoto. He went on to tell me that each member of the imperial family is given a personal crest or badge at birth (or through marriage) and that he had sentimentally chosen the birch tree for his bride.

The Empress Michiko's other great interest is calligraphy and she has a fine collection of prints and woodcuts, some of which were shown to me by her ladies later. The Emperor is a serious ichthyologist, whose special field of study is tropical freshwater fish. He contributes an average of one paper a year to the world's scientific publications. The crown prince was at Oxford and read History at Merton, but his youngest son is also a scientist whose speciality is catfish. The family were delighted when, last year, both father and son had articles on their own subjects in the same issue of a learned journal. As soon as I mentioned that I wanted to identify a particular Japanese lily,* Emperor Akihito rushed off to his library and returned with an armful of books and all the enthusiasm of a schoolboy. He told me that his work was truly his hobby, and I told him how Winston Churchill once told *me* that this was the secret of happiness. He still enjoys playing tennis and the annual holiday at Karuizawa, where the family leads a much less formal life; there they do a lot of walking, meet friends, socialise and are seen by the local population. When I asked if they ever would go 'on walkabout' like our own royal family does, they both looked puzzled and paused, as if weighing up the term. When I explained it, the empress nodded eagerly and told me that was a little bit like what they managed to do in Karuizawa.

At this moment we were deftly served, so deftly that I was hardly aware of it, with some more golden tea and a plate of the prettiest sweetmeats I have ever seen, which tasted as good as they looked. The emperor told me that his younger son, Prince Akishino, had greatly enjoyed his terms at Oxford, where he read Zoology at St John's. He also liked Scotland where he had visited our friends and neighbours, the Chief of Clan Cameron and Lady Cameron of Lochiel. We talked about nature and nature conservancy, which is the young prince's greatest

---

* Lilium auratum, the golden-rayed lily of Japan.

interest. I did *not* bring up the subject of whales, or over-fishing, but I had to bite my tongue not to!

The Empress walks in the palace gardens at 7 a.m. every morning for a good hour, looking at flowers and listening to birds: 'It is the best way of restoring peace, regaining equilibrium – when the children were small it used to be 6 a.m., but now I can be lazy!' Princess Sayako, who is twenty-one and still at university, has also a great love of nature and animals. She is interested in the training of guide dogs for the blind, to whose problems she gives much time and understanding.

Before I left I gave the Emperor a bottle of our own brand of Old MacPhunn malt whisky and told him the true story of MacPhunn, the impoverished Laird of Driep, who was hanged for stealing sheep but revived by a timely dram of whisky, which made him laugh, and I gave the empress my husband's book of *West Highland Tales* from which it comes. I told her this was all about clans and myths, like much of Japan's history, but failed to tell her that that was where the likeness ceased. In the West Highlands we say, as we put off till tomorrow what should be done today: 'When the good Lord made time, He made plenty of it.' In Japan, they have fixed the calendar and everyone is in a hurry. Yet, as I curtsied and left, I felt I had found a missing key to at least some of the mysteries of Japan – through the humanity of the 'First Gentleman' of the land, who is also the symbol of state and the subject of 100 million people's aspirations and dreams.

It was quite simply a mutual sympathy, which is the beginning of all understanding. I would like to meet Emperor Akihito again.

19

THAILAND

King Bhumibol Aiulyades

'There's such divinity doth hedge a king,
That treason can but peep to what it would.'

WILLIAM SHAKESPEARE

*The histories of the three south-east Asian countries that I visited next
were sometimes similar and often interlinked, but the style of the
monarchs who rule them today could scarcely be more different.*

*The Thais have never been conquered by a foreign nation; they are
traditionalists and monarchical to a man. They cheerfully play musical
chairs with their generals and prime ministers, but their king is sacro-
sanct (quite literally so, as he also happens to be God) and his subjects
could no more stop worshipping him and enjoying the whole delightful
paraphernalia of royal pomp and circumstance than they could stop
chewing betel-nuts, or holding funeral cocktail parties over the corpses
of their late lamented, or flying kites, or, simply, looking beautiful.
They are right to do so, for he probably works harder for his subjects
than any other monarch I visited.*

*The Sultan of Brunei is also an absolute king, probably more
absolutely absolute than the kings of Bhutan, Oman or Thailand, but
although he can adopt any foreign policy he chooses, his tiny country
is historically and economically linked with Malaysia and Singapore.
He is also a 'one-off' monarch. There are no rules for an absolute
king who is a billionaire except, perhaps, moral ones, and it is fortunate
for the people of Brunei that His Royal Highness is a convinced
Muslim and the head of Islam in his country, so that his life and
actions are circumscribed by his faith – even if, on occasions, Islamic
law bends a little in his favour.*

*The Sultan of Malaysia is a British-trained lawyer as well as a
Muslim. He is a prince of ancient lineage, but also a down-to-earth,
practical ruler, bound by constitutional parameters and happy to clarify
these by refining and improving Malaysia's young and still-emergent*

legislation. His country is one that has enjoyed lasting benefits from colonial rule and, with Independence, its legacy of a Westminster-style constitution. Without doubt it was its colonial rulers who saved the country from the horrors of a Communist take-over and laid the foundations of a reasonably high standard of education and of a market economy which has flourished.

It is fascinating to think about what will happen next in this part of the world. Will the resurgence of Eastern dynamism be concentrated in this fertile triangle of countries and will their monarchs play a significant part in directing it? Or will the increasingly fundamentalist direction of Islam become a threat to them, and it?

Will their giant neighbours, China and Japan, become ready markets for their manufactured goods – or will they be deadly rivals? A counterpoise or an alliance? Or simply, one day, swallow them up?

T he gentleman from Bombay in the seat beside me had a curious way of sleeping: a hitching up of one leg – the one nearer to me – into the lotus position, which involved appropriating more than his fair share of air space, and a long night for his neighbour.

I scrunched myself still further into my window-corner and thanked goodness that, below us, dawn was breaking over the Andaman Sea. Soon its dove-coloured surface gave way to solid land – a strip of yellow, a tuft or two of green and then a wilderness of flat mud intersected by writhing café-au-lait waterways. A little later the jungle took over, a verdant, furry rug thrown over the landscape, though snaky rivers still twisted between its humps and bumps and cut it into segments. Then, quite suddenly, the scene changed and we were flying over patchwork cultivation, criss-crossed this time by straight roads and still straighter *klongs* (canals), winking jewel-bright in the early-morning sun. The ribbon roads were crawling with ants which turned into lorries and cars, a traffic so dense that, as we came into land among the glass towers and concrete boxes of a modern city, they disappeared altogether in the miasmic cloud of their own pollution, through which buildings occasionally poked, as if carefully packed in cotton wool.

So great is the pollution, and so snarled the traffic in Thailand that it had already reached crisis point when the latest military junta took took over in February 1991, and it was one of the first things they promised to do something about. What followed is typical of all Thai government, military or civil. The many traffic authorities have been rationalised into one, very properly called the Committee for Solving

Traffic Problems. Wheel clamps have been introduced and the Thai Treasury has been persuaded to provide twenty gas masks for the traffic police. The public has been asked to be patient and told that in time . . .

Nevertheless, the car that came to meet me was on time. It had been sent by Son Excellence M. Gérard André, ex-Ambassadeur de France to the court of King Bhumibol, and an old and dear friend who had also been en poste in London for many years.

French ambassadors seem to have an affinity with Thailand. Men of taste and discrimination, they have chosen this country above all others for their retraite and, at one time, there were two of them around, though Gérard is the one who spends much of the year away from the city in an island paradise where he lives in that kind of sumptuous simplicity that is, to my mind, the perfect lifestyle.

I had put Gérard André in charge of my Thai education, and he suggested that, before I joined him in Phuket among the orchids and amaryllis, I spend at least a week in Bangkok doing some serious home-work. My audience with King Bhumibol was fixed for the penultimate day of my visit and both he and our hospitable British ambassador, Ramsay Melhuish, hoped that by then I could at least appear to know a little about his country and his people.

And so, not to let them down, I toured around Old Bangkok, its temples, klongs and waterways. I cut my teeth on ancient capitals, Ayu-thaya, Sukothai and Lopburi; I compared beautiful, serenely superior Buddhas of seven different periods and I learnt to recognise the various styles of stupas (chedi in Thai) and temple adornments: Pranga, Mongkuts and Sky-tassels, as well as encountering in their courtyards the largest caste of mythical monsters, demons and giants that can be met with anywhere in south-east Asia.

I discussed with anyone who would discuss with me the mysterious death of King Ananda, the king's elder brother, the disappearance in Malaysia of Jim Thomson (an ex-OSS officer who founded the Thai silk industry and vanished seven years ago), the dearth of albino elephants, which belong, like swans on the Thames – only larger – to the monarch.

I was saddened and shocked by the Allied war cemeteries od Kanchan-aburi – where 9,000 prisoners-of-war of the Japanese lie buried – the infamous Death Railway, and the Bridge over the River Kwai.

I wondered what could be done about Thailand's endemic problems: the Cambodian refugees and Khmer Rouge guerrillas in the north-east, the drug barons in the Golden Triangle, now exacerbated by the new regime in Burma, and the porn padrones in the sun-sin cities of the coast.

We talked about corruption in high, low and middle places, the economic boom that is making Bangkok a second Singapore, its feeble infrastructure, appalling pollution and endless traffic jams – the contrast between Western and Thai tradition (that was easy, there seems to be no clash, for their culture always comes out on top!). By the end of the week various facts, impressions and opinions had begun to emerge.

Although modern Bangkok surrounds them, and has almost gobbled them up, the shimmering, glittering golden temples, with their curved, gabled roofs repeating each other like shuffled cards, remain the heart and treasure of the town. They are unique and quite superb, the eighteenth-century ones particularly pleasing to Western eyes; and the Wat Phra Keo, the residence of the Emerald Buddha, the finest. The Thais have a genius for incorporating the heavens in their architectural plans, and some of the buildings really look as if they are poised to take off and fly. On the other hand, the crumbling pink and grey ruins of ancient cities, with their endless repetition of writhing bas-relief motifs, left me cold – they are not all that ancient, and, to my mind, it is only their immense scale and unfamiliarity which impress.

The people are extremely religious and, at least in the part of the country I visited, unwavering monarchists. The royal family – whose ramifications are great, thanks to King Chula and his seventy-seven children – seems to have a finger in most pies, but this is popular for Thai royalty is simply on a different plane from other mortals, deeply respected, if not worshipped, and I mean that literally so. The rest of the population is divided into a caste system in which there are not only different rules but also different languages.

From almost my first day in Bangkok I decided that I could never even think of learning Siamese. The alphabet is bad enough – it consists of forty-six wiggly consonants, that look like immature tadpoles, and thirty-one vowels. It was devised by King Ramkamhaeng the Great in the thirteenth century. The language itself has developed from a mixture of Pali, Sanskrit and Cambodian tongues and is of the Sino–Tibetan family of languages. The spoken language (like Chinese) is monosyllabic, has five different tones, and you use different words for people in different stations in life. Even before you say 'Hello!' in Thailand, you must shrewdly estimate the social status of the people you greet. (If this status is too low you do not say 'Hello'.)

For Clare Hollinger, an American diplomat's wife who taught at Chulalongkorn University, and wrote an enchanting book about it, the language 'was difficult enough without the added burden of social analysis, and I ended by addressing all my pupils with the words meant for the level just below royalty, which at first caused consternation and much hilarity'. But the Thais are the politest people on earth, and shun anything socially disagreeable or rude – so she could easily have done worse. It was not necessary to learn the royal form of address. 'Nearly all the royal family,' she adds, 'have been educated in England, and speak better English than you.' Prince Prim Parachatra, head of the English Faculty at Chulalongkorn at that time, was educated at Harrow and Cambridge, and spoke Siamese with an English accent. He was a liberal in the broadest sense of the word and, when asked why all members of the English faculty at Chula were 'so odd', he answered with regal and icy brevity, sounding every syllable: 'It is a pre-requisite of the appointment.'

The Europeans with whom I made friends in Thailand told me that to become integrated with its people you have to forget as many things as you learn. Time, for instance.

Time, as I was soon to find out, is a commodity that has a different meaning for the Thai people. Perhaps it is because they believe in reincarnation and therefore know there is plenty of it. In Thailand, if one asks 'When?' they will answer 'Soon', or sometimes even 'Immediately' (to please one) but they do not mean it, for to them time has no urgency – and in their ancient wisdom they regard all *fahrangi* (white foreigners) as foolishly frenetic.*

And honesty. Western ethics of honesty do not apply and certainly will not survive in Siam. The Thais are not dishonest, according to their own lights – in fact, most are extremely honourable people, it is just that they live under a different system which is too complex for fahrangi to fathom, and they operate within its structure. To them corruption is not a bad habit, but a way of life. Even important officials receive very small legal wages, and bribes are considered part of their salary. A country which, when castigated by others for 'corruption in high places', issues a proclamation that: 'Henceforth all bribes over 200,000 baht [$US 40,000] will be declared illegal', is probably more honest than the ones who refuse to admit that corruption exists at all.

They are a very beautiful people. From the alert, saucy faces of street urchins to the elegant, graceful Thai youth who, with a twirl or twist of brightly coloured cotton and a flower behind the ear, can transform their *pakimas* (or simple, sarong-like dresses) into carnival creations, to the gracious saffron folds worn by the ubiquitous Buddhist monks, the

---

* To be tyrannised by time is the sign of a barbarian. The Thais basically believe all foreigners to be barbarians.

population is a delight to behold. Even the 'goody-men', who trundle their colourful carts or dangle their wares from their shoulders in flat baskets hung from curved teak poles, are beautiful. They have an elegance and an individuality which is instinctive. No two people are dressed in the same way, and whether they are arranging fruit in a wooden bowl or a packet of bean-curd on a banana leaf, it is always done with style.

The Chao Prya river is still the heart of Bangkok life. Away from the hectic streets and hamburger joints, the ageless timeless water-traffic has scarcely changed since the days of Rama I in the eighteenth century, who founded the city on its banks. Nose-to-nose, flat brown teak boats are still lived in by a large part of the population. They are home and factory and marketplace for thousands of families, and it is here that one comes face to face with the poignancy, the fierce reality of the East.

Walking down a narrow street one evening, I came upon a group of old men with wispy beards and ancient Asian faces. They were standing outside a garish shop painted red and white which sold gold, and were bumping and bowing to each other in the formal, lacy cadences of elderly orientals. Looking around, I suddenly realised I was in Bangkok's Chinatown, a large and pullulating area near the river, called Sempeng.

Before my week was over I had come to the conclusion that the Thais are a happy, fun-loving, resilient race and that their religious certainty and acceptance of man's venality makes them strong. Their romantic ideal of 'seemliness' is an elegant and sophisticated one, their very sure sense of identity, which no Western veneer can ever alter, comes from their never having been colonised, but also maybe because, like the British, they are a mongrel race, their nationhood having been forged from many different cultures and peoples.

Before I came to Thailand, I had not realised the significance of the old name 'Indo-China' for a part of south-east Asia, or the importance of the trade winds. I now learnt that, although settled by a non-Mongoloid, possibly Polynesian people as far back as the fourth millennium BC, Thailand was subsequently over-run by waves of immigration from the north (China) and, because of the prevailing winds' direction, from the west (India and Ceylon).

In the second and third centuries of our era, Indian merchants would sail with the trade winds across the Bay of Bengal to the Malay peninsula; they would do business there and then lie up all winter until the winds changed and the summer monsoon blew, when they would put to sea again and continue their journey to points further south and east. Slowly and surely their higher civilisation left an indelible mark on the whole of south-east Asia. Indians intermarried with the local population, and the teachings of the Lord Buddha gradually replaced the animism of earlier times. Local rulers would invite Indian Brahmins and scholars to serve as administrators and astrologers in their courts, and Brahminism, the ancient form of Hinduism, with its central hierarchical concept of god-kings, once heard of, was enthusiastically embraced by the Khmers of Angkor and the Mons of central Thailand.

And it still plays a part in the formal court life of Bangkok today, palace Brahmins being in charge of most of the royal religious rites which cocoon King Bhumibol and the royal family in a web of ancient and sacerdotal ceremonial.

As well as Indian culture from across the sea, three indigenous civilisations influenced the emergent Thais, who did not become a cohesive or united nation until the thirteenth century, with the founding of the kingdom of Sukothai. The most important was that of Dvaravati, a collection of more or less united city states in central Thailand with a mainly Mon population that flourished from the sixth to the eleventh centuries. It first imported Theravada Buddhism from Ceylon, and left behind beautiful temple architecture and very pure, other-worldly, religious sculpture.

By the beginning of the thirteenth century, the power of the Khmer Empire had begun to fade and two Thai chieftains united their forces and founded the first Thai capital at Sukothai, the name meaning, in their flowery language, 'the dawn of Happiness'. The happiness did not last very long, Sukothai being eclipsed by Ayuthaya only a hundred years later, but during that short time it established a distinct Thai style of art and architecture. The Sukothai period also produced an enlightened king – Ramkamhaeng the Great (1279–98), who created the Thai alphabet – and installed the first monks of the Singhalese school of Buddhism in the capital, whose tenets and forms of worship are followed in Thailand to this day.

The Thais, who are great builders, had a very pragmatic approach when it came to a shift in the fortunes of one dynasty or another. They simply abandoned the city that had been the old capital and built a new one. As Sukothai faded, Ayuthaya waxed and it became the state capital for central and southern Thailand for the next three hundred and fifty years.

In the north, however, a separate state emerged, centred on Chiang Mai and known as Lanna. It was ruled over by a Thai-Lao prince called Mengrai, who died in 1317, struck by lightning, a suitably dramatic end for a separatist. He had succeeded, however, in creating a dynasty of princes in northern Thailand who ruled even until the 1930s, when they were finally reabsorbed into the central government of Bangkok.

The Thais themselves have never been great merchants, the lower orders being agriculturists or fishermen, the nobles, administrators. They allowed other races to trade – under the royal monopoly, of course – and with China and Japan virtually closed to all foreigners, Ayuthaya became a major entrepot for the fast-growing European trade with the Orient. First came the Portuguese in 1511, then the Dutch, followed by the English (in 1612) and the Danes, and lastly, in 1662, King Louis XIV sent two magnificent French embassies to King Narai's court at Lopburi in order to spike the influence of his Dutch and English competitors.

It is a pity that we do not have more detailed accounts of the merchant adventurers of those days: greedy, resourceful men like the Englishman, Samuel White, who, purporting to serve the interests of the Thai kings, amassed vast fortunes for themselves, and as quickly lost them, in dangerous initiatives and conspiracies which often ended in penury or violent death.

One of the most extraordinary of these was Constantine Phaulkon, known as 'The Falcon', a British seaman of Greek origin who rose to such heights in King Narai's service that eventually he became the king's Chief Minister, and the second most powerful man in the country. It would seem that he served the king faithfully, but he inevitably made enemies and his downfall was brought about by his advising the monarch to favour the French, and in particular the embassy to Siam of the Chevalier de Chaumont. Unfortunately, this embassy overplayed its hand, for besides fishing for trade concessions, it was rumoured that the Jesuits in its train were preparing to convert King Narai to Roman Catholicism, and a band of outraged courtiers, led by Phra Paetracha, started what became known as the Revolution of 1688 (not to be confused with the English one!), which ended by 'the Falcon' being tried for treason, tortured and executed, the French being kicked out of the country, and Thailand itself becoming closed to all foreign trade or relations for the next 150 years. King Narai shortly afterwards died of natural causes, but his successors, lesser men, became increasingly weak and inward-looking.

There had existed for a long time a kind of *guerre sourde* between the Burmese and the Thais, which occasionally erupted into a major battle. Ayuthaya was finally attacked and razed by the Burmese in 1767; but a previous attempt to take the city in 1592 had failed after a great battle was fought and won by the Thais. It was a kind of eastern Agincourt:

the Crown Prince of Burma and the young ruler of Thailand, mounted on fighting elephants, engaged each other in single sword-to-sword combat in front of the drawn-up ranks of their two armies. Nerusuan, the Thai prince, won and a fine 'chedi' (Wat Yai Chai Mongkol) was built to commemorate his victory.

It was after the sacking of Ayuthaya, however, that the Thais showed their remarkable resilience. General Taksin had set up a resistance base across the river from what is now Bangkok, at a village called Thonburi, and within a year of the sacking of Ayuthaya he established a new capital there, set himself up as king and, in a series of masterly counter-attacks, drove the Burmese out of the country once and for always.

Unfortunately, the new ruler's pride in his military success eventually turned into a dangerous megalomania and his courtiers, seeing he had become incurably insane (at one time he thought he could levitate), sent for another remarkable general, Chao Phya Chakri, who had been campaigning in Laos and was only too pleased to take over. Taksin was disposed of in the only way that was thought seemly for royalty. He was placed in a velvet sack and beaten over the head with a sandalwood club until he was very dead (presumably so that no one should witness the dreadful sight of royal blood being spilt).

The new King Chakri, or Rama I, the Great, as he came to be known, was the founder of the Chakri dynasty and King Bhumibol's direct ancestor. He was a man of action and lost no time in abandoning his predecessor's capital at Thonburi and once again building a new one across the river – the capital we now know as Bangkok.

Rama I had brought back with him from his campaign in Laos a fifteenth-century statue of the Lord Buddha, 'the Emerald Buddha', which is made not of emerald but of green jasper, and unlike many Buddha images is small and precious – only 24½ inches high. It was supposed to have been discovered in Chiang Rai, the northern capital, when an old stupa split open, but it was covered in plaster and it was only when this also split that its true beauty was revealed. It became the Chakri dynasty's most potent symbol, and the first act of the new monarch was to build a temple worthy of it at the centre of his new city. It now resides in the Wat Phra Keo, an ethereal, fantastic and dazzlingly elegant royal chapel in the grounds of the royal palace, and has its three costumes changed personally by the present king at special ceremonies at the beginning of the hot, rainy and cool seasons of the year.

Two other remarkable members of the Chakri family brought Thailand out of its mediaeval past and into the modern world, making it one of the most stable countries in the Far East. One was the present king's great-great-grandfather, King Mongkut (or Rama IV), who ascended the throne in 1851 after serving twenty-seven years in a monastery as a Buddhist monk. He was both clever and intellectually curious, a scholar of considerable achievement and no mean statesman. Determined to bring Thailand back into the international scene, he signed a mutually favourable trade agreement with Sir John Hoskyns, Queen Victoria's envoy, which safeguarded his country from any Western colonial designs, and very soon brought it new prosperity. His only mistake was, perhaps, to employ Miss Anna Leonowens as governess to his many children, for her romantic reminiscences of court life in Bangkok during the 1850s and 1860s, though they inspired the musical *The King and I*, are laughably inaccurate and have done a disservice to this remarkable king's memory.

The other was King Mongkut's son, an altogether different character. King Chulalongkorn the Great was a jovial monarch who did not believe in doing things by half. To begin with he is said to have been the happy father of some seventy-seven children, and the present ramifications of the Thai royal house can, to a large extent, be laid at his door (he would greet a child bowling a hoop or catching frogs in the royal park with the benign 'And which mother is *yours?*'). But he was a good king and during his lifetime many important reforms were carried out. He abolished slavery, and reorganised government administration on Western lines, creating the first Thai national bank and bringing education, justice and public welfare generally up-to-date; he also rebuilt much of the capital, filling in many of the klongs and laying out wide, tree-lined avenues, round which he used to motor cheerfully in a custom-built electric car. When the royal apartments of the eighteenth-century Grand Palace became overcrowded he built a charming Swiss-chalet-cum-Turkish-cum oriental wooden palace for himself and his elastic family, which, set among exotic yet curiously English-suburban watergardens, is one of the architectural and tourist treasures of Bangkok. It is built of golden teakwood, and its architect was the king's brother, Prince Narisaranuwatiwong. On Chulalongkorn's death in 1910, Vimanmak Palace was abandoned, and suffered eighty years of neglect, but fortunately Queen Sirikit recognised its charm and importance and under her guidance it has now been beautifully restored as the museum of King Rama V and his period.

Reforms and modernisation continued, but more slowly under the next two kings, Vajivarudh and Prajadhipok. Compulsory education was introduced and the granting of a constitution was actually considered by Chulalongkorn's grandson, King Prajadhipok, a naturally liberal-minded sovereign. But his good intentions were forestalled in 1931 when a bloodless revolution led by young officers in the army and young intellectuals brought matters to a head. Still greater and much faster political reforms were demanded, and granted, and the Thai kings, who had been absolute monarchs and 'Lords of Life' for centuries, became constitutional ones overnight.

A strange interim period followed – the king was unhappy about the consequences of the new constitution and seemed to have lost the will to reign. He spent less and less time in the country and, in 1935, he abdicated in favour of his schoolboy nephew, Prince Ananda. He then retired to England where he lived the life of a country gentleman in Sussex until his death in 1975. Young King Ananda was not so fortunate.

His father, Prince Mahidol, one of King Chulalongkorn's innumerable sons, had been educated at Harrow, had served in the German army, and then graduated in medicine in America at Harvard where he married a fellow Thai student. During the 1920s the young couple had lived for some time in the States, in a quite humble way, practising medicine and bringing up their small family. Prince Mahidol died when he was only thirty-one and his younger son was only a year old. After returning to Thailand for a brief period, his widow decided to continue her children's education in Switzerland where they lived for some time in Lausanne, the boys first attending excellent schools and then the university there.

When King Ananda came of age, they returned to Bangkok to prepare for the coronation ceremonies, but one morning, six years after his father's death and only a few months before he was due to be crowned, Ananda was found dead by his younger brother Prince Bhumibol – shot through the head, and no one to this day has explained the mystery of how it happened, or why.

In 1850 the Deputy Prahlang, an important official of King Rama III's court, threw out the American envoy who had come to re-negotiate the first American treaty with Siam because he did not conform with his idea of courtly and polite procedure. He informed him that 'since he had arrived in Bangkok alone, without any ceremony, it was contrary to royal custom to arrange for him to have an audience with the king'.

I was determined not to make the same mistake and so, politely and, I hoped, suitably dressed, gloved and hatted, I sat in solitary splendour behind the smartly uniformed chauffeur of the British ambassador's Rolls-Royce and worried that there were not more of me, and that perhaps I should have asked for a few attendants to accompany me on my mission.

The embassy car purred slowly round the boundary walls of the Khitada

Vika Palace, which is separated from Swankhalok Road by a fifteen-foot-wide canal and a high, thick-set hedge. It was important to arrive 'on the dot', so at exactly three minutes to four we crossed a stone bridge, negotiated the guard at the gates and swept along a beautiful avenue of feathery rain trees in full flower. At one minute to four we drew up at a side door of Rama VI's palace, a solid white Victorian building which looks rather like Sandhurst, or a 'Grand Hotel' on the south coast of England.

Several royal ADCs in sparkling white uniforms and a bevy of royal servants sprang out of nowhere to meet and escort me up a steep marble staircase to a large and impressively palatial ante-chamber. There I was sat down between two charming courtiers, Khun Patrapas and Morn Luwang Thawisan Ladawan, who proceeded to entertain me in a delight-fully relaxed and easy way.

Within minutes, palace servants had materialised like friendly djinns, gliding between us in the slithering, deft crouch that I was soon to accept as part of court life, leaving behind them three little white-clothed tables, an assortment of *bonnes bouches* (*pâté de foie gras*, toast, tiny cakes, exotic fruits in flowery silver baskets) and, in front of Khun Patrapas, a silver tea-kettle and wafer-thin porcelain cups. *

The conversation that followed was sprightly and one could not have wished for more elegant and entertaining hosts, but there was an under-current, all the same, of tension that made me jump when large doors were suddenly thrown open behind us and a much grander official – the Court Chamberlain, I assumed, though he was dressed as a general in white and gold uniform and medals – entered the room, accompanied by several aides-de-camp as retinue. After formal introductions and a lingering look at the comparative cosiness of our little tea-party, I fol-lowed the escorting party across marble halls and down a long corridor into His Majesty's presence.

The room I was shown into was not at all what I expected. It was large and lofty, but with no particular style. There was a conventional

---

* The crouch. In Thai custom it is not considered good manners, even today, for any servitor to approach his master, or superior, except at a lower physical level. This tradition is strictly adhered to at His Majesty's court, on all occasions, and by every member of it except the royal family. To stand while the king is sitting would be considered *lèse-majesté* and his whole entourage is adept at this kind of slithering motion, when they pass by, talk to him, or hand him anything on a salver, for lowly hands must never touch his royal person. I felt they were exaggerating *tout de même* when a charming lady-in-waiting who showed me over the royal palace the next day slithered past King Mongkut's ancient and *empty* throne at foot-stool level! But the 'Book of Palace Laws' clearly and unequivocally states that the punishment for standing in front of or touching the king is death; and this was so strictly observed that on one occasion in 1881 when, during a procession of royal barges one of King Rama V's queens fell overboard, no one could rescue her, so, poor soul, she drowned.

grouping of over-stuffed chairs around low tables at one end of the room, but the other end seemed to grow into a study-cum-spaceship command cabin and, seated among the banked computers and antennae, or whatever they were – I am not mechanical – was the slim, rather stiff figure of a man whom I first thought too young to be the king. But the cringing slither of my escort, who now faded backwards behind me, made me realise I was wrong, and we advanced rather warily towards each other across acres of (modern) Persian carpet, to the middle of the room.

King Bhumibol Aiulyades was born in 1927 and is therefore in his mid-sixties, but his spare, wiry figure, black hair and unlined face make him look half that age. He is tall for a Thai and un-smiling, which is also untypical. It is an intellectual face, yet surprisingly sensitive. Broad, high brow, regular features, large ears, he has always worn spectacles, but losing an eye in a teenage car crash, and having it replaced by an unconvincing artificial one, gives him, at first sight, a rather severe and professorial appearance which belies his personality for, though serious and somewhat tense, he is also eager and friendly, with an almost youthful charm and the touching vulnerability of all people who live in glass cases. He loves to communicate: we had hardly sat down before His Majesty started talking and I realised that his eloquence would leave no room for the carefully prepared and boringly bland questions I had submitted for approval to the court – which was a considerable relief.

He is talented in so many ways and interested in so many things that one's first thought is: there will never be enough time to talk about all of them, and then that this poor, clever man, this powerful king, is *starved* of conversation. Apart from his close family, there can be few people with whom he can have ordinary discussions or enjoyable arguments. He is perpetually surrounded by sycophants, or men whose tongues are tied by the elaborate protocol of the court, while his own is equally circumscribed by the need for discretion and tact.

He is, without doubt, a polymath. His skills as a composer and artist may have (to Western eyes and ears) been somewhat exaggerated, but he is a serious and inventive scientist, a brilliant linguist, a good musician, a poet, yachtsman, photographer, as well as being an able politician – though he would strenuously deny this. He is, above all, a technocrat: space-age machinery and techniques, linguistics, harmony, science and engineering, hydraulics, these are the things that obviously fascinate him and even when he is working flat out to alleviate poverty and improve the Third-World conditions in which many of his subjects still live, it is the technological approach and the scientific solution which he enjoys

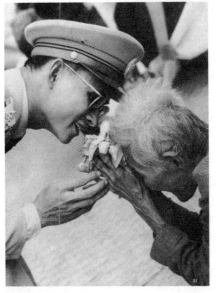

HM King Bhumibol Aiulyades of
Thailand and the King being greeted
by a hundred-year-old woman in
north-east Thailand.

bringing to bear on each and every problem, and which he finds the most satisfying. The other side of his character comes over as rather touchingly simple, and perhaps even a little romantic.

His courtship of Princess Sirikit was certainly that. As a young student in Lausanne University he drove fast cars, and, after his accident, he was taken to Paris for a critical eye operation. Before it his mother asked if there was anything at all he wanted, and he told her he would like to see the beautiful schoolgirl daughter of the Thai ambassador to France, whom he had met once but barely spoken to. Princess Sirikit came to his bedside, and that, in a sense, was that.

The surgeons operated, successfully as it turned out, though he has been only partially sighted ever since. Later the young couple became engaged, and they were married in 1950, seven days before his coronation. Judging by Queen Sirikit's looks today, and by early photographs, it was a very sensible request for what might have been his last moments of sight in a lifetime of blindness.

Bhumibol's early life and his dramatic and unwanted accession were unlike that of any other king I visited. He had been born in America, educated in Europe, outside his own country, even continent, but, like many Siamese kings and three-quarters of the Thai male population, he also served his apprenticeship in a Buddhist monastery, where he lived as an unprivileged monk for a short time and was eventually ordained. Perhaps it was this, rather than foreign influence, that made his opinions of a king's role so refreshingly different.

He told me that he believed in the Lord God Buddha's ten precepts for the 'Practice of Kingship and Righteousness', the first of which is 'Auirouha', or 'No opposition', which means that a king must always be *in harmony* with his people. *

'But what if your people want two different things?' I asked him – and he smiled a superior, Lord Buddha-ish smile (he is thought by millions to be the personification of Narai, who is the mortal form or avatar of the Hindu God, Vishnu) and suggested that that was the domain of politicians, and that he would leave it to them.

He reminded me that he had already reigned longer (forty-five years) than any of his predecessors and that, for all its political upheavals and military coups, his country was more stable than any other in south-east

* According to a different source the ten precepts in the Buddhist 'Code of the King' are *alms-giving*, i.e. charity to individuals; *morality*, i.e. proper observance of the moral precepts; *sacrifice*, i.e. the giving away of something one holds dear for public benefit; *straightforwardness, courtesy, self-restraint*, i.e. refraining from all temptations; *non-anger, non-violence, patience*, and *impartiality* – *not* an easy road to follow, but the path of the righteous seldom is.

Asia, implying, no doubt, that this was *because* the monarchy was above politics, yet the final arbiter in any dispute. He then added that he did not like politics and never interfered in them.

'But Your Majesty appoints the Prime Minister, and can dismiss the government!' I exclaimed.

'Only after consultation, and only in an emergency,' he answered firmly, and shut his mouth like a trap.

Yet we talked a few minutes later about the students' revolt in 1973 when he effectively defused a national crisis. He had insisted on seeing the ringleaders, and he told me how they had knelt before him and wept and begged his forgiveness, before he sent them home through the back door of the palace, for their safety's sake, but how he had afterwards sent for the politicians and sorted out their grievances. He believed in minor explosions like these, and the abortive coup by a group of young military officers in 1981, when once again his initiative had taken the heat out of a political impasse, showed the excellence of a constitutional monarchy in its best light. It prevented *violent* change, he explained, and the amendments to the 1932 Constitution which had been brought about by these events were all steps on the road to real democracy, which should be the eventual goal of every country – a democracy firmly held in place by a constitutional and paternalistic monarchy which leads from behind, I could not help thinking, and wondered if it would work in other countries, nearer to home.

'We have seen Communism,' he continued, 'and it does not work.' Most Thai people are too individualistic to be seduced by any totalitarian regime, and the horrors they have witnessed in the rest of Indo-China have been warning enough.

We talked about the endless guerrilla warfare in Cambodia that spills over into the north of Thailand; about the refugees and the compassion the Thais show them, but we did not speak about the rebel armies who use Thailand as their refuge and springboard. Instead he told me a story about a poor leper who, returning to his lonely house one evening, found all his seed corn stolen by Khmer Rouge soldiers. He had only two fish in his basket, but he gave one to the robbers. 'Why did you do that?' asked the king. 'Because they are hungry too,' the leper answered, and this had obviously made a deep impression.

We did not talk about the corruption and vice of the 'sin cities' of the coast – our two disparate cultures being perhaps equally responsible for the demand and its notorious supply – nor did he mention the growing problem of Muslim fundamentalism in Malaysia and the south of Thailand. He told me the enormous gap between rich and poor in his country would widen, then gradually narrow down; that education was the surest weapon against poverty and the greatest hope for the future; that teachers were the *real* heroes and heroines of his country, revered by the tribespeople but also targeted by the Communist guerrillas and their sometime allies, the drug traders – that they were frequently intimidated and even murdered but that there were always more brave volunteers to take their place.

The king and queen and their two younger daughters, Princess Chakri Sirindhorn, who is not married, and Princess Chulabhorn, who is, as well as the king's eighty-year-old mother and his sister, Princess Galyani Wattana, are all actively involved in schemes that promote education and help poor rural communities in Thailand. They are themselves a formidably gifted and educated team. The Princess Mother is a doctor in her own right and is the founder of a volunteer flying doctor service which has nearly four thousand doctors and dentists, and over ten thousand nurses belonging to it. Through radio contact with medical clinics and cottage hospitals all over Thailand, they can bring expert help to sick people in even the remotest areas. Queen Sirikit is the active head of the Thai Red Cross Society, which has worked now for years, giving expert medical care and services to the hundreds of thousands of refugees who have flooded (and still flood) into the country from the wars in the rest of Indo-China. In order to help the poorest women in the most backward areas she has set up her own foundation, which is known as SUPPORT. It teaches them how to make the most of local talents and crafts – how to weave and sew, and then how to market their products. She has been awarded the Ceres Medal for her work by the Food and Agriculture Organisation of the United Nations, a rare honour for a queen.

The king and queen's eldest daughter is married to an American chemical engineer, Peter Ladd-Jensen, whom she met while graduating in Physics at MIT, and they live in the United States. Princess Chakri Sirindhorn, known to the family as 'the Hurricane', and her sister Princess Chulabhorn, are equally clever, holding doctorates in sociology and biochemistry. They often accompany their father on his journeys into the interior, and are fearless and hardy campaigners in what are often tough conditions. The king himself spends eight months of every year 'on the road', travelling up and down the country and overseeing and encouraging his various projects.

Bhumibol's only son, the crown prince, is a soldier by profession. He is a colonel in the Royal Guard and often fills in for his father when the latter is on tour. He is married to Princess Soamsawali and they have two children.

Outside the cities and away from the coast, eighty per cent of Thailand's population live by subsistence farming. There is too much water in the south, too little in the north, and one of King Bhumibol's greatest achievements has been to set up irrigation and drainage systems which have transformed swamps or deserts into good farming land. He not only uses engineers and experts from the Royal Irrigation Department (which he set up himself) for this, but also personally surveys the area concerned, and when all data has been collected, computed and studied, it is the king who decides what type of water control – barrage, weir, dam or canal – should be built, and who sometimes designs himself the details of construction.

Land reform for landless farmers, farming cooperatives, initiatives for marketing, reafforestation, fish culture and fish farming, water purification, electric power generation are all projects started up by him and there seems to be no end to his creativity and energy.

Did I know, he asked me, that the introduction of water hyacinths into its ditches and klongs can purify the water supply of an entire village and greatly reduce the infant mortality?

Did I realise that a few specimens of *Tilapia nilotica*, tropical fish from the Nile delta that were originally sent to him by the Crown Prince – now Emperor – of Japan had revolutionised fish farming in Thailand?

My mind reeled from an avalanche of facts and figures, and then His Majesty seemed to change gear – or pause merely to catch his breath – and he told me about his country's endemic problems that have *not* yet been solved.

Despite all the royal family's endeavours, Third-World conditions exist in many parts of his country: leprosy and disease, famine, hurricanes and floods. In the beautiful mountains and steep valleys of the north the drug trade still flourishes. Growing opium poppies is the easy and traditional way of life for the hill farmers of the Golden Triangle, and Thailand, Burma and Laos still produce more than half of the heroin consumed in the world today. There the international drug barons are largely in control – and until poverty and demand, smugglers, traffickers, pushers and users are all eliminated, there is little hope that the evil trade will stop. At best it can be discouraged by restrictions and precautions, but these are all too easily evaded.

At one time King Bhumibol worked almost single-handed on pioneering schemes that would stop opium growing among his hill-tribe farmers, but now the Thai government and the International Narcotics Control Board help him set up research stations and crop replacement centres for the introduction of alternative cash crops that are more valuable than opium growing, and are marketing these successfully. At last these schemes are catching on, and in the last few years there have been some encouraging results.

King Bhumibol has set up his own emergency command post in his drawing-room. The palace bristles with antennae, and he has a private wireless station (hidden somewhere in that bank of technology at the other end of the room?) and can get in touch with any part of the country within minutes in case of crisis or disaster, so that immediate relief can be organised.

The conversation then turned to more peaceful topics. We talked about music, and His Majesty told me that Queen Sirikit was studying to be a concert pianist when he married her, and that all his children are musical and that, when they were young, they frequently played together, both classics and gentle jazz. He has made and written an analysis of Bach's piano works, *Das Wohltemperierte Klavier* – enlisting his computers to help him – and also using them to discover the (mathematically) 'true' scale. This was all a bit above my head.

He asked me if I knew anything about a Scotsman called Mackintosh, a merchant adventurer or soldier of fortune of the eighteenth century – or a similar, but much earlier, entrepreneur called da Silva. They are both known to have had adventurous careers in Siam and he would like to trace an imaginative link between them, even to write a romantic/ historical novel – a chronicle – about these men, which would embrace the old and new worlds – the East and West. It sounded an ambitious and slightly wild project, but he has already collected a lot of material and dreamt up a lot more, and he has studied ancient Sanskrit to help him transcribe various contemporary documents he has come across. Here's another intellectual challenge, I thought, and given the king's dogged determination in any task he sets himself, I do not doubt that he will succeed. Meanwhile, I promised to consult the Mackintosh of Mackintosh, Chief of Clan Chattan, who will no doubt be amazed by my request, but I hope will also be helpful.

Bhumibol had not wanted to be king, and he spoke movingly about the horror of discovering his brother's dead body, for he had loved him, and he knew the consequence of the tragedy only too well. 'There was no investigation,' he told me, 'no proper police investigation . . .' and it was obvious that he thought the young king had been assassinated. I remembered then a story I had heard in Phuket of a bewildered young man driving wildly along the tangled dirt tracks of the island's interior in a desperate urge to escape, only to end up, inevitably, in a village where someone recognised him; the headman arrived, the village went into hysterics, the ADCs caught up and the king (I was not told which) was once more ensnared by his destiny and returned to his golden cage.

After forty-five years of it, Bhumibol must have grown used to being a king. His marriage, his children and their close family circle have made his life perfectly acceptable. He recognises that strict protocol and religious ceremony are a necessary part of his functions (he is, fortunately, a convinced Buddhist) and that in no other life would he have been able to achieve so much for the good of his people.

Like all Thais he loves tradition, and I think he now enjoys the ceremony, the mystery, the apartness that keeps him on the throne. He sees nothing odd about being a demi-God revered and worshipped by all his subjects, and at the same time a very modern-minded monarch.

On my way out I passed the door of another room which was half-open and I glimpsed a pile of smart-looking umbrellas, done up in gaudy ribbons and bows, on a table. There was also a queue of soberly dressed Thai gentlemen awaiting His Majesty's pleasure in the passage. I put two and two together, and wished I had done something laudable enough in the king's opinion to be given one too!

Postscript – May 1992

In spite of King Bhumibol's claim of his country's stability and his telling me that he 'never interfered in politics' there have, in fact, been seventeen military coups in Thailand since 1932 and he himself, whether visibly or invisibly, has been largely responsible for defusing the crises they have caused.

But in May 1992 it looked at first as if the crisis would turn out differently. For the first time in the country's history there had been free elections. Democracy was growing, albeit slowly, and so was a prosperous middle class which was no longer altogether willing to play in with the military.

However, when the unelected General Suchinda Kraprayoon seized power (he had been responsible for the 1991 coup which had toppled ex-diplomat and would-be reformer Chatichai Choonharin) and declared himself Prime Minister, the population of Bangkok exploded and took to the streets in mass demonstrations of protest. When the army then opened fire on the demonstrators and Suchinda arrested his rival, General Chamlong, a much loved and respected politician, the people appealed once again to King Bhumibol to stop what was fast becoming a serious and bloody revolution.

Pictures appeared in the press of student demonstrators facing the army, which reminded the world of Tianenman Square in Peking, but these students were holding up portraits of the king as if they were holy icons. Then after King Bhumibol had appealed to the nation (on his drawing-room radio station) there were TV clips of the two protagonists in the Palace, slithering their way to his feet and begging his forgiveness, while he once more – from his incorruptible apolitical, semi-divine position – delivered a lecture and (presumably) told the erring general that he must go, and then, with his usual patience and forbearance, forgave him. Five days later Suchina resigned and left the country for 'an unknown destination', a new government was formed with General Chamlong's party winning a clear majority, and, quite literally, 'the King's peace' – at least for the time being – returned to the country; a triumph, one might conclude, for monarchy at least in one faraway but important part of the world.

Whether these events will have seen the end of military power in Thailand is, however, unlikely. Democracy is still more an ideal than an actuality, and outside Bangkok votes can still be bought for the price of a pair of shoes (one shoe before the election, one shoe after it); corruption is still rampant and government by a military junta has become almost an ingrained tradition.

Under the new army-dictated constitution an unelected military-dominated senate still sits above the elected House of Representatives and still has the power to throw out elected governments that it does not like. Good generals, rather than no generals, is perhaps the best one can hope for in Thai politics and the survival of their wholly estimable and admirable monarch, King Bhumibol, who, 'above it all' but with great and benign influence, works continuously and indefatigably for eventual democracy and more equitable governance in his troubled and beautiful country.

20

MALAYSIA

Sultan Azlam Shah of Perak, the Yang di-Pertuan Agong IX

'The Sovereign has, under a constitutional monarchy such as ours, three rights: the right to be consulted; the right to encourage; the right to warn – and a King of great sense and sagacity would want no other.'

WALTER BAGEHOT

The first sign that visitors read when they arrive at Kuala Lumpur airport is: '*If you bring in DADAH you will be liable to a death sentence.*'

It alarmed me enough to enquire nervously who or what *DADAH* was. It is such a friendly, innocent-sounding word, and might I possibly have some in my luggage without knowing it was forbidden? I was told sternly by a uniformed customs official that it meant narcotics, and covered any and every kind, from marijuana to heroin, and that carrying even the smallest amount meant immediate arrest, imprisonment and a trial that could well end in capital punishment.

The Malays, unlike their neighbours, are deadly serious about fighting the opium trade and, even as I spoke, six young idiots from Hong Kong, who had probably been duped, were appealing against just such a sentence, an appeal which was unlikely to be granted.

I did not have any dadah in my luggage, only two important letters: the first an assignment for an audience with His Majesty, Sultan Azlam Shah, the IXth King, or Yang di-Pertuan Agong, of Malaysia, written on beautifully embossed paper from the palace secretariat, the other, on the writing paper of a famous British merchant bank, was a letter of introduction to a friend of a friend with whom I would be staying.

With a placatory smile at his handler, I patted the yellow sniffer-labrador as I passed, and emerged, blinking, into the blazing sunshine of the peninsula. To my considerable relief, a tall soldierly figure stepped forward and immediately took charge.

This was Colonel John Carruthers, late of 2 King Edward VII's Own Gurkha Rifles, a soldier turned merchant banker who, in spite of his name with its 'Clubland Heroes' overtones, tuned out to be the most sympathetic and broad-minded economic empire-builder one could wish to find, with a delightful sense of humour and a profound and realistic knowledge of the country and its ways. He is married to Rukiah, the half-Malay, half-Baba-Chinese daughter of a Malaysian general and ex-Minister of Defence, a bubbling, happy, hospitable young woman whose warmth and enthusiasm make her the centre of a large circle of cosmopolitan friends. Ruki loves shopping in London, gardening and animals. The Carruthers do not have any children, but they do have dogs – in every size and shape – and Ruki seems to have space in an expandable home and heart for every four-legged refugee in the country.

John Carruthers had first-hand experience of the Emergency, the anti-Communist civil war of the 1950s which preceded Malaysian independence, and he has seen a backward, uneducated population, deeply divided by racial tensions and divided loyalties, and ruled by a foreign power and autocratic sultans, grow into a self-governing, homogeneous community which has swallowed and almost digested democracy and capitalism and now stands on the verge of great economic prosperity. It is a lot to have happened in one lifetime.

There were always comings and going in the Carruthers' home, and it was the ideal background for a beginner to start learning. Between them they knew just about everyone, and had been just about everywhere in Malaysia but, best of all, they had the patience and kindness to share their knowledge and answer my insatiable questions.

Ruki was very proud of her Baba-Chinese blood, and began by explaining to me how this sophisticated community within a community had roots which went back to the sixteenth century and beyond. The Baba-Chinese claimed descent from a Ming emperor who had given his daughter in marriage to Mansur Shah, a Malayan sultan; she had arrived in the country with a suite of many hundred handsome young men and beautiful handmaidens who eventually married and settled, though they proudly preserved much of their courtly Chinese customs and style. The fine antique furniture in Ruki's house, and the magnificent costumes I saw later in Kuala Lumpur's museum, bore witness to this. Sadly, Baba-Chinese identity is slowly disappearing and it is now only a tiny drop in the extraordinary ethnic mix that forms Malaysia today.

First of all there are the Malays, and they are a mixed enough race in themselves: they form 49 per cent of the population, and include only those people among the original inhabitants of the peninsula (and Malaysian Borneo) who have embraced Islam. Then there are the mostly Animist peoples of the jungles and coasts – Negritos, Orang Aslis,

Senois, Proto-Malays; the aborigines of Sabah and Sarawak; Kadazan, Murut, Rungu, the Dayaks of the Sea (Iban) and Land (Bidayuh), the shy and nomadic Punan – these are only some of the innumerable tribes and ethnic groups who constitute a further 10 per cent of the native population.

Today the majority of Malays and tribal aborigines live a leisurely existence at subsistence level, fishing and farming a little, and – sad to relate – cutting down more and more of the magnificent Malayan jungle, the oldest primal forest in the world. They are easy-going, polite and dignified people, whose lives revolve around their *kampongs* (villages) and families. Nature has supplied them with almost all their basic needs and, without undue exertion, they can earn a little extra by planting a few rubber trees at the bottom of their gardens. Natural rubber, which was grown originally from seedlings smuggled out of Brazil and germinated at Kew Gardens by the British, now supplies more than half of the world's needs.

But as a race they are singularly uninterested in making money, leaving that to the Chinese and Indians whom, though they nowadays get along with them well enough, they privately despise. In the past the Malays accepted a hundred years of British authority with polite indifference; they reserved their reverence, and that is the right word, solely for their sultans.

It was the colonialists, Portuguese, Dutch and, most of all, the British, who were largely responsible for the incomers – the remaining 41 per cent of the present population: 32 per cent Chinese and 9 per cent Indian, for as the development of the country proceeded, the Europeans found they needed skilled, but cheap, labour for their rubber plantations and tin mines, and could not find it locally.

It may have upset the old racial balance in which the indigenous population was dominant, but there is no doubt that the incomers, and particularly the Chinese, were and still are the workers – the engine that provides the dynamism that runs the economy of the country today. The half-million Indians, if they are not lawyers, merchants and medics, mostly provide a floating labour force for the rubber plantations. They come from the Madras area of India, speak Tamil and, when they have made enough money to buy themselves a plot of land in their own country, usually return there. They live in their own areas of the city and, one day as I wandered round Kuala Lumpur, I came on such a community, living in an entirely different style and at an entirely different pace from the bustling, crowded streets and organised frenzy of the Chinese quarter. Here, doe-eyed women sauntered by in brightly

coloured saris, men squatted in doorways or stood in groups, shirt-tails
flapping, talking, talking, while an all-pervading smell of curry and spices
hung heavily on the dusty, breathless air, or rather the smog that counts
for air in modern down-town Kuala Lumpur.

Kuala Lumpur, like Singapore and Hong Kong, is an object lesson built
in concrete of what capitalism and entrepreneurial genius can achieve in
half a century. You may not like it, but you cannot help being impressed.
Yet at the very centre of the soaring skyscrapers, the sparkling new
mosques, the stadiums, conference halls and museums, you can still find
the ghost of Empire.

The wide open 'village green' campus is still there, where the British
once played cricket, or gathered on Sunday afternoons in striped blazers
and immaculate whites before wandering across to the Selangor Club,
or 'Spotted Dog', for a *stengah*, though now it is more of a public park
than a playing field. 'The Club' and the long bar of the 'Coliseum' were
privileged haunts of the European colony and had been out of bounds to
'natives' for generations, until General Sir Gerald Templer's iron broom
swept the city clean of every kind of racial discrimination (and half the
club committee resigned).

Facing the Spotted Dog on the other side of the campus are the exotic,
grandiose and many-domed buildings of the legislature. They look like
an exotic palace in Rajistan but still fulfil the purposes of modern government; they were built no doubt to fit in with the nearby, famous, and
even more exotic Kuala Lumpur Railway Station, said to be the largest
white elephant in south-east Asia. It was originally intended for a busy
terminus in northern India but, owing to frontier disputes and skirmishes,
the economically-minded British Office of Works switched its location
to Malaya, a country which had then but one railway line and one train
a day using it.

One night we dined at The Club and I read with interest, and perhaps
a twinge of nostalgia, a board which listed the fading names of past
Presidents, English and Scottish members of the old colonial establishment. It served as a memorial as well as an archive to men who had
loved the country, and on the whole who had served it well. Their
British names were followed, after the 1960s, by Chinese and Indian
ones. The restaurant was crowded, mostly with Indian family parties,
and there were very few Europeans at the long bar.

Another night Ruki gave a dinner party and the guests, as well as
some very grand Malay relations, included an ex-cavalry officer of enormous charm who had 'stayed behind' and who now swapped stories and
jokes with John Carruthers about the Emergency, their superior officers,

the jungle and the terrorists, which made the whole period come start-
lingly alive. After dinner we sat on, long into the starry night, and they
told me about Malaysia, and how our involvement in the country had
first started.

At the beginning of our era, Indian traders were blown across the Bay
of Bengal by the same convenient trade winds that had helped colonise
Thailand, and they brought Buddhism, Hinduism and a much more
advanced civilisation to the peninsula. As in the rest of south-east Asia,
some settled and intermarried. They traded in gold, pepper, spices and
sandalwood and soon small entrepots and trading ports appeared along
the coast.

The most important by far of these was Malacca, which was founded
by King Paramesvara, or Iskander Shah, as he was known to the Arabs.
During his reign, Malacca quickly became one of the most prosperous
cities and trading posts of the East, for not only was tin discovered and
mined in its hinterland but it was geopolitically the centre of the spice
trade, halfway between the Cocos Islands and the Muslim entrepots on
the Arabian coast. The town grew from a small village to a city of some
fifty thousand souls in less than half a century, and even the Ming
Emperor Yangho recognised it and granted it his protection.

But the independence and prosperity of the small Malayan kingdom
lasted only a hundred years. King Paramesvara died in 1414, having been
converted to Islam by Indian Muslims. In 1450 his successor, Muzzafar
Shah, declared Islam the official religion of the kingdom, and from
thenceforth Malaya's kings became sultans, and adopted a form of
Arabic/Malay as their written language, called *Jawi*.

The royal palace was the centre around which Malaccan life gravitated, and its incumbents were absolute rulers of great magnificence,
with powers of life and death over their subjects. Only the royal family
could wear yellow garments, only the sultan could be shaded by a white
ceremonial umbrella or wear golden anklets. He was assisted in governing
the kingdom by a *bandahara* (Prime Minister), a *temenggung* (Chief of
Police) and a *laksamana* (Admiral). It all seemed to work reasonably well
until the beginning of the sixteenth century when Sultan Mahmud, a
rather feeble ruler, became jealous of his remarkable bandahara, Tun
Marahir, and had him assassinated, with many other high dignitaries of
the court, an impulsive act which he later regretted. Indeed his conscience, it is said, was so stricken that he went into a decline and
abdicated in favour of his son, Ahmed, an even feebler character.

It was unfortunate for the Malayan monarchy that these events coincided with Vasco da Gama's discovery of the round-the-Cape route to China and thereby his royal master Henry IV of Portugal's decision to capture the Far Eastern spice trade; an ambitious design but one which King Henry hoped would simultaneously destroy the hated infidel's monopoly, weaken Venice (the Arabs' European distributors and Portugal's maritime rivals), reinforce St Francis Xavier's missionaries, who had recently landed in Malacca, and last and perhaps least, discover whether Prester John, the mythical priest/king, who had temporarily ruled half of Africa, really came from these parts or, indeed, had ever really existed.

A Portuguese ship arrived off Malacca in 1509, its captain requesting trading concessions. The negotiations failed, an armed squabble followed and several Portuguese sailors were taken prisoner. A few months later, a Portuguese war fleet under the command of Admiral Alfonso de Albuquerque appeared on the horizon and that was the end of Malacca's independence. The Portuguese built a huge fort on a hill above the port, which they called A Famosa, and for nearly one hundred and fifty years their merchants did, in fact, dominate the Far Eastern part of the spice trade. It is difficult for us to realise what desired ingredients pepper, capsicum, cinnamon, cloves, ginger and allspice were on the tables of the Europeans, but in the sixteenth century, if a ship laden with spices loaded, say, at Malacca, escaped the perils of piracy – and there were plenty of pirates off the coasts of Malaya and Borneo – the dangers of shipwreck, malnutrition and mutiny, it would make a tenfold profit when it landed its cargo in a West European port, after having defrayed the cost of the voyage and of the ship itself.

The Dutch took over from the Portuguese as the major European traders in the East in the late sixteenth century, after the annexation of Portugal by Spain and the subsequent closure of the port of Lisbon to Dutch and British merchant ships. In response to the embargo, the Dutch traders founded the Dutch East India Company and duly captured the spice trade and also, after a long siege, the fort of A Famosa in Malacca. They occupied the port for another one hundred and fifty years, but their interests were purely obstructive, a tactical dog in the manger to prevent the British (and possibly the French) from replacing them, for they had made what is now Djakarta the centre of their Far Eastern possessions.

The British already had a toe-hold in Malaya. Their East India Company was founded in 1600, with the blessing of Queen Elizabeth, who had a weakness for merchant-adventurers. One of them, Sir Francis Light, had been approached by the Sultan of Penang, who was frightened of the growing might of the Siamese, and who agreed to lease Sir Francis trading facilities on a large off-shore island, north of Malacca, in return for his protection.

Sir Francis double-crossed the sultan, took over the island for the nascent company, and began the massive task of clearing it of jungle and establishing a free port, now Penang, in its excellent natural harbour. Before long, ships from all Asia were calling in and the population of the island prospered and exploded.

The French Revolution was the unlikely cause of the British occupation of Malacca. In the Napoleonic wars that followed it, Holland, having lost her home ports and most of her trading fleet, asked the British to act as caretakers for her Far Eastern possessions, and Malacca became a British protectorate in 1795, under the aegis of the East India Company. A British merchant company's idea of 'protection' at that time was perhaps curious, for the systematic destruction of the Portuguese-built Dutch fort, A Famosa, began as soon as they arrived to take it over, and with it Holland's power in the region. After Waterloo and the allied victory, the Dutch reoccupied Malacca for a short time, but without the fort to defend it they lost interest and it became a British possession in 1826.

Although the Dutch returned only briefly to Malaya, they repossessed their other bases and soon controlled a large part of the East Indies which alarmed, amongst others, the first of the British Far Eastern merchant potentates, an ex-civil servant called Sir Thomas Raffles. He believed that another British trading port in the region was necessary to redress the balance and, in 1819, he privately bought the little island of Singapore from the Sultan of Johore for less than one hundred pounds.

It was a shrewd move. Singapore was then inhabited by 1,000 Malays and Orang Lants living at subsistence level in primitive conditions. Within five years, owing to its strategic position and the establishment of a Free Port in an excellent harbour, the trade of his new possession boomed. It soon became a microcosm of what Malaysia is today, with Chinese, Indians, Bugis, Arabs, Armenians and Europeans jostling each other in the marketplace. By 1824, its population had grown to 11,000. Today it has a population of several million.

With so much trade being carried on under the British flag, it soon became clear that the three free ports of Malacca, Penang and Singapore would be better off amalgamated and, a few years later, they joined forces and interests to become 'The Straits Settlements', a sort of south-east Asia twin to the East India Company.

Malaya is rich in tin, a mineral found in only a few countries of the world, and because of the growing canning industries of Europe and the

USA the tin mines of the Malay Straits Settlements were becoming increasingly valuable. Their owners had imported a large and quarrelsome (but cheap) labour-force from the Chinese mainland to deal with the more skilled and technical operations of the mines, and this soon became a wasps' nest of intrigue, secret societies, quarrels and unrest. The sultans had no authority over the incomers, did not like them and were unco-operative. By the early 1860s the industry seemed on the verge of collapse and the traders appealed to the British government for intervention and help.

The Colonial Office sent out a governor, Andrew Clark, who pulled off a coup by exceeding the terms of his assignment. He summoned the Malaysian sultans to a meeting on his yacht, anchored off the coast of Penang and, after lavish entertainment, he put forward some far-reaching proposals. The Sultan of Perak was the first to succumb to both his hospitality and his blandishments and signed a treaty on the spot, by which a British 'Resident' would, in future, assist him in all aspects of his kingdom's development, excepting those of religion and indigenous customs.

It was the thin end of the wedge.

Selangor signed a similar treaty before the year was out and three years later the Malay Straits Settlements became colonies of the British Crown. One by one of the Sultanates of the Peninsula, and eventually Sabah in Borneo, followed suit and accepted British rule, or more pre-cisely British participation in government through the Resident who 'advised' the monarch on how to run his country. There were some bad 'Advisers', but mostly they were good, tactful and efficient, and nearly always 'originals'. Many of them forged deep friendships with their royal colleagues and lived extraordinary lives of isolated oriental splendour.

Of course there were occasional rebellions against the system but these were small and easily limited. Malaya had its Che Guevaras who have entered into their folklore as heroes of the resistance and pioneers of Independence: Mat Saleh in Sabah, Dat Bahaman and Mat Kilau in Pahang. But by 1896, a loose 'Federation of Malay States' was established and a governor-general was appointed to supervise the state governors. The legislature and law courts, except those that dealt with local cus-toms, which remained in the hands of the local sultan and his Adviser, were moved to Kuala Lumpur. At first the sultans accepted being organ-ised into a federation, thinking it would give them more collective power, but later they were not so sure. In fact it proved to be another name for centralised British government.

Each of the nine Sultans: of Johore, Kedah, Kelanton, Melaha, Negri

Sembilan, Pahang, Perak, Perlis, Penang, as well as Sabah in eastern Malaysia, and to a much lesser extent Sarawak, despite their newly limited powers, still maintained a royal court of considerable magnificence. On formal occasions they sat on their golden thrones beneath a giant State Umbrella (a royal monopoly) with the insignia of their office – jewel-studded *kris*, seal of state, sceptre and betel-box laid out before them, immobile and unsmiling (immobility is a sign of divinity) while innumerable tribal chiefs would drag themselves forward at crouching level in painful but loyal homage to the very steps of the throne – but never further – for the sultan's person was sacred and no one was allowed to touch him.

These displays were in accordance with custom and for the edification of the many thousands of their devoted subjects. In private, most of the sultans and rajahs were a sophisticated, jolly lot, who had often been educated at Sandhurst or Oxford, were good at games, owned race-horses, bought Rolls-Royces, and enjoyed the good things of life in an uninhibited way.

Only one indigenous race in Malaya refused to bow to the powers of the sultans, or the British – the aborigines. Shy and gentle, they lived (and still live) in the unexplored parts of the deepest, darkest jungle, long-haired, pale brown people who hunted small game with bamboo blow-pipes and poison darts, were expert trackers and believed that every animal, stick and stone had its own living spirit, which they respected and sometimes feared. They had never been counted but probably numbered between fifty and one hundred thousand people.

Such was the 'State of the Nation' between the wars and up to 7 December 1941, the moment when the Japanese, joining the Axis powers, bombed Pearl Harbor and started their invasion of south-east Asia.

On 8 December 1941, they bombarded Singapore and the coast. There was no defence, and within twenty-four hours they had destroyed every airfield in Malaya. Two days later their aircraft sank two British battle-ships, the *Prince of Wales* and *Repulse*, and the war at sea and in the air was lost. Allied land forces held out a little longer, but the British were in no position to reinforce or adequately defend Singapore, the peninsula or Sarawak, and Japanese tanks, followed by waves of infantry on what John Carruthers' cavalry friend described as 'bloody bicycles', rolled unopposed down the country's few trunk roads, or hacked and crawled their way through the jungle in a campaign that barely lasted three months.

North Borneo capitulated in January 1942, and on 16 February, Singapore fell.

In the Japanese occupation, which lasted three and a half years, the population, both indigenous and European, suffered horribly under a fanatical military dictatorship and an army that thought all prisoners who let themselves be taken alive were abject traitors and should be treated as animals. A great many Europeans and many thousands of Malays died in the prison camps from overwork, disease or plain starvation.

There was little active native resistance, except from the more dedicated communists of the Chinese community, who were anyway planning a social revolution and who had hated the Japanese (even more than the British) ever since their invasion of their motherland. A substantial number of them were recruited by Colonel Freddie Spencer Chapman who, after the fall of Singapore, 'stayed behind' in the jungle with a handful of other British officers, to harass the enemy and prepare for an eventual British army of liberation. This tiny nucleus of brave and highly skilled guerrillas were known back in London as 'Force 136', and they were soon joined by other British soldiers dropped in by parachute or secretly landed by submarine.

It is ironical to think that these Chinese Communist terrorists, who at that time called themselves 'the Malay Peoples' Anti-Japanese Army' or MPAJU, were trained in jungle warfare and the use of modern weapons by the British, who would soon be finding themselves at the receiving end of their hard-learned skills. They only had to change one word. From June 1948, MPAJU became MPABU. *

Spencer Chapman regarded the young Chin Peng in those days as 'Britain's most trusted guerrilla', and several of the Chinese communists who had fought so bravely with Force 136 – including Chin Pen and Osman China (the Communist terrorist who loved Shakespeare) – came to London at the end of the war to take part in the victory parade.

In the event the British army never liberated Malaya for, in August 1945, the atom bomb dropped on Hiroshima, in one horrific hour, dramatically and terribly ended the war in the Far East. Special troops returned to Malaya the following spring to set up a provisional military government until conditions could return to approximate normality, and with the long-distance objective of preparing the country for eventual self-government.

* 'The Malay Peoples' Anti-British Army'.

'Normality' meant to many returning Europeans, who had spent most of their lives developing or administering the country, and who genuinely loved it, a return to the status quo of before the war. This was no longer possible.

The Japanese had joined the four northern protectorates of Kedah, Perlis, Kelantan and Trenggann to Thailand in 1943, and these were returned and, together with the Malay Straits Settlements of Malacca and Penang, now became the 'Malaysian Union' under a provisional British administration. Singapore, having a predominantly Chinese population, remained outside the 'Union' and became a separate British Crown Colony, as did Brunei. It was decided in London that the 'Union' was to be governed as a single entity, from central administration in Kuala Lumpur, but with local affairs still in the hands of the native rulers and their British Advisers.

The sultans' reaction was mixed.

Some pro-British heads of state (the wise and ebullient old Sultan of Johore, for one) willingly cooperated, but others were less accommodating. Indeed there was considerable Malay opposition to this new and overtly British form of government, which would deprive the sultans of their individual sovereignty and of many of their ancient rights and privileges, while it gave a modicum of power to the much-disliked Chinese population. To resist the terms of the Union the Malay people formed a political party called UMNO and, in 1946, demanded its abrogation. The Colonial Office did what is usual in such cases. It appointed a commission to look into the problem. After this had sat and pondered the question for two years it decided that the Union should be dissolved, and it was succeeded, in 1948, by a Malayan Federation whose more flexible statutes favoured the Malays.

For the moment the sultans were propitiated, but both the Chinese and the Malay Communist Parties were not. The Communist movement, which had helped the British in their guerrilla war against the Japanese, had been outlawed by the post-war government. It immediately went underground, though it still remained a cohesive force of some five thousand highly trained ex-guerrilla-type soldiers whose speciality was jungle warfare.

The fact that the British government was slowly moving towards establishing an infrastructure that would lead to Malaya's eventual independence and self-government did not deter the Malayan Politburo one jot from their purpose: to establish a Communist Republic in Malaya, immediately, or certainly the sooner the better.

Chin Pen knew that his revolution would be led by two million active, industrious Chinese, many of whose grievances had already festered into strikes and industrial unrest, for though they believed they were largely responsible for the booming post-war economy of Malaya, they thought themselves underpaid by the British and resented being treated as aliens by the Malays – a revolution they felt sure would change all this. They would drag the Indian and Malay workers along with them, throw out the British and the sultans and create a new Communist state, loyal to their motherland and their hero, Chairman Mao. It would be accomplished by a carefully planned, minutely plotted campaign of terror.

In the spring of 1948, nearly fifty leaders of the underground Malayan Communist Party met in a stoutly built, well-organised camp, hidden deep in the jungle, near Raub in the state of Penang.

Osman China, ex- Force 136, was one of them, and it was to him and the others that Chin Pen, their Secretary-General, exposed his battle plan. 'The dedicated Communists and CT* sympathisers would be split into two groups – one would be a small and deadly striking force, operating from secret jungle bases, and using not only the expertise they had learnt from the British, but also the ammunition and food stores they had hidden and sometimes even the same camps that "Force 136" had built and used during their guerrilla war against the Japs. The other would be a large and dispersed civilian force of ordinary citizens, secretly CT members, who would be responsible for supplying the striking force with money, food and information. They would be called "Min Yuen" or the "movement of the masses".'

On 16 June 1948, the killing began. That day, on many estates and rubber plantations throughout Malaya, unsuspecting British were systematically assassinated by Chinese CTs who walked into their unprotected offices and, in front of terrified native clerks, coldly murdered them with revolver or machine-gun, after which they vanished, like smoke, back into the jungle whence they had come.

And it was not only the British.

In Johore, on the edge of the Voules Estate, five terrorists in jungle green with red stars on their hats walked into a kampong (village) and knocked on the door of a Chinese rubber tapper foreman called Ah Fung. They demanded subscriptions from every tapper on the estate and, when the wretched headman pleaded that this would be impossible, they tied him and his wife and daughter to nearby trees. With a deadly, flat-bladed *parang* they cut off one of Ah Fung's arms above the elbow

---

* Communist Terrorist.

and, as the blood spurted, their leader shouted: 'Keep their eyes open!' The soldiers forced the women's heads round towards him as he hacked off the other arm. Above the sagging, bleeding body of the headman they pinned a notice for all to read: 'Death to the Running Dogs'. *

At first it seemed to the horrified British community that these were random killings, that there was no sense, no pattern to the savagery. But soon one emerged. The Communists' message was to *all* the people of Malaya. This was a war of terror against the British, and no one could escape from it. In all but name it was a war that lasted for twelve and a half long years, and there were moments, especially at the beginning, when it was nearly lost. It was called 'The Emergency' for its duration, in order to protect the interests of British planters and firms. If it had been called a 'war' they would have lost their insurance coverage.

That the Emergency was won was due to the courage and dogged tenacity – some might call it sheer bloody-mindedness – of the British civilian community who organised themselves, when there was no other organisation, into a closely knit, brilliantly resourceful resistance force. There were twelve thousand of them: planters and their families, members of the Malay civil service, tin-miners, doctors, businessmen. All, it is true, with a prestige that was slowly declining in the surging post-war aspirations of a new Asia, but all with a genuine affinity and deep love for the beautiful country in which they had lived for most of their lives and had made their home.

Some of them had been soldiers during the Second World War, which gave them an edge. Some of the more intelligent ones, including the remarkable Bob (later Sir Robert) Thompson, had recognised, as early as 1947, that things were seriously wrong and had warned the High Commissioner, Sir Henry Ghent, and the security forces of their misgivings. But complacency in high places was unshaken, and it was not until an ex-police colonel, who was going home to England, sent a private report to Malcolm MacDonald, the Supremo for political affairs in southeast Asia, who was appalled by the information it contained, that Whitehall began to wake up. Ghent was recalled to London 'on indefinite leave', but his life was brought to an abrupt and tragic end when his aeroplane collided with another over London airport.

The lull that followed and the squabbles that frequently arose between a peace-time police force, an un-prepared, ill-equipped army and a

---

* 'Running Dogs' was the name the CTs gave to any Malay, Indian or Chinese, who co-operated with the British and it was the title Noël Barber used for his 'The War of the Running Dogs', the best book I have read about the 'Emergency', and from which I have taken much information.

civilian administration benefited no one except the Communists. Fortunately, the newly appointed High Commissioner, Sir Henry Gurney, was a man of vision and vigour who on arrival immediately set things into motion. He realised at once that this was a war of political ideologies that could never be won by arms alone, and that what was needed was armed support for an alternative and *superior* ideology, rather than political support for an army. And so a campaign was begun to 'win the hearts and minds' of the people of Malaya, and to coordinate a counter-insurgent policy, which would fight the terrorists on every front, but always with this in mind.

The sultans and their advisers, the emerging right-wing Malay politicians, among whom Tunku Abdul Rahman was soon to shine, educators, and propagandists all played their part. A 'Director of Operations', Sir Harold Briggs, was appointed and, though it was not easy for him as a civilian to coordinate the anti-bandit operations of the police and fighting forces, he and Bob Thompson, his civil staff officer, devised a strategy which marked a turning point in the war. The Briggs Plan aimed 'to support and protect the vulnerable civilian population from the terrorists, by achieving control of the populated, and especially the squatter areas on the edge of towns, to break up the Communist organisation within these areas, to isolate the CT bandits from their food and information-supply organisations, and to destroy them by forcing them to attack British forces on their own ground'.

A central War Council was formed which planned policy in detail, and a similar council was organised in each of the nine states, headed by a State Prime Minister, an office appointed by the sultan and his adviser. The Police, and especially 'Special Branch', were reinforced from Britain and eventually the latter elevated intelligence-gathering to a state of the art. Soon all Malaya was engaged in fighting terrorism.

Gurney himself was responsible for many new ideas. With the sultans' help, who all gave him parcels of land, he was responsible for re-settling the 'squatters' into new villages, where they could no longer be terrorised into helping the CTs. He insisted on granting extremely generous bounties for valuable counter-insurgent information, and he started a system of National Registration which meant that everyone had to carry an ID card.

Sir Henry Gurney's ambush and murder was an accident, a tragic trick of fate – or perhaps, as some think, a deliberately courageous act of self-sacrifice.

On 6 October 1951, a platoon of thirty-eight guerrillas, led by Siu Mah, a friend of Chin Pen's, were at ambush stations on the winding road that led to Fraser's Hill, a mountain resort in Pahang. They were after arms, not men, and were expecting a military convoy to pass, which they hoped to jump. Their information had been faulty, and they were just about to give up and withdraw when a three-car convoy appeared, climbing slowly up the road. At its head was a Land-Rover full of armed Malay policemen; in the centre a large black Rolls-Royce flying the Union Jack and the Malay flag, while the third car trailed some way behind as its engine had stalled on the steep hill.

When the CTs opened fire they had no idea that the High Commissioner, his wife and private secretary were the Rolls's passengers. In the first burst, all the policemen were killed except for one sergeant, who bravely returned their fire. The High Commissioner's chauffeur was killed instantly and the big car slewed round and stopped. Suddenly its door opened and out stepped Gurney. He banged the door shut and walked slowly towards the roadside bank behind which the CTs were hidden. There he seemed to hesitate for a moment, then there came another murderous hail of fire and he crumpled and fell at the verge of the road, hit by a dozen or more bullets, while Lady Gurney and Mr Staples crouched shaking, but safe, on the floor of the Rolls.

A bugle sounded and the guerrillas faded back into the jungle just as the third car rounded the corner and its armed guard leapt out. But Gurney, the man who had initiated the greatest social revolution in south-east Asia, lay dead, and when the news broke, it produced world-wide reaction, being hailed in the Communist press as a triumph for the terrorists' cause.

The recognition of Red China by the Attlee government in 1950 had been a distinct setback to the 'war of ideas' being waged in Malaya, but the murder of the British High Commissioner in 1951 seemed to those waging it very much worse.

Strangely enough it was also a time when Chin Pen first realised that the war of terrorism was not going according to plan, and that the guerrillas, far from winning it, were becoming hated as much as they were feared. In October 1951 he called another jungle meeting of all his commanders and issued what has become known as the October Directive.

It was an astonishing volte-face and may have been directly influenced by intervention from Mao's mainland China. All unnecessary civilian bloodshed was in future to be avoided; there were to be no more attacks on civilian institutions; Min Yuen would in future attempt to control the masses 'legally' by penetrating the trade unions and other positions of importance.

We now know that Chin Pen from then on, recognising military stalemate, if not defeat, committed himself to wage war on two fronts, terrorism against the police and army on the one hand, legal infiltration on the other. It was the classic Maoist principle.

The year 1951 was indeed a fateful one in the history of Malaya. Fortunately it fell to Winston Churchill, the incoming Prime Minister of the new Conservative government, to find a High Commissioner for Malaya worthy of replacing Gurney, and again, fortunately, though several other generals were approached and refused, it was Sir Gerald Templer who was summoned to Ottawa, where Churchill was presiding over a 'council of war' on Commonwealth problems.

Lord Ismay and General Alexander were both present at the conference and they and other members listened with dismay when Oliver Lyttelton, the new Colonial Secretary, who had just returned from Malaya, reported the existence there of an 'appalling situation'. 'From a long life in administration,' he ended sombrely, 'I could find no parallel.' For several months the country had been without a High Commissioner, a Director of Operations (Briggs's term of office had come to an end) or a Chief of Police (the somewhat discredited Nicol Gray had quietly left the country, leaving behind him a letter of resignation).

Britain, after six years of a socialist government, was practically bankrupt, and the war (Churchill called a spade, a spade) in Malaya, where three thousand men and women had been killed in the last two years, was costing half a million pounds *a day*. The problem of Malaya, one can guess, was high on the council's list. Winston Churchill had not lost his empirical view of world politics, or his statesmanship. His realisation of the global gravity of the Malayan situation and his determination to resolve it was perhaps one of his greatest achievements.

At the end of dinner on the first night of the conference, Churchill and Templer talked, and when he was offered the appointment by the cigar-puffing premier, the young and little-known general did not hesitate to accept it. 'I regarded it as an order,' he said afterwards, and three weeks later he had taken up his command, this time a High Commissioner with military and political powers 'greater than any British soldier had enjoyed since Oliver Cromwell'.

Gerald Templer was far from being a typical soldier. He was strikingly good-looking in a pale, intense, rather nervy kind of way; indeed there was a tension about him that was almost electric and exploded every now and then in outbursts of impatience or rage or – if sorely tried – a flood of withering, barrack-room language.

I knew him when he was Chief of the Imperial General Staff in London and my husband Under-Secretary at the War Office under Antony Head. We called him *le Comte de Paris*, a silly joke – but his name had once got mixed up with the Royal Pretender's when being announced at someone's party, and it suited him, for there was something both foreign and authoritarian about his slim, slight figure. We dined several times at his house in Chapel Street, and I was amused when I once found him cooing over a sick kitten in the kitchen. He was highly intelligent, extremely shrewd, deceptively frail (he had been a member of a British Olympics hurdle team and was once bayonet-fighting champion of the army) and amazingly sensitive to the political nuances of an international situation.

He believed that his predecessors had learnt by their mistakes, but that both Gurney and Briggs had been on the right track in trying to win over 'the hearts and minds' of the Malayan people. He hated any show of British old-style colonial superiority or racial prejudice and believed that if the federation was to hold together after Independence there must be closer integration and cooperation between its different races, for the way forward would not be a British way, but should and must be a united Malay way, and much of his energies, as well as winning the war, were directed towards achieving this result.

By the end of Templer's assignment to Malaya he had built and opened racially integrated primary schools and technical colleges for the entire population; he had sent Malay-speaking teachers on training courses – sometimes as far away as England* – he had raised a Chinese Home Guard and given the somewhat surprised regular officers and NCOs of crack regiments of the British army the task of training them.

But perhaps his greatest political achievement was that in September 1952, with the encouragement of the Tunku and the somewhat reluctant acquiescence of the sultans, after a stormy session of the Conference of Rulers ('After all, this *is* their country and they *are* the sovereigns') 1¼ million Chinese and 180,000 Indians were given Malayan citizenship. This, and the protection the 'new villages' gave to them, did more than anything else in winning the confidence of the Chinese and Indian population.

But it was not all benevolence and bounty. When a particularly horrible ambush and massacre of British soldiers occurred near the town of Tanfong Malim, Templer used methods to smoke out the Commmunist sympathisers in the town which would have done credit to the Black

---

* When no suitable school could be found to accommodate them he would 'borrow' superfluous buildings on some rich friend's estate.

and Tan, and were much criticised by readers of the *Guardian* and other liberals back home. But they worked – the informers were arrested, and a very dangerous CT brigade broken up and dispersed.

After the Second World War and a spell on the Intelligence Staff of the occupying army in Germany, Templer had been Director of Intelligence at the War Office, and he emphatically believed in the importance of intelligence gathering. One of the first things he did when he took up his command was to upgrade the services of the police and especially of their Special Branch, until they were as well equipped and trained, brilliantly led and deadly effective as any force in the world. Soon information gathering, a network of double-agents, a campaign of misinformation, propaganda (including 'Voice' aeroplanes and the dropping of millions of pamphlets) and psychological warfare matched and surpassed anything the Communists could produce.

The aborigines, the gentle, terrified people of the deep jungle, who had only helped the CTs under duress, now had the jungle forts of the British army to protect them from reprisals. These strategically placed forts, built far into the jungle, allowed British troops to remain for long periods in aborigine areas. They also served as advance intelligence posts, and played a significant role in winning the jungle war.

In 1952 the first CT defectors began coming in, and by the end of that year four of the CTs' major commanders had been killed, and the trickle of defectors became a flood. The following spring, Chin Pen, the CTs' political leader, fled to a new base in so-called 'neutral' southern Thailand. Though he continued to direct the war from there, it was an admission of defeat, and a shattering blow to the morale of his half-starved and exhausted jungle army.

Templer had told Churchill, with whom he conferred in London after Queen Elizabeth's coronation, that he believed his job was nearly finished and that it was time to let the emerging Malayans 'have a clear field'.

During his early days, the first municipal elections ever had been held in Kuala Lumpur, and he had immediately spotted Tunku Abdul Rahman, a young lawyer-turned-politician who had taken twelve *years* in England to pass his bar finals ('I spent too much time at the races . . .' he would explain later, with a charming smile) as a serious and right-thinking potential leader, and the two had become great friends.

The Tunku had come into politics almost by chance when, during the municipal elections, the leader of the UMNO party resigned and, at the last minute, he took his place. He formed an alliance with the MCA (the Malayan Chinese Association) and by not contesting each other's seats they had won the election hands down and formed a new party, the Alliance, with the Tunku at its head, a party which was now to have considerable influence in shaping the eventual development of the country.

Before he left Malaya in May 1954, General Templer was able to promise that by the middle of the following year the country would be ready to hold its first *national* elections for the Federal Legislative Council, and that the nation would be voting for fifty-two elected and only forty-six nominated members, a clear majority of Malayan politicians, and a historic step in the march towards self-government.

Independence finally came to Malaya two years later. Tunku Abdul Rahman then became Minister of Internal Defence and Security, as well as Chief Minister, and the British soldiers, police and civil servants packed their bags and began to leave, often with great regret. The role of the advisers to the sultans was abolished, again not without sadness on both sides, for they had been a distinguished and loyal, although sometimes an eccentric lot. *

The war was over, Independence had been achieved, but the peace and political stability had still to be won. In the years that followed Tunku Abdul Rahman and his Alliance party dominated the political scene. The 1957 Constitution was a complicated one, for it had of necessity to reach a compromise between the powers of nine different heads of state and the new-found principles of democratic government. In the end the Federal Legislative Council, together with the Conference of Rulers, decided that a rotary system be instituted whereby each sultan would rule in turn as a constitutional monarch for a five-year period only, and then hand over to his successor, another of the nine.

The Federal Constitution of Malaysia further provided that the Yang di-Pertuan Agong would be the Supreme Head of the Federation and would take precedence over all persons in the Federation. It then provided that the Raja Permaisuri Agong would come next in the order of precedence, and that neither of these offices would be hereditary.

The order of succession in 1957 was established by the sultans' length of tenure in their own states, and it has been followed ever since, unless an incumbent wishes to be excused from serving *or* if a Conference of Rulers is called and a majority of five or more rajas considers him unsuitable for the office.

---

* On the first dramatic day of the Emergency, Bob Thompson remembers, the Adviser to the Sultan of Perak had driven up in his large official Humber to the scene of Christian and Allison's tragic murder, to see for himself the outrage which had marked the outbreak of the war. While Gurkhas and policemen stiffened to attention he got out, asked a few questions and offered assistance in his usual kindly way, but when Thompson asked if he would like an escort on his drive back to the palace, he had exploded: 'An escort? Good God, why on earth should I need an escort? I've got my walking stick and my wife!' (I particularly like the order in which they came!)

HM Sultan Azlam Shah of Perak, Yang di-Pertuan Agong IX of Malaysia.

His Majesty, Sultan Azlam Shah of Perak, who is the Yang di-Pertuan Agong IX of Malaysia today, is a constitutional and democratic monarch, but he still retains considerable powers and, in effect, he still enjoys among the Malays, and in particular in his own state, the devotion and reverence that Malay people still feel towards their sultans. In a general election, it is the king who appoints the Prime Minister of the victorious political party, and many other functionaries who sit on statutory boards or commissions. He alone can grant pardons, refuse permission to dissolve parliament, issue a proclamation of Emergency or summon a meeting of the Conference of Rulers, which deals exclusively with the positions and privileges of his fellow rajas. He is head of the Executive, Legislature and Judiciary. He is Supreme Commander of the Armed Forces and, in the Islamic territories of Kuala Lumpur and Labuan, he is the head of the religion of Islam.

Sultan Azlam Shah has already shown a considerable flair for foreign affairs and has proved an astute ambassador in promoting Malaysian interests internationally; a practical man with a shrewd legal brain, he is not slow to see where they lie. Before his turn came to be head of state two years ago, he was both ruler of Perak and Lord President of Malaysia, the highest legal office in the land.

His Majesty was educated in Malaysia, but he read law at Nottingham University, winning a degree in Law there in 1953. He was admitted to the English Bar a year later. On his return to Malaysia he held many legal offices in Perak, Pahang and Johore before being elevated at the age of thirty-seven to the Bench of the High Court of Malaysia.

Although a member of the royal family of Perak, as a legal officer he has always been in touch with both humble people and the elite and it has been his understanding of the problems of the ordinary citizen that has enabled him to make a substantial contribution to the development of Malaysian law. His judgments have now been published in a book which is much admired by the legal profession.

The palace of the Yang di-Pertuan Agong in Kuala Lumpur once belonged to a rich Chinese merchant who cannily built it on top of a hill and surrounded it with parkland. It has magnificent views in every direction and a much cooler temperature than the steamy heat of downtown Kuala Lumpur. The palace itself is modern, sparkling white and golden domed – the Islamic touches being added later.

As we drove up to a side door, we could see an alfresco dinner-party being prepared on the wide terrace in front of it. A dolly blue pavilion had been erected and servants were bustling round it with napery and flowers.

John Carruthers steered me into a small office where the queen's sister, a very elegant and sophisticated lady who speaks perfect English, is in charge of the palace's protocol department. She was wearing an emerald green and blue silk sari that looked as if it had been made in Paris by one of the 'top ten'. I had been told by Ruki that she is married to the best-looking general in the Malaysian army, and this was verified when he looked into her office a few minutes later. She told us her brother-in-law had only just returned to Kuala Lumpur and that as usual he was frantically busy. Later that afternoon he would take part in a public reading of the Koran, have an update on affairs from one of his commissioners and then give a reception and dinner for the visiting dignitaries of some Indian province. John Carruthers is an old friend and they gossiped happily together till it was time to leave; we then passed through a series of winding passages which led to a large hall and a suite of reception rooms at the front of the palace.

A small crowd of petition presenters and favour-seekers were in the outer hall, seated stiffly on ballroom chairs, and gazing anxiously at the grand staircase, down which they hoped His Majesty would eventually descend. ADCs in white and khaki uniforms hovered, but we passed on to one of the big reception rooms whose many windows overlooked the terrace. It had scarlet walls, beautiful chandeliers, black and red chairs arranged round the walls, but was otherwise empty, no doubt for the reception that evening. It was a formal and rather intimidating room and I was glad to have the genial company of Colonel Carruthers.

Suddenly he stopped talking and got smartly to his feet, and there was the Tuan-Ko, standing quietly waiting by a side door, a solid, dignified, imposing figure in a dark-grey European suit. He has thick, grizzled grey hair, a big strong face, unsmiling at first, and an air of authority. One would not be surprised to see him in a periwig on a British bench, or even the woolsack. He was accompanied by an aide, also in civilian clothes but with a red tarboosh on his head, who only spoke once, to say goodbye.

His Majesty waved us into chairs and, after John had introduced me, he briskly conducted the business he had come to talk about and then bowed and left.

His Majesty had just returned from Penang where he had taken part in a grand review of the FPDA (Five Power Defence Agreement) fleets. The weather had been awful and the sea very rough. 'I'm afraid the wives of the officials and diplomats did not enjoy it very much,' he told me ruefully, 'but it was too late to cancel and so we decided to go ahead.'

We talked about Malaysia's armed forces and he told me that, unlike

Brunei, where there is still a British military presence, his country now has its own military and naval academies, 'though we still send some officers abroad for training, particularly to Sandhurst'. The army, unlike Thailand's, is not involved in politics, but the king and his government are very much aware that the Communist danger, which it had taken twelve long years to overcome, might one day return, if security in the country – for which the monarch is responsible – was weakened. 'The last of the insurgents,' he told me, 'only laid down their arms *last year*, and a treaty was signed only *last November*,' under which the remaining Communist guerrillas agreed not to carry on their armed struggle against the government. 'Thirty years after the so-called end of the so-called "Emergency"! The collapse of Marxism in Europe has, I'm afraid, nothing to do with the situation here; their ideology has not changed and remains a danger I am very aware of.

'There is a rich–poor gap,' he continued, 'in Malaysia and in most of south-east Asia which will get worse before it gets better. That is the real danger, and it can only be solved by economic measures. A balance must be found between the two extremes, a ceiling to the riches that the clever, hard-working entrepreneurs can accumulate, and a safety-net for the less gifted or skilled poor. Fortunately, a steady and solid middle-class already exists in Malaysia.'

We agreed that a middle class brings stability and culture to a developing nation, even though it may complicate the political scene.

I told him about my visit to Nepal during its recent troubles, where there is an emerging and quarrelsome middle class. 'They are all lawyers or politicians,' I told him somewhat tactlessly, and then, realising I had put my foot in it, looked nervously at the monarch. But his eyes twinkled and he laughed.

'We are not *all* lawyers here,' he countered, but then added seriously, 'a developing country cannot stand still. Change must come in its search for democracy, and change cannot be held back.'

I explained about my book and why I was in favour of a monarchical system, with safeguards, and we quoted Walter Bagehot to each other, he knowing much more about him than I did. He firmly believes in Bagehot's definition of the few remaining duties of a constitutional monarch: to be consulted, to encourage, to warn. 'A very good recipe,' he concluded.

'But Your Majesty, you do a bit better than that,' I objected. 'You have more power than almost any other constitutional king. I understand you were even able to dismiss a large proportion of your judiciary last year and replace them with men of your own choosing, on whose probity you could really count. No king in Europe would dare to do that' (except perhaps, I thought privately, the King of Spain). 'And what about the 1957 Constitution?' I asked. 'If there were parts of that which time showed could be improved, would you try and push legislation . . . ?'

'That is delicate ground,' the King interrupted rather firmly. He hesitated, then continued, 'I have my advisers, the first of whom is the Prime Minister* . . . and then there is always the Council of Rulers.'

'So, you might jointly . . . ?'

'There is always that possibility.'

We talked about British law and how the past and the present Lord Chancellors have been trying, not always successfully, to bring it a bit more up to date. He told me about the recent Heads of Commonwealth meeting in Kuala Lumpur that had taken place immediately after his accession. 'For me, it was going in at the deep end. I had only just taken over, and then all these heads of state and Queen Elizabeth descended on us . . . but in fact I thoroughly enjoyed it.'

I had heard through the grapevine, I told him, that Queen Elizabeth had been delighted with the visit, and that all the arrangements had been perfect, which seemed to please him.

We talked about modern communications which made every country in the world neighbours. Today, he concluded, you cannot stand alone, Malaysia belongs to the Commonwealth, and to the ASEAN, the Association of South-East Asian Nations. 'To co-exist in peace is the aim of all small nations, and I believe there is more hope today for peace – especially in our part of the world – than ever before. Of course there are problems, but problems exist to be solved. The refugee question and the increasingly strong Fundamentalist movement that is sweeping through the Islamic states are certainly worrying. There are twenty thousand refugees living in camps, and I have had to refuse to take any more. An international city should be built for them somewhere, with every nation contributing.'

'You should make a speech about it in the UN,' I suggested.

'No one would listen to me,' he answered sadly. He believed the Americans who, after all, had been largely responsible for it, were particularly backward in helping. There does not seem to be much love lost between the USA and the Yang di-Pertuan Agong.

'The tariffs that are imposed on Malaysia by America are *particularly* unfair. They amount to us being taxed twice, and if the economic miracle of Singapore and Hong Kong is repeated here . . .'

* Dr Mahathir Mohamed was re-elected shortly after I left Kuala Lumpur.

At that moment there was a hullabaloo in the room next door and I was just in time to see a small posse of beautifully dressed children cross it and make for the wide marble staircase which led to the private apartments of the palace. They were trailing balloons and carrying brightly wrapped parcels. 'It's my little granddaughter's birthday,' he explained, looking a little embarrassed, 'and I promised . . .'

I quickly rose to my feet and the interview was over. He may be a powerful king, but he is also a good grandfather, and I liked him all the better for ending it in such a human way.

21
BRUNEI

Sultan Sir Muda Hassan al Bolkiah

'The Spartan legislator, Lycurgus, on being asked why he had not made Sparta's constitution democratic, answered: "Try the experiment on your own family".'

A *TIMES* LEADER

I did not fly on from Kuala Lumpur to Singapore and thence to Brunei, as I had planned, because I learnt that unfortunately His Royal Highness the Sultan had delayed his return to his own country and was still in residence at The Aviary, his country estate outside London – 'unfortunately' because I would dearly have loved to visit Borneo and the small Islamic kingdom in its north-west corner, which is all that is left of Brunei today, especially, of course, the mega-palace that the Sultan of Brunei has just finished building for himself and his family. If reports are true, it must be an amazing sight, for HRH Sir Muda Hassan al Bolkiah is mega-rich and has two wives and two sets of children who will be accommodated (we are told by a reputable Sunday newspaper) in two separate wings of the new homestead, in conditions of sumptuous magnificence.

It has indeed been claimed that the Sultan is the third richest man in the world. Forbes magazine, which usually gets this sort of thing right, has at least placed him among the top ten, but this can only be an informed guess, as the royal family of Brunei is understandably reticent about such private concerns.

The money – and there is certainly lots of it – comes from off-shore oil wells, which only began being seriously developed twenty years ago, so I suppose you could call the ruler of Brunei nouveau-riche, or at any rate nouveau-seriously-riche, a condition which excites the tabloids to a frenzy whenever his name crops up in the news.

Riches bring power, and absolute power – as we all know – is bad for commoners, let alone kings. I was curious to see what the effect had been on the Sultan of Brunei and his large and happily homogeneous family.

And so, on this occasion Brunei proved to be a taxi-ride away from our flat in London. The Aviary, the sultan's palace, off the M4 motorway to the west, is a large neo-Regency villa-type country house that Nash might well have run up for a Hanoverian princeling, but which, in fact, was built about 1920 around the shell of an older and smaller house.

It has a high, Dr No-type fence around its perimeter, but except for this and the guard at its lodge gates, you might just as well be driving up to take tea with the local squire rather than an oriental prince who is also one of the last absolute monarchs in the world.

My mini-cab driver, suitably thrilled, dropped me off in a courtyard where about half a dozen cars of different types awaited their owners' pleasure, and Major Christopher Hanbury, an ex-cavalry officer, who is a friend of my son's and the sultan's co-ordinator and aide, came out of his office to greet me. We walked round together to the quite ordinary front door of the house – ordinary, that is, until it opens and you look inside. Then it's a case of 'amaze your friends!'

The floors of the vestibule are marble intaglio, and the inner hall is painted scarlet and gold. It soars upwards to a semi-oriental glass drum and gilded cupola of immense size, from which hangs the tallest, fattest, most glittering chandelier it has ever been my pleasure to be dazzled by.

Dazzling too are the white silk sofas, the Ritzo-Rothschild *bureaux plats* and *tabouret* tables, jewel-coloured cushions, crystal and ormolu ornaments ('glāss and brāss,' Lord Curzon would have called them) of the split-level, open-plan drawing-room – where potted orchids spill down steps to long plate-glass windows and a vista of patio and park beyond.

Christopher Hanbury hurried me through this nest of luxury to a more austere waiting parlour beyond it. Here there was only one circular marble table and lots of 'Louis Quinzy' chairs arranged around the walls. Despite the overpoweringly sumptuous decor, the house still has a rather homely, untidy and casual atmosphere, with parcels and toys lying about in the usual pre-Christmas mess.

The sultan had an appointment elsewhere at 3.30, and I was being squeezed in for a mini-audience before he left. After a few minutes' gossip, Major Hanbury looked at his watch. 'I'll come with you,' he said, and stubbed out his cigarette. '*Toi, moi et le Roi – nous faisons trois*' ran

HM the Sultan of Brunei, Sir Muda Hassan al Bolkiah

irreverently through my head as I followed him meekly back to the double drawing-room, and there, on the top level of the split, was the Sultan of Brunei, Sir Muda Hassan al Bolkiah, who came forward to meet us, and shook hands.

He is delicately constructed – small, neat, wirily slender and much younger and better-looking than I had supposed from my daughter-in-law's portrait (which is mostly concerned with his horse). He wore a dark V-neck cashmere pullover, narrow black trousers and very beautiful hand-made jodhpur boots, the overall effect being a little theatrical – man of action cum freedom-fighter off-duty – but very becoming.

Brunei's only attempt at democracy was ended when a Communist-inspired rising, in 1962, was put down by his father, the late Sultan of Brunei, with the help of the British army. The present sultan had no stories to tell about the State of Emergency. He was, after all, only a young boy at school in Kuala Lumpur when it all happened, but he was well aware of jungle fighting in Brunei and 'a lot in Sarawak'. He clearly remembered the crisis when the last 'Union' of Malaysia was formed. Would or would not Brunei join it? By that time he was seventeen, and he recalled Lord Cobbold visiting his father in the wooden palace he lived in, built out on stilts over the sea. 'I also remember the Tunku's

[Tunku Abdul Rahman] very long speeches, and then there was a referendum, which we won' – by which he meant that Brunei remained a
separate and eventually independent state.* He beamed when we talked
of Lee Kwan Yew, who is an old friend. 'He has just retired,' he told
me, but added with a chuckle, 'but only in theory – he will never really
give up running Singapore till he dies.'

It was the old sultan, Sir Omar's decision to stay out of the new
Malaysia, 'and a wise one,' said his son, 'for they would have absorbed
all our oil revenues, and given us little in return'.

Of the three countries I had so far visited where the sovereigns wield
almost unlimited power – Bhutan, Oman and Brunei – I suppose Brunei
is the only one where you could say that the Sultan's rule is absolutely
absolute. He is his own Prime Minister and Minister of Defence. He has
a Council of Ministers and a Privy Council (which is like our cabinet)
and two of his brothers are members of it. When I asked him whether
he appointed all his ministers, he answered unblushingly, 'Yes'.

'And have powers to dismiss them?' An equally frank 'Yes'.

'Lucky you,' I couldn't help saying, thinking of our own leadership
drama that was taking place at that very moment only a few miles away
(it was the week when Margaret Thatcher's leadership of the Tory party
was challenged and she resigned as Prime Minister).

This made him laugh. 'Not always lucky,' he answered. 'It depends
how you view responsibility and hard work.'

'But you *do* have more power to fix things than any other monarch in
the world?'

He looked rather smug as he agreed, but added that Brunei was a small
Islamic state and that, as head of state, he was also father to his people,
not always an easy role and that he did his best to be a good one; that
they were a very religious people; and that under Islamic law they had
great respect for their imams and leaders.

I asked him if there were fundamentalists in Brunei, and he looked
rather shocked and answered that there were no extremists of any kind
in the population.

According to Islamic law a man can have four wives. The sultan has
two, who live with their children in two separate establishments, both
at 'The Aviary' and in Brunei, the sultan sleeping in each of them

* In 1971 Brunei became internally self-governing, the UK temporarily agreeing to retain
responsibility for its defence. In 1979 the British government signed a treaty with the sultan by
which Brunei would become a fully independent state from 1 January 1984. In February 1984 the
Legislative Council was disbanded. In October 1990 the sultan declared his country to be a 'Malay
Islamic monarchy' (Melayu Islam Beraja).

alternately. When he was nineteen he was married off to his seventeen-year-old cousin, Raja Isteri, by whom he had six children. But, when he was twenty-eight, he fell in love with a Royal Brunei Airline air hostess (uniforms again) who was a commoner, had half Japanese, half Malayan blood, was enchantingly pretty and thought quite unsuitable by the formidable old sultan, his father.

Nevertheless they married in a private ceremony and have three children, including a six-year-old son. The two spouses are treated equally, though, as the senior wife, Raja Isteri walks a step ahead of Princess Mariam at formal functions. As in many Muslim households, they are said to get on very well in private, and the children, as I was to see later, have a ball. He hoped one or more of his three sons would go to Sandhurst, where he himself had been very happy. The eldest was at the moment at a school in Singapore, where there was a high standard of teaching. 'If he reaches university level, he will probably go to a university in England.'

We talked about education and its effect on awakening the political awareness and the ambitions of the Third-World countries – its inherent advantages and inevitable risks if those ambitions could not be satisfied. He seemed determined not to impede progress towards what will eventually be a more democratic form of government in Brunei. He told me his father had given the people a written constitution, the first they had ever had. 'But I do not believe the time is ripe yet for full democracy in Brunei. Education must come first, and it will bring responsibility, the concept of good citizenship to our people. We are building our first university; the lecture halls are nearly finished and the faculty and students have already begun working on the half-completed campus. Women are even more anxious for higher education than men – 'and often more clever,' the sultan concluded. (In Brunei women are completely emancipated, unlike in most Arab states.)

I asked him if he had visited his recent acquisition, the about-to-be reopened Dorchester Hotel, and he said he was keeping away until it was completely decorated before viewing (I told him I wished my husband would do the same when I re-decorated a room at Strachur). I did not ask him about his youthful involvement with the Al Fayed brothers, or about Harrods, a subject that I find a dead bore.

The sultan's brother, Prince Jefri, is now his Minister of Finance and, according to those who know him, 'Min Fin' is not only extremely good-looking and dashingly extrovert, but also very sharp. If the sultan was badly advised (through those always fatal 'friends of friends') and impulsive about dealings with his personal fortune when he was twenty-three, he is not likely at forty-three to be so again. For today he has professional advisers; a Brunei Investment Agency (BIA) was set up in 1983 within the Ministry of Finance, which deals with both the national and the sultan's private fortune, and their accounts are audited by a respectable British firm. Brunei's investments in real estate, hotels and other commodities are extremely diverse and known to be worth many billions of pounds. As to the value of the monarch's private portfolio, that is a secret which few people know and even fewer would be foolhardy enough to divulge.

We talked about his army, in which he is a Field Marshal, and of which he is very proud. Brunei has 3,500 men under arms, 'but it is only for internal use,' he told me, rather chillingly. I learnt later, from an officer who had served in it, that the Royal Brunei Malay Regiment is trained by British officers, predominantly from the Special Air Service, and is as well equipped as any small force anywhere in the world. It has two infantry battalions, an air wing and a flotilla. It also possesses the latest in deadly weaponry: Exocets, Rapiers and, no doubt, by now all the lethal machines that performed so efficiently in the Gulf War.

The Sultan of Brunei also has two Boeing 757 aeroplanes for his private and personal use as well as two smaller aeroplanes and a helicopter or two, which he can pilot himself and frequently does. My daughter-in-law, Susan Crawford, can bear witness to that. She was summoned to the Istana Nurui Iman Palace in Brunei to paint the sultan on his favourite polo pony – (he had seen some of her paintings in England and liked them). The appointments for the sittings had been carefully set up weeks beforehand, but as she descended the steps of the Royal Brunei Airline's latest turbo-jet she happened to notice a small white plane taking off on another part of the runway. *That*, she was told by the welcoming party, was the sultan. 'His Royal Highness has an important match he is playing in Johore but he will be back at the end of the week!' It was Saturday, and she did not in fact get her first sitting for another ten days. The oriental idea of time is wonderfully independent. Or, as the Thais believe it to be, *civilised*.

Records of Brunei's civilisation before the fifteenth century are patchy: Sindbad, the explorer-sailor of Baghdad, is fabled to have visited the island. Kubla Khan tried unsuccessfully to conquer it and Marco Polo describes the considerable junk trade that existed between Brunei and China. Friar Odoric, that peripatetic priest whose missionary zeal carried him all over the Far East in the fourteenth century, visited Borneo in 1323 and recounts how the Great Khan constantly engaged war with the King of Borneo, 'but the King always vanquished and got the better of him'. Borneo was then covered in deep tropical jungle, and the various Malay tribes that lived beneath it and on the coast differed little from their cousins across the Strait. At that time it would have been under the suzerainty of the Javanese Majahapit empire, but this in turn gave way to a new power: the Islamic empire of Malacca.

The first Islamic Sultan of Brunei was Awang Alak Bekatar (Alak ber Tata) and there is a romantic story of how Alak, one of fourteen brothers, bade his siblings find him a beautiful bride. They swept the oceans in their search, but finally returned with the (kidnapped) daughter of the Sultan of Johore – and the couple were happily wed. But the Sultan of Johore had a rukh, or mythical bird, who had observed these proceedings and reported back to its master. A raiding party was sent, the princess was re-abducted and returned to her Muslim father; but when she told him how happy she had been, he allowed Alak Bekatar to visit him, there were proper nuptials and the bridegroom (and all Borneo) were converted to Islam. It all sounds very like clan legend in the Highlands of Scotland, except that there it would have been a golden eagle.

The golden age of Brunei came with the reign of Sultan Bolkiah in the sixteenth century. At that time 'the Singing Pirate', as he was called (because he carolled with joy as he made his victims walk the plank), included in his domains all of Borneo, Sulu and half the Philippines. The Italian historian Antonio Pigafetta, who accompanied the Portuguese explorer Ferdinand Magellan on his voyages, arrived in Brunei in 1521 and gives a vivid account of the sumptuousness of the King of Brunei's palace at that time; 'and not to forget it, I will add our men reported . . . that the King wore two pearls in his crown as large as goose eggs'. He also adds, rather less approvingly, that the monarch chewed betel nut 'constantly'. By the end of the sixteenth century, with the incursions of the Dutch, Portuguese and British to the region, Brunei's power began to wane. Towards the end of the eighteenth century the British East India Company started a factory in Brunei with its sultan's permission, and then abandoned it. Piracy throughout Indonesia was endemic in the nineteenth century. It seems to have been the Bruneians' main activity – that, and shipping slaves to Arabia and the various slave markets of western Asia.

But in the 1830s, when British trade in the 'Straits Settlements' of Malacca, Penang and Singapore increased tenfold, the piracy became unacceptable and Admiral Keppel, with a squadron of Royal Naval gunboats, was sent to deal with it. At first he had the cooperation of the then Sultan (or Rajah) Muda Hashim, but when civil war broke out in Sarawak, the sultan's attention became diverted. The fighting continued for several years and it was not until his son succeeded him that the warring tribes were finally pacified with the help of a young British adventurer called James Brooke. Brooke was the son of a 'Company' official, and was born in India. He served in the Indian army but, after his father's death, he inherited enough money to sail around the China Seas and the South Pacific on a voyage of discovery and adventure in a small boat he called *The Royalist*.

In 1839 he found himself anchored off Sarawak, the beautiful but rebellious province that the new Sultan of Brunei's father, Rajah Muda Hashim, had tried so many times and without success to discipline. The young sultan, in desperation, now enlisted James Brooke's help. With it, order was swiftly restored and peace at last returned to his kingdom. To show his gratitude (and perhaps to avoid further trouble), the sultan then handed over the rule of the province to the young Englishman, who became the first white rajah in the world at the age of thirty-eight.

His rule was a wise and liberal one. He never attempted to change local custom and traditions, and he firmly believed that European government of under-developed countries should put the interests of the natives before those of their own pockets, a rare enough credo in the nineteenth century. He finally retired to England in 1868, and was succeeded as rajah by his nephew, Charles Brooke, possibly a more practical administrator, but a somewhat morose and less sympathetic character, without the charm or bonhomie of his adventurous uncle.

Towards the end of the century, a third family of British entrepreneurs, the Dent brothers, in association with an Austrian named Overbeck, formed a company to develop the northern tip of Borneo which is now called Sabah, and which was also once part of Brunei's empire. After disagreements between the partners, Overbeck resigned, and the Dents alone formed a company which they called the British North Borneo Company (BNBC) to which the British government gave support, although at this stage the three members of the Malay Straits Settlement – Singapore, Sarawak and the Dents' BNBC – were all trading ventures of the companies or individuals concerned, and in no way Crown possessions.

Sabah, the largest part of the island, and Sarawak in the south, eventually broke away from Brunei and became Crown colonies of the British Empire, at first in the loose Federation of Malaya, and then in the 'Union of Malaysia' in which a much-shrunken Brunei, by then no more than a bite out of the north-west corner of Borneo, did not join.

In 1888 it had become a separate British protectorate; in 1906 King Edward VII signed a treaty with the Sultan of Brunei by which he accepted a British Resident, or Advisor, to assist in the administration of the country, as they were already doing in Malaya. In the Second World War, Brunei was overrun by the Japanese army, which did not leave till 1945. Brunei was also, though marginally, involved in the Communist rising, or 'Emergency', in Malaya.

According to a soldier friend of mine, who knew him well, the present sultan's father, the late Sir Omar Ali Saif al Bolkiah, was a jovial, simple and likeable monarch. He had been harshly treated by the Japanese when they invaded Borneo, thrown into a prisoner-of-war camp and made to carry and break stones (he would show off a calloused hand to prove it). He was a good Muslim and lived according to strict Islamic law in a traditional wooden palace built out on sticks at the mouth of the river estuary, with a small garden on the landward side. Though strongly pro-British, he had felt no wish to join the new Malay Federation. In this, Brunei's discovery of off-shore oil, which he did not wish to share with any other country, was one consideration, and the proud history of her former ascendancy in south-east Asia another.

The sometimes heavy-handed 'advice' of the British government no doubt irked the sultan, who was perfectly happy to go on reigning in the same way as his forefathers had reigned, but in the end he gave in to pressure and in 1959 he granted his people a written constitution, which established a Privy Council as well as an Executive and Legislative one. Whether this precipitated the events which were to follow is a matter of conjecture.

In 1962 all elective seats in the Legislative Council were won by the 'People's Party', led by Sardar Asahari (who had been educated in Indonesia). They favoured the creation of a single independent north Borneo state comprising Brunei, Sarawak and Sabah which would enjoy a special relationship with Indonesia. This promoted a revolt against the sultan backed by Indonesia and their ambitious left-wing President Sukharno, and soon Brunei became absorbed in the 'confrontation' between the Indonesian Communists and the 'Imperialist Powers'. Brunei, unlike Sarawak, did not have a common frontier with Indonesian Borneo and the fighting was more a case of rebellion and infiltration, than invasion, but it was on a large scale and posed a considerable threat.

Fortunately Brunei, in the 1960s, was still under the protection of the United Kingdom, and British troops were immediately rushed in from Malaya to stiffen the small British-trained army of the sultan. These had been battle-hardened in the cruel jungle warfare they had already fought in that country's Emergency and the same tactics, in which the Special Air Service now played a part, were used in Brunei. The campaign lasted two and a half years; it was a hard-fought, dirty war, but by 1965 the rebellion had been put down, the invasion repulsed and the sultan was re-established on an increasingly secure throne, whose feet were firmly planted in the rich black oil wells that were soon to bring his family and his countrymen unheard-of prosperity and peace.

But the Labour government's zest for de-colonisation put further pressure on the sultan in the years that were to follow. In 1965 and 1966 there were more talks about extending a ministerial and more democratic form of government and by 1967 the old sultan must have felt he had had enough.

On 24 September 1967 Crown Prince Sir Muda Hassan al Bolkiah was summoned home from Sandhurst, and on 4 October, his father abdicated in his favour, probably considering that younger and broader shoulders could withstand criticism better than himself (and that he could continue ruling his country, as before, from behind them). Although the accession was announced the following day, the coronation would have to wait until the next year when Sir Muda would be eighteen and would come of age. And so on 1 August 1968 the present Sultan was crowned and took over his new responsibilities.

The coronation ceremonies were magnificent and conducted according to Brunei Islamic tradition. These were started by elaborate cleansing rituals, when seven different fragrances were mixed in turn in an enormous 'gong' of spring water – rose, jasmine, kusume wijayak, ylang-ylang and scents derived from three sweet woods, cinnamon, aloe and sandalwood – with members of the royal family taking turns in pouring the perfumed waters over the sultan. When the ablutions and the chanting that accompanied them ended, a 21-gun salute was fired 'signalling the conclusion of the royal bath'. Then the magnificently robed young sultan and his royal attendants were pulled through the streets of the capital on a 100-foot-long gilded palanquin by forty strong men to the new lapan, or ceremonial hall, with its 'imported Australian grass lawns, Viennese chandeliers and Japanese escalators'. Brunei today is nothing if not cosmopolitan.

The sultan was actually crowned by his father, Sir Omar Ali Saif, with a multi-tiered gold crown, studded with diamonds, rubies and emeralds; and after the crowning the royal family drove through the streets of Bandar Sari Begawan, to the acclamation of their subjects.

There are 250,000 of these, and they now enjoy nearly the highest per capita income in the world – certainly in the east. Though off-shore oil-wells were discovered in the late 1920s the oil bonanza did not really arrive till the 1970s. It is now supposed, though this is perhaps an inflated guess, to bring in an annual income of $US25 billion.

Despite this seemingly heaven-sent wealth the people of Brunei still prefer to live in their traditional wooden houses, built on stilts above a river or coastline, but their homes now have refrigerators and televisions, and a motor car (or two) stands outside the door. There is no income tax in Brunei and the State looks after everyone from the womb to the tomb. The sultan told me that one of the main economic problems of his country is that everyone wants to work for the government, because of the extra bonuses and pension this entails. 'Part of my new five-year plan is to encourage self-employment in the service industries, and to start diversification, so that we are not solely dependent on the oil industry which, after all, will end one day.'

The first of his five-year plans was to transform the infrastructure of the country, the second to tackle education. The sultan is very aware of the dangers of too much Westernisation – neither tourists nor political parties are encouraged (the largest had 245 members, and another was dissolved after it formed illegal links with a 'foreign group').

The Permanent Secretary to the Treasury, who was educated at the London School of Economics, told Susan Crosland, who was interviewing him, 'We are a Muslim country with seven hundred years of a continuous monarchical system. Western journalists come here for two days and tell us that overnight we should substitute democracy . . .' and he shrugged his elegant shoulders – then no doubt smiled at her and took her out to lunch.

The sultan is said by some to be less open and friendly than his father, who loved entertaining and made many friends among the British officers who were stationed in Brunei. But he could not have been more friendly to me and, as we said goodbye, he urged me to visit his country one day as his guest. I left the way I had come, colliding with a gang of merry, balloon-carrying, partying children and helpers in a busy outer office, from which I was whisked back to London in one of His Royal Highness's custom-built cars. I ought to know which, but I can only remember that it was not a Rolls-Royce.

22

SAMOA

Sir Malietoa Tanumafili II

'I know an island,
Lovely and lost, and half the world away . . .'
RUPERT BROOKE

I had almost given up looking for the semi-mystical religio-magic link between modern kings and their priest-king, king-god progenitors that the Stuarts and Holy Roman emperors believed they possessed – even in Japan and Thailand there seemed no flicker of divine majesty about their sovereigns – but at last, and quite unexpectedly, I found it in Samoa.

I do not believe for a moment that King Malietoa, or his especially extraordinary sister, Sasooga Salamasina, were conscious of having such a link, or would have seemed to most people to be more than just naturally good, very human, human beings. But I was conscious of it, and that moment of spiritual awe, which had nothing to do with emotion, that they both inspired in me, however briefly, has not vanished from my mind since I left Samoa.

In Auckland the airport lounge was filling up. I had been dozing on a green plastic chair between planes but now, as I looked around it, my self-esteem rose, and I sat up and felt good. So often in exotic parts of the world, especially the east and south-east, I had often felt large and fat and foreign. But these splendid fellow-travellers were at least twice as big as I was! Tall, wide and frequently handsome, they all had a fine dignity and great style. The children, and there were dozens of them, from babes in arms to pretty teenagers, were particularly engaging, and the grown-ups of what seemed like over-extended families carried on lively conversations with each other from every corner of the room, in a completely unselfconscious and cheerful way.

They all had pale, honey-coloured skins, well-shaped heads and large, rather flat faces. In fact they looked exactly like Gauguin's Tahitians, only dressed in less becoming – a good deal less becoming – modern clothes. But they were not Tahitians (whom most Polynesians now regard as a mongrel race) but pure-blooded Samoans, and we were all bound for Upolu, the main island of Western Samoa where, in Apia, its capital, I was to take a cup of morning tea with their Paramount, Kingly High Chief and Head of State, His Highness Malietoa Tanumafili II.

Pacific Islanders belong to one of three races: Melanesians, the 'black islanders'; Micronesians, 'the people of the small islands'; and Polynesians, 'the people of the many islands'. The Samoans are probably the oldest civilisation in Polynesia, and there are many theories as to how they got there, but that the islands were inhabited since at least the third century of our era is now an accepted fact, reinforced by the latest archaeological discoveries. The Tongans, the Cook and Ellice Islanders, the native inhabitants of Tahiti and Fiji, the Hawaiians and lastly, those most mysterious of all peoples, the Easter Islanders are all believed to have come originally from Malaysia to Samoa, where they prospered, and then spread from island to island over all the eastern archipelagoes.

Pacific Islands are either the result of volcanic eruptions, or coral atolls. The Samoan group manages to be both. Its volcanic islands are mountainous, covered in incredibly lush vegetation and watered by heavy rainfall, while its coral atolls are circular or elliptical crowns of rock that have been slowly built up over the ages on the lips of the craters of submerged volcanoes by the patient but misguided polyps, tiny South Seas crustaceans called coelenterates. They are low-lying, seldom reaching more than about fifteen feet above sea level, the reason for this being that the poor polyp dies when it reaches the surface. They frequently enclose lagoons as large as the crater is wide, with an opening to the outside sea beyond the 'reef', and consequently have excellent harbours.

It was still dark when we landed at Faleolo airport, which is about twenty-four miles from Apia. A warm, scented darkness. My companions, and their extended families, climbed quickly into the waiting trucks and lorries already half-full of other welcoming family, and sped off into the night. As there was no welcoming party for me, I accepted the offer of the first taxi-tout and sank gratefully back into a battered old limo whose driver turned out to be as capable as he was loquacious.

It was an exciting drive. We rattled along a roughish road to a flow of free information, which I did my best to absorb, while a rosy dawn broke over the Pacific and first palm trees, then churches, loomed out of the night.

I asked: 'Why are there so many churches?'

'Churches, Mrs?' he answered. 'We have them all – LMS, that's the main one, used to be London Missionary Society, only now they call it Christian Congregational Church of Samoa; gone up in the world, it has . . . Then there's RC, Roman Catholic, that's me and all my family, then Seventh Day Adventist, Mormon, Wesleyan, even Muslim, mosques, minarets and all . . . You name it, Mrs – we have it. Samoans are *very* religious people!'

An amazing, sparkling white edifice with golden trumpeting angels on its twin Notre Dame towers at that moment flashed by, and I humbly accepted his verdict.

The villages seemed a good deal more modest: groups of neat, tin-roofed cottages, with here and there some older, more dilapidated ones, thatched with palm branches. Some had screens, some open sides through which one could see early-morning life stirring.

My taxi-driver told me he had just been made a *matai*, that is, the head or 'chief' of an extended family, or *aiga*, and therefore the custodian of the property and land belonging to their community. He was also eligible to become their political representative. I was impressed, as I was meant to be, and we talked politics for the rest of the journey.

Samoa has only two political parties: the SHRPP, or Samoan Human Rights Protection Party, which was in power, and the SNDP, the Samoan National Democratic Party, the opposition.

Only the chiefs are eligible for the legislature; the parties do not have any significant difference in policy; voting at the last election (which had just taken place) was by universal suffrage. It did not sound exactly like the House of Commons but, 'It's a big change from tradition,' my taxi-driver told me proudly.

By this time we had arrived in Apia where, at first sight, it looked to me as if tradition had held firm – more churches, a waterfront of single-storeyed clapboard or concrete shops, a covered market, a few free-standing stone buildings and, as they petered out, a tall, wooden Edwardian-cricket-pavilion-type building of considerable charm and grandeur: Aggie Grey's hotel, and my destination.

After checking in, I was led out of its welcoming foyer, across a painted wooden veranda at its back, down some pavilion steps into a large tropical garden, already sparkling in the morning sun. Narrow paths wound between flowerbeds crammed with creamy frangipani, scarlet hibiscus, yellow acacias and purple orchids, while fountains of tree fern, bright green banana trees and feathery bamboo groves screened a few quiet corners of shade. After my long dusty journey it seemed like paradise.

The swimming pool had an island with a palm tree in the middle of it which we passed on our way to the *fale* (traditionally built native house), which was to be my very own. Its wooden walls and glass windows, its plumbing and air-conditioning were acceptable improvements, but the hand-hewn beams and beautiful, intricate patterns woven into the palm-branch roof, were the real thing. No chocolate-mint on my pillow, thank God, no 'guest-friendly' extras in the simple shower room, the kettle on a neatly laid-out tea tray did not always work, but I was happy. I had left Holiday-Inn-ship far behind.

By noon, when I woke, it was too hot to bathe, or even eat, and the grass by the pool burnt my toes as I walked across it. I made a half-hearted attempt to do both and then weakly retired to bed and the coolth of my *fale*, once more completely discombobulated by being told it was now yesterday (I had crossed the dateline), but that I had a whole extra day to play with before I visited the King of Samoa.

The first European visitors had been a lot tougher.

In 1722 a Dutch ship on an East Indian voyage of discovery hove to off the islands, and the inhabitants came out in their boats 'bringing fish, coconuts, Indian figs and other refreshments'. An eighteenth-century geographer's account of the journey continues: 'It soon appeared that these Islands were fully populated since many thousands of men and women, most of the former armed with bows and arrows, came down to the shore to look at them. Among the rest they observed a very majestic personage, who, from his dress and the honours that were paid him, they easily discovered to be the Prince or Sovereign of the nation.'

The French followed the Dutch at the end of the eighteenth century, but their experience was less fortunate. First came the Comte de Bougainville (guilty of bringing back to the West that puce-coloured shrub that every garden should be without), and then La Pérouse, both of whose eager landing parties came to sticky ends, largely, it must be said, from their own misjudgment of the islanders' character and intentions.

In 1791, the British frigate *Pandora*, in search of the surviving mutineers of HMS *Bounty*, visited both Savaii in Western and Jutuila in Eastern Samoa. Though her captain was a man of few words, the ship's surgeon, George Hamilton, has left a lively account of close encounters between the natives and the ship's company: 'One woman, among many others, came on board. She was six feet high, of exquisite beauty, and exact symmetry; being naked and unconscious of being so, added a lustre to her charms; for, in the words of the poet: "She needed not the foreign ornaments of dress; careless of beauty, she was beauty's self".' He is equally lyrical about the delights of both Tahiti and Samoa: 'What poetic

fiction has painted of Eden or Arcadia is here realised; where the earth
without tillage produces both food and clothing, the trees loaded with
the richest of fruit, the carpet of nature spread with the most odoriferous
of flowers, and the fair ever willing to fill your arms with love.' But then,
after describing the generosity that is characteristic of the Polynesian
race, he concludes on a gloomy note: 'Happy would it have been for
these people had they never been visited by Europeans; for, to our shame,
be it spoken, disease and gunpowder is all the benefit they have ever
received from us, in return for their hospitality and kindness.'

And sadly, it was with gunpowder once more that the *Pandora*'s mission ended, and ended badly, for her tender, which had become detached
from the frigate in a local storm, was attacked by a raiding party from
Upolu on the very night they set sail from the island, and defended
herself with vigour, many Samoans being killed – 'our seven-barrelled
pieces making great havoc amongst them'.

The first missionaries appeared in Samoa in 1838, some forty years later
and, good men though they were, full of good intentions, their coming
may well have caused greater havoc than any that had gone before, for,
as Robert Louis Stevenson was to write: 'Experience begins to show us,
at least in Polynesian Islands, that change of habit is bloodier than a
bombardment.'

But the missionaries were not the first white men to inhabit the islands.
By the beginning of the nineteenth century, a good many desperate men
had found refuge among the kindly chiefs and hospitable communities
of Samoa. Like the *Bounty* mutineers they too were on the run, escapees
from the press-ganged crews of the Royal Navy's men-o'-war, or prisoners
from the convict ships which had already begun unloading their cargoes
of human misery in New South Wales. A bad lot, on the whole, who
exploited native innocence, stole and plundered, and often behaved with
greater brutality than their supposedly uncivilised hosts, they brought
with them a new kind of violence and corruption to the islands.

By contrast, the *papalangi* – John Williams and his small party of
missionaries from the London Missionary Society – must have seemed
to the islanders an entirely different race, and the one they had long
been waiting for. These good men had fortunately brought with them,
as guide and interpreter, a young Samoan chief called Fakea, who had
been converted to Christianity in Tahiti. He had accompanied them
with some misgivings, for the Samoans were being terrorised by a particularly brutal 'sacred' king called Tamafuinga, and he foresaw they would
make no converts as long as this tyrant reigned.

The missionaries had indeed arrived at a dark and unhappy moment. Not only had the islands been stirred up by the white convicts, but a brutal civil war had broken out among themselves, with some of the convicts supplying one side or another with guns and gunpowder.

For many generations the title of *O Le Tupu*, the Samoan equivalent of Paramount Chief, or King, had been confined to members of the Muangututi family, one of several princely families who constituted the aristocracy of Samoa, but on the death of the last of that line, the title remained vacant for several years and was eventually usurped, without the all-important traditional formalities, by Tamafuinga, a ferocious war/priest – 'devil's man', or 'Sacred-King in whom the Spirits of the Gods dwell'. He came from Manono, a tiny island between Upolu and Savaii which is still a blueprint for heaven-on-earth, and where I picnicked and swam and snorkelled the following day with a party of Swedish blondes. But, to go back to Tamafuinga . . .

At first no one challenged his despotic rule for fear of offending the Gods, then Malietoa, the rightful claimant to the title of *O Le Tupu*, and his brother Taimalelagi, gathered together an army to defeat him in battle, but they were forestalled by the people of A'ana, a province of Upolu, who, goaded beyond endurance, upped and murdered the tyrant in his sleep.

The rules of warfare in Samoa are different from those of the West. There is an element of formality and of chivalry about them, and though all the islands rejoiced at the death of the devil-king, nevertheless Malietoa and the other high chiefs who had been related to him were under an obligation to avenge his murder, for dishonour had been done to their family, and so they declared war on the people of A'ana. Several skirmishes had taken place already, and a great battle was expected at any moment when the battered, hurricane-torn *Mission of Peace*, carrying the missionaries, stood off the coast of Savaii and weighed anchor. Indeed, almost the first thing they saw and heard was the smoke of burning villages and the murmur of distant battle. But they also heard from the delighted natives who came out in their canoes to greet them that Tamafuinga the tyrant was dead, and John Williams wrote in his journal that night: 'I could not be otherwise than deeply affected with the seasonable interposition of a gracious providence.'

The next day, King Malietoa himself visited the new arrivals, and made a great impression on them. He welcomed them as 'the true sailing Gods' to the islands and told them he and his people had heard of the *Lotu* (Christianity) which had already come to the Tongan archipelago. He was thankful they had now come to Samoa, and would receive their teachers and treat them with kindness, for they too were ready to be instructed, but now, he added on a somewhat different note, he and his people must go over to Upolu (the home of the assassins) and finish the war. Immediately after his return he would become a worshipper of Jehovah and place himself under the instruction of the teachers. He then departed in his war-canoe and that night a storm drove the missionary ship once more out to sea.

The description of the feast given by Malietoa, on his return from the war, is the best part of the journal. The exhausted missionaries, carried like parcels over the heads of a hundred eager warriors; a torch-lit procession from the shore to the High Chief's *nu'u** through wondering crowds; the ceremonial mats spread before them in the *malae*† by the High Chief's own daughters, whom the good Mr Williams modestly described as 'fine looking young women, about eighteen and twenty years of age, each wearing a beautiful mat about the waist, a wreath of flowers as a head-dress and a string of blue beads around the neck. The upper parts of their body were uncovered and anointed with scented coconut oil'.

There must have been ceremonial drinking from the *kava* bowl, feasting on fish and fowl, roast pork and breadfruit, pineapples, mangoes, bananas, followed by dancing in which the missionaries 'saw nothing bordering on indecency' (it must have been the *kava*) and an exchange of gifts. 'The missionaries then ordered one of their people to open a basket and place their gifts before the two chiefs, Malietoa and Taima-lelagi' (Son of the Skies) whose role of *Tulafale*, or Orator and Spokesman, was complimentary to, and almost as important as, that of his brother's, the O Le Tupu. 'As soon as the articles were laid out, the Chief took up first an axe, and placing it upon his head exclaimed: "*Faafetai le toi tele*," or "Thank you for this large axe," and having observed this same ceremony with every other article he concluded by saying: "Thank you for all. Thank you for all".'

The Samoans took to Christianity enthusiastically, not least because it had been introduced to them by two men (Mr Williams and Mr Stair) whom they believed to be 'great English chiefs' for had they not brought with them a *tulafale*, or talking man/orator (the young chief, Fakea) according to correct Samoan etiquette? And were they not fulfilling a prophecy that had been believed on the islands for generations: that new learning would come to them with new Gods from across the sea? There

---

* *Nu'u* – village, but it also means the entire polity and community of a village.
† *Malae* – ceremonial meeting-house at the centre of every Samoan *nu'u*.

were also more mundane considerations – some thought that by adopting Christianity more ships would now visit them, with whom they could barter goods; others that it would prolong their lives and preserve them from the malignity of their own Gods; and a few hoped that the Christian teaching of love and peace would finally put an end to their bloody and desolating wars. Was not the sailing Gods' ship called the *Mission of Peace?*

But in this respect Christianity did not change things over much. True, Malietoa, in a new-found spirit of forgiveness, allowed the people of the A'ana District, whom he had driven from their lands, to return, but after his death in 1841, fighting broke out again on every side.

It seemed endemic in Samoa during the nineteenth century, and it was usually about succession to chiefly titles, the murder of high chiefs or women. The story of Taimalelagi's conversion and final apostasy could well be the subject of an epic poem, or the libretto of an opera. His Christian obligation to pacifism vanished after Tupapua, his favourite son, died and the holier-than-thou newly baptised Christians of a nearby *nu'u* attributed the death to God's punishment for sin. Taimalelagi, in grief and anger, put his new faith to the test by committing the same sin with the same woman once again, daring the Christian's God to kill him for it. He lived, and together with Malietoa's son he renounced the London Missionary Society's creed and left his village for the war, cursing the mission there, and all the people who refused to follow him.

The war that followed, and continued until 1851, was the last Samoan war in which European intrigues played no substantial part, and the first to be influenced by European weapons.

Before guns were introduced to Samoa, wars were conducted, with the utmost savagery and brutality, in hand-to-hand fighting, and to the death, for victory required the utter humiliation and destruction of the enemy if the victors were to gain ascendancy for any length of time. According to an early missionary, the heads of enemy warriors killed in battle were cut off and presented to the Chief leading the 'war party'. 'After a fight, the heads of the slain enemies are paraded in the presence of the assembled chiefs and people, when the individual heroes are thanked and their personal prowess and daring are publicly acknowledged. The excitement of the successful warrior is intense as he passes before the chiefs with his bleeding trophy, capering in the most fantastic evolutions with blackened face and oiled body, throwing his club high into the air and catching it behind his back or between his legs . . . sometimes himself carrying his enemy's head, sometimes dancing around a comrade who carried it for him, all the while shouting in the loudest voice: "Ou Ite Mau Tagata!" – "I have my man!"

'To a young Samoan warrior, that was the realisation of his highest ambition.'

It would be pleasing to think that the advent of Christianity put an immediate stop to this kind of behaviour, for it certainly changed other aspects of traditional Samoan life, and often for the worse, but despite the missionaries' zealous teaching of brotherly love and the merits of peace, the islanders' fondness for a good fight and inter-village skirmishes continued until the very end of the century.

At this point I must confess to a prejudice against missionaries and if I exaggerate the physical damage done to Fa' Samoa* by their advent and underestimate the spiritual advantages, then I apologise, but, practising Catholic though I am, I personally find it hard to accept the need for missionaries, especially of the self-righteous, fundamentalist kind who played so large a part in the development of Samoa. That a Christian ethic and the lower end of Christian civilisation should be arbitrarily imposed on a reasonably moral but totally different civilisation and be accepted as 'salvation' for 'heathens' seems to me an arrogant and questionable assumption. And that an all-knowledgeable, all-powerful, all-loving God cannot, in His infinite wisdom and mercy, find room for these 'poor ignorants' in an eternity of which we understand very little, also seems to me as insulting to Him as it is to His creation, the human race. But many saintly people have thought otherwise.

Apart from their propensity for killing each other – and this was only spasmodic – the Samoans had reached a remarkable level in a seemingly unique civilisation in which a gentle and idealistic communism, patriarchal and monarchical authority and rudimentary democracy all played a part. It was the destruction, or near-destruction, of this civilisation and the traditional role of its high-chiefs by missionaries, and later on by the colonial governments of the West in 'the making of modern Samoa', that is to be regretted. According to the very bright young Samoan historian, Dr Malama, whose book† is called just that (and with whom I talked long into the night at Aggie's cosmopolitan cocktail bar), the events of the years following the arrival of the Mission of Peace were as much influenced by the ideological confusion of the Samoans as by the intrusion of greedy white settlers and insensitive or despotic white rule.

---

* Samoan tradition – the Samoan way of life.
† The Making of Modern Samoa by Dr Malama (University Press of Java).

The main trouble with the missionaries was that, though their message was the best, they were such very second-rate messengers. In accordance with the promises made by John Williams to Malietoa, six white missionaries of the London Missionary Society (LMS) and their wives duly landed in Samoa in June 1838. Their belief was not solely 'that a civilising and religious influence might be exerted upon the countless thousands of benighted heathen', but also that a settlement could be made whereby ships, in particular the whalers who operated from New South Wales, might 'refresh and refit without danger' and that trading initiatives might eventually follow, for after his second visit to the islands, John Williams reported: 'If it be not already proved, the experience of a few more years will demonstrate the fact that the Missionary enterprise is incomparably the most effective machinery that has ever been brought to operate upon the social, the civil and the commercial, as well as the moral and spiritual interests of mankind'.

The advantages to British and Australian commerce were no doubt considerable. Within a few years the newly converted heathen had discarded their native lava-lavas, wreaths and garlands of forest flowers, for the long gowns, bonnets and shawls of 'Christian women' or, if they could not afford these, for 'Mother Hubbards', long tubular garments, like nightgowns, designed by the missionaries to hide 'the lower limbs'. These hideous objects not only trailed in the dust and were rarely washed, but they also soaked up the rain and stored perspiration, trebly encouraging germs of influenza, dysentery and tuberculosis, which Europeans had already brought with them to the islands. Indeed, in the New Hebrides – where poor John Williams was later clubbed to death by xenophobic natives (there is a contemporary print of his stove-pipe hat floating dismally in a palm-fringed lagoon, which was very popular in Wales) – the missionaries were known by a name which literally means, in their language, 'the bringers of disease'.

But it was not only the unfortunate side-effects of conversion and enforced 'civilisation', the stamping-out of innocent and delightful practices, that upset many critics of missionary zeal, it was the manner of conversion itself which was, in Samoa, particularly obnoxious. In his diary, the Reverend A. W. Murray, who was in charge of the main LMS mission in Samoa from 1838 onwards, and whose fiery sermons promised eternal damnation to all those 'who did not repent', wrote as follows:

'On Sunday a most plentiful shower . . .' (of God's grace, one presumes). 'Eighty-three persons were on that day deeply convinced of sin for the first time . . . On Monday the chapel was also filled; at least one thousand people. The service was carried on *as the people could bear it*, with address, prayer and praise . . . Sometimes the whole place was in a move with the carrying and the carried' (those overcome and fainting with emotion). 'The voice often quite drowned in the cries and groans of awakened sinners.'

In another extract he wrote: 'Women were carried out by the dozens, convulsed and struggling, so as to drive five or six men about like trees in the wind, who were exerting all their strength to hold and convey them away. I had heard of beating breasts and tearing hair before, but I have now seen and shall not soon forget it . . .'

Before long, the LMS found it could not cope with the demand for redemption, and it established a training institute for indigenous pastor/ teachers at Malua. The quality of some of these native missionaries was lamentable. Puffed up by their new importance and greedy for more converts and more revenue for the mission, they encouraged a kind of personal and inter-village rivalry to see who would give most to their periodic cash collections, and the cash would be silver only, dearly earned, and often leaving individuals or even whole communities in debt. What is more, a large proportion of the money collected was sent away from Samoa and did not even benefit the islanders.

No wonder J. R. Brenchley, a visitor to Samoa in 1865, wrote: 'The Samoans are distinguished by some remarkable qualities which, if not deteriorated by so-called civilised people, give promise of a superior civilisation. It is much to be regretted that they are not assisted in their advance by men of a more polished order than the greater part of those who have undertaken to elevate them.'

That Fa' Samoa survived this period was due to the extraordinary resilience of its traditionally minded people, and also to their failing, after the death of Malietoa and his brother, to find a central authority, an *O Le Tupu*, who without doubt would have been manipulated and then eliminated by foreign intervention, as happened in nearly all the other Polynesian islands.

Fa' Samoa was basically a form of idealistic 'Communism', on which all Samoan customs and social privileges were built, but it had nothing to do with Marx or Lenin.

The Samoan *nu'u*, or village, was more than a settlement, it was a territory which was collectively owned and controlled by what the anthropologists call 'a number of bi-lateral corporate descent groups' which in Scotland is called, a good deal more simply, a 'clan'. A *nu'u* averaged a population of 200 to 500 people, was politically autonomous, had its own hierarchy of leaders or chiefs and its own historical traditions. These were summarised in the *Fa' Alupega*, or clan, 'charter' which on every formal occasion, and there were many of them, would be recited by the *Matai's Tulafale* (Chief's orator) at great length, together with his chiefly titles and any complimentary tit-bits he cared to throw in, much as a Celtic Senachie of yore would recite the genealogy of his clan's chiefs, and the history of the clan.

These extended family groups, *aigas*, had their elected chief or *matai* who, as my taxi-driver had explained, was the custodian of the property of his *aiga* and had the authority to allocate land and other resources to its members. If, however, he abused his powers the *aiga* could replace him by a democratic process, the consensus of the village council, the *Aiga Potopoto*.

Inequality in Samoa lay only in the dispensation of certain symbolic objects, like fine mats and headdresses, drinking cups or conches, and the titles and roles of those chosen to be in authority. There was no substantial difference in the standards of consumption between the highest ranking chief and an un-titled man (though this was less evident in early times). All the members of an *aiga* were expected to divide what they had between the relatives and families that formed their community. If there was a surplus, it was simply and enjoyably removed by the *matai* ordering a period of feasting and jollification; if a dearth, then a similar period of belt-tightening and conservation would be observed. The title system had, therefore, a firm economic base.

Titles belonged to the nobility and were of two main kinds: *Ali'i* and *Tulafale*. *Ali'i Pa'ia* or sacred High-Chief, were those nobles who could trace their origins back to the Gods, and finally to Tangaloa-a-Lag, the Creator, through enormously lengthy genealogies, which of course, as they go back in time, link noble family to noble family (in the same way that almost every aristocratic family in England can trace its ancestry back to John of Gaunt).

Ali'i Pa'ias were regarded as having supernatural power which they received from their divine ancestors, and this power was fundamental to their high-chiefly authority. When the missionaries landed there were still twelve families who could claim divine descent, including of course Tamaifuinga, the tyrant-King, but they seem to have dwindled as time passed.

Great aristocrats, both male and female, became *aitu* after death, that is spirits or ghosts. They could take human form or appear in plants, fish, birds, animals or even be transmogrified into another living person. These beliefs were the basis of the old Samoan religion, which they abandoned for Christianity, with some relief, for the spirits were not all benign. Some were definitely dangerous and much feared.

The Reverend John Stair, one of the pioneer missionaries who landed on Samoa with John Williams in 1838 and stayed for seven years until his wife's health failed her, was persecuted by a particularly malign domestic *aitu* when they moved into a new mission house at Falelatai on the south-west coast of Upolu. The spirit, or possibly spirits, constantly rolled balls down the passage outside their bedroom, banged on doors, rang bells and generally behaved in such a tiresome and upsetting way that Mrs Stair, who 'was a brave woman, and battled with dangers and difficulty in a surprising manner . . .' finally 'felt the constant strain too heavy to bear, and gave way under it'. (It is not exactly recorded how.)

That Samoa was full of these creatures in 1840 there seems little doubt, but what the Reverend found 'a question of much interest, and difficult to answer' was 'whether the Samoans and other nations of Polynesia were more directly under what is usually called "Satanic Agency" in their heathen state than (immediately) after the introduction of Christianity'. He is surprisingly cautious, in view no doubt of his experiences, in believing they were.

Manifestations of Tangaloa, the Creator, were benign and known as *atua*, and this was the word adopted by the early missionaries to convey the conception of a single Christian God, or Jehovah, to their postulants.

The Samoan aristocracy depended on the granting or removal of titles which were in the gift of certain districts and therefore were subject to change. *O Le Tupu O Samoa* was the regal title, an approximation to 'King of Samoa', and meant that its possessor held two distinct great titles, conferred upon him by the five most important provinces, the decision being made by another class of aristocrat, the *Tulafale* (or groups of *Tulafale*). Succession to these titles was not automatic or hereditary, but to hold all five of them meant that the possessor had the support and recognition of the leaders of every district in Samoa.

After Tamafuinga's demise and the introduction of Christianity, these five titles were conferred on Malietoa, who was the first of his family to attain them and be declared *O Le Tupu O Samoa*. He was also the last independent king to rule over all Samoa. On his deathbed he mistakenly divided the five titles that conferred kingship, with disastrous results. His brother, Taimalelagi, Son of the Skies, retained the title of Malietoa until his death when two claimants arose, and there was no agreement on the disposal of the other four titles. The 'throne' remained empty for thirty years while the Chiefs and *Tulafales* bickered, and for the rest of the nineteenth century competition for the titles, in which rested supreme authority, dominated Samoan politics.

The adoption of Christianity had a levelling effect on the Samoans. It replaced the power that the great chiefs possessed through their blood-lines being linked to the ancient Gods, and re-defined that power as secular authority. Thus it made the criteria for succession more rather than less complicated. It reduced the crucial distinction between *Ali'i* and *Tulafale*, which became henceforward more ceremonial than actual, and it did away with the 'great warrior' element, which had always been one of the key factors of chieftainship.

The seekers of titles had now to find new ways to acquire prestige and maintain their titles: in the Church? in government? Or by economic means?

It is ironic, Malama points out, that while the Great Powers sought and failed to find a centralised political authority in Samoa, the effects of the Europeans' religion, Christianity, de-centralised that authority by weakening the beliefs that gave legitimacy to the power of the Great Chiefs.

Christianity also brought social change and a host of new taboos. The missionaries disapproved of the population's nakedness, their lovely orchid garlands and scented headdresses, the elaborate tattooing of young men which, in a land where everything comes easily, almost amounted to an initiation ceremony and a test of their virility and manhood, and so was deeply prized. Rumbustious and obscene dancing and games, singing – except for hymns – was outlawed. Communal village bathing places, and *lomi-lomi* – the massage that was always awarded tired travel-lers by village maidens – were forbidden, and the keeping and taming of wild pigeons, the presentation of ceremonial mats, and a host of other delightful and harmless habits were discouraged. But conversely, and to their credit, the village schools were extremely well run, and native farming methods greatly improved. By the end of the century, almost the entire population could read and write.

The missionaries preached middle-class individualism, the very oppo-site to *Fa' Samoa* traditional authority and communal sharing, which, according to my anthropologist, was 'a unitary system of dispersed power'. They set up their village pastors as models of the family life they wished Samoans to adopt. The Samoans, however, soon transformed the pastors into a new kind of sacred chief, each village providing their minister with the largest and finest house, sending their children to wait upon him and his family and providing him abundantly with the best of the food available. So, although Protestantism became the greatest ideological influence in the later nineteenth century, and destroyed much that was beautiful and good, the Samoans somehow managed only to adopt the parts of it they liked. In some ways it too became part of *Fa' Samoa*, and was used, like the old religion, to legitimise their own institutions.

The missionary 'take-over' and the squabbling among the High Chiefs coincided, in the second half of the nineteenth century, with an awakened interest in Samoa among the foreign powers as a valuable trading post with splendid anchorages. From the late 1860s, France (who had already occupied Tahiti, and eliminated its king), Britain, Germany and America prowled around Samoa like growling dogs around a bone.

It was a period of confusion, intrigue and rivalry on every side, between the various Christian denominations, between the Great Powers and between the High Chiefs.

Confusion had also arisen over the ownership of land and of trading rights, and this was the primary cause of more trouble. Under the government of the chiefs, every family in every community was assured of a piece of land to cultivate and live off, land which meant shelter and protection and care in old age; but land was now being bartered, leased and even sold to Europeans and then reclaimed by Samoans as 'illegally' come by.

To legitimise their land and trading claims, it was imperative for the Europeans to deal with a central authority, but in Samoa, despite all their efforts, this seemed constantly to elude them. In a gradually deteriorating situation the British were the first to whom the Samoans turned for help and protection. Queen Victoria sent them a gunboat and a resident consul, but her government was not prepared to do more.

In 1878 America cobbled up some kind (possibly an illegal kind) of a treaty with Eastern Samoa by which, in return for 'trade protection', she acquired the harbour and other rights at Pango Pango – the best anchorage in the whole of the Southern Pacific.

The young New Zealand government also made an attempt at protective hegemony. In fact, what all the foreign powers wanted was trade and land concessions, and good harbours to trade from and shelter in – without any kind of responsibility towards the legitimate owners of these amenities.

It would seem that finally the Gods – whether Samoan or Christian, who can tell? – lost patience and took a hand, for one night in 1889, a terrific hurricane blew up and sank the rival fleets of Germany and America who had been sitting in Apia harbour, glaring at each other, dashing their ships against the coral reef of the bay and drowning many of their crews. A solitary British warship managed by supreme seamanship and more than a peck of common sense to escape from the harbour and ride out the storm at sea, but the grim skeletons of the German ships can still be seen at low tide from Aggie Grey's front porch.

The deaths of so many sailors was international news, and it influenced the provisions of an international agreement, the Berlin Act of 1889, which was signed by all three rival powers and which declared Samoa a neutral territory, giving equal rights to the three signatory powers (Britain, Germany and America), independence to a Samoan government and the free right to elect their king and choose a form of government *according to their laws and customs*. A European Chief Justice was appointed, and a European President of the Municipality of Apia.

It all sounded too good to be true. And so it was – the rivalry of the three powers still grumbled on and the rival chiefs, Malietoa and Mata'afa, still competed for supremacy.

In 1889 Robert Louis Stevenson arrived in Samoa and built himself a most beautiful native-style house – with a few mod-cons – on a perfect site on the hill above Apia where he led a most agreeable and civilised life, making friends among the Samoans and with the remarkable mix of white settlers, traders and officials who now lived in and around Apia, and who were known collectively as 'the Beach' – characters who were larger than life and could have walked straight out of a novel about the South Seas. Furthermore R.L.S. somehow managed, in this remotest of retreats, and while slowly dying of tuberculosis, to preside over a kind of international literary and political salon (visitors came from far and near) which had considerable influence in the islands, and beyond.

He very soon declared himself for *Fa' Samoa* and supported the candidature of Mata'afa for the supreme title – indeed, he wrote a book about Samoa, *A Footnote to History*, which is almost a party political pamphlet.

The climax to the squabbling of High Chiefs and foreign powers came in 1899 amid great confusion, when the young Malietoa, grandson of the great chief and grandfather of the present king, made a bid to succeed his father, who had just died, as king. He was supported by an internationally appointed judge, by the Tamasesi party and by Mr Gurr, a respected citizen, and editor of Samoa's only newspaper. But the coup failed, and the small Malietoa party was obliged to take refuge in HMS *Porpoise*, a British warship which was standing by in Apia harbour.

The Germans, who supported Mata'afa (a more malleable character), and the allied British and American navies the Malietoans – now faced each other in a distinctly warlike stance. The New Zealanders offered a Volunteer Corps to defuse the situation, but it was refused, and to solve the impasse a joint commission of the three powers was formed and arrived in Samoa towards the end of the year.

Without consultation with the inhabitants, and without serious deliberation, it decided on a solution worthy of King Solomon – the partition of the island archipelago.

Great Britain was already unhappily involved in the Boer War, and needing to placate Germany on that front she was awkwardly placed for negotiations. She therefore conceded that the interests of the other powers, Germany and the USA, were greater than her own, and retired from the bargaining table (for which she was later rewarded by being granted new territory in the Solomon Islands and German Tonga). Germany and America then divided up the archipelago between themselves, the USA taking the still commercially unimportant Eastern Islands, with their strategically important harbour of Pango Pango, which soon became a busy coaling station and naval base; the Germans taking Western Samoa, the two large islands of Savaii and Upolu, and the small islands around them, of which Manolo and Apolina were the most important.

In all this the consent of the Samoan people was neither sought nor given. They had three times asked to be annexed by Britain, and once by the USA, but the very last thing they wanted was to be cut in two, like a cake, or dominated by Germany.

Dr Solf, the first German Governor of Western Samoa, is a controversial figure, judgments about whom differ sharply, but that he was an intelligent, efficient and loyal German functionary of the first order, there is no doubt. He began his career in Samoa as President of the Municipality of Apia, and was already well versed in Samoan habits; he had himself tattooed, gave cocktail parties for the white settlers and other entertainments for the chiefs, with whom he got on very well. He viewed, no doubt with anthropological interest, probably the last display of obscene dances and games to be held in Savaii. He acted as his own secretary of native affairs, he built roads, bridges and public buildings, and he (in Newton Rowe's opinion) 'set himself the task of deliberately offsetting certain influences of the Protestant missions', which is a polite way of saying he tried to end their worst abuses. To many of the white traders and settlers, life under German rule was lived 'as one happy family'.

Yet, according to later Samoan historians, he was a sinister figure who deliberately dismantled the last remains of all that was important in *Fa' Samoa* – and superimposed complete German hegemony ('for which no-one can blame him', added my Samoan informant, 'after all, it was his job').

Dr Solf had studied British administration methods in Fiji and, two months after raising the German flag in Western Samoa, he called in arms from the two warring parties, and paid for them. He then called a meeting of the Samoan chiefs and dictated the future foundations of the new German/Samoan administration. 'The head of the Samoan administration shall be one single High Chief: Mata'afa Iosefo, who will be styled: Le Ali'i Sili. This designation of Mata'afa (as Ali'i Sili and not O Le Tupu) spelt out Solf's policy and signalled the end of any further attempt to create a monarchy that would reconcile European and Samoan ideas about rank and authority. The German emperor, Kaiser William, was then designated Tupu Sili or 'Highest Ruler'. The new hierarchy in Samoa could not have been made more clear.

And to underline German authority still further, the powerful senior groups of Tulafale were abolished. Dr Solf was determined that only his administration should fulfil this role and referred to Tumua and Pule as 'that body of indolent intriguers' (which they probably were). In the Governor's view, the Kaiser was to be the source of all honour and no other, and he himself was the representative of the Kaiser. Dr Solf may have understood Samoan culture better than any previous or later European, but that did not mean to say that he approved of it. He also had the Teutonic wish for orderliness: the country needed tidying up and organising, German interests and rights being always paramount.

Chief Mata'afa, the Ali'i Sili, proved as deferential and submissive an ally as was expected. He recognised that, for the moment anyway, his position depended more on support from the Governor than from his backers among the Tulafale of Tumua and Pule.

But on the island of Savaii the chiefs were less subservient, and there began there the first stirrings of a resistance to the colonial overlords, a resistance called the Mau (meaning 'Opinion'), which of course Dr Solf disapproved of and at first had no difficulty in suppressing.

After Mata'afa's death in 1912, the title of Ali'i Sili was abolished and a new title and role for the High Chiefs was created by the German Governor – that of Adviser, or Fautua, to the administration. It was given jointly to Malietola Tanumafili I and Tupua Tamasese Meaoli I. Thus, though it recognised the titles of certain High Chiefs' families and their eligibility to be Paramount Chief, this ended all attempts to install a 'King' or single supreme chief as leader of the Samoans. In fact, the Germans had fundamentally altered a traditional system that had existed for centuries.

However, God, or Fate, was once again on the side of the Samoans. In 1914, on the outbreak of the First World War, the Germans departed, behaving very decently, even giving all native administrators a year's salary in advance. They were immediately succeeded by a detachment of New Zealand troops, who called themselves The New Zealand Expeditionary Force and annexed the islands of Western Samoa without a shot being fired by either side.

The military administration of New Zealand's Colonel Logan during the next five years seems to have passed without incident, except for one horrendous misjudgment, which originated in Auckland, at its end. In 1918, a ship, bearing the disastrous and worldwide epidemic of pneumonic influenza, left Auckland for Samoa and on its way was duly quarantined in the British Crown Colony of Fiji; it reached Apia without the Governor being advised of any danger, and its passengers were allowed to land. Within a few days the epidemic was raging in Western Samoa, although Eastern Samoa, sixty miles away, owing to a strict quarantine, escaped the plague. The American Governor there radiographed Colonel Logan from Pango Pango offering medical assistance but, inexplicably and unforgivably, this was curtly refused and Western Samoa closed down all wireless communications with its Eastern relations.

Twenty-two per cent of the native population died in the epidemic, and a second Island petition (the first was from the British residents in 1915) was made to the British Colonial Office, 'praying to God that Great Britain will take over the control of Samoa from New Zealand and that New Zealand and those responsible . . .' but this was later withdrawn. It should be pointed out that Colonel Logan, except for his unfortunate antipathy for Americans, behaved well and bravely throughout the emergency, and that the missionaries, with the exception of a few Roman Catholics, did not. In spite of an embargo on movement, they continued their annual silver collection, moving from village to village and spreading the virus, for some were 'carriers', wherever they went. When one missionary complained to Colonel Logan that grave-diggers had drunk whisky on holy ground, the good colonel arrested the man and set him to burying corpses, often in a high state of putrefaction, in his own cemetery; after two days of this he begged for liquor, which was the only thing that made the grisly task bearable (and also acted as a disinfectant) and was refused it.

In 1921, under the Treaty of Versailles, Western Samoa became a C-class League of Nations mandate under the administration of New Zealand, but again without consultation with its inhabitants. In view of the excellent relations that Western Samoa and New Zealand have had since its independence, and the high standards of the post-war New Zealand High

Commissioners, it would be churlish to dwell on the inadequacies of their first Governors under the League of Nations' mandate, who, after all, had no experience in colonial rule, and rule over what was in some ways an essentially civilised population with an extremely complicated social/political organisation far older than their own. Unfortunately they did not try, or simply failed to understand the Samoans, their love of tradition and ceremonial, their inborn instinct for courtesy and 'good form', their natural kindness and good humour, and this led to conflict, repression and ill-will on both sides.

It would, on the other hand, be only fair to the Samoans to recall some of the misguided 'reforms' and glaring injustices of Colonel Tate's, General Richardson's and Colonel Allen's administrations, and the dubious part played in them by Mr H. S. Griffin, the LMS printer-turned missionary-turned civil servant who acted as their Secretary of Native Affairs, for they have a bearing on present government and the present Head of State. If they had not been so awful, there would probably not have been a *Mau* movement, a 'Citizens' Committee', a King Malietoa Tanumafili II and an independent Samoa today.

I wish I had known, as Robert Louis Stevenson, and later Rupert Brooke, Lloyd Osborne and Newton Rowe all knew, the remarkable white and half-white traders who made up the European colony, 'The Beach' or, as one of General Richardson's ADCs once unwisely called them: 'the riff-raff of Apia'. It was this courageous little group who did the almost unthinkable thing, in the climate of those days, and formed a 'Citizens' Committee' which actually supported a rebellious native movement, the *Mau*, and who made the world outside the Antipodes aware that the administration of Western Samoa was disastrous, and that serious acts of injustice and malpractice were being committed daily.

At first they had done their best to support the new order, for most of them were men with long local and professional experience, but when they witnessed the flood of petty and ignorant legislation that poured out of the Governor's office, and saw the harm that was being done in appointing yes-men to local councils, they would have nothing more to do with it. There were nonsensical schemes for rubber and cotton plantations set up in a climate where neither could possibly thrive; a 'village planning campaign' which involved the destruction of traditional *nu'us* and the building of Western-style model villages; a drive of 'hygiene for the natives' which ordered every village to build wooden privies on their shorelines, thus creating unheard-of pollution, and total bewilderment (I saw the relics of these and puzzled over them on a visit to Manoa). There was also unwarranted and irresponsible interference with the marriage laws and the social life of the villages (the Fine Mats Ordinance). But when it came to reorganisation of land tenure, which is the crucial element, the core of the *Fa' Samoa* economic system, it was too much. The ordinance stated: 'Samoa will never prosper until a change is made in the Native system of land ownership. The present system must be changed to individual holdings.' To individualise land tenure, however, was to rob the Chiefs and Orators of their last vestige of authority, and would have meant the overthrow of the whole social and economic machine. The Samoans realised this and the population joined the resistance movement in their hundreds.

Public meetings organised by the Citizens' Committee were attended by large numbers of Samoans and Europeans, and an individual protest was made to the Government of New Zealand by Dr O. F. Nelson, a much-respected citizen and a member of the Legislative Council. Promises were given and eventually a Royal Commission met in Samoa and reported back to Auckland, but the only result of this was that the *Mau* were declared a dangerous and subversive organisation and that three members of the Citizens' Committee, Mr Nelson, Judge Gurr (an American who ran the local newspaper) and Mr Smyth, a leading merchant, were deported from the Islands without proper trial.

To General Richardson, a former British NCO gunnery instructor and quartermaster-sergeant who had received a commission in the New Zealand Militia and worked his way up to Brigadier-General in the 1914–18 war, the *Mau* was simply a bunch of tiresome natives, led by agitators, who must be taught a sharp lesson. He had no understanding or sympathy for Samoan tradition or national pride.

The *Mau* was in fact a non-violent, passive resistance movement, whose aim was perfectly clear. Self-government for the Samoans under the direct protection of Great Britain, and not New Zealand, and a return to *Fa' Samoa*. Its acknowledged leader was the good-looking and romantic young advocate and High-Chief, Tamasese Liolofi II, who was a natural leader, and the grandson of the former king. Tamasese came into collision with the Administration in 1924, when he planted a hedge on his own land, which obstructed the view of the native pastor of the London Missionary Society, and ignored an order to remove it. For this he was banished for life, and without trial, from the country his forefathers had ruled over for centuries.

For several years he visited Upolu clandestinely and would hold secret meetings in a small pavilion in the centre of General Richardson's first model village, which is today a memorial to him and to the founding members of the movement. Eventually he was allowed back, as was Mr

Smyth, who returned to Samoa after three years' banishment on 27 December 1929. Tamasese led a peaceful and permitted procession of *Mau* members to the Tivoli Wharf to welcome Mr Smyth home, but as it passed the courthouse, a white policeman suddenly made a foolish, if not pre-arranged attempt to arrest a man who was playing in the *Mau* band. Blows were exchanged and then revolver shots were indiscriminately fired into the unarmed marchers. Some fell, mortally wounded, and as the procession broke up in panic, Tamasese tried vainly to calm his followers, shouting repeatedly, 'Samoa, please keep the peace,' when a single shot rang out and he fell, 'and then machine-gun fire opened up from the Police Headquarters and all the Samoans went down. A kinsman of Tamasese, a boy who protected with his own body the wounded chief, was riddled with bullets . . .'

That evening Tamasese, lying mortally wounded in hospital, issued a manifesto to his people: 'My blood has been spilt for Samoa, I am proud to give it. Do not dream of avenging it, as it was spilt in maintaining peace. If I die, peace must be maintained at any price.' Towards morning it was seen that there was no hope, and he was removed from hospital to his village of Vairioso, where he died soon after dawn.

The murder, for such it was, of two high chiefs and nine others, plus sixteen seriously wounded Samoans, made headlines in the world's press, the more so as the latest enquiry by the Mandates Commission had finally uncovered some disturbing facts about the Administration's 'staffing, finances and attitudes to the Native population' – this after ten years of its own appalling laziness and incompetence – the understatement of all time!

New Zealand, however, sent a warship to Samoa and declared the *Mau* a seditious and illegal organisation, with heavy penalties for anyone joining it. As, by now, several thousand of the island's population were already members, this did not greatly disturb them. They went underground, or took to the bush, the perfect hiding place, where they were supported by their relatives from the villages. A situation of stagnation and civil disobedience developed. Raiding parties were sent to hunt them down, but they did so half-heartedly and with little success.

In 1936, New Zealand went to the polls and elected a Labour government which cancelled the order of banishment against the *Mau* leaders and recognised the movement as a political party.

Relations between the two countries improved slowly, but it was only in the Second World War that they reached a turning point. US Marines were stationed in Upolu, where they constructed roads, built an airport (still the only one on the islands) and by their friendly and cheerful kindness, restored the islanders' confidence in the '*papalangi*', as white men have been called in Samoa since the time of the 'Sailing Gods'.

Samoa did not see any fighting during the Pacific War, although invasion from Japan was a constant threat, and at the end of it she became a Trustee of the United Nations, although still administered from New Zealand. But New Zealand had learnt a lot during the intervening wartime years and immediately began preparing Samoa for self-government. It was not as easy as it sounds, and the difficulties of finding common ground between the traditional system of *Fa' Samoa* or *Aga Nu'u a Samoa* (government in the Samoan way) and a rational legal system of parliamentary democracy with a modern structural bureaucracy were acute.

How a formula was finally arrived at, with both parties sitting on either side of the table, bewildered UNO representatives looking on and neither side really understanding what the other side of the table was talking about, was a triumph of patience and diplomacy, but also, in the context of everything that had gone before, it was a renewal of mutual faith in each other's race.

The United Nations supervised a plebiscite which was held in 1961 in which all Samoan citizens were asked: a) whether they approved of the new constitution, and b) whether they wanted independence. The result was a foregone conclusion and independence finally came to Samoa on New Year's Day, 1962.

In the days of the first missionaries there were at least twelve 'sacred' High Chief titles in Samoa – noble lines, who could claim descent from the Gods and were called *Ali'i Pa'ia*. By the end of the nineteenth century, these *Tama a Aiga*, 'Sons of the Families', titles had dwindled to four, which were recognised as being of paramount rank by the whole nation – Malietoa, Tupua Tamasese, Mata'afa and Tuimaleali'i Fano. After independence, the *Tama a Aiga* were given the highest ranking positions. The constitution provided for a single Head of State, called in Samoa *O Le Ao O Le Malo*, to be elected by the legislative assembly (parliament, or in fact an elected council of chiefs) for a term of five years. However, in the first instance, it was decided that the two High Chiefs who had been titled the *Fautua* since 1947 – Tupua Tamasese and Malietoa Tanumafili II – should become joint heads of state and have a lifetime tenure of office. Chief Tuimaleali'i Fano became a member of the Council of Deputies (or 'Cabinet') and Chief Mata'afa was elected Prime Minister.

In 1963, Tupua Tamasese died, and the sole Head of State since then has been His Highness Malietoa Tanumafili II, on whom I was going to call the next morning.

I am not sure what I expected as my car and driver (kindly lent by Adrian Simcock, the New Zealand High Commissioner) rolled up the beautiful driveway to Vailima, Robert Louis Stevenson's last, and favourite home; General Sir George Richardson's residence; and now the tidy little palace of the Samoan heads of state. After all I had learnt about sacred High Chiefs, guerrilla leaders and political martyrs, perhaps I imagined its present incumbent would be an other-worldly aesthete, or an aggressively articulate politician. I certainly did not expect a benign and cheerful country squire – no, not exactly a squire since, for all his simplicity, there is a touch of grandness and hauteur about King Malietoa that places him among the aristocrats, the early nineteenth-century grandees. He could easily be mistaken for the somewhat sunburnt great-grandfather of Lord Airlie, or the Duke of Rutland, and, if he had been wearing plus twos and gaiters and carrying a gun under his arm, it would not have looked out of place. Instead he was wearing a long *lava-lava* and tunic-style batik shirt. A guard in a uniform of the 1900s with a cream-coloured topi with a spike on it opened the car door, a deft and bare-footed steward in white shirt and *lava-lava* embellished by a scarlet sash fielded me neatly and guided me up the stairs of the veranda to where the Paramount and Sacred Chief, the Kingly-Ruler and Head of State was waiting, with Tina Hellafoe, his smiling and matronly Chief of Protocol, by his side.

Malietoa's hair is thick and wavy and only slightly grizzled. He has the well-shaped head, bull neck and strong face of most Samoans, and he is tall and fit and looks younger than his sixty-three years, but his old-world courtesy and kindliness – one can only call it that – is the first thing one notices. A kind of happy, patriarchal benignity, which makes you smile back at him: it is so rare and natural – and nice.

We sat down in comfortable chairs round a low tea table at one end of the glassed-in veranda, which runs the whole width of the house, and which commands a magnificent view over the valley and coast below. Immediately a generous morning meal, or sumptuous 'elevenses' (or old-fashioned nursery tea) was brought in and set before us. Large and delicious egg sandwiches, sardine and ham ones, too; little cakes and savoury tartlets, and then a truly magnificent carrot cake, of surely missionary inspiration, was handed round.

A bird fluttered against the mosquito-mesh of an open window and I asked King Malietoa if he had kept up the royal tradition of taming wood pigeons and keeping them as pets. 'Alas, no,' he answered. 'It is one of the nice old Samoan customs that has come to an end. It was a delightful way of relaxing, and bird and master became good friends. Indeed the High Chief's pet bird used to be carried in a cage in front of him when he travelled around the island. No, I'm afraid for relaxation I play golf.'

This brought me down to earth with a bump, but at least it introduced the subject, and so I thought it a good moment to give His Highness my present. I fished it out of my Bhutanese book-bag and handed it over with a little speech. It was a large Royal Worcester china breakfast cup, liberally strewn with golf clubs and flags and with an eminently suitable message written round the rim – 'For a Very Important Person'.

It went down a fair treat. He took it and, with a delighted smile, placed it carefully upon his head, saying, just as his ancestor, the Great Malietoa, had said about his axe: 'This is a very fine cup, for which I thank you. I thank you very much.'

We then talked about his role as head of state and the referendum that had taken place a year ago and which had sought the population's opinion on three issues: universal suffrage; a second chamber to parliament; and a prolongation of its term. Only the first of these proposals was adopted and elections had just taken place, for the first time, by universal suffrage.

Everyone agreed that the election was well conducted. It does seem possible, however, that as only *matai* (village chiefs) can be candidates for the legislature and their numbers seem to have suddenly increased, that a few extra ones may just possibly have been created (for instance, my taxi-driver?) to bolster the chances of a political party in districts where their support was weak.

My new friend, Dr Malama, thought that this might eventually endanger the *matai* system, but Princess Momoe, who now joined us – a pretty young woman with a yellow Puataunofo flower behind one ear – did not agree: 'On the contrary,' she protested, 'it will give women, ordinary women of every village, political responsibility – and power they have never had before.'

She is small and slim and obviously used to arguing with her father. 'And they deserve it,' she continued, 'for they are sensible and level-headed traditionalists, and I believe their vote will counteract the rashness of all the young men who want change, any kind of change, and believe it will make them rich.'

The princess, besides being something of a feminist, is also a poetess.

The next day she presented me with a book of her poems which were lyrical and romantic and, like Samoan singing, nostalgic for the past.

We munched our way through the sandwiches, and brooded over the thought of what promises unscrupulous *matai* might make to win election from conservative rivals. And His Highness, in beautifully sonorous, perfectly spaced phrases, recounted the terrible fate that had befallen other Polynesian islands in the name of Western 'progress'. 'In Hawaii,' he told us, 'there are now only a half of one per cent of full-blooded Hawaiians left on the islands. In Fiji, because of a United Nations crusade for human rights, and the British colonial legacy of imported Indians as a cheap labour-force, those Indians can, and certainly now do, protest and appeal internationally against any "discrimination" shown to them – and soon they will swamp the Fijians and take over the islands.

'In Samoa,' he continued, 'there was the same problem but on a much smaller scale,' with the Chinese people whom the Germans had imported to work in their coconut plantations. Fortunately, they have been absorbed into the population and 'now our immigration laws are much stricter – but human rights,' he added, and shook his fine head – 'human rights as a universal and flatly applied principle of reform, without taking into account local circumstances? It could lead to disaster in the long run.'

I asked him why one of the Samoan political parties had called itself the Human Rights Party. 'It was a fashionable word, I imagine,' he answered, 'a modern catch-phrase that sounded good, and vague enough not to compromise a political programme.' There was no finer form of justice, he believed, than that dispensed in Samoa by the old *matai* system. It was strict, but it was merciful, and everyone understood and accepted it.

We talked about the Gulf War, about the troubles in India and about education. Apparently there had been a recent UNESCO test in literacy throughout Polynesia and Samoa had come out of it badly, nearly bottom of the league. The Head of State felt the shame of this deeply. Apparently, since independence, the teacher associations had become more and more political, and education was now administered centrally by the government instead of each school being under the guidance of the village pastor and the chiefs. The result had been an increase of illiteracy from 2 per cent to a frightening 43 per cent. His Highness sadly admitted that everything was not yet perfect. 'Democracy is still a new concept among my people, and we must go slowly, gradually adapting ourselves and, when necessary, the constitution to bring about its true benefits.

'The Polynesian people,' he told me proudly, 'started here in Samoa.

You will hear theories of how we came here from somewhere else, but I believe we have *always* been here. God gave us a land of plenty, and we slowly developed in it a system which was good, the *matai* system. And then Christianity came and God doubly blessed us.' His Highness Malietoa has a deep, rumbly laugh, and when he says 'Saamoa', with a long, dark 'aah' for the first syllable, it is almost like hearing the murmur of waves breaking over a coral reef. I had a sudden vision of a square-rigged barque sighted against the low clouds that always line the Pacific horizon, between blue sky and turquoise sea, and a bewildered people's first sight of those they called 'the Sailing Gods'. 'Papalangi,' they shouted to each other in terror, as the billowing sails came nearer – 'The clouds are broken' – and 'Papalangi', or 'heaven-burster', is what the white man is called to this day. How little they knew then what an apt description it would prove to be.

The royal family are very proud of Vailima, and they assured me the central part, in which we were sitting, had been little changed since Robert Louis Stevenson had built it. As we talked I tried to sum up my impressions of this gentle, courtly old man. There was an element of relaxed bonhomie, an element of wisdom and astuteness, an element of kindness and – grace?

'Does Your Highness know the word "Manna"?' I asked him, 'and do you still have it?'

He looked startled, and asked in return if I knew what it meant, to which I answered I had heard it spoken of as the supernatural power that the Sacred High Chiefs of Samoa had inherited through descent from their Gods. Was it like charismatic power – or grace? The 'divine right' of kings? But he shook his head and said slowly, 'In the old religion, we believed it was a gift of the Gods that set High Chiefs apart. I suppose you could call it a supernatural gift,' and he changed the subject.

I wish now that I had stayed longer, but I knew too little about *Fa' Samoa* etiquette and did not want to overdo it, so after we had talked for a few more minutes I took my leave, my host accompanying me down the steps of the veranda and handing me into the High Commissioner's car with the most exquisite courtesy.

The following day Princess Momoe sent a message round to Aggie's. 'Would you like to have tea with Sasooga To'oa Salamasina at her Papauta school? I will pick you up at 3.30.' The High Commissioner of New Zealand, Adrian Simcock, had told me I would learn more about Samoa from this high-born lady, the eldest sister of the king, than from anyone else alive today. 'She is as wise as she is good,' he told me, 'and what is more she is great fun too.' Sasooga Salamasina never married.

Instead she has spent all her life and her considerable talents in the service of others as mistress, head mistress, and then Governor of the school where she still lives, which is a sort of Samoan Young Ladies' Academy and, though now old and ill, she remains a tremendously strong and forceful personality. She reminded me of my formidable but lovable Scottish aunt, a most capable and holy woman who became a nun and ran a hospital for many years with equal devotion and vigour.

We talked for several hours in the central mal'ae of the school campus and she explained things that I had not understood before: mats, for instance, which seems such a silly word for something that was so central to Samoan life. Fine mats (*tonga*) are made of the reed-like Pandanus plant which grows everywhere on the islands. It is gathered, sun-dried, split and woven into intricate patterns, ending with a texture and a suppleness so fine that it equals coarse linen. The circulation of fine mats was said to promote good fellowship among chiefs, but it was much more than that. They were used as clothing, payment for houses, boats and property, and were given by chiefs to their orators for services rendered. Presentations of fine mats were made at births, weddings and funerals, to parents on their deathbeds and on almost every formal occasion. They were in fact the currency of the islands and their value depended on their quality and fineness of texture. In General Richardson's 'Fine Mats Ordinance' of 1923, he prohibited *malangas*, or formal visits, by chiefs from one district to another to present fine mats. As one young chief said at his trial for disobeying this order: 'Unlike Western currencies, I have never heard of anybody through fine mats committing adultery or murder.'

They are still used and, when I said goodbye to Sasooga Salamasina, she presented me with one, which I value so much that I would almost be prepared to murder anyone who took it from me.

N. B. and Vale:
It was with great sadness that I heard, in the summer of 1992, that Sasooga Salamasina had died. Our meeting made a great and lasting impression on me. It was not how she looked or what was said, but what I suddenly realised: here is sheer, unadulterated, unequivocal goodness – and that, for a brief moment, I warmed my hands at it.

23

TONGA

King Taufa'ahau Tupou IV

'It is back to the sweetness it has destroyed, that ultimately the course of progress must return.'

On my last night in Samoa, at Aggie's, there was a party. The tables under the roof of the dining *malae* were piled high with exotic flowers and fruit, our waitresses had transformed themselves into Dorothy Lamours for the occasion by garlands of orchids, a flower behind the ear and a kind of festive wiggle that did justice to both; the open-sided building had been closed at one end by mats and a large stage erected . . . an electric current of anticipation buzzed around the place.

'What's up?' I asked, and was told, with a lot of giggling, that Aggie's family and the staff were laying on an 'entertainment' at the beginning of the *fia-fia** and everyone was preparing for it. Having sat through a good many amateur concerts in odd corners of the world, I confess I was not all that thrilled at the prospect, but in due course, and to show willing, I put on my only best dress and joined two amiable Aussies at a table in front of the stage, with some long cool drinks to support us. What happened next was, to put it mildly, sensational.

The lights suddenly dimmed, flickered and went out; then, through the tropical darkness came from each and every side of us the throb of a thousand native drums, gentle at first, like the buzzing of bees, then louder, clearer, like the heartbeat of some sleeping child, then man, then monster, as it rose, slowly, menacingly, inexorably in deadly crescendo, to a final ear-splitting *crash*, an explosion of stunning, mind-blowing sound as a thousand lights dazzled and the empty stage erupted into a chanting and leaping frenzy of formidable warrior-killers. Near-naked, with oiled and gleaming skin, fringed armbands and little else they formed themselves into club-brandishing, spear-waving phalanxes of perfect symmetry. Chanting in unison a deep-throated, rhythmic war-song which seemed

---

* A *fia-fia* is a celebration, feast, or party.

like the invitation to a massacre. They ended each stanza with a double stamp and a kind of short, coughing bark, 'Ugh-Ugh-Uuuuugh', followed by a wild screech which was quite simply blood-curdling.

The placid Australians gripped their drinks, or each other, and one little boy stood frozen in the aisle between tables, too frightened to move. And then it was all over, and the next item was a languorous love-song whose predictable harmonies rose and faded like the gentle waves of Samoa's palm-fringed beaches.

It was all good stuff but nothing, not even a charming, nostalgic 'Goodbye R.L.S., we miss you so' which had obviously been composed after their hero's death in 1894, or a grand finale sung by Aggie's daughter and grandchild in a *hula hula* skirt, matched the excitement of that first war-dance. And what would have interested an anthropologist was that at least one-third of our undressed 'warrior' waiters were tattooed from naked knee to naked hip.

Fa' Samoa lives on, in spite of universal suffrage.

The next morning was 10 April, and I flew out to Tonga by Samoa Air for my midday audience with King Taufa'ahau Tupou IV the following day. At least that was what I expected. The airport bus decanted us at the tiny airport in good time and all went well until halfway over the sea, when the aeroplane suddenly made a U-turn from its south-west direction and the captain told us over the intercom that we were returning to Samoa as part of the landing gear had come adrift and it could not be repaired in Tonga. He hoped the missing part could be found in Samoa and was going back to see.

I sat on a green plastic seat for the next three hours and worried. Could it? Would it? Wouldn't it? And, if the spare part was not found, what then? The airport buzzed with rumour, some passengers spoke of delays lasting for days, others thought it was the coffin in the hold, slipped in after our luggage, which only a few people had noticed. 'Perhaps he doesn't want to leave Samoa?' was suggested by a tow-haired wit. We drank cup after cup of musty airport coffee and I bit my nails and fumed. But at last, after nearly four hours, the little plane was in the air again with, we could only hope, every bit screwed on properly, and, sure enough, we landed safely in Tonga as dusk was falling.

Tongatapu, the main island of the Tongan group, looked very flat from the air, and so it should, being a coral atoll, but not nearly as flat as I felt a few minutes later on reading the polite but firm letter I was handed by the government protocol lady, Mrs Akosita, who had come to meet me.

It was dated Friday 11 April and informed me that, owing to the aeroplane's late arrival and His Majesty's departure the next morning for Auckland, it was much regretted etc., etc. My audience, which I had flown halfway round the world to obtain, had been cancelled! 'But it's for *tomorrow!*' I protested, and sat down in the nearest VIP chair in the VIP lounge, feeling a good deal less than a VIP. 'They've got the date wrong! This is Thursday and I'm seeing His Majesty on *Friday* . . .' My voice trailed off in sudden and miserable doubt.

Mrs Akosita looked at me more in sorrow than in anger and explained as one would to the stupidest child in the class that as I had crossed the dateline when I flew from Auckland to Samoa and gained a day, so when I recrossed it on my return I must inevitably lose one. This was indeed 6.00 p.m. on *Friday 11th*, and my audience had been for noon. The second half of Thursday had floated off into the ether somewhere between Samoa and Tonga!

The letter kindly suggested that His Majesty could see me the following week in Auckland, and would I please inform his Secretariat if this were possible 'as time was of the essence'?

There was no possible chance of this as I was booked all the way back to Britain on a round-trip ticket starting that weekend. "What is His Majesty doing *now?*" I asked in desperation.

'Giving the prizes away at a school cricket match.'

'What will he be doing tomorrow before the plane leaves?'

'His Majesty always jogs and takes exercise in the early morning.' There was absolutely no solution.

We motored towards Nuku'alofa in gloomy silence, while I thought up wild schemes for circumventing fate, but when Mrs Akosita deposited me at the International Dateline Hotel (why rub it in?) on the water-front, we had both agreed that my only chance of seeing the king was to catch up with him the next morning in the VIP lounge at the airport we had just left, and *hope* to be presented, for we were both booked on the same plane to Auckland, the first leg of my long journey home.

The kind protocol lady had done all she could to help and she now left me with, no doubt, a sigh of relief and two telephone numbers: the public relations office of the Foreign Ministry and His Majesty's private secretary. I also had our own High Commission's chargé's name and telephone number in my diary. The first two proved useless, but Martin Fidler, who was acting British High Commissioner in his boss's absence, turned up trumps. He sounded calm and reassuring on the telephone and responded to my wail of woe with a practical suggestion. He and his wife were going out to dinner but they would meet me for a drink in the bar of my hotel in an hour's time and we would put our heads together and think out a plan of action.

The best two hotels in Tongapatu lie off-shore and the International Dateline is described as 'moderate' in the guide books and travel articles. It is built around a dusty courtyard in great concrete slabs, with bedrooms leading on to concrete passages and concrete stairways, weather-stained and somewhat chipped. I looked round the grand 'suite' I had been booked into and found that, after the idiosyncratic comforts of Aggie Grey's, I didn't like it. The view from my concrete balcony was also uninspiring – acres of tarmac with a palm tree here and there, a long empty quay and a distant ocean beyond the reef. However, bathed and refreshed, I came down to find the Fidlers already installed in a corner of the bar. He is a sandy-haired East Coast Scot, small and intelligently positive, with a friendly and engaging manner, indubitably of the breed that ran the British Empire successfully for over a hundred years, though such an unfashionable thought could not be voiced today and I quickly stifled it.

His wife is a pretty young woman, small and slender, with equal enthusiasm and considerable charm which she now proceeded to exercise on a large and rumbustious High Chief whom they had recognised drinking in the bar and whom they called over to our table.

He was a cosmopolitan, not to say Americanised Chief, called Kai-huai, and he had just returned from Hawaii and was working off its inevitable hangover on a dog's hair, or whatever the expression is. Dressed in a smart tropical suit with an abundance of gold chains over his massive shirt front, he reminded me of Lhendup, the Queen Mother's flashy brother in far-away Bhutan, with the same larger than life bon-homie and clubability. He thought it a great joke that I had mislaid a day on my journey to Tonga, but also that it would be an inconceivable slight on his country and his king if they were not fully represented in a book about reigning royalty. He was on my side from then on and we plotted tactics over glasses of double whiskies, his size precluding any other, and lots of cheer. There would be no difficulty, he told us, in reaching the VIP lounge next morning, though of course it would be off-limits to ordinary travellers that day. Mrs Akosito should simply tell our chauffeur to drive through the guard at the gate and he himself would arrive early and be there to greet me. The king usually rested in the lounge before departure and held a kind of informal court with most of his cabinet and the members of the diplomatic corps who always came to see him off. It would be easy to slip me in, and then ask if I could be presented.

The Fidlers went off to their dinner-party and, considerably reassured, I found a quiet table in a corner of the very formal Dateline dining-room where I ate a surprisingly well cooked and served dinner (including savoury), straight out of 'Mrs Beeton'. Towards the end of it a tall, middle-aged New Zealander, with the pinch-faced countenance of an accountant or income-tax inspector, came into the restaurant with not one, but *three* very young Tongan tarts.* They wore micro-skirts, off-the-shoulder flounces, sequins and feathers wherever there was room for them, and four-inch spike heels. They winked at the old waiter, blew smoke-rings like 1930s cinema vamps and giggled charmingly with each other, and only occasionally with their escort. I longed to know whether they were theatrical bimbos, trainee bank clerks or cousins of his wife, and who went upstairs with whom, but they were still eating when I left the dining-room and the next morning I saw their host paying his bill, equally stiff and correct, but looking distinctly tired.

That evening I revised my notes about Tonga and finished Sir Harry Luke's breezy biography of the King's famous mother, Queen Salote, who had made such waves at Queen Elizabeth's coronation in 1953.

Tonga is a Polynesian word meaning 'south'. Its early history is much the same as Samoa's, by whose inhabitants it was almost certainly colonised. White explorers seeking the conquest of new territory, white missionaries seeking the conquest of souls, white men on the run, seeking asylum from convict-ships or press-gangs, all played their part in the 'European-isation' of these islands, but in Tonga, as in Tahiti and Fiji, there were regular kings and regular dynasties (in fact, a multiplicity of them) and a less complicated system of succession than in Samoa.

A seventeenth-century Dutchman called Tasman was the first navigator to discover Tongatapu. He called there briefly on his way south (no prize for guessing where he went next!); but no other Europeans followed him until Captain James Cook, that best of Yorkshiremen and finest of explorers, was sent by the Admiralty to the southern Pacific in HMS *Endeavour* to observe the transit of the planet Venus across the sun's face in an eclipse that the Royal Society had worked out would occur in 1769. Captain Cook made three voyages of discovery in Polynesia. On the second he called at Tongatapu, but did not stay. On the third he returned in HMS *Resolution* and, having at last found a good anchorage, made the archipelago his base, staying for many months,

---

* At least, I think they were Tongan, but had no means, or inclination, to confirm it.

afloat and on shore, in what he had christened 'the Friendly Isles'. In 1779 he left Tongapatu and sailed for Tahiti, calling in on the Sandwich Isles where, on the night of 14 February, he was most cruelly and wantonly murdered.

Captain Cook's journals, besides being entertaining reading, give an acutely observed and detailed overview of Polynesia in the eighteenth century and from them we have learned (once he had sorted out the confusion surrounding it) a lot about the Tongan monarchy, or rather, the large number of Tongan monarchs who seem to have co-existed at this time.

According to ancient tradition the Tongan kings descended, like the high chiefs of Samoa, directly from the Gods (the first Ha'a king was considered to be the son of Tangaloa, the Sun God) and for many centuries were the sole and hereditary rulers of the archipelago, combining both spiritual and temporal power. But it would seem that in about 950 AD the Tui Tonga dynasty grew tired of being kings and decided to appoint a temporal and executive ruler who would take over the day-to-day burden of monarchy (settling disputes, conferring honours, planting trees, going to war – the usual) and they retired into a passive, but much revered spiritual leadership of the community which, though retaining considerable power, necessitated no work, of any kind, ever again. The new dynasty of temporal rulers became known as *Tui Ha'atakalau* and ruled successfully for at least three centuries when exactly the same thing happened again. About 1470 the *Ha'atakalau* elevated themselves into the position of much revered spiritual leaders of the nation, and intermediaries between the *Tui Tongas* and a third ruling house, the *Tui Kanokupolu*, on whom they unloaded all the more tedious and difficult duties of temporal rule while they themselves retired into a kind of permanent monarchic sabbatical. This situation lasted another three hundred years, which brings us to the time of Captain Cook's visit.

It was King Fatafehi of the Kanokupolu dynasty whom James Cook eventually recognised as the supreme and legitimate ruler of Tonga and it was with him that he formed an amused and affectionate friendship. Initially, however, there had been considerable confusion – a treacherous but charming High Chief of the northern islands of Vava'u and Ha'apai, called Finau, had been the first to welcome the British, guide them to safe anchorages and entertain them with dancing, feasting and fun, while a silent but impressive grandee known as Latou Lipolu had followed the Captain's ship wherever it anchored, attaching his sailing canoe to its stern, but never speaking or coming aboard. (He was once heard to laugh, but no one knew at what.) They were both believed to be kings of some kind and it is indeed possible that the silent one was a descendant of the original *Tui Tonga* kings, for the natives treated him with great respect; once King Fatafehi turned up, however, it was clear he was the supreme ruler of the islands and he helped the British expedition in every possible way. The final parting between the two unlikely friends is most touchingly described in the last pages of Cook's journal.

By some strange quirk of history or fate, a second and even more closely observed account of Tonga and its exotic monarchy was to entertain the British public only a generation later. Dictated to a Dr Martin, and published under his name, this is the classic South Seas adventure story of all time and almost certainly the source of R. M. Ballantyne's famous book *Coral Island*. What made it exceptional was that it was true. Not unnaturally it had an immediate and international literary success.

It is the strange tale of a thirteen-year-old clerk who, beguiled by a sea-captain's romantic descriptions of the South Pacific islands, abandoned his career as an apprentice in a London lawyer's office and sailed with Captain Duff in the *Port au Prince*, a 500-ton privateer which, after many adventures (and the death of the captain), anchored in a leaking and storm-racked condition off Lifuka, one of the Ha'apai islands of the Tongan archipelago. Now captained by a stubborn and credulous First Mate, the crew mutinied and half of them left the ship, to be robbed and clubbed to death by the islanders, while the other half, without anyone in command, remained on board to be robbed and clubbed to death by a raiding party of the same. Young Will Mariner, by now fourteen, was fortunately mistaken for a High Chief's son and his life was spared. Indeed he was treated very kindly and subsequently adopted by the King of Ha'apai, who was none other than the son of Captain Cook's roguish friend, Finau, and went by the same name. This Finau had finally achieved the regal status his father had pretended to by murdering the son of Fatafehi, supreme King of Tongatapu, in his sleep. But he was still only King of Ha'apai and Vava'u and though he coveted it, Tongapatu, the principal island of the group, had fortifications which had so far remained impregnable.

One of the most enjoyable parts of the book is how young Will, the brains behind a new assault, and four other survivors from the ill-fated *Port au Prince* use the ship's twelve-pound carronades as artillery to capture the fort, which they bombarded for several hours. The defending chiefs hold a consultation sitting on a large wooden canoe: at the moment when they are deciding on a last desperate rush to capture the white men, a carronade ball hits the canoe they are sitting on and blows it and them to pieces. Sensation! And end of chapter.

Soon afterwards the island submitted to King Finau and he was proclaimed King of Tongapatu.

It is all good 'Boy's Own' stuff and there are many other stories of treachery and savagery, loyalty and deep affection, superstition and pragmatism in the book – the strangest perhaps being when young Mariner is nearly killed by his 'blood brother', the old king's son, for *sneezing* when the king was about to perform a ceremony of 'head-breaking' in memory of his father's death. This is when Tongan mourners bash and cut themselves about the head to demonstrate their grief; for in Tonga it is taboo to sneeze when anyone is making plans, especially on such a formal occasion.

Finally, after seven years of exile, a British ship is sighted on the horizon and the young castaway's account of his final dash for freedom is as exciting as anything in the book. When Will finally reaches England he rather disappointingly settles down to a life of admirable rectitude and extreme dullness. It is rather like Ella Maillard, Peter Fleming's dauntless travelling companion, who brought 'News from Tartary' and ended her life by being run over by a bus. But one can't have everything, and too much excitement is perhaps best kept between the covers of a book.

In Britain, towards the end of the eighteenth century, the news of Captain Cook's tragic end and the publication of his journals and maps brought images of an exotic and hitherto unknown world to an eager and receptive public. It was a heathen world where natural beauty and innocence mingled with savagery and horror, and where the real and fictional heroes of later publications stirred not only the imagination of the Romantic Movement of the day, but also, strangely enough, that of the sober and earnest followers of the Evangelical Church. To these Christian enthusiasts the power of demagogic preaching to simple people had already been demonstrated at home, but now the idea of the 'noble savage', patiently awaiting conversion to a better life which they alone could bring, the possibility, even likelihood of a martyr's crown, the warm and sunny climes in which they would labour, must have seemed particularly alluring in the rain-sodden valleys of Wales and Scotland. It certainly produced, almost overnight, an army of volunteers to preach the gospel and save souls in foreign parts, and they were ready to sail wherever ships could be found to carry them.

In 1796, ten years before Will Mariner's adventure began – and while Samoa was still waiting for the *Mission of Peace* – the London Missionary Society sent a small band of brave and dedicated, but hideously unprepared Christians to Tongatapu. They were not ordained ministers, these were to follow later, but simple artisans. They had no interpreter and could only tell the gospel story in sign language, which must have looked pretty silly. They did not impress the Tongan chiefs, who cast covetous eyes on their tools which, it soon became obvious, were more appreciated than their message. They made no converts and before long three of them had been massacred, six had returned to England and only one, who had 'gone native', remained in Tonga.

They were followed, some twenty years later, by an expedition of Methodist missionaries from Australia. It was led by an ordained minister named Walter Lawrie, a tough and acerbic character who at least had made some effort to learn the language, but his stumbling use of it caused at first merriment and then misunderstanding and deep suspicion among 'the heathens'. Their comment on his impassioned preaching was: 'Your religion is very good for you and ours is very good for us,' and the poor Reverend was stumped for a reply. After only fifteen months and in spite of the protection of an outsize Chief called Palau, it became evident that this mission had also failed and that the lives of the missionaries and their families were in grave danger. As soon as it was feasible to do so they returned to Sydney, the Reverend Walter leaving this rather jaundiced opinion of the natives' character as his Tongan *vale*: 'The Navigators who first visited these islands and the castaway mariners who have lived with them for some years have attempted to wash these Ethiopians white. The fact is, however, they follow their natural inclinations and are earthly, sensual, devilish. It is not considered a disgrace to lie or steal unless detection follows; and then it is very rarely punished; and as to chastity, it is little regarded. Their whole lives are a scene of corruption . . .'

Ten more years passed before a new effort was made to convert the tough Tongan heathen and this time the challenge was taken up by a young village blacksmith from Worcestershire, a very extraordinary village blacksmith with simple and invincible faith, a good deal of charm with it, but above all, gentle and patient ways. John Thomas sailed from England to New South Wales in 1825, but it took him over a year to convince the Australian Methodists that he was the right man for Tonga. He landed at Nuku'alofa in 1826 and set up his mission at Hififu under the protection of a chief called Ata, whose sister was the local sorceress.

At first things went badly and it looked as if he would be no more successful than his predecessors, but John Thomas was a survivor and, though he made no converts, he did slowly and gradually make friends, Eventually he was joined by two more missionaries and their families, which gave the faltering establishment new heart. Together they began using Will Mariner's Tongan grammar and vocabulary, recently published in England, composed cheerful hymns in the Tongan tongue and opened schools, which soon flourished. Then one day Nathanial Turner, who had set up a mission house at Nuku'alofa, received a letter from King Finau, in Vava'u (the very same Finau who had wept when he said goodbye to Will Mariner, and had begged to be taken to England with him). In it he wrote: 'I am tired of my Spirits: they tell me so many lies that I am sick of them . . . My Island, Sir, will turn to the Great God because I am the only Chief on the island. I have no-one to control me. When I turn they all turn . . .' and so he did, though not before a personal missionary had been specially sent out from England to convert him and to teach his people the advantages of the *Lotu.*

Tubou, King of Tongatapu, was already a secret Christian and there only remained the conversion of Taufa'ahau, the handsome young King of Ha'apai, a monarch of great strength and character – who, incidentally, was Queen Salote's great-grandfather – to complete the christianisation of the archipelago.

King Taufa'ahau did not do things by half and before long he invited the principal people of his kingdom, or 'Tout Tonga', to a great feast at which he publicly declared his new belief in Christianity. 'After which he marched to the *mala'e* and destroyed the heathen temples before the eyes of the people.' It was a brave thing to do, but as he had not been struck dead by either one of his own subjects or their *aitu* (heathen Gods) his example was followed by many of the people of Ha'apai.

At his request John Thomas, the holy blacksmith from the Welsh borders, now joined him on Ha'apai. They evidently formed an incongruous but deep and lasting friendship which influenced King Taufa'ahau throughout his reign. It was a friendship which probably also saved his life.

When Taufa'ahau decided to *marry* his favourite wife according to the rites of the Christian Church (and presumably abandon any other ones) he crossed a Rubicon, but as usual he did it with style, inviting a huge company of the Tongan Establishment to witness the event and to join in the usual great feast that would follow it. But the handsome bridegroom had only just risen to his feet to propose a toast to his Christian bride when the wrath of the aitu struck and he suddenly collapsed in agony, followed by strange convulsions, and was carried off in what the onlookers felt sure was a moribund condition. The 'heathen' faction among his guests wished to transport him immediately to a nearby island whose powerful spirits might just possibly stave off what looked like certain death, but the king had enough strength left to resist this and he was carried instead to his private quarters where John Thomas joined him. A powerful emetic was quickly administered and though it was touch and go throughout the night, a weak but well Taufa'ahau emerged from his *fale** the next morning and the festivities were resumed – no doubt to the carefully concealed chagrin of some of his guests.

In 1831 Taufa'ahau was baptised and took the name George, or as Tongans write it, 'Jorji',† 'out of respect of our good old King George [III] whose memory is cherished in these islands,' John Thomas wrote home. His three children were baptised Charlotte (Salote in Tongan), David (Tefita, but surely this is a *Welsh* David?) and Josiah (Josaia). Two years later Finau, who had finally received his 'special' missionary and also been baptised, died 'In the arms of the Lord' and bequeathed his kingdom of Vava'u to Taufa'ahau, who now became the ruler of all three of the main groups of islands in the 'Friendly' archipelago.

Though the missionaries in Tonga had, in less than a dozen years, made great progress in christianising and thereby inevitably Europeanising the islands, the great majority of their inhabitants remained true to their 'heathen Gods' and a long period of danger and unrest followed the conversion of the three kings.

To anyone who takes the trouble to rummage among the dusty accounts of Wesleyan Church history, it soon becomes clear that the early Methodist missionaries to Tonga were not only a brave but also a tolerant lot, who believed more in example, education and patient prayer than in wild sermons that induced hysteria; the bullying and the often naked cupidity, which gave their brothers of the London Missionary Society in Samoa such a bad name, do not seem to have existed in Tonga.

But nevertheless there were disagreements and disputes, which sometimes ended in bloodshed and tragedy, and poor King Tubou never lived to see the 'wars of religion' resolved for he died a sad and worn-out old man who had only really wished to be left (like many of his predecessors) in happy idleness and peace.

He was succeeded by his kinsman, King George of Ha'apai and Vava'u, who was then elected *Tubou Tu'i Kanokupolu*, and became George I of Tonga, supreme monarch of all the Friendly Isles.

King George reigned for an astonishing seventy years. He had been

---

* *Fale* – native house.
† Tongans usually write foreign words which they have adopted in the same way that they pronounce them.

born at the end of the eighteenth century and died at the end of the nineteenth, in 1893, aged ninety-six. In that time he not only succeeded in unifying his dispersed and disparate kingdoms into a small but vigorous nation, and in christianising and educating its peoples, but also in giving them their first taste of democracy and, most important of all, a constitution.

It was a written constitution based on the British one, which of course does not in fact exist, so it too was a bit vague, frequently tinkered with and often violated, but it did give the islanders a voice in their country's affairs, a voice that grew stronger as the years went by.

During the second half of the nineteenth century the European powers suddenly became interested in the South Pacific. Their beautiful sailing ships had given way to hideous ironclads and steam, and the acquisition of good harbours and coaling stations was an important element in their growing rivalry and competitive trade. Warships prowled around Polynesia while their governments and nationals bought up concessions and real estate, promising rich rewards to the gullible islanders and their kings. By 1900 all the islands of the South Pacific, except the Friendly Isles, had come under the control of one or other of the Great Powers, and it was perhaps King George's greatest achievement that he maintained the independence and sovereignty of his own islands when all about him were losing theirs.

King George's last years were clouded by the emergence of an eccentric and rather comic adviser, a Methodist minister of dubious character called the Reverend Shirley Baker, whose influence over the ageing King became paramount and dangerous. While still a Reverend, Baker involved King George in a fortunately nebulous deal with the Germans over the lease of a coaling station in Vava'u, which earned Baker a German medal and an unspecified financial award. He then left the Church, went into politics and became Prime Minister, accumulating, they say, a small fortune on the way.

The Reverend Baker advised the king to set up a State Church, which split the Methodists in Tonga into two bitterly opposed and warring factions, and he accused the Free, or traditional, faction of plotting with the British Vice-Consul in an unsuccessful attempt to assassinate him. This was going too far, and the wrath of Queen Victoria's Empire descended on him. He was neatly disposed of by Sir John Thompson, Governor of Fiji and High Commissioner for the Western Pacific, who visited Tonga and, discovering how far the country's books had been cooked by Baker, ordered him to be immediately deported from the islands.

After his death in 1893 King George Tubou was succeeded by his son, George II. King George I had been much respected and loved and, until his health failed, he was universally regarded as the doyen of the Pacific Islands, whose goodwill (and good advice) was sought by everyone. Tonga was desolated by his demise and plunged itself into a period of extravagant mourning which further depleted the almost empty national coffers – vast sums being spent on enormously expensive funeral feasts which went on for months. No one in their sorrow felt able to work. During the last years of his life King George had leant heavily on the advice of the remarkable Basil Thompson, an excellent diplomat whom the British government had sent out to repair the damage done by the disastrous ex-Reverend. He had acted as an Assistant Prime Minister and 'elder brother' to the late king and he had warned Lord Curzon, the Foreign Secretary, 'that Tonga's seizure (by a foreign power) was only a question of months, *unless she had a powerful protector*'. Now, in her greatly weakened state, she seemed even more vulnerable and the British government decided to send a Commissioner to Tonga to negotiate a Treaty of Friendship and Protection (something that had eluded the people of Samoa on numerous occasions). The task fell, somewhat naturally, on the protean British administrator.

Sir Basil, who had, since leaving Tonga, become Governor of Northampton Prison, was given temporary leave of absence and sailed for Nuku'alofa in HMS *Porpoise*. It was a delicate situation, a case of putting a reliable and home-grown dog in the manger. Britain had no territorial ambitions in Tonga, but she had to persuade a young and inexperienced, and probably suspicious King George of this, assuring him that her concern was purely for Tonga's survival. Under the treaty that Sir Basil hoped to negotiate, Tonga would place itself under the protection of Great Britain and undertake not to make agreements with other nations. Foreign affairs would be transacted through the British Agent and Consul, who was to be responsible to the High Commissioner for the Western Pacific, on Fiji. The British Consul would be entitled to review the budget and veto unwise expenditure. He would also, through a Consular court, try any British or foreign subject accused of a major crime.

Through Basil Thompson's delicate diplomacy all went smoothly, and the treaty was signed in 1900 despite the convoluted intrigues of Père Oliver, a Catholic missionary who also happened to be a zealous French citizen.

So, in 1900, Tonga became a completely autonomous independent

state and a self-governing kingdom which voluntarily, and only for specific purposes, placed itself under British protection.

Tonga played a very minor role in the Great War, some of its English-
speaking nationals enlisting in the New Zealand forces, and the few
German firms on the island being liquidated. George II never lived to
see the peace that followed, however, for he died in April 1918 to be
succeeded by his daughter, Princess Salote.

Many people remember Queen Salote, Tubou III, and her triumphant
progress in an open landau through the streets of London in Queen
Elizabeth II's coronation procession. It rained, she smiled and waved and
there was something about her that captured every Cockney heart.
'Who's *that?*' a voice in the crowd shouted, and its owner pointed to a
much smaller individual who sat beside the very large Queen Salote.
'*That*'s her lunch!' came the typical Londoner's answer, and the joke
went round the world and is even said to have been appreciated by the
queen herself. And that would not surprise me, for there is something
about them, so unaffected and friendly, so dignified yet down-to-earth,
that nothing can assail the poise, the natural kindliness and warmth of
these extraordinary Polynesian women, whose charm, as well as their
size, has become legendary.

Just like Queen Victoria, Princess Salote was only eighteen when she
succeeded her father on the Tongan throne, but she had already married,
aged seventeen, Uilame Tungi, a Tongan noble who was a direct
descendant of the Tui Ha'atukalau kings.

Salote's grandfather, George I, had succeeded to the spiritual rights of
the Tui Tongas, as well as being nineteenth Tui Kanokupolu himself, so
when Salote and Tungi's eldest son was born on 4 July 1918, he united
three of Tonga's most ancient royal lines, a good augur for the future. Tungi
was an able man and Salote made him her Premier quite early in her reign,
as no doubt Queen Victoria would have loved to have made Prince Albert.
But Tungi died quite suddenly in 1941 and a high chief called Ata was
appointed to bridge the gap until her son, the crown prince, finished his
education in Australia. Prince Taufa'ahau returned from Sydney University with an honours degree in jurisprudence, but he had also distinguished
himself in another dimension – as a fine athlete: he had played rugger,
and rowed in his university's champion teams. Almost as soon as he
returned to Tonga he became involved in the government of his future
kingdom. He was first made Minister of Education, with cabinet rank,
and this was followed by various other portfolios, until he succeeded Ata
as his mother's Prime Minister, a post he held for sixteen years.

*   *   *

The next morning Mrs Akosita and I were almost the first to arrive at Longatapu airport and we passed through the guard at the gate without any difficulty. A military band and a company of Tongan soldiers were practising their drill on the dusty parade ground beside the VIP compound, their sergeant's voice occasionally shattering the polite murmur of the royal guests who now gathered around the veranda of the small wooden building.

Tongan voices, one of them told me, are even more powerful than Samoan ones. In earlier times the king's commands were passed from one end of the island to the other by people lying down and *shouting* his messages on to their neighbours. It was known as 'making proclamation while reclining', and, as a system of communication, it has much to recommend it, once you begin thinking about it.

Soon Kaihuai arrived, with even more gold chains and a mat around his middle, followed by the Minister of Justice, the Premier (who is the king's brother) and other members of the cabinet. Two ancient and venerable nobles, with whom I talked briefly, had the same aura of old-fashioned courtesy and grace that I had just encountered in Apia, with the Samoan head of state. All wore neatly folded 'fine mats' around their middles above their *lava-lavas*, which someone assured me were absolutely *de rigueur* on formal occasions in Tonga. There were more ceremonial mats below the king's throne, a black and gold brocade armchair of immense size that I could see through a window of the VIP lounge.

The diplomats arrived in pairs: Chinese from Taiwan, Japanese, Swedes and Germans, Australians and New Zealanders. Then, to my joy, Martin Fidler, looking very smart and official. Soft drinks were handed round and talk was desultory and difficult if tried with the Chinese, who spoke no European language.

Then, with a growl of motorbikes, whose outriders preceded it, a long, sleek black Cadillac drew up, number plate 1 TON and a large lumbering figure emerged from it. His Majesty King Taufa'ahau Tupou IV. He acknowledged the salute of the officer in command and disappeared with him to inspect the guard of honour while we stood at attention and the band played the Tongan National Anthem.

The VIP guests then trooped into the VIP lounge, the Fidlers sweeping me in beside them in fine style, and took their places in a formal circle round the edge of the room.

I talk, I think, to the Premier, His Royal Highness Prince Fatafehi Tuipelehake, which is heavy going as we, neither of us, are quite sure who the other is, and then to the Minister of Justice, an Oxford man who has just returned from London and is mad about rugger (as is Kai and almost everyone else in the room). I am not very good at this and before I make a complete fool of myself I am saved by the arrival of the king, who makes a stately entrance and proceeds with great dignity towards his outsize black and gold armchair. He is wearing a navy-blue city suit, a shirt and tie, a navy-blue solar topi and dark glasses. He is very large, a bit lame and very impressive. For about three long minutes there is a complete and somewhat Elysian silence. Then the New Zealand High Commissioner, who is seated next to the throne, bravely breaks it and everyone relaxes.

A servitor in a white *lava-lava* and scarlet epaulettes brings His Majesty a glass of orange juice in a kind of slithering crouch that reminds me of Thailand, and I ponder on the enormous contrast between the royal styles of Samoa and Tonga. Eventually someone I have been talking to suggests that I should be presented and he goes over and explains my presence to the king, who seems to nod affably in my direction, though this is difficult to ascertain because of the shades (Oh why, oh why will they wear them?). I advance nervously to the throne, curtsy and apologise for the aborted audience. We talk about aeroplanes and their disadvantages. His Majesty flew in one lately whose cargo door blew off in mid-flight. Out streamed the luggage, to the dismay of the passengers who watched their cherished possessions flow past them into space. I tell him about the fireball Fitzroy and I once encountered over Vienna. He regrets that I cannot stay longer and I promise to return and visit *all* the islands and His Majesty at a more propitious time. After such pleasantries I return to my seat and shortly afterwards our flight is called. On the way out I am presented to HM Queen Halaevelu Mata'Aho of Tonga, a pleasant and good-looking matron of quite ordinary size. Both king and queen shake hands with the assembled company, who bow and curtsy.

The procession to the aircraft is swift and orderly, though at one moment the band strikes up the National Anthem again, which causes everyone to freeze, but this allows my brilliant protocol lady, who has been hovering, to shove my boarding card, tickets, etc, into my hand and say goodbye. I wonder whether to kiss her, but decide she might think it a lapse in formality, and Martin Fidler and I follow the royal party at a respectful distance to the steps of the plane. At the top of them I collide with the queen and her three-year-old grandchild, who is tugging her into its cabin. 'Is he good?' I ask.

'Hardly ever!' she answers with a charming smile, and allows herself to be pulled inside.

On the journey I was able to have a few more words with the queen, whom I found to be a comfortable person, easy, sympathetic, with a happily compatible sense of humour. The baby prince wriggled his way between her, the ADCs and his nanny, who may well have been a noble's daughter, and sat with me and the private secretaries, below the salt. He is an impish child, strong and good-looking, clearly destined for the rugger field.

There was a very old Tongan in my row who had only a smattering of English and was going to join his son in New Zealand. The stewardess and I filled in his landing forms for him and I only hope that Immigration was as kind to him as she was, for he was very inarticulate, half-blind, only just literate – and lovable.

So that was Tonga, a Polynesian nation utterly different from Samoa, its neighbour across the South Pacific Ocean, with a different social organisation and a different history for its kings. Both nations have clung to their independence and to their traditions, but they have gone separate ways.

In Samoa I felt the tug of a half-forgotten knowledge, of something that was unique and good, and nearly, but not completely, lost; its monarch the very embodiment of Fa' Samoa, and the natural heir to his forefathers. In Tonga there was a stiffness and unnaturalness about the protocol surrounding the king which seemed imported from a British court in Queen Victoria's time.

The mourning that succeeded the death of the king's grandfather showed how devoted the Tongans are to their royal family, and the Fidlers impressed on me that this is still so today. King Taufa'ahau Tupou and his brother, the Prime Minister, direct the government of the islands skilfully, and without opposition, for they are both learned and capable and, more important, good men; but the spontaneously happy, abundantly beautiful, naturally enchanting Polynesian element that is immediately visible in Samoa seemed somehow to be lacking in Tonga – though it is unfair of me to come to any conclusion after such a short and truncated visit, an accident which was entirely of my own making.

Next time I shall bring with me to Tonga a calendar and a pocket calculator, and I shall visit all the islands of the archipelago, and I will almost certainly change my mind.

CONCLUSION AND
POSTSCRIPT

'May you live in interesting times.'

TRADITONAL CHINESE CURSE

THE ONES THAT GOT AWAY

There were two monarchs in Europe that I had not visited, two in the Middle East, and one in North Africa.

The Court Chamberlain of Queen Beatrix of the Netherlands advised me, with impeccable promptness and courtesy, that he regretted, etc, etc, but Her Majesty never gave interviews, and that was that.

After a very long wait I finally received an answer to my letter to King Baudouin of the Belgians from his ambassador in London, passing on a curt turn-down from the office of the king in Brussels. Regular visitors to Beaufort, when I was a child, had included his grandparents, King Albert and Queen Elizabeth – and I must confess that I was slightly hurt by this apparent lack of reciprocity – but I have since learned that His Majesty has been more or less an invalid for the last two years, and very likely was never shown my letter.

Sadly, one cannot help thinking that a monarch who has to abdicate when he wishes to express an opinion on a matter of conscience – as did King Baudouin, a devout Catholic, when he felt unable to give his assent to a Bill legalising abortion – represents a monarchy which is an anachronism and which may well disappear with his eventual demise.

The Gulf War intervened just as I was starting to wangle an interview with His Majesty, King Fahd of Saudi Arabia, and my helpful go-between and I decided that he had more important things to think about.

This was also, à plus forte raison, the case for the ruler of Kuwait, King Javer Al Hamad Al-Sabah.

But it is His Majesty King Hassan of Morocco that I am most disappointed not to have visited. He is a clever and cultivated king who has led a very interesting life. I have read and enjoyed his autobiography and I believe his country in spring is one of the most beautiful in the world. He has a very pleasant ambassador in London who was not only helpful, but also did his best to get things moving. But, alas, for the purpose of this book, King Hassan has one fatal fault – he very rarely answers letters, and in my case he didn't.

Of all the twenty reigning monarchs I did visit, plus one ex-empress/queen, and one king, as it were, in the slips, I can truthfully say I found no prototype and no clone. In fact there was a good deal less similarity between them than I had expected.

General Franco had told the young Don Juan Carlos, 'You will have to do it your own way,' and I soon discovered that the monarchs' individual ways, though surprisingly different, were all conditioned by their country's history, which is, of course, another way of saying by the story of their own ancestors.

I found in my travels that the present incumbents of the world's thrones were thoroughly aware of that history, family and dynastic pride being one of the few constants among all the kings I visited.

Their own roles today may be humbler but are more diverse and varied than those of their forefathers. I talked to representative monarchs, who led by example; business and entrepreneurial kings who helped make their countries rich; aesthetic and scholarly kings who inspired their subjects; anchormen kings who kept the peace; tutor-kings who taught their peoples the hard lessons of democracy; paternalistic kings who cared for their countries' poor and disadvantaged.

I found that strongly religious nations revere their monarchs more than pragmatic and materialistic ones, and show them more devotion.

I found that 'leadership', a kingly virtue, still existed, perhaps not in the style of Tamerlaine and Alexander but in a quiet and skilful way that, despite its modesty, was impressive.

I found that most monarchies have adapted and evolved to meet the exigencies of the modern world and that it is the inflexible ones that have been or are likely to be overthrown – that in Britain our monarchy, in the Prince of Wales's own words, 'has always adapted to different circumstances, and that *that* is its strength'.

Of all the monarchs I visited I did not find a single bad, idle or unuseful king or queen, and only one or two dull ones. I found that, though some of them, whether through their ambience or their personality, were more alarming and majestic than I had expected, others were a lot less frightening than I had been led to believe; but on the whole, yes, monarchs *are* different and they *do* command respect and, quite often, by their mere presence, a quite inexplicable awe.

But of that early, semi-religious, mystery-magic element of kingship that used to inspire armies and cure scurvy and pardon sinners, I sadly found little trace. A faint breath of it still lingered, perhaps, in Samoa, in the person of a good and simple king whose islands' beauties and ancient traditions have not yet been extinguished and where bare feet still touch the earth. But otherwise . . . no.

After nearly two years of travelling round the world inspecting kings, I came home in the aftermath of the Gulf War to find everyone concerned with new problems – the collapse of Communism and the fragmentation of the Soviet Union in the East, the EC's pressure for political union and perhaps a new kind of Holy Roman Empire emerging in the West.

'But how about our hallowed independence?' I asked. 'Our sovereignty? . . . patriotism? . . . "this sceptred isle" and all that sort of thing?'

'Oh, *patriotism*,' everyone answered. 'The trouble with patriotism is that it leads to nationalism, and nationalism, we all know, is a very bad thing. It leads to war.

'We must now all think,' they went on brightly, 'as *Europeans*, well, as Western Europeans, anyway. It's the only way to stop wars for ever, and it will also make us exceedingly rich.'

But thinking like a Western European does not have much appeal for me, neither does it make me feel any richer or safer than I felt before.

'Safer?' I retorted with some asperity. 'It looks to me as if wars, revolutions, mass starvation, rampant nationalism, massacres and mayhem are raging in almost every corner of the globe; that atom bombs are rolling around Eastern Europe like carpet bowls, that Eastern bloc nuclear scientists, driven mad by hunger, are putting themselves up for auction, that the southern Slavs are committing genocide, and that the world has never been a more dangerous place to live in.

'It is surely only a matter of time before Europe is caught up in some major conflagration, and when it is I doubt very much that the EC countries will act in unison. I think they will react as they have always done in the past: each country in its own, its very own interest, and the devil take the hindmost!

'And what is more,' I said, warming to my old fogey opinions, 'I do *not* believe that the days of individual nations and Christian kingdoms in Europe are numbered. On the contrary, when their solid and idiosyncratic citizens realise they are being bamboozled by the soothsayers, politicians and economic witch-doctors of today, they will suddenly wake up and rush to the ballot box – or at least write letters to *The Times*,' I finished on a rather weaker note.

What worries me most, however, is how such complex and open-ended issues can ever be understood by Joe Bloggs the ordinary voter, and how much our clever politicians really know about its effect on the status and equilibrium of our own sovereignty, our own constitution and our own monarchy.

Sir Edward Heath has said that sovereignty in Britain is a doctrine of a period that is past, but our sovereignty, by which I mean the authority of the Crown, acting through ministers who are accountable to parliament, is for me and many others a prized possession, dearly won and infinitely desirable, while the authority of unknown bureaucrats in Brussels – who are accountable to no one, have built-in political bias and different standards of honesty from our own – is not.

If the authority of Britain's ministers and parliament is diminished in certain respects by reason of the higher authority of a Federal Europe, then the Crown must surely be diminished too. And if we accept Walter Bagehot's doctrine that a constitutional sovereign has three rights: 'to be consulted, to encourage and occasionally to warn', then Queen Elizabeth herself is diminished, for these rights do not extend to the Council of Ministers in Brussels.

The British Constitution, based on Common Law and the devolution of power to an elected parliament has never been written down in black and white. It is a mystery, just as the Queen's Prerogative – the powers that the unwritten constitution has left the Queen – is also a mystery, for neither of them has ever been clearly or exactly defined.

I do not believe that, search where you will, there is any more explicit information available today as to what the Queen can actually do in a new situation of political and national crisis than there was in Walter Bagehot's day, when he believed that 'the Queen [Victoria it was then] has a hundred [such] powers which waver between reality and desuetude and would cause a protracted and very interesting legal argument if she tried to exercise them'.

That Queen Elizabeth II has no legislative power is clear and certain, the rest is a grey area of deliberate vagueness, some would call it 'obfuscation', others 'latitude', but this very mystery has its advantages. It brings with it a kind of accepted reverence and 'in times of transition' (Bagehot again) 'the traditional strength of hereditary monarchy is of incalculable use'.

'When there is a select committee on the Queen', he continues, 'the charm of royalty will be gone. Its mystery is its life. We must not let in daylight on magic. We must not bring the Queen into the combat of politics or she will cease to be reverenced by all combatants. She will become one combatant of many.'

The Queen is above politics and politicians, that again is certain, but might there not come a time when and if she felt the break-up of the United Kingdom was about to occur, or the sovereignty of her country was threatened by a European legislature – situations which have no historical precedent – when she possibly might wish to use, or try to use, her Royal Prerogative in a more dramatic way?

Bagehot wrote his much-quoted pronouncements on the British monarchy, the constitution and the Royal Prerogative in 1865. To find a more up-to-date version, just before the General Election of April 1992 and when it looked as if its outcome might be a 'hung' parliament, I went to see my old friend Lord St John of Fawsley (Norman St John-Stevas) in the suitably magnificent president's office he has settled into at the Arts Council's headquarters in St James's Square. He was both illuminating and encouraging.

I asked Norman what he thought, and what he thought was that I was being over-dramatic. He reaffirmed what I had already been told by Prince Charles. The strength of the British monarchy is its ability to adapt. The Queen is equally Queen of England, Queen of Scotland, Queen of Wales and Northern Ireland. Whether these nations choose to separate from the United Kingdom or form a different sort of federation will not affect her position, indeed in some ways it may strengthen it.

As for Europe, a political union is a long way off but, should it ever occur, the position of European monarchs would in the same way be greatly enhanced, for they would uniquely represent, in a harmonious yet un-homogenous way, the individuality of their countries – something that no ephemeral and forgettable president could ever do. Monarchy is above politics and therefore in countries where the population wishes to retain their national identity monarchy becomes more, not less, important as the most obvious repository and visible symbol of the nation's heart and soul.

I asked him whether Royal Prerogatives had now become RIPs and Norman explained to me better than anyone has ever done before our own Queen's Royal Prerogative.

I asked him whether Royal Prerogatives had now become RIPs and Norman explained to me better than anyone has ever done before our own Queen's Royal Prerogative.

All that was left, he said, of the Queen's historic Royal Prerogative was that if, for one reason or another, there is a deadlock in the election of a Prime Minister she has the right and duty to appoint one who, in her opinion, 'can form an administration which will command a majority in the House of Commons'. This she did on two occasions: in 1957 and 1973, but since their last unseemly leadership wrangle the Tory Party has altered its rules and a new apparatus for choosing their leader has been put in place, so that now even this small political power has disappeared – no doubt to the great relief of the Queen. Today, it would only be if a Prime Minister suddenly died, and a caretaker government had to take over until an election could be called, that Her Majesty might be called to re-exercise her ancient powers. In a hung parliament the Queen *is* still involved and the situation is more complicated. A basic rule would be that she would first send for the leader of the party that believed it could command a majority in the House of Commons. It would probably be the party with the greatest number of seats won in the General Election, but this could be tricky, and not necessarily follow, because of the horse-trading and alliances that another party could cook up.

We then talked about Bagehot, about whom Lord St John has written an excellent book, and our mutual belief that monarchy must always be a *show*, and a dazzling one at that. 'It is better to spend a million in dazzling when you wish to dazzle than three-quarters of a million in trying to dazzle and yet not dazzling,' wrote our hero. Add a couple or so of noughts today and the situation remains unchanged.

What has changed is the general public's attitude towards the expense of dazzling. Until quite recent times there was a sense of pride in the 'show' that was put on for royal and State occasions, but now that seems to be suffering a sea-change: grudging envy and discontent have crept in, with a good deal of misrepresentation by the tabloids and/or republican propaganda. The facts are that currently our royal family costs the British nation some £57 million a year – nearly £8 million under the Civil List and £49 million for the upkeep of royal palaces, overseas visits, yachts, trains and aircraft. In return, a cautious statistician would estimate that they promote at least ten per cent of Britain's £25 billion a year tourist trade (the British Tourist Authority says that fifty per cent of *all* overseas holidaymakers coming to London watch the Changing of the Guard at Buckingham Palace and hope to see the Queen); that they fill – and sell – at least five per cent of our national newspapers, and that they probably double the heavy end of our export market through state visits and royal hospitality. As well as this they support and invigorate half the charitable, social, health and defence organisations in the country and fight the evils of unemployment, poor housing and inner-city decline through the Prince of Wales's Trust schemes, which now contribute as much towards this end as a small government department (and cost the country nothing). In addition, they contribute the entire profits of the Crown Estates to the Exchequer (some £61 million annually), and the Queen has now decided to pay Income Tax on her private fortune, which is found not to be as large as the public expected. The country would, in fact, be a good deal poorer without them.

Another unhappy change there has been in my lifetime is the gradual trivialisation of the monarchy, encouraged once again by the media, and the public's insatiable hunger for prurient royal gossip, which, until the laws of the land are changed or our royal family all behave with greater circumspection than Caesar's wife, will continue to sell newspapers and make their owners richer – but will not, in my view, seriously rock the throne.

At the end of my visit Norman told me something so extraordinary that I am still at pains to believe it: the majority of people living under free, democratic systems of government in the world today are living under constitutional monarchies.

I said goodbye to this ardent monarchist, feeling much more cheerful about our royal family's fate, but also thinking, should not what we had talked about encourage other countries to bring back their kings?

Some of them certainly seem to be thinking about it seriously.

In Brazil, where the people are preparing for a referendum in two years' time in which the country will vote for either a presidential republic, a parliamentary democracy, or a constitutional monarchy, they are arguing that monarchy is the only system which has already proved itself efficacious in their country (Brazil has had only two monarchs, emperors, who ruled from 1822 to 1889) and that it would 'protect the people from the government' (my italics). What is more, they aver, it appeals strongly to the poor and underprivileged and has the support of many of those democratic politicians who would prefer a constitutional monarch to an authoritarian president.

This link between democracy and monarchy is new, but in May 1992 it was very vividly demonstrated in Thailand, and it has caught on in Brazil and may well be the deciding factor in the country's future. Monarchists there also claim that a king would 'revive liberal traditions, reduce the threat of military intervention, alter the moral climate in public life, provide stability and continuity, restore dignity to the country and its institutions and protect the threatened ecological environment'.

What more could you want? Roll over Boris Yeltsin, and make room for a tsar!

The second new factor that may affect the survival and even the increase of monarchies in the world is the one that Lord St John and I talked about: small and newly independent countries are keener than ever on their cultural identities. Nationalism, outside the corridors of the 'Community', and despite its 'wickedness', is very much alive and a king can be the very symbol of a new country's identity, the guardian of an ancient nation's soul.

Yet, if more kingdoms do emerge, I doubt whether I shall visit them, for I have proved to my own satisfaction that our existing kings and queens are what Messrs Sellar and Yeatman would call 'a good thing'; and that when all is said and done (as Professor Hugh Thomas points out), 'it is not really necessary to have a theory about monarchy or to explain its present popularity. It is based on an ancient custom that is accepted by people in most European countries – in their bones.'

Postscript

THE ONES THAT MIGHT
COME BACK

To anyone who attended the funeral, in Vienna's beautiful Stephansdom, of the ex-Empress Zita, the long-lived widow of the last Austro-Hungarian emperor, it would have immediately been apparent that there is no dearth of royalty 'in waiting': ready, willing and anxious to re-ascend European thrones that their forefathers vacated a generation or two ago. Many of them will probably never do so, but since the collapse of the Soviet Empire, the end of apartheid and the wars in Afghanistan, Ethiopia and Cambodia, followed by the confused vacuum that has succeeded these convulsions, their expectations have certainly changed.

Suddenly the world seems to have woken up and rediscovered the merits of monarchy. At least the questions now being asked are more serious than the silly ones (who is marrying, divorcing, 'carrying on' with whom?) that usually fill the 'Royal' magazines.

Afghanistan: could a constitutional king unite the quarrelsome and quite disparate elements in the Mujahideen imbroglio and bring the country the stable government it so desperately needs?

Might the Romanian Hohenzollerns or the Austrian Hapsburgs (who were also Emperors of Hungary, Bohemia and most of what is now Czechoslovakia) replace the increasingly contentious and largely stopgap politicians who were thrown up by the recent revolutions in these countries?

Might the exiled King Michael of Romania, who has an impeccable record of patriotism and was forced in 1947 to abdicate at Communist gunpoint, be willing to make a comeback, and is there any practical chance of it?

Although Zita's son, the clever and serious-minded Dr Otto von Hapsburg, has personally renounced all claims to the imperial throne (believing he can achieve more for his country by membership of the European Parliament), he has not done so on behalf of his children and heirs; so might Austria or Hungary reinstate a king, just for starters, and then, maybe, an emperor?

In Georgia the Royalist Party (and, being Georgian, there are several of them) actually sent for a member of the Bagratid dynasty to take a look at him (and he at them). Unfortunately, neither seems to have liked what they saw, but the party has not given up, and is now trying again with another member of what some claim to be the oldest royal family in the world (said to descend from the biblical King David).

In Serbia King Alexander plans to return to what was once Yugoslavia this year, though how the most Serbian of Serb families can help to unite opposition to President Milosevic or bring about a peace settlement between his country and Bosnia or Croatia is a mystery to me.

In North Africa the Senoussi are waiting in the wings to replace the dictator, Muammar Qaddafi of Libya.

Further south Shaka's descendant, King Goodwill Zwelithini KaBehekezulu, Ngonyama (Lion) of the Zulus, may actually reign again one day as an elected monarch, and Abyssinia's Crown Prince Asfa Wossen (Emperor Haile Selassie's grandson) might be asked back, as a figurehead, to unite a Commonwealth of Independent Ethiopian states. This is doubtful, though, for the imperial family, though they suffered dreadfully in the Communist take-over, were probably more popular outside than inside their own country.

In the Far East, Cambodia could well restore King Norodom Sihanouk, who abdicated in 1955, yet is still a powerful political figure, while a new emperor in Brazil – as has been mentioned – is being strongly advocated by a growing number of its people.

There have been several more ex-royal funerals (duly attended by their exiled ex-royal relations) which may point in the same direction. The remains of King Nicolas of Montenegro were solemnly reinterred at Cetinje two years ago, an event which probably stirred up nationalist passions there even more than dynastic aspirations.

Then in February 1992 thousands of Russians packed St Isaac's Cathedral in St Petersburg for the funeral service of Grand Duke Vladimir Kyrilovich. He died in exile in Miami, USA, but he had asked for and been given permission by the present Russian government to be buried in the Alexander Nevsky monastery of St Peter and St Paul, whose slender golden spire, across the grey waters of the Neva, catches every gleam of sunshine and lights up the view that his ancestors must have gazed on from the windows of the Winter Palace. He had been brought up by his parents as heir to the imperial throne, but when he was allowed back to Russia for the first time in November 1991, he promised to help his country and his countrymen 'in any capacity'. Though debarred his own, he had never taken out citizenship in any other country, and Patriarch Aleksei of All-Russia reminded the staunchly Tsarist congregation in his funeral oration that the Grand Duke 'had seen the only reason for his existence as being to serve his Motherland'. His grandson, Grand Duke Georgy Mikhailovic, is now the eleven-year-old pretender to the once-mighty throne of what used to be called 'All the Russias'.

Finally, and apparently with no less pomp and ceremony, the remains of the last Emperor of Abyssinia, Haile Selassie, were re-interred in Addis Ababa in July 1992.

A great deal of monarchical zeal has gone into the organisation and attendance of these dead (and therefore uncontroversial) monarchs' last appearances. The next decade will show us if there is enough left in the world to waft their live successors on to their vacant, but still golden thrones. What is at least certain is that, although people once knew they needed protection from the 'divine' right of kings, they are beginning to feel that they now need protection from the ambitious and often mis- guided plans of over-reaching politicians – and that a constitutional monarchy might best safeguard them from these and once more redress the balance. They could be right.

Index